A Critical Companion to Spenser Studies

A Critical Companion to Spenser Studies

Edited by

Bart van Es

palgrave
macmillan

First published 2006 by
PALGRAVE MACMILLAN
Houndmills, Basingstoke, Hampshire RG21 6XS and
175 Fifth Avenue, New York, N.Y. 10010
Companies and representatives throughout the world

PALGRAVE MACMILLAN is the global academic imprint of the Palgrave
Macmillan division of St. Martin's Press, LLC and of Palgrave Macmillan Ltd.
Macmillan® is a registered trademark in the United States, United Kingdom
and other countries. Palgrave is a registered trademark in the European
Union and other countries.

ISBN-13: 978–1–4039–2027–0 hardback
ISBN-10: 1–4039–2027–3 hardback

This book is printed on paper suitable for recycling and made from fully
managed and sustained forest sources.

A catalogue record for this book is available from the British Library.

Library of Congress Cataloging-in-Publication Data
A critical companion to Spenser studies / edited by Bart van Es.
      p.   cm.
   Includes bibliographical references (p.) and index.
   ISBN 1–4039–2027–3 (cloth)
   1. Spenser, Edmund, 1552?–1599—Criticism and
interpretation—Handbooks, manuals, etc.   I. Van Es, Bart.
   PR2364.C68 2006
   821′.3—dc22   2005054606

10   9   8   7   6   5   4   3   2   1
15   14   13   12   11   10   09   08   07   06

Transferred to digital printing 2006

To Anne Marie

Contents

A Note on Quotation

Unless otherwise stated, quotations from Spenser's poetry are taken from Richard A. McCabe, ed. 1999, *Edmund Spenser: The Shorter Poems*, London: Penguin and A. C. Hamilton ed. 2001, *The Faerie Queene*, 2nd edition, Harlow: Longman. Quotations from *A View of the Present State of Ireland* are taken from Edwin Greenlaw, *et al.*, ed. 1949, *The Works of Edmund Spenser: A Variorum Edition* Baltimore: Johns Hopkins Press, Vol. 10, *The Prose Works*. Quotation from the commentary in the *Variorum* are acknowledged in parenthesis.

Notes on Contributors

Elizabeth Jane Bellamy is Professor of English at the University of New Hampshire. She is the author of *Translations of Power: Narcissism and the Unconscious in Epic History* (1992) and has published widely on psychoanalysis and literary theory.

Patrick Cheney is Professor of English and Comparative Literature at Penn State University. He is the author of *Spenser's Famous Flight: A Renaissance Idea of a Literary Career* (1993) as well as other studies on the careers of Marlowe and Shakespeare. He is editor of *Worldmaking Spenser: Explorations in the Early Modern Age* (1999) and *Imagining Death in Spenser and Milton* (2003) and is co-editor of the new Oxford edition of the collected works of Spenser.

Andrew Hadfield is Professor of English at the University of Sussex, and Director of the Centre for Early Modern Studies. He is the author of *Spenser's Irish Experience: Wilde Fruit and Salvage Soyl* (1997), and editor of the Longman Critical Reader *Edmund Spenser* (1996) and *The Cambridge Companion to Spenser* (2001). He has co-edited Spenser's *A View of the State of Ireland* (1997) as well several other works. In recent years he has published *Shakespeare, Spenser and the Matter of Britain* (2004) and *Shakespeare and Republicanism* (2005) and worked on the 4th edition of the Norton Critical edition of Spenser's selected works.

John N. King is Distinguished Professor at Ohio State University. He is the author, amongst other works, of *English Reformation Literature: The Tudor Origins of the Protestant Tradition* (1982), *Spenser's Poetry and the Reformation Tradition* (1990), and *Milton and Religious Controversy: Satire and Polemic in Paradise Lost* (2000).

Theresa Krier is Professor of English Literature at Macalester College. She is the author of *Gazing on Secret Sights: Spenser, Classical Imitation, and the Decorums of Vision* (1990) and *Birth Passages: Maternity and Nostalgia, Antiquity to Shakespeare* (2001). She is the editor of *Refiguring Chaucer in the Renaissance* (1998), co-editor of *Luce Irigaray and Pre-Modern Culture: Thresholds of History* (2004), and a former editor of *The Spenser Review*.

Raphael Lyne is a Fellow of New Hall and Lecturer in the Faculty of English at the University of Cambridge. He is the author of *Ovid's Changing Worlds: English Metamorphoses 1567–1632* (2001) and of a forthcoming study of Shakespeare's late work.

Richard A. McCabe is a Fellow of Merton College and Professor of English Language and Literature at Oxford University. His publications include *Joseph Hall: A Study in Satire and Meditation* (1982), *The Pillars of Eternity: Time and Providence in 'The Faerie Queene'* (1989), *Incest, Drama and Nature's Law* (1993), and *Spenser's Monstrous Regiment: Elizabethan Ireland and the Poetics of Difference* (2002). He is the editor of *Edmund Spenser: The Shorter Poems* (1999).

Willy Maley is Professor of Renaissance Studies at the University of Glasgow. He is the author of *A Spenser Chronology* (1994), *Salvaging Spenser: Colonialism, Culture and Identity* (1997), and *Nation, State and Empire in English Renaissance Literature: Shakespeare to Milton* (2003). He has co-edited *A View of the State of Ireland* (1997) as well as several collections of critical essays, including *Representing Ireland: Literature and the Origins of Conflict, 1534–1660* (1993) and *British Identities and English Renaissance Literature* (2002).

David Lee Miller is Professor of English and Comparative Literature at the University of South Carolina. He is the author of *The Poem's Two Bodies: The Poetics of the 1590 Faerie Queene* (1988). In recent years he has published *Dreams of the Burning Child: Sacrificial Sons and the Father's Witness* (2003) and worked on the 1590 *Faerie Queene* for the new Oxford edition of the complete works.

Anne Lake Prescott is Helen Altschul Goodhart Professor of English at Barnard College, Columbia University. She has published extensively on Spenser and the Renaissance, focusing in particular on the influence of French writing on English literature. Her books include *French Poets and the English Renaissance: Studies in Fame and Transformation* (1978) and *Imagining Rabelais in Renaissance England* (1998). She is a co-editor of *Spenser Studies* and the Norton Critical Edition of Spenser's poetry.

Bart van Es is a Fellow of St Catherine's College, and Lecturer in English Language and Literature at Oxford University. He is the author of *Spenser's Forms of History* (2002).

Andrew Zurcher is a Fellow of Queens' College, Cambridge. He is co-editing Spenser's diplomatic letters for the Oxford edition of the *Collected Works* and is working on a book on Spenser's legal language and thought. As well as articles, he has produced numerous online resources for the study of Spenser.

Brief Chronology of Spenser's Life

c. 1552–54	Spenser born in London
1561	Enrols in Merchant Taylor's School, London, as 'poor scholar'
1569	*Feb.* Publication of Jan van der Noot's *A Theatre for Worldlings* containing Spenser's translations of 'Visions by Petrarch' and 'Visions of Du Bellay'
	May Enters Pembroke Hall, Cambridge, as a sizar (or poor student); friendship with Gabriel Harvey Begins.
1573	Takes his BA degree at Cambridge, 11th out of 120 candidates
1576	Takes his MA degree at Cambridge, 66th out of 70 candidates
1577	*July* Possibly in Ireland, as Irenius in *A View of the Present State of Ireland* claims that he witnesses the execution of Murrogh O'Brien
1578	*Apr.* Secretary to John Young, Bishop of Rochester
	Dec. In London, dwelling at Mistress Kerke's
1579	In London, dwelling at Leicester House
	Oct. 27 Marries Maccabaeus Chylde in Westminster, with whom he will have two children, Sylvanus and Katherine
	Dec. 5 The Shepheardes Calender entered in Stationers' Register, printed soon after
1580	*July 15* Lord Grey appointed Lord Deputy of Ireland, Spenser to be appointed his secretary
	Nov. 10 Grey orders massacre of Irish rebels at Fort d'Oro, Smerwick, Spenser possibly a witness
	Dec. Spenser-Harvey *Letters* printed
1981	*Mar. 22* Spenser becomes Clerk to the Controller of Customs on Wines
	Dec. 6 Spenser Granted lease of a Friary and Mill at Emniscorthy, Co. Wexford
1582	*Aug. 24* Obtains lease of New Abbey, Co. Kildare
	Aug. 31 Lord Grey recalled to England, Spenser remains in Ireland
1583	*May 12* Spenser appointed Commissioner for Musters in Co. Kildare
1584	*July* Probably becomes Clerk of the Council of Munster, serving as deputy to Lodovic Bryskett
1588	Quotations from *The Faerie Queene* appear in Abraham Fraunce's *Arcadian Rhetorike*
1589	*by 24 Mar.* In occupation of Kilcolman Castle

1590   Spenser in England
        The Faerie Queene printed
        Dec. Complaints entered in Stationers' Register
1591   Spenser in Ireland
        Daphnaïda printed.
        Feb. 25 Granted life pension of £50 by Elizabeth
        Complaints printed.
        Dec. 27 Colin Clout Come Home Againe dated at Kilcolman
        Ongoing disputes with Lord Roche over land.
1592   Publication of *Axiochus* (probably wrongly) attributed to Spenser
1594   Further disputes with Lord Roche
        June 11 Marries Elizabeth Boyle with whom he has one son, Peregrine
1595   *Colin Clouts Come Home Againe* printed. *Amoretti and Epithalamion*
        printed.
1596   Second edition of *The Faerie Queene*, Books I–VI, *Fowre Hymns*, and
        Prothalamion printed. *A View of the Present State of Ireland* composed.
1598   *A View of the Present State of Ireland* entered in Stationers' Register,
        but not printed.
        June Tyrone rebellion breaks out
        Sept. 30 Spenser made Sheriff of Cork
        Oct. Spenser's house at Kilcolman falls to the rebels
        Returns to London, paid £8 for delivering a letter to the Privy
        Council
1599   *Jan. 13* Dies in London. Buried at the expense of the Earl of Essex
1609   First folio of *The Faerie Queene* printed, including Mutabilitie Cantos
1611   First folio of collected poetical works printed
1620   Funeral monument erected in Westminster Abbey
1633   Publication of *A View of the [Present] State of Ireland*

Acknowledgements

Sincere thanks are due to those who helped make this book a reality. All of the contributors have been a pleasure to work with, offering a true embodiment of the ideal of a scholarly community. In particular I would like to thank Patrick Cheney for his generous investment of time at the design stage of this book and to Andrew Zurcher for judicious scrutiny at the close. Other friends and colleagues—Andrew Hadfield, Richard McCabe, Colin Burrow, David Norbrook, Christopher Tilmouth, Bruno Currie, Tore Rem, Michael Suarez, Peter McDonald, Sos Eltis, Duncan Wu, Jeremy Dimmick, and David Womersley to name but some—have also provided invaluable support along the way. I am grateful to Paula Kennedy and Helen Craine at Palgrave Macmillan for their commitment to the book over the years and to Jaya Nilamani and her team for their careful work of copy-editing. Finally, love and thanks go to my children—Josie, Beatrice, and Edgar—and to my wife, Anne Marie, to whom this book is dedicated.

1
Introduction

Bart van Es

The 'Theory Revolution' and a View of the Present State of Spenser Studies

In 1973 Alastair Fowler published an essay on 'Neoplatonic Order in *The Faerie Queene*'. In it, the Bower of Bliss, the deceitful garden of lust destroyed by the knight Guyon at the end of Book II of the poem, comes under discussion. 'Everyone', Fowler tells us, 'has noticed the correspondence and contrast that Spenser develops between the Bower of Bliss and the Garden of Adonis' (Fowler 1973, 70–2). Careful reading, however, can reveal more rewarding parallels. Acrasia's pleasure garden, placed alongside others that appear later in the poem, can thus be recognised as an element within an 'extraordinarily unified' structure: a 'delicate order' in which 'moral emblems, mythological entities, and symbolic attributes' echo one another across the great span of the poem (70). The cultural context that informed such 'multiplicities of dazzlingly intricate forms' (71) was to be found in the period's dominant philosophy: Neoplatonism. Knowledge of this tradition, Fowler explains, allows a reader to understand the Bower of Bliss as a vital component within a composition of aesthetic and moral balance.

Less than a decade after Fowler, Stephen Greenblatt also produced a study in which the Bower of Bliss provided a central example. Greenblatt's account of the episode, however, is so different from Fowler's that it at first seems scarcely credible that the two critics are discussing the same piece of literature. Where Fowler sees harmony, abstraction, and a context of high cultural values, Greenblatt finds dissonance, ideology, and bloody genocidal violence. He locates the Bower not within the narrative structures of *The Faerie Queene*, but in relation to what he sees as the poem's ideological purpose: that is, its aim 'to fashion a gentleman or noble person in vertuous and gentle discipline' ('Letter to Ralegh', quoted in Greenblatt 1980, 169). This act of fashioning—as Greenblatt understands it—is premised on the eradication of the cultural 'other'. For Spenser, as a colonial official in Ireland, that 'other' was in the first instance a recalcitrant Irish populace.

Spenser demanded its absolute surrender, and where this was not forth-coming advocated a policy of slaughter, burning, and deliberate starvation. That activity finds its cultural parallel in Guyon's merciless destruction of the Bower of Bliss:

> all those pleasaunt bowres and Pallace braue,
> *Guyon* broke downe, with rigour pittilesse;
> Ne ought their goodly workmanship might saue
> Them from the tempest of his wrathfulnesse,
> But that their blisse he turn'd to balefulnesse:
> Their groues he feld, their gardins did deface,
> Their arbers spoyle, their Cabinets suppresse,
> Their banket houses burne, their buildings race,
> And of the fayrest late, now made the fowlest place.

(II.xii.83)

All the 'rich complexities' of the episode, Greenblatt insists, 'are not achieved in spite of what is for us a repellent ideology—the passionate worship of impe-rialism—but are inseparably linked to that ideology' (174). Spenser 'worships power', and his ultimate offering to that deity is *The Faerie Queene*.

The contrast between Fowler and Greenblatt's readings, though extreme, is not unrepresentative.[1] The last quarter century has seen a revolution in Spenser studies, and the distance between these two interpretations is a testament to the magnitude of that event. Indeed, if anything, Fowler shares more with Greenblatt (the central critic within New Historicism) than he does with equivalent figures in other movements of the 1980s and 1990s, such as Deconstruction, Feminism, and Lacanian Psychoanalysis. All of these movements have had a significant impact on the interpretation of Spenser's texts. The poet, for long a respectable but somewhat fusty subject for scholarship, has become politicised and controversial. His work has come to stand at the centre of critical debate. Books and articles on Spenser have appeared at an ever-greater numbers, even to the extent of displacing other major writers of his time.[2] Whatever one's assessment of the value of this material, there can be little doubt that Spenser speaks in profound ways to the current critical moment.

---

[1] Criticism of the Bower of Bliss, including Greenblatt's reading, is the subject of more extensive treatment in David Miller's chapter in this book.

[2] In the 1970s monographs on John Donne, for example, by some way outnumbered those on Spenser. In the last two decades that trend has been reversed: a search of the MLA bibliography shows the publication of scholarly books running more than two to one in favour of the earlier writer.

Prevailing judgements on the period in which Spenser lived have themselves changed significantly, and it is partly as a consequence of that re-evaluation that earlier conceptions of the nature of his work have been overturned. Emphasis on a 'Renaissance' based on the rediscovery of classical knowledge was for much of the 1980s and 1990s replaced by concentration on an 'early modern' period characterised by cultural and political unrest.[3] The orthodoxy that a poet was best understood in the context of a 'world picture' consisting of literary allusion, Christian wisdom, and harmony of design was displaced by a new set of concerns, including violent colonial expansion, psycho-sexual drama, and religious strife.

This change in the perception of Tudor and Stuart society affected the characterisation of all literary figures. But the shift for Spenser was dispro-portionately large. Ireland and the detailed politics of Elizabeth's court, for example, were in the 1970s still commonly looked upon as mere distractions from Spenser's literary endeavours. At best, the troubles of the age drove the poet in a search for transcendence; at worst they were corrosive influences that damaged his imagination in the final stages of his life. For many in the 1980s and 1990s, however, such conflicts became central to the poet's art; Spenser's engagement with power was seen as inseparable from his literary achievement.

Along with the dominant perception of the period, the prevailing sense of the nature of 'literary achievement' itself has also changed. An earlier generation of critics (led by Leavis, Empson, Frye, and others) tended to value moral depth, verbal subtlety, and complexity of form. For much of the twentieth century it was possible to consider a poem in terms of a kind of architectural unity. In the 1980s, however, critics (influenced by Foucault, Lacan, and Derrida) focused much more on moments of repression, crisis, and open-endedness. If a poem was fractured, indeterminate, marked by lacunae, it became all the more rewarding as a subject of criticism. A text that was stable and authoritative was an uninteresting or simply an impossible thing.

Again, it appears that writing on Spenser was affected especially strongly by these developments. Critics such as Fowler find *The Faerie Queene* both morally and aesthetically balanced. They locate the work's greatness in its intricacy of patterning, the beauty of its images, and the richness of its verbal art. For the subsequent generation of writers this language of appreci-ation becomes much more muted. Certainly, complexity is still appreciated; but it is a complexity that tends to be observed under stress. If *The Faerie Queene* is acknowledged to be beautiful, that beauty is often a dark and disturbing phenomenon. Moreover, the close reading that writers such as Greenblatt apply to 'historical' documents like Spenser's *A View of the Present State of Ireland* makes the issue of 'literary value' a nebulous concept. While

---

[3] For an authoritative brief overview of these developments, see 'Afterword' in Norbrook 2002.

Fowler insists on a fundamental difference between a 'background' of Neoplatonic tracts and the foreground of Spenser's original composition, such distinctions are much less apparent in Greenblatt's work. There are a number of reasons why the work of Spenser proved particularly open to the new kinds of reading that came to dominate English studies in the last part of the twentieth century. For one thing, Spenser—unlike Shakespeare, Donne, Marlowe, or any number of other poets writing in Elizabeth's time—appeared to write poetry as a means of transforming his readership for both moral and political ends. Critical movements like New Historicism and Cultural Materialism, which tended to approach literature in terms of the 'cultural work' that it performed, found in Spenser an author who was himself quite explicit about this kind of instrumentality. Again, unlike many of his contemporaries, Spenser could be identified with historically specific causes: militant Protestantism, the cult of the monarch, and the fate of the English inhabitants of Ireland. Critics—including John N. King (1982) and David Norbrook (1984)—who were newly interested in more detailed political history could track the poet's responses to particular disputes (such as those surrounding the Queen's plans for her marriage in 1579). Those looking for political engagement in the Renaissance could find few subjects as rewarding as Edmund Spenser.

It is also true that Spenser's texts (artfully unfinished in the case of the Mutabilitie Cantos; ludically annotated in the case of *The Shepheardes Calender*) proved especially fertile ground for those—influenced Barthes and Derrida—who were interested in the instability of meaning. For Jonathan Goldberg (1981) especially, Spenser's epic, haunted by its ever-deferred central signifier (the Fairy Queen), provided a model text for the Derridean practice of Deconstruction. Simply by virtue of its length and complexity of plotting, *The Faerie Queene* was more open than other poems to the reading practices that had worked so well in relation to the great novels of later periods. Individual lyric poems, or even plays, were far less amenable to this interpretative strategy, but *The Faerie Queene*—full of unfinished tales, transformations, and authorial self-referentiality—constituted a supremely 'writerly' text.[4] A theoretically minded readership, especially one that was often determinedly out of step with the values of mainstream non-academic culture, found in *The Faerie Queene* a work at once expressive of a hegemonic order, and indicative of that order's ultimate collapse.

This newly exciting openness in Spenser's creation also proved rewarding for other audiences. 'Fairyland' (with its monstrous females, lost identities, and sexual pursuits) could be read in psychoanalytic terms by a new generation

---

[4] The term 'writerly' (as opposed to the more restrictive 'readerly' text, which is resistant to interpretative play) is coined in Roland Barthes' *S/Z* (first published in French in 1973) and is a central concern of Jonathan Goldberg's *Endlesse Worke* (1981).

of critics—including Elizabeth Jane Bellamy (1992) and Susan Frye (1993)—working within feminist and Lacanian paradigms. Book III's 'Legend of Chastity', especially, was seen to contain a series of deeply resonant episodes: not least Britomart's vision of her sexual future in a prophetic mirror (III.ii) and the torture of Amoret's heart in a house whose walls are decorated with the depictions of sexual conquest (III.xi–xii). The fact that Spenser's poem was dedicated and addressed to a virgin queen added another dimension to its sexual drama. *The Faerie Queene*'s Amazonian women and feminised men provided exemplary instances through which to explore the pressures involved within the formation of gender identity—above all within a society whose patriarchal assumptions were put under tension by the veneration of a female ruler. Spenser, in a manner that appeared at once more direct and more ambiguous than that of his contemporaries, addressed the problematic combination of gender and power within the Elizabethan state.

From whatever perspective his work was approached, Spenser seemed unusually well suited to the new reading practices that existed at the high point of 'Theory'. As a result, the critical attention paid to the poet can rarely have been as varied as it was during the 1980s and the early 1990s. We are now in what is often characterised as a period 'After Theory'.[5] The undiluted currents of critical thinking identifiable a decade and a half ago have now mingled to the point where it is often difficult to isolate them. New interpretative trends have emerged: interest in book history and the materiality of the text, fascination with national identity, and concern with the recovery of Early Modern reading practices. Older modes have resurfaced, including attention to religion and the reception of classical literature. Yet, at the same time, the more theoretical modes of the preceding decade continue to make their presence felt.

The 'present state' of literary studies is more difficult to define than was the case in the 1970s or 1980s (the moments at which Fowler and Greenblatt produced their respective readings of the Bower of Bliss). There is neither a consensus nor a conflict between easily identifiable camps. Yet, just as strongly, work on Spenser continues to function as an exemplary matrix through which to analyse today's debates. This fact again appears to be tied, at least in part, to the qualities of Spenser's work that connect to the critical zeitgeist. If today's modes of reading are a hybrid of traditions that were previously distinct, this is also true of Spenser's poetry. The poet, as he is most commonly celebrated by contemporary criticism, has a voracious, synthesising intelligence. He plays upon the influence of Virgil, Ovid, Chaucer, and Ariosto (to name but a few of the most prominent examples),

---

[5] The notion that literary studies are in a post-theoretical phase is widespread, although also widely contested. Notable recent publications on the subject include Kastan, *Shakespeare After Theory* (1999), Cunningham, *Reading After Theory* (2002), Eagleton, *After Theory* (2003) and *Life.after.theory*, ed. Payne and and Schad (2003).

and he mingles genres including pastoral, epic, lyric, and complaint. This syncretic drive is at the same time understood in relation to a divided historical condition. Spenser is seen not only as a poet of empire, but also as an exile far from the centre of power; he is a prophet of national achievement, but equally of global apocalypse.

It is useful here to turn to a reading of the Bower of Bliss in a study published at the beginning of the twenty-first century: Richard McCabe's *Spenser's Monstrous Regiment* (2002, 131–41). What is revealing is just how much McCabe has learnt from earlier generations of critics, from nineteenth-century scholars on mythology to twentieth-century New Historicists. As a consequence, McCabe's reading calls upon an extraordinary range of intertertexts: Irish bardic poetry, English colonial propaganda, pro-Spanish engravings of the New World, but also Homer's *Odyssey*, Virgil's *Aeneid*, and Tasso's *Gerusalemme Liberata*. His picture of the Bower (carefully placed in relation to other episodes in Book II) is neither one of Neoplatonic balance nor that of imperial triumphalism. For McCabe, the episode needs to be understood in the context of a long European literary tradition. Yet it is also shaped by a horror of the Irish 'other', a culture that Spenser's writing distorts in significant ways. McCabe's analysis traces a multitude of narrative modes and historical pressures; there is no single consistent aesthetic design or ideological end. The representation of the witch Arcrasia, for example, points two ways. In part she does reflect the transformative power of the Irish: a people who, in Spenser's contention, can lure English Protestants to a degenerate end. At times, however, Acrasia's representation also touches upon anxieties about Spenser's own monarch: a female ruler accused of enfeebling English men. Spenser's poem, modelled on the achievements of Western culture, is thus flawed in fundamental but fascinating ways.

It would be misleading to claim that McCabe's study was 'representative' of the present state of Spenser studies, but his work does illustrate something of the inclusive perspective of current work; in a sense he has mapped Greenblatt's politics onto Fowler's world picture. Without doubt, McCabe is indebted to New Historicism. Though his methods are different, it is also true that his judgements are influenced by the insights of Feminist critics, as well as Marxist political theory on nationhood. Behind these influences lie other traditions, including the philological close readings of the New Critics and the factual discoveries of the 'Old' historicists. In no sense could McCabe be said to 'belong' to any of these schools of criticism, but it would also be simplistic to claim that his approach was unaffected by theory of any kind.

What is true of McCabe's study applies equally to other academic work. At this juncture, therefore, it is more important than ever to have an accessible guide to criticism on Spenser's texts. The excellent existing guides to Spenser's work—such as Hadfield's *Cambridge Companion* (2001) or the fine overviews by Burrow (1996) and Oram (1997)—are of relatively little assistance here. Indeed, taken in isolation, such surveys can sometimes work to obscure the realities of critical dispute. For students and scholars to be empowered—for them to be able to investigate and challenge current assumptions, and develop new readings of their own—it is vital for them to know what has been written, where today's scholars stand, and where the debate appears to be heading.

One thing that becomes clear from a survey of Spenser 'in history' is the fact that the 1980s and 1990s were not the first period during which there was a major shift in the poet's critical reception. Neo-Classicism, Romanticism, 'Old' historicism, and New Criticism each brought perceptual revolutions every bit as spectacular. Still less can the last quarter-century be isolated in terms of individual studies. Earlier academic publications—Greenlaw (1932), Lewis (1954, 1967), Alpers (1967), MacCaffrey (1976), and Nohrnberg (1976) to name but a few—have made contributions that remain central to any understanding of Spenser's achievement. This is also true of pre-twentieth-century writers, such as Coleridge, Johnson, and Pope. In spite of their hybrid modes of interpretation, there is still a tendency amongst today's readers to foreshorten critical history. There is a curious willingness to declare work 'outdated' and therefore to leave it unread. A narrative of Spenser criticism can help to reconnect us to the achievements of earlier interpreters. It can make us think anew about our own reading practices, and push readers onwards to make new discoveries.

The broad lines that emerge from an overview of the reception of Spenser provide a useful paradigm for the course of Renaissance studies. Yet, at the same time, each text and each subject for study has a subtler story to tell. Ultimately, we are concerned at least as much with individual texts and readers as with the issue of generational change. It matters, for example—as David Miller shows in his chapter in this book—that when Milton read the Bower of Bliss episode he took it as an allegory for the experience of the way-faring Christian, a figure who must experience the moment of temptation in order to prove his power to resist. This companion aims to direct its readers to a succession of such moments of interpretation. As a result, it prompts questions about what remains permanent in a work of literature, as well as what alters over time. It is rewarding, in this light, to conclude with the verdict of Spenser's goddess Nature, who famously concludes *The Faerie Queene* with the declaration that

> all things stedfastnes doe hate
> And changed be: yet being rightly wayd
> They are not changed from their first estate;
> But by their change their being doe dilate:
> And turning to themselues at length againe,
> Doe worke their owne perfection so by fate.

(VII.vii.58.2–7)

'Perfection' is not an achievable goal in criticism, but we can learn a great deal from the contemplation of change.

The objective and structure of the companion

It is not a difficult thing to find a good general introduction to Spenser. Recent years have seen the publication of a number of such studies, and the multi-author 'companion' has become a publishing phenomenon. Arguably, the 'Post-Theoretical' era has made the design and commissioning of such volumes more straightforward. On one level, the general reader has never been so well-served. As has already been suggested, however, there is a potential downside to this positive development: for by presenting what looks like a consensus picture, such studies can come to close the door on further debate. Paradoxically, the more authoritative a guide becomes, the firmer the boundaries set on further exploration. Put bluntly, an overdependence on today's authoritative companions can lead to dull, predictable work.

The object of this book is to equip the reader—from undergraduate student to expert Spenserian—to produce fresh interpretations of Spenser's poetry and prose. It aims to do so by giving that reader a sophisticated understanding of the poet's critical history, from the first responses of his contemporaries to the academic criticism of today. Both elements in the pairing 'works' and 'readers' are important, and as few assumptions as possible have been made about prior knowledge in either case. The contributors to the *Companion* quote liberally from Spenser's poetry, and summaries are provided where these are likely to be of help. In this way, often through specific examples, the chapters illustrate how the most influential readers have responded to the poet's work over time. By pointing to the specifics of critical interaction, the book thus not simply offers a general insight into the works of Spenser but opens the way for participation in an ongoing debate.

For those starting out to write something new on the work of Spenser, the *Companion* provides a way of establishing the 'state of criticism' on a particular issue or text. To that end, the essays are—broadly speaking—chronological, they are subdivided into sections, and each concludes with an assessment of current trends and a brief bibliography. An index allows rapid searches for more specific queries (on such subjects as 'C. S. Lewis' or 'Allegory'). In this way, the book provides access to a network of reading—interaction between critics as well as between the lone critic and 'primary' text. Of course, the full bibliography of Spenser studies is vast and cannot be covered in a single volume, nor would such exhaustive presentation be desirable. Instead, it is the most prominent episodes and approaches that are examined in detail, providing a dynamic vision of the existing field. With this information behind them—knowing the strengths, the weaknesses, and the gaps in what has been done—readers can strike out to make a contribution of their own.

The 'facilitating' quality of the book is one key target. It is perhaps most practically embodied in Andrew Zurcher's concluding chapter on 'Texts and

Resources', which sets out the principal scholarly instruments for the study of this poet. All the chapters in the book are, in one way, 'resources' in the sense that Zurcher describes them. Yet they are also individual critical essays. The style, structure, and judgement of each piece is distinctive; each has its own—sometimes contentious—argument about the direction of criticism and the value of specific work. Across the book, methods of explication vary considerably, and few follow a straightforward chronology. While authors strive to be representative, they can also write with passion about the successes or shortcomings of a particular approach. If this makes the book something less than a clinically objective work of reference, it also makes it more enjoyable to read.

The contributors and chapters

This book aims to make readers more aware of critical debate. One way it does so is through the provision of accessible narrative surveys. Another, however, is by bringing together scholars who are themselves representative of the diversity it wishes to expose. It would be naive to presume the book's structure did not of itself encode certain intellectual preferences. Inevitably, its survey element implies that literary values are historically determined, and that works of literature owe their significance, at least in part, to their interpretative contexts. Yet that unavoidable fact should not be allowed to suppress the vitality of other approaches operating within, or occasionally chafing against this framework. It would be ironic if a collection concerned with the exchange of critical views were itself slavishly to follow a single set of assumptions. The individual contributors to the book, therefore, all bring their own traditions to bear on the questions proposed by this study, and they will not always agree on the best answers to give.

The essays collected here demonstrate that there is no easy consensus amongst contemporary writers on Spenser. The chapters by Theresa Krier and Andrew Hadfield, for example, stand out as strongly argued, at times polemical, pieces of writing. There are fundamental issues on which these two scholars would not agree. Hadfield's sense of Spenser's political engagement, and the importance of this to the study of his poetry, for example, stands in contrast to Krier's insistence on the primacy of narrative structures and the experience of the individual reader of *The Faerie Queene*. Where Hadfield works to define the political radicalism present in Spenser's work, Krier argues that the lessons to be found in the poetry are fundamentally of a literary kind. David Miller and John N. King, equally, come with very different angles in their perspective on the poet. Miller's critical practice has been shaped by Freud, Lacan, and Derrida amongst others. King, in contrast, has much stronger ties to historians of the Early Modern period, in particular those concerned with the character of Protestantism in Tudor England. Their two essays, while courteous in their treatment of all reading traditions, work on different assumptions about what is valuable or central to the work of explicating literary texts. The critical position of Richard McCabe has already been broached, but it is worth stressing his historicist roots. In other areas (such as Patrick Cheney's chapter on Spenser's life, Elizabeth Jane Bellamy's on gender, or Willy Maley's on the *View*) one could also argue that contributors implicitly provide a 'justification' of a particular way of approaching an author. These critics have certainly been central figures in the emergence of the specialisms they describe: they have territory to defend.

Less explicitly, but no less strongly, the essays by Anne Lake Prescott and Raphael Lyne also adhere to a distinctive critical ethos: one that insists upon the foundational significance of Spenser's humanist education, and that tends to privilege a high cultural context consisting of literary and philosophical works. They have beliefs about the value and nature of literature, and these cannot be excluded from the essays they write. My own chapter (on texts published before 1589) is particularly marked by historical relativism, which seeks to explain critical insights in relation to wider cultural trends. This too is a defined position, and it sets the boundaries for the argument I propose. Finally, while we might consider Andrew Zurcher's chapter on texts and resources 'neutral', it is worth remembering that he is very much part of a current movement in scholarship that stresses the importance of Renaissance manuscript culture and the history of the printed book. On the whole, it is fair to say that his essay operates in the spirit of that endeavour.

As much as it is a reference work, therefore, the *Companion* is also a forum: a meeting place for traditions of reading—both within and between individual essays. It constitutes a snapshot of at least some aspects of 'Spenser studies' as it currently exists. There is no single dominant ethos but, in as far as it is inclusive and methodologically eclectic, this collection may itself be taken as representative of the age. Each of the essays described in this book thus gives access to both past and present strands within an ongoing debate.

Patrick Cheney's chapter on Spenser's life takes a look at what is currently one of the most vibrant of these strands. It begins by telling the story of the construction of a life narrative for Spenser. Having set out the ways in which the facts and legends about the poet's life came to be established, the chapter moves on to consider the rediscovery of interest in biography amongst today's scholars. In particular, Cheney explores the contributions of 'author' and 'career' criticism, illustrating the way 'life' and 'work' are increasingly recognised as intertwined within Spenser's texts. As this chapter illustrates, present day interest in a multitude of competing histories, combined with sophisticated attention to the physical production of texts, makes the literary life an integral part of the contemporary understanding of Spenser.

The physical production of texts is again a concern in Andrew Hadfield's chapter on politics, which begins with the partisan publication of sections of *The Faerie Queene* by a Royalist editor during the English Civil War. Set against this edition, Hadfield documents some of the responses to the political content of Spenser's work by his contemporaries, notably the irate reactions of Lord Burghley and King James VI of Scotland to the supposed slanders in the *Complaints* and *The Faerie Queene*. In the light of this initial reception history, Hadfield goes on to examine Spenser's politics in a number of areas, including the representation of Elizabeth and the contentious issue of female rule. Overall, Hadfield sketches the recovery of politics as a key issue within Spenser studies, in particular stressing the importance of the succession crisis and the Irish wars. His chapter notes a tendency amongst recent critics to view Spenser as a political radical, but also documents the emergence of counterblasts to that opinion. The picture of the current state of criticism he leaves us with is of strongly argued conflict, in which a host of historical assumptions are coming under increasingly fierce scrutiny.

While Hadfield concludes with ongoing controversy, the subject of John N. King's chapter—Spenser's religion—has on the whole had a more stable position within critical debate. King begins with the annotations of John Dixon, who, during the poet's lifetime, already produced a detailed commentary touching on *The Faerie Queene*'s biblical allusions. The tradition established by Dixon is still in existence more than four hundred years on, but, as King observes, it has grown enormously in scope and sophistication. The chapter tracks debate through the eighteenth and nineteenth centuries concerning the religious and aesthetic value of Spenser's Protestant allegory. Early twentieth-century scholars sharpened the discussion by writing more explicitly about distinct strands of religious thinking, including Calvinism and the position of the Puritans. Post-war critics—in what was in part a break from their predecessors—introduced new ways of approaching religious material: first through the study of iconography, and later through more explicitly theory-governed ways of reading. Throughout this period, however, detailed historical awareness of the sixteenth-century religious picture remains a vital component. While essentialist assumptions have been challenged, and while a new understanding of the poetics of religious experience has emerged, there remains remarkable continuity in the debate upon this subject.

Elizabeth Jane Bellamy's chapter on gender, in this respect, provides a stark contrast with the preceding chapter by King. Where work on the religious content of Spenser's poetry can be traced back to the sixteenth century, the subject with which Elizabeth Jane Bellamy is concerned does not emerge as a specific focus for enquiry until the 1970s. At the opening of her chapter, Elizabeth Jane Bellamy spends some time examining this 'blind spot' of earlier criticism, and throughout her essay she shows the way in which the study of such concepts as 'Petrarchanism' does offer a kind of pre-history for the subject. The bulk of this chapter, however, is concerned with the developments in Feminist criticism of the last quarter century. Elizabeth Jane Bellamy focuses especially closely the treatment of Britomart in key episodes of *The Faerie Queene*'s Books III and V, which have been the subject of sustained attention during this time.

In the closing stages of the essay, she identifies a number of phases within this debate on gender, including earlier historical work on the female monarch, and subsequent psychoanalytic criticism influenced by Lacan. Elizabeth Jane Bellamy concludes on emergent subjects of interest, such as the representation of Ireland, masculinity, the body, and Spenser's reception amongst Early Modern women poets. While, in these areas, Feminist thinking has accommodated the influence of other movements, the chapter demonstrates that it will also continue to function as a powerful and coherent tradition in its own right.

Where Elizabeth Jane Bellamy examines a defined school of criticism, Anne Lake Prescott's chapter—on sources—considers a category that cuts across all critical movements and texts. In a way that bears comparison with King's identification of a long tradition of commentary on religion, her chapter takes a subject that has always been crucial to the readers of Spenser's poetry. Indeed, the essay begins with a study of the influence of religious works that very much complements King's. Subsequently, Prescott moves to consider Spenser's treatment of Classical, Medieval, and—finally—Renaissance texts, all the while tracing their influence in specific examples of Spenserian verse. While on the one hand she observes a continuity of commentary, however, Prescott also addresses a major conceptual shift in the treatment of this subject. The dominant model, she argues, has changed from an earlier interest in the identification of single sources to a present day celebration of the mixing and multiplicity of influence. The very term 'source' has become inadequate, needing to be replaced, perhaps, by 'complex of intertexts' or even 'magnetic field of recollection'.

Prescott's is the last chapter of the book to focus on an issue rather than a specific group of texts. Subsequent chapters move chronologically through Spenser's published works. My own—on *The Shepheardes Calender, Letters*, and *Theatre for Worldlings*—is the first of this section. It begins and ends with Spenser's own printed commentaries: first, as an instance of the way he anticipated his reception at the hands of Early Modern readers, and—eventually—as a focus for present-day interest in intertextual play. Between these two points the essay charts a chronology of response that, for the *Calender* at least, is remarkably passionate and sustained. The fortunes of this text—under the scrutiny of Neoclassicists, Romantics, and others—are testament to the vicissitudes of literary fashion, as well as the genuine onward progress of criticism.

If it is tempting to take the history of the *Calender*'s reception as a small-scale paradigm for the development of the discipline, the body of writing on *The Faerie Queene* (1590) rebukes all such attempts at schematisation. David Lee Miller, nevertheless, achieves an extraordinary feat of synthesis in his chapter on this text. His chapter begins with the moment at which the work was printed, at the shop of John Wolfe in early 1590. Even so, it proceeds to move further back in time, to explore the years of the poem's composition and the early responses of contemporaries. From there Miller charts the poem's reception over centuries, starting with Dixon's annotations of 1597 and ending at the twenty-first century. Yet the structure that Miller adopts is only part historical. Long sections of his chapter consider topics without recourse to chronology, as in the case of the Spenserian stanza or the form of the poem as whole. Throughout, he makes extensive use of close reading, both his own and that produced by other critics of Spenser's texts. The effect is to produce a genuinely comprehensive reading, although one that also acknowledges the limits of any attempt to encapsulate the critical history of this work.

Richard McCabe's chapter, which follows Miller's, is concerned with poetry published between the two instalments of *The Faerie Queene*: the *Complaints* collection, *Daphnaïda, Colin Clout*, and *Amoretti and Epithalamion*. The range of modes and genres touched on by these texts is remarkable, and one of the things that McCabe's text-by-text survey chronicles is a developing awareness of Spenser's generic innovation. McCabe also points to a recovery of interest in Spenser as satirical poet, a role whose importance is confirmed by the sixteenth- and seventeenth-century responses to the *Complaints*. In these areas recent criticism has made considerable advances, but this chapter also directs attention to the achievements of earlier close readers, who made major discoveries about the structure and patterning of these works. Overall, the shorter poems published between 1590 and 1596 have grown in critical importance. They are no longer to be labelled 'minor' works. A collective effort of scrutiny has shown them to be vital intertexts for Spenser's epic, and also profound and complex poems in their own right.

Richard McCabe's chapter begins with the contemplation of 'ruin' in the *Complaints*, and Theresa Krier's essay—likewise—opens by entertaining notions of dissolution. The second instalment of *The Faerie Queene*, she observes, has for a long time been seen as both expressing and provoking disappointment. Her essay charts and explores the critical responses to this experience, from the laments of early twentieth-century commentators to the welcoming of narrative frustration amongst more recent writers on this text. Krier's chapter pays careful and sustained attention to the major voices of the 1960s and 1970s, setting out the full complexity of their insights into the poem's form. Historicist critics of the 1980s and 1990s, she observes, shifted attention from narrative to political discontent. While these contributions were certainly valuable, Krier argues that they should not distract attention from the experience of readers or the long and ongoing tradition of commentary on the pleasures and Freudian drives of the 1596 text.

If Krier warns against the deleterious effects of a reductive historicism, Willy Maley's chapter—on the *View*—addresses the text around which that historical impetus has centred in recent years. Maley's chapter charts the process that has effected this development, tracing the tract's shift in status from political and antiquarian treatise to literary intertext. The chapter explores the complexity of the work's current reception, even noticing its status as a source for present-day Irish poetry. The *View*, Maley contends, catches the conscience of contemporary critics, and poses troubling questions about the nature of academic practice itself. Looking in detail at three of the work's most important passages, the chapter offers a challenging assertion of the primacy of prose in the current characterisation of Spenser both as individual and as poet.

Almost as if in answer to Maley, Raphael Lyne's chapter on the late verse (including *Two cantos of Mutabilitie*) presents a more contemplative, more literary, figure. While some contemporary critics have emphasised the political backdrop to these poems, most acknowledge a drive for transcendence and retrospection in these works. Looking one by one at these three late publications—rarely considered as a body—Lyne sets out the way in which commentators have explored their distinct historical and generic contexts as well as their shared universalising themes. Perhaps most consistently, he suggests, they explore the interaction of the philosophical and material, and therefore need to be located with intellectual dexterity in the last stages of Spenser's life and work.

Where Lyne looks at responses to closure, Andrew Zurcher—in the final chapter of this volume—looks ahead to further research and at the resources that will enable its progress. Zurcher's chapter describes the nature of the first printed texts, the location of key manuscripts, the important scholarly editions, and finally the available research tools for finding information in the study of Spenser. The chapter itself is followed by an appendix, in which Zurcher lists all Early Modern publications of Spenser's work, and also the major editions of the centuries that follow. The appendix closes with a section detailing Internet resources, accurate at time of going to press. Zurcher's chapter makes it possible to conclude the book with a vision of the modern reader empowered: newly equipped—like the Redcrosse Knight—with tools that have a venerable history, however inexperienced their current user may be.

The future of Spenser studies

In the third canto of the third book of *The Faerie Queene* Merlin provides Britomart with an extended prophecy of the future. The sage presents the lady knight with a neat chronology of events to come that stretches the length of Canto iii. It is only when he looks beyond the reign of Elizabeth that Merlin narrative falters: 'But yet the end is not' (III.iii.50.1). In reality, of course, what Spenser gives us here is really history, a chronicle of past happenings transmuted to the future tense. Prophecy is easy as long as we learn this lesson—beyond this it is best to remain cryptic or run the risk of exposure. Critics of the past have never been good at envisaging how future readers would come to understand Spenser, and a prediction of the future of Spenser studies can only really be an extrapolation of what is known— history taking on a prophetic guise. All the same, because this guide is composed with an eye to the requirements of future scholars, it is worth taking a moment to reflect upon the road ahead.

Chairing the closing 'round table' discussion at the International Spenser Society conference of 2001, John Watkins cited Thomas Kuhn's classic thesis on the structure of scientific revolutions: rare events that involve a momentary transition from 'normal science' to 'tipping points' where change is momentarily possible. Watkins—looking back at the intellectual upheavals of the 1980s—described the state of Spenser studies in 2001 as 'normal science'. The 'science' he witnessed was certainly a many and varied thing. Sessions held at this five-yearly gathering of Spenserians included papers on 'Elizabeth', 'Topographies', 'Antiquity', 'Irigaray', 'Memory', 'Thinking', 'Pain', 'Poetics', 'Allegory', and 'Book III'. The 'normal' state of this discipline is certainly productive and diverse.

There is still a great deal of ongoing work in the areas touched on by the Cambridge conference. Spenser's scholarliness (he appears to have thought seriously about almost all of the major intellectual developments of his time, from anatomy to historiography) makes him a rewarding subject for a context-centred approach to literature—without doubt, we will continue to see an ever-widening search for valid intertexts. Yet, if in one way the Cambridge convention can be taken as a picture of intellectual stability, in another it also holds the seeds of new developments. The theme of the conference was 'The Place of Spenser', and work on 'places' (in multiple senses, from the geographic to the institutional) have come to stimulate fresh thought on the poet's writing in recent years. As the boundaries defining 'the Renaissance' and 'English Studies' receive ever more sceptical scrutiny, that 'place' looks to be increasingly, and productively, uncertain.

One of the 'places' likely to be the subject of sustained attention over the coming decade is the Elizabethan printing house. Even as recently as 2001, interest in the materiality of the text was less prominent than it is today. The specifics of the production and consumption of the printed and written word are now central concerns in the study of Spenser. Current work on a new edition of Spenser's poetry and prose at Oxford University Press is certain to generate new issues for debate. The editors are looking in unprecedented detail at the condition of Spenser's printed texts and also at a much wider range of manuscripts. Especially because today's readers are more alert to the complexities of patronage and shared authorship, this kind of scholarship has repercussions far beyond straightforward bibliography.

One consequence of the critical revolutions of the 1980s has been the development of more subtle sense of the interconnection between bibliography and the biographical. As almost all the contributors to this book testify, amongst the strongest recent collections in this area is Anderson, Donald Cheney, and Richardson's 1996 *Spenser's Life and the Subject of Biography*. As has been noted, the debate here has moved from the 'autobiographical' to what Richard McCabe (1999, xvii) has termed an 'auto-referential' sense of the poet's identity. The pieces in Anderson's collection offer productive new ways of approaching an author whose conduct might otherwise have become the subject of reductive ideological disputes. They acknowledge the reality of an identity that is accessible only through texts, and is therefore never unmediated. Combined with new knowledge about the production and preservation of the written word, fresh thinking on identity looks set to stimulate significant original work in the future.

As is apparent from the essays by McCabe and Lyne in the *Companion*, publications such as the *Complaints* or *Fowre Hymnes* have only recently taken a more prominent place in our appreciation of Spenser. The development highlighted in Anne Lake Prescott's chapter in this book is also pivotal here. The movement from the concept of 'sources' (neutral raw materials whose individual elements disappear once transformed by the author) towards 'intertexts' (pieces of writing that remain distinct within the mind of the reader and thus remain the subject of allusive play within the literary text) allows a new kind of appreciation of these poems. Many of Spenser's shorter works reward a form of reading that concentrates on such allusive strategies, in particular when it is combined with an awareness of the author's artful self-presentation in print. With prevailing critical opinion moving away from monolithic conceptions of originality and authorial control, it is possible for such works to play a key part in a new stage in the development of Spenser studies.

As writers on Renaissance literature come increasingly to question the validity of an immutable 'author function' it is perhaps possible that the exclusive study of Spenser will itself become less common in future years. The single author monograph is said to be an endangered species. Many, it appears, prefer to focus on specific epochs or issues, examining a cross-section of works and authors in this light. Such concern with both specifics and pluralities may make 'Spenser', as an individual, a less common focal point. Yet, if in one way the study of Spenser may become a more diffuse phenomenon, in another it could itself become the subject of probing scrutiny. One expanding area of interest—usefully served by this book—involves the examination of specific moments of reception, for the history of reading has itself become an increasingly important element in literary studies. Scholars have become interested not simply in the way in which a poet was understood in his or her 'own time' but also in the manner subsequent generations made sense of that work. As Elizabeth Jane Bellamy points out at the conclusion of her chapter in this book, for example, recent studies come to look at the way in which women poets such as Wroth and Lanyer responded to Spenser's work. There seems no reason why later responses should not, equally, reveal productive points of connection. Literature exists *in* history not just at a particular contextual moment, but always, ongoingly, being re-read and thereby changed.

Finally, there are also signs of a reaction against historicism—in particular a reaction against a historicism that is felt to have been too reductive in its presentation of a functionalistic, purposive, Spenser. Foremost here is Richard Chamberlain's *Radical Spenser* (2005), which argues that the poet is, in practice, determinedly resistant to critical domination. In line with this argument, Chamberlain reads the Bower of Bliss neither as part of an ordered pattern of persuasion, nor as a reflection of Spenser's colonial experience, but rather as an allegory of the failure of critical endeavour itself. Attacking Greenblatt (1980), and reaching back to the insights of William Empson (1935), he suggests that Spenser's output is best approached through the methods of a 'New Aesthetics' that combines the methods of Formalism with the insights of more recent literary theory.

Even as it contemplates new directions, work on Spenser continues to require a complex awareness of its critical past. It seems that, in the future, Spenser studies will continue to grow in awareness of its history, and it is to be hoped that this *Companion* will help to place the reader at the focus of this endeavour. More importantly, the individual chapters of this book should illustrate the pleasures and rewards of this perspective on the past. It is certainly in the best tradition of Spenser's own compositions for us to be made aware of the blending of old and new in any literature. Equally, the recovery and preservation of past achievement is a very Spenserian concern. *The Faerie Queen*, in its opening stanza, sets out the poet's objective to 'sing of Knights and Ladies gentle deeds, / Whose praises hauing slept in silence long, / Me, all too meane, the sacred Muse areeds' (I.Proem.1.5–7). Spenser himself has been lucky in receiving the attention of able critics, scholars who have worked tirelessly to maintain an understanding of his poetry. In its 'all too meane' way, this collection strives to preserve those acts of preservation.

Acknowledgement

Amongst many other debts, I would like to acknowledge Andrew Zurcher's extensive suggestions for improvement produced in response to an earlier draft of this introduction; the remaining faults are, of course, my own.

2
Life
Patrick Cheney

> ... this Lifes first native source ...
>
> *Prothalamion* (1596)

State of the art

Readers looking for a short and authoritative overview of Spenser's life would do well to consult Ruth Mohl (1990) and next Donald V. Stump (1996). Willy Maley (1994) assembles the full biographical facts in his detailed chronology. The standard book-length biography remains that by Alexander C. Judson (1945). A more recent "literary life" by Gary Waller (1994) is idiosyncratic but still accessible for the disciplined nonspecialist. A collection of essays recently edited by Judith H. Anderson, Donald Cheney, and David A. Richardson (1996) supplies a superb "fin de siècle" vantage point for re-thinking "Spenser's life and the subject of biography." On Spenser's "career" as an author who presents himself fictionally, the originary twin essays are by Richard Helgerson (1983) and David Lee Miller (1983), followed by Joseph F. Loewenstein (1986) and later by Anne Lake Prescott (2000), while Patrick Cheney (1993) contributes a full-length study. In a groundbreaking book and two follow-up essays, Richard Rambuss (1993, 1996, 2001) examines Spenser's "secretarial" career intertwined with his career as a poet. Colin Burrow (1996) and William Oram (1997) write useful short overview books on Spenser's life and career(s) in popular series for the general reader and the specialist alike. In different formats, national foci, and methodology, Louis Montrose and Richard A. McCabe produce valuable complementary studies: Montrose's seminal series of essays (1983, 1996, 2002) on Spenser's career as an English author in reciprocal relation with Queen Elizabeth; and McCabe's authoritative monograph (2002) on Spenser's career as an "exiled" author in conflicted relation with the bards and other leaders in Ireland. In this opening chapter, we shall look into this "state of the art" on Spenser's life and career, and trace its origins.

Origins and orientations

In 1679, the anonymous editors of the third folio edition of Spenser's *Works* printed the *second* formal commentary on Spenser: "A Summary of the Life of Mr Edmond Spenser."[1] This commentary is not merely inaugural but paradigmatic, because it uncannily predicts the singular feature organizing Spenser commentary for the centuries to follow: the fusion between biographical and literary criticism. Among English Renaissance writers, Spenser is the first to make his life central to his literary career as an author, sometimes obtrusively so. Thus, in his last published poem, *Prothalamion* (1596), he interrupts his allegorical swan vision of the betrothal ceremony for Elizabeth and Katherine Somerset, daughters to the earl of Worcester, to remind us of his own origins:

> At length they all to mery London came,
> To mery London, my most kyndly Nurse,
> That to me gave this Lifes first native source:
> Though from another place I take my name,
> An house of auncient fame.
>
> (*Prothalamion* 127–31)

Ever since, Spenser scholars have worked to comprehend his historic invention of English authorship.

In the sections following, we shall inventory scholarship and criticism on the history of Spenser's authorial invention, beginning with his self-presentation in his extant works and following with five subsequent phases of commentary: (1) the sixteenth and seventeenth centuries, when colleagues of his era offer the first biographical reports; (2) the eighteenth and nineteenth centuries, when scholars print the first official biographies, including the first free-standing one, by Ralph Church (1879); (3) the early twentieth century, when Judson relies on a 1930s surge of research to produce the first fully modern biography; (4) the late twentieth century, when post-structuralist scholars effectively turn from the frustrations of biographical criticism to "career criticism" (see Rambuss 1996, 11); and finally (5) the early twenty-first century, when scholars even now are following up on the fin de siècle return to biography. As we shall see, the chronology for this classification is messier than the scheme might indicate, but it nonetheless provides a starting structure for mapping a complex terrain stretching across four hundred years. Moreover, the phases are not equal in magnitude; the first

---

[1] The first was Sir Kenelm Digby's *Observations on the 22 Stanza in the 9th Canto of the 2d Book of Spenser's Faery Queene* (1643).

three serve primarily as evolutionary origins for the last two. Since effectively *all* criticism written on Spenser fits under the rubric of the present chapter, we will necessarily concentrate on those works formally important to a study of Spenser's life and/or career. The goal will be to help readers bring the presence of earlier biographical commentary to bear on the range of commentary being produced today. This strategy should enable us to determine just where we are even as it indicates how we have arrived.

A Life in the Works

As the example from *Prothalamion* intimates, Spenser is the first canonical author of his time and nation to write both his own biography and his own literary commentary. From his inaugural publication in 1579, the pastoral *Shepheardes Calender*, through to *Prothalamion*, he uses the nascent medium of print and book to advertise himself as England's "new Poete" (E. K. "Epistle", *Shepheardes Calender*), the heir to the "old [native] poet" (1), Chaucer, and to Virgil, the great classical poet of imperial destiny for the Roman nation. In writing pastoral, Spenser follows Virgil in particular, who began his career with the *Eclogues*, progressed to the genre of husbandry or farm labor, the *Georgics*, and put both forms in service of his national epic, the *Aeneid*. Following Virgil and the long tradition of commentary on him, Spenser publishes the twelve-eclogue *Calender* with two important sets of information relevant here: 1) the verse eclogues themselves, which feature Colin Clout as the author's persona; and 2) a complex set of prose, verse, and pictorial documents designed to comment on the poem proper. The latter include a prefatory poem, "To His Booke," seeking patronage from Sir Philip Sidney, signed by one "Immerito" (the unworthy one); E. K.'s dedicatory "Epistle" to Spenser's mentor at Cambridge, Master Gabriel Harvey;[2] E. K.'s "Generall Argument"; an anonymous woodcut and an "Argument" by E. K. preceding each eclogue; and, closing each eclolgue, Immerito's emblem and E. K.'s detailed gloss. Although the name of Edmund Spenser nowhere appears, the effect of his book is paradoxical: it uses anonymity to draw attention to the biographical fiction of "the Authour['s] selfe" (133). Thus, in his "Epistle" E. K. reports that the "Author" uses "Colin" to "shadow" himself (133–4). Repeatedly, the book draws attention to its biographical and historical origins, from Colin's difficulties with the shepherdess Rosalind, "a feigned name," says E. K., "which being wel ordered, wil bewray the very name of hys love and mistresse, whom by that name he coloureth" (p. 39); to Colin's Song of Eliza in "Aprill", which is "purposely intended to the honor and

---

[2] Early biographers, as well as Judson, identify E. K. with Edward Kirke, a classmate of Spenser's at Pembroke College. Recently, however, scholars confirm longstanding suspicion that E. K. is Spenser himself (Schleiner 1990).

prayse of our most gracious souereigne, Queene Elizabeth" ("Argument"). From the outset, in other words, Spenser makes the fiction of his own role as national poet central to his works.

This may not be quite the topic of his next publication, the so-called Spenser–Harvey Letters of 1580, but these documents remain priceless biographically. They reveal Spenser's first name, comment upon the commercial success of *The Shepheardes Calender*, show Spenser on familiar terms with Sidney and Edward Dyer, and altogether present the poet and his friend as "university wits" not simply with a humanist education but with a national future.

Spenser's next publication, the 1590 installment of his national epic, Books I–III of *The Faerie Queene*, fulfills these early expectations by opening with a career announcement, this time under the imprimatur of the poet's full printed name, which now appears on the title page as "Ed. Spenser":

> Lo I the man, whose Muse whilome did maske,
>   As time her taught, in lowly Shephards weeds,
>   Am now enforst a farre vnfitter taske,
>   For trumpets sterne to chaunge mine Oaten reeds:
>   And sing of Knights and Ladies gentle deeds.
>
> (*Faerie Queene* I.Proem.1.1–5)

Here Spenser identifies himself as the author of *The Shepheardes Calender* and presents his turn from Virgilian pastoral to Virgilian epic, cut along the romance lines of Ariosto's *Orlando Furioso* (as "Knights and Ladies" indicates; see Hamilton 2001, 29).

As Robert Durling (1965) and Jerome S. Dees (1971) show, Spenser follows the tradition of romance epic by inserting his role as poet into his fiction initially through the voice of a first-person narrator. For instance, in Book I, Canto xi, the poet prepares for his narration of the Redcrosse Knight's battle with the dragon through an authorial pause modeled on the Virgilian tradition, during which he invokes the Muse for strength: "Now O thou sacred Muse, . . . / O gently come into my feeble brest" (I.xi.5.6–6.1). In Book III, Canto ii, the narrator uses his authorial voice to rebuke "men" for their injustice to "women kind," although again the voice is borrowed from Ariosto: "Here haue I cause, in men iust blame to find, / That in their proper praise too partiall bee" (III.ii.1.1–2). While Spenser uses his authorial voice to frame the narrative—the first-person "I" appears in the first and last stanzas of the 1590 installment—periodically he inserts a fiction that allegorizes his own art. Perhaps the most obvious in Books I–III is the episode involving the magician Merlin, who makes a magic mirror that reveals the political operation of *The Faerie Queene* itself: "It was a famous Present for a Prince, / And worthy worke of infinite reward, / That treasons could bewray, and foes conuince;/Happy this Realme, had it remayned euer since" (III.ii.21.6–9; see Williams, 1966, 94).

The 1596 installment of *The Faerie Queene* (which adds Books IV–VI) enlarges the printing of the poet's name on the title page as "EDMVND SPENSER" (Hamilton 2001, 26–27) and continues to frame the poetic fiction through the author's voice. This voice again appears in the first stanza of Book IV and in the concluding stanza of Book VI. In both places, the author's voice refers to the same troubling event: the criticism of Spenser by Elizabeth's closest adviser William Cecil, Lord Burgley. It is Cecil who appears at the outset of the poem as "The rugged forhead that with graue foresight/Welds Kingdomes causes" (IV.Proem.1.1) and at its close as "a mighty Pere" (VI.xii.41.6). Additionally, in Book IV, Canto xi, the poet tells us where he went to university: "My mother Cambridge, whom as with a Crowne/He doth adorne, and is adorn'd of it/With many a gentle Muse, and many a learned wit" (IV.xi.34.7–9). Again, Spenser inserts allegories of his role as poet. Most memorably, he situates Colin in the epic landscape of Fairyland, where the hero of courtesy in Book VI, Calidore, stumbles upon the poet's Dance of the Graces on Mount Acidale (Canto x), long understood as an allegory of Spenser's relation with a patron, perhaps Sidney or Essex (Greenlaw, 1932–57, 6: 349–64). Yet an earlier biographical portrait emerges in Book IV, Canto viii (P. Cheney 1993, 111–48), when Spenser uses the friendly Dove to bring about the reconciliation of Timas with Belphoebe, an allegory for the poet's role in reconciling his two chief patrons in the mid-1590s, Sir Walter Ralegh and Elizabeth herself, after Ralegh secretly married and impregnated Elizabeth Throckmorton, one of the queen's maids of honor.

In between the two installments of *The Faerie Queene*, Spenser publishes a series of shorter books that bear on his biographical fictions. In the 1591 *Complaints*, he pens a form that *foregrounds* the poet's voice, almost always addressing the realm's mighty peers: Sidney and Leicester in *The Ruines of Time*; Leicester again in *Virgils Gnat*; Burgley (surreptitiously) in *Mother Hubberds Tale* (see Peterson 1998); poets and patrons generally in *The Teares of the Muses* and in *Muiopotmos*. The *Complaints* are also invaluable for their dedications to the three Spencer sisters celebrated subsequently in *Colin Clouts Come Home Againe* as Phyllis, Charillis, Amaryllis (540): *Muiopotmos*, dedicated to Elizabeth; *Mother Hubberds Tale*, to Anne; and *Teares of the Muses*, to Alice. In the 1592 *Daphnaida*, Spenser writes a funeral elegy for Douglas Howard, wife to his friend Arthur Gorges (a kinsman of Ralegh), and he hints that he himself has undergone a similar grief, perhaps over the death of his first wife, Machabyas Chylde (Oram 1981, 154, 158n21). In the 1595 *Colin Clouts Come Home Againe*, Spenser transplants his pastoral persona from the *Calender*'s fields of Kent to his new home in Ireland, and narrates his trip with Ralegh back to Elizabeth's court in 1589–90. In the 1595 *Astrophel* (and the appended *Doleful Lay of Clorinda*), Spenser belatedly produces his memorial elegy on Sidney (who had died in 1586) and brings himself into relation with the grieving sister, Mary Sidney Herbert, Countess of Pembroke. Also in 1595, the marriage volume of *Amoretti* and *Epithalamion* memorably records the poet's courtship of and marriage to Elizabeth Boyle, daughter to Richard Boyle, the earl of Cork. *Amoretti* 60 has long been used to date Spenser's birth to 1552 (see D. Cheney 1984); *Amoretti* 74 mentions that the poet's mother, future wife, and queen are all named "Elizabeth"; and *Amoretti* 33 and 80 both identify Spenser as the author of *The Faerie Queene*, while sonnet 33 specifically names Lodowick Bryskett, a friend and fellow diplomat who provided, in his *Discourse of Civil Life*, one of the earliest accounts of Spenser's cultural life and acquaintances in Ireland (see Judson 1945, 105–7).

Finally, in the last year of his publishing career, 1596, England's New Poet publishes two other volumes. *Prothalamion* is biographically valuable for telling us that Spenser was born and raised in London, and that he is related to the Spencer family of Althorp Castle (the present burial site of the late Princess Diana). In this poem, too, we see Spenser not simply in association with the earl of Worcester, his two daughters, and their grooms, but he is still in mourning for Robert Dudley, earl of Leicester, who had died in 1588, and thus he now seeks a new patron, Essex. In *Fowre Hymnes*, Spenser makes his only known foray into contemplative or religious poetry, suddenly eschewing all mortals in order to depict the author's relation with God, Christ, and Dame Sapience.

From this overview of the life within the poetical works, we can glimpse how consistently Spenser uses the art of poetry to foreground his own biographical fictions. The same is true of his main prose treatise, *A View of the Present State of Ireland*, where the bureaucrat relies on the dialogue form to debate English colonialist policy in Ireland. In a way that is unusual for its time, Spenser's fictions look autobiographical in character. In his edition of the shorter poems, Richard McCabe prefers the term "auto-referential," since "the Spenserian 'I' is never truly autobiographical": "Autobiography is the condition it never quite attains, auto-fabrication the condition it never quite escapes" (1999, xvii). The auto-referential feature of the author's corpus becomes something of a Spenserian signature, and helps explain a good deal of the commentary to follow.

The sixteenth and seventeenth centuries

The principal source of material from Spenser's contemporaries is reprinted in R. M. Cummings (1971), which usefully collects 179 reports, written between 1579 and 1715. These are the polar dates connecting E. K.'s dedicatory epistle to the *Calender*, which presents the first self-printed view of Spenser as a man and an author; and John Hughes' "Life of Mr Edmund Spenser" in his edition of the *Works*, which presents the first signed biography and thus is the basis of modern commentary. Even though Hughes' "Life" appears during the eighteenth century, we will include it here because of the convenience afforded by the Cummings volume. This compendium includes a useful introduction orienting readers to the documents and a short bibliography.

Readers interested in contemporary reception of Spenser will find Cummings' volume indispensable. It includes important tributes (and occasional criticism) from such important authors as Sidney, Ralegh, Samuel Daniel, Michael Drayton, Ben Jonson, Francis Beaumont, John Milton, John Dryden, and Alexander Pope. Most pertinent here is Cummings' final section, "Biographical Notices" (315–41), which includes eleven documents, penned between 1600 and 1715 and ranging from short passages by William Camden and Thomas Fuller to the first two official biographies already mentioned, the 1679 folio and the Hughes edition, both of which occupy only a matter of pages (324–7, 334–41). These eleven documents are notable for outlining the main archival events in Spenser's life and career, for recording certain biographical anecdotes (which may or may not be true), and for etching the main features of the author's biographical portrait. These three phenomena have an afterlife in subsequent commentary.[3]

The main archival events appear in the chronology of this book. They include Spenser's birth in London to parents of poor stock, and his claim to be related to the Spencer family of Althorp; his education as a poor scholar at Cambridge; his brief job as secretary to the earl of Leicester; his conflict with Lord Burgley over *Mother Hubberds Tale*; Spenser's (subsequent) "exile" to Ireland, where he served as secretary to Lord Grey; his trip back to England with Ralegh and audience with Queen Elizabeth; his acquisition of land at Kilcolman Castle in Cork; his flight from Ireland after Irish rebels sacked Kilcolman; and finally, his poverty-stricken death after which Essex paid for his funeral and ordered the construction of his monument beside Chaucer in Poets' Corner, Westminster Abbey. Starting with Edward Phillips (Milton's nephew) in 1675, some of the documents include an inventory of Spenser's works, beginning with the *Calender* and usually concluding with the 1596 *Faerie Queene*. Yet Cummings' biographical documents are also notable for what they leave out: for instance, the name of Spenser's second wife, Elizabeth Boyle, let alone reference to the three known children who survive him; nor do the documents refer to such works as *Fowre Hymnes* and *Prothalamion*, although beginning with James Ware in 1633 *A View* occasionally attracts attention.

The biographical anecdotes tend to be intriguing. After graduating from Cambridge, it is said that Spenser lost a university fellowship to Lancelot Andrews, who went on to become Bishop of Winchester and to play such an important role in the composition of the King James Bible (1611). John Aubrey tells us that Rosalind "was a kinswoman of Sir Erasmus Ladys" and

---

[3] On the seventeenth-century lives of Spenser, see Judson (1953).

that the "chamber there at Sir Erasmus' is still called Mr Spencers chamber" (322). The anonymous life of 1679 first records the charming "Despair" incident, when Sidney read "the Twenty-eighth Stanza of Despair" in Book I of *The Faerie Queene* and told his servant to give the poet who penned it 50 pounds, only to up the award 50 pounds after reading the next stanza, and so forth up to 200 pounds, so that the servant feared that if his master kept reading, Sidney would squander the family estate (325).

Yet what is finally striking about these early biographies is the particular portrait of the author they etch. In its broadest narrative, they tell how an obscure Londoner of poor birth rose up to become "the Prince of Poets in his time," in the words of the Westminster monument. Yet inside this triumphal narrative, the biographies tell a darker tale, all the more haunting for its circular, romance pattern. For it begins in London, where the poet is born; it moves to Ireland, where the poet spends most of his adult life in exile; but finally it returns to the place of origin, where Spenser dies broken in his birth city. From Camden through Hughes, early biographers appear obsessed with Spenser's life for its fusion of *poetics* with *economics*, the "Muse"' (Camden, 316) with "Business" (Hughes, 318). It is astonishing to discover how much biographical information pertains to the financial and institutional rewards this "poet" received: the early patronage of Sidney; the official crown pension that Burghley blocked; the status of "Poet Laureat" that Elizabeth finally secured (325); the land she gave; the poverty Spenser embraced upon his final return home; and lastly, Essex's generosity in paying for Spenser's burial. Jonson gives us our starkest report:

> the Irish having robd Spensers goods, and burnt his house and a little child new born, he and his wyfe escaped, and after, he died for lake of bread in King Street, and refused 20 pieces sent to him by my Lord of Essex, and said, He was sorrie he had no time to spend them. (Cummings, 136)

Yet it is Hughes who most fully expresses this romantic narrative of authorial defeat: after Sidney's death, Spenser "seems to have spent the latter part of that time with much Grief of Heart, under the Disappointment of a broken Fortune" (339). Recurrently, we hear of a poet besieged by "Discouragement" (336), and in the end the early biographers agree: Spenser "died...of...a broken Heart" (1679 "Life", 326). As we shall see, the story of Spenser as the poet of final disaffection is still powerfully with us.

From these contemporary reports, we acquire a few other important contours. Around 1639, Robert Johnston provides the first formal glimpse of the "Spenser" we inherit today, both a poet and a secretary: "He excelled by a long way all English poets of the century before, and went with the Lord Deputy Grey to Ireland, to forestall poverty, and that he might give his energies to Apollo and the Muses in peace and leisure" (319). Around 1697, Aubrey first fixes the enduring template with which we began, when he records the phrasing of the Westminster monument, the life in the works: "Edmund Spencer, the Prince of Poets of his tyme, whose divine spirit needs no other witnesse, then the workes which he left behind him" (323). Spenser's "workes" are "witnesse" to the "divine spirit" that animates the author's life. From the 1679 life forward, commentators attempt to find Spenser in those works. In fact, Hughes succinctly formulates the entire enterprise: Spenser is "much better known by his Works than by the History of his Life" (334). Accordingly, he concludes with a lament shared by subsequent biographers: "I wish I cou'd give the Publick a more perfect Account of a Man whose Works have so justly recommended him to the Esteem of all the Lovers of *English* Poetry" (340). This predicament forces biographers to rely on the works to structure the life.

In sum, from these early documents two principal narratives emerge: the story of how the Elizabethan system of politics and economics broke the greatest poetic heart since Chaucer; and the story of how this system finally could not impede the poet's own triumphal flight to immortality. No one inscribes the latter narrative more eloquently than the anonymous biographer of 1679:

> He was a man of extraordinary Accomplishments, excellently skill'd in all parts of Learning: of a profound Wit, copious Invention, and solid Judgment: of a temper strangely tender, and amorous.... He excelled all other Ancient and Modern Poets, in Greatness of Sense, Decency of Expression, Height of Imagination, Quickness of Conceit, Grandeur and Majesty of Thought. (Cummings 1679, 326)

Whoever penned these eloquent lines, they powerfully speak to Spenser's own self-portrait in the "November" eclogue; as the shepherd Thenot tells Colin: in England and throughout Europe, Spenser is the "Nightingale... souereigne of song" (25).

Two subsequent works valuably augment Cummings: Wells (1971, 1972), printing 205 works alluding to Spenser between 1641 and 1700; and an update by J. C. Boswell (2003), which adds 49 new allusions. On the history of Spenser's reception, from the sixteenth through the twentieth centuries more broadly, three volumes are important, especially the last, which is the most recent: Wurtsbaugh (1936); Mueller (1959); and Radcliffe (1996).

The eighteenth and nineteenth centuries

Beginning with Hughes at the outset of the eighteenth century, editors of Spenser's works routinely include a short life of the poet.[4] We shall mention

---

[4] On the eighteenth-century lives, see Judson (1946). Dr Johnson does not include Spenser in his *Lives of the Poets*, for reasons outlined by Frushell (1999, 123). Frushell also includes a judicious evaluation of Hughes' life (106).

four biographies, together with the first freestanding life, which together significantly extend the short biography of Hughes, even if much in them now looks fanciful and speculative. While mentioning the earlier known facts and extending them in important ways, the principal information continues to come from Spenser's own works.

By the mid-nineteenth century, Francis J. Child (1855) in his "Memoir of Spenser" can call the author "the poet's poet" (1: vii), and include copious footnotes. Child discusses the so-called lost works of Spenser at length (1: xvi–xx) and sifts through the information about Spenser's departure for and stay in Ireland (1: xx–xxxi), while also mining the poems between the two installments of the national epic for biographical detail (1: xxxi–xlii). As Child acknowledges, his "sketch, while it is a summary of all that can now be ascertained of the uneventful life of the writer, does not afford a satisfactory insight into the character and spirit of the man" (1: xlix). This, he adds, "can only be attained by reading his works in the light derived from a knowledge of his life and fortunes" (1: xlix). Child thus concludes with some judicious insights about that character and spirit: "if Spenser's imagination was not comprehensive, precise, and bold, it was fertile, rich, and various. If he was destitute of profound passion and warm sympathy with his kind, he manifests a natural gentleness, a noble sentiment, and an exquisite moral purity...The most characteristic quality of his mind is undoubtedly sensibility to beauty" (1: lv). Whether we agree with such insights, today they appear from a forgotten age concerned to mark the precise terms of Spenser's genius.

Toward the end of this phase, we are standing on the threshold of modern biography. John Payne Collier (1862) includes a detailed life in his edition (1: ix–clvi), again complete with copious footnotes. Collier still does not know that Spenser was educated at Merchant Taylors' School (1: xi), or that his second wife's maiden name was Boyle (1: xv), but he speculates that Spenser had a first wife, although he does not know her name and mistakenly cites the register of St Clement Danes in the Strand for evidence that Spenser had a daughter named Florence (1: xv–xi). Collier knows that Spenser had two sons, Sylvanus and Peregrine (1: cliii), and a daughter, Katherine (1: cliii–iv), but he erroneously includes a third son, Lawrence (1: cliv). He believes E. K. refers to Edward Kirke (1: xxv–xxvi), provides detail about Spenser's positions in Ireland (e.g., 1: xlviii–lii), and examines the poet's relations with such figures as Harvey, Sidney, Grey, Bryskett, Ralegh, Essex, and Gorges, as well as with William Ponsonby. An inventory of both the lost works and the extant works takes up much of his space. Collier concludes by expressing surprise at how long his biography turned out to be (1: clv) and by reporting that he has been able to "add some new particulars" to Spenser's life (1: clvi).

A few years later, J. W. Hales (1883) contributes a shorter biography in R. Morris' edition, usefully summarizing nineteenth-century views: "No poet ever more emphatically lived in his poetry than did Spenser... His poems are his best biography" (xv). Hales divides Spenser's life into chapters, according to sets of years (e.g., chapter 1: 1552–79). He relies on William Winstanley to locate Spenser's birth in East Smithfield, London (xvi), and he rejects Collier's identification of Florence as Spenser's daughter (xxiii). He does not yet know the maiden name of Elizabeth Boyle, but he cites the incident, now notorious, in which Spenser quarreled litigiously with Maurice, Lord Roche over Irish land dominion (l–li). Like previous biographies of the time, Hales strings Spenser's life together primarily through his poems and prose.

Probably, however, the major contribution of the century was Church's single-volume biography of Spenser (1879), the very first full biography, and thus the great precursor of Judson.[5] Church structures his monograph-length life around six chapters; strikingly, one chapter title features *The Shepheardes Calender* and three *The Faerie Queene*, with the chapter separating the pastoral from the epic titled "Spenser in Ireland." For Church, in other words, Spenser is the poet who completes the Virgilian career pattern despite his exile in Ireland (103–04). Church identifies Spenser's education at Merchant Taylors' School (7–8), and he infuses the conventional chronological order with much contextual material, such as the John Whitgift–Thomas Cartwright controversy at Cambridge (14–15). Anticipating Judson, this is very much Spenser in his life and times (minus, we shall see, Judson's talent for *storytelling*). Principally, Church sees Spenser as "the harbinger and announcing sign" of "a new poetry, which with its reality, depth, sweetness and nobleness took the world captive," the fulfillment of which emerges where we should expect: with "Shakespere" (35–6). Church is admirably aware of the historical significance of Spenser's time in Ireland: "The first great English poem of modern times, the first creation of English imaginative power since Chaucer, and like Chaucer so thoroughly and characteristically English, was not written in England" (87). Indeed, the landscape of Ireland is "a feature of his work on which Spenser himself dwells" (88): "The *Fery Queen* might almost be called the Epic of the English wars in Ireland under Elizabeth" (91). Compelled to inventory Spenser's faults at length (119–38), Church responds with a matching inventory of his strengths (138–65). Most incisive is his observation that Spenser's premier achievements are two (165): his invention of the "English gentleman" (157), a national form of "manliness" (151) that he modeled on Sidney, Grey, and Ralegh (159–63); and his creation of modern English poetry: "It is not merely that he has left imperishable images which have taken their place among the consecrated memorials of poetry and the household thoughts of all cultivated men. But

---

[5] Pask (1996) calls Church's life "the most widely circulated biography of Spenser in its time, ... representative of ... Victorian understanding" (98).

he has permanently lifted the level of English poetry by a great and sustained effort of rich and varied art" (165). Church laments that "the family name [of Spenser's second wife] has not been thought worth preserving" (169), and he is forced to rely on Camden and Jonson for details of the poet's death (177–8): "We only know that the first of English poets perished miserably and prematurely" (178). *The Mutabilitie Cantos* thus become "fit closing words to mark his tragic and pathetic disappearance from the high and animated scene in which his imagination worked" (181). Somber yet exalted, passionately moved to the stony edge of reason, Church's story of Spenser prepares for the modern age.

Technically speaking, however, the late nineteenth-century biography by Alexander Grosart (1882–84) takes Church's work a step further and thus competes as the great transitional life to modernity. Grosart's biography, we might say, is a self-conscious scholarly one. This makes it less readable than Church's; in fact, difficult to read at all, for spliced in are long quotations, documents, and so forth. Still, Grosart has found significant new information. In his Preface, he asserts that he has written "a more matterful and adequate Life of the 'Poet of Poets' than any hitherto—from Todd to Professors Craik and Hales, and from Collier to Dean Church" (1: vi). To back up the assertion, he claims that "on almost every point of the Biography new light is thrown" (1: vi). Most importantly, he has succeeded in determining that Spenser's second wife's last name is Boyle, as announced in the title to chapter XII: "Wooing and marriage.—Wife's Name for the first time disclosed" (1: 190–202). But Grosart opens with a lengthy "Introduction" detailing "The Ancestry and Family of Spenser," which he traces to the Lancashire Spensers (xi–lxiv). Grosart identifies Rosalind as Rose (or Elisa or Alice) "Dineley or Dynley or Dinlei" (50); he includes detailed information on Jan Vander Noot (15–43), John Young, the Bishop of Rochester, and the Spenser–Harvey letters (61–76); and he explores Spenser's life in Ireland (140–71). Of particular interest is Grosart's polemic project to overturn the "deplor[able]" narrative that "allege[s]" Spenser's "dying of a broken heart and in beggary" (vi; see 235–41): "it is mere idle fiction to write him as dying broken-hearted. A broken-hearted man never could with such statesmanly resolve have addressed his Sovereign as we have found him doing" (236). Grosart is particularly proud of another accomplishment: to have "made luminous the Poet's attitude toward the 'great ones' of the period" (246), and he may have a genuine point— "I look in vain for another equal intellect's verdicts on the outstanding personalities and events of his time approaching Spenser's. You do not find the like in Shakespeare or Bacon—not even in Milton, except casually" (247). Despite such claims and his polemic, Grosart is also genuinely moved by something we appear no longer able to express:

> the Life of EDMUND SPENSER was surely one of the "beautiful lives" that not only elevate the human ideal, but inspire approximation to that

ideal... It is questionable if ever there has been human imagination so steeped in colour or so capable of shaping subtlest or swiftest thought. Few tongues can ever have been more voluble, as scarcely any pen more fluent... He also comes before us as a man of iron will, of decision, of masterful resolution, of thoroughness against all odds... his Poetry stands second only to the English Bible of 1611, in enriching our (poetical) language. (Grosart, 1882–84, 1: 250)

The early twentieth century

Twentieth-century scholarship itself is ushered in by the edition of Spenser's "poetical works" that remains standard today: J. C. Smith and Ernest de Sélincourt (1909–10, 1912), which includes an introduction to the poet's life and works. Because this edition was issued in paperback as late as 1970, and is still in print, students of Spenser continue to be drawn to de Sélincourt's introduction. Indeed it is true that this text feels modern in comparison with nineteenth-century approaches, for the biographical voice tends to stick to the facts in ways that readers today might find familiar.

It would not be until mid-century, however, that Spenser would be subject to his first full-length modern biography. In 1945, as part of the monumental eleven-volume *Variorum Edition of the Works of Edmund Spenser*, Judson gives the profession a life that is still readable and reliable today, however fanciful many find it (Rambuss 2001, 34). Judson's opening sentence reveals what had changed so dramatically by his time: a reliance on *narrative* for the voice of the biographer: "On June 29, 1552, there was born to Sir John and Lady Katherine Spencer, of Wormleighton and Althorp, their third daughter, whom they named Elizabeth" (1). Unlike previous biographers, Judson begins with the Spencers, as if trying to catch the reader's attention. Repeatedly, we are invited to imagine a lost scene, as this from Chapter 5 on "Cambridge": "Through streets dotted by students wearing such garb, we may imagine Spenser making his way as he paid his first visit to Pembroke Hall on a spring day in 1569" (29). Complete with illustrations of some of the central sites of Spenser's life, Judson's biography divides into eighteen chapters, with titles that still have the feel of biographies today: "The Southern Shepherd's Boy," "Last Years," and "Sleep after Toil."

Judson has himself done archival work, and he has benefited from a surge of research during a remarkable period in Spenser scholarship, the 1930s, by W. H. Wepley, Percy Long, Ray Hefner, Edwin Greenlaw, Douglas Hamer, Josephine Waters Bennett, Mark Eccles, Raymond Jenkins, and others.[6] Judson speculates that the poet's father was named

---

[6] For citations to these and others, see the bibliographies of Judson (1945) and Mohl (1990).

John (8), that he had a sister named Sarah (9), and that he was educated at Merchant Taylors' School in London (9) under head-master Richard Mulcaster (15). At Cambridge, we learn further about the religious debates between Whitgift and Cartwright (31–6). There is still, however, much imagination: "Warmhearted and interested in people, Spenser must have acquired other friends during his college days. One of these may have been Edward Kirke" (39). Above all, Judson's life is *congenial*.

He knows that "Spenser was a secretary, but he was also a poet" (49), and he has new facts: "On the title-page Harvey recorded in Latin the fact that the book [*The Traueiler of Ierome Turler*] was a present from Edmund Spenser, secretary of the bishop of Rochester [John Young], 1578" (53). Judson relies on Hamer to report that Spenser was indeed married early to Machabyas Chylde, and that she is the mother of Sylvanus (62–3). Judson also knows Spenser's positions in Ireland, and he narrates Spenser's life there with remarkable detail, devoting a chapter to the land, its history, and its people ("The Salvage Island," 73–83). For the first time, we realize what it might have been like outside the pale with Lord Grey. Judson includes detailed reports on the major figures of Spenser's life, from Grey and the Earl of Ormond, to John and Thomas Norris, to Ralegh and Bryskett, to Ponsonby and the printer John Wolfe. Most importantly perhaps, Judson has a chapter titled "Elizabeth Boyle."

Judson concludes with analysis and reproduction of three portraits that have been proposed for the author: the Kinnoull, the Chesterfield, and the FitzHardinge miniature (208–10). Given the dispute over them, Judson remarks, "we should probably do well to content ourselves with the vivid impression of his personality conveyed by his works and create an image of him from our own fancy":

> And what a sharply defined personality emerges from a close study of his works and life! As a foundation, there is poise, sanity, persistence in attaining worthy ends…He gains learning, he founds a house, he acquires, a decade before his death, the reputation of being England's principal poet. (Judson, 210)

From this, we can see that Judson privileges the first of our two main life narratives for Spenser: the poet's triumphal ascent to fortune and immortality. Hence Judson closes with the following sentence: Spenser's "distinction probably consists less in his innovations, notable as some of these were, than in his remarkably complete embodiment of the spirit of his age in poetry of lavish profusion and extraordinary beauty" (212).

Judson's "Preface" self-consciously reflects on his own historic contribution: "The present life differs most from its predecessors in the attention given to the atmosphere in which Spenser moved. I have undertaken to place him in his environment, surround him with his friends and associates, and study the influences both physical and human upon him" (vii). In reading Judson sixty years later, we can easily discern why his successor has yet to emerge; this is a seminal moment in Spenser studies.

The late twentieth century

Between the 1940s and the 1980s, Judson's life seemed to leave little room for biographical work. With it and with the text of Smith and de Sélincourt as the foundation of modern scholarship, by the late 1950s and 1960s, and in the 1970s, scholars rely on New Criticism and on archetypal criticism to revolutionize interpretation of Spenser's allegory. What we notice at this time is the emergence of a new biographical form in Spenser studies: the "chronology." During this period, we might say, *chronology replaces biography* as the convenient textual staple of the Spenser edition. In fact, this is the particular historical phase we now occupy: in command of Maley's *A Spenser Chronology*, we lack an updated biography.[7] Other examples right at hand are the two editions used for this book: Hamilton's *The Faerie Queene* (2001); and McCabe's shorter poems (1999). Unlike editions of Spenser from the seventeenth into the twentieth century, neither edition includes a "life," but both include a helpful prefatory "chronology."

The post-Judson turn from biography no doubt paved the way for post-structuralism during the 1980s, and especially the New Historicism, inaugurated by Stephen Greenblatt (1980), who includes an influential chapter on the colonial energy at work in Sir Guyon's destruction of the Bower of Bliss, situated historically in terms of English policy toward the Irish. Greenblatt's model of self-fashioning informs the next major phase of Spenser commentary: "career criticism."[8] In this phase, critics turn from reading Spenser's allegory to reading his literary career.

The pioneering works are Helgerson's chapter on Spenser in *Self-Crowned Laureates* (1983), and Miller's "Spenser's Vocation, Spenser's Career" (1983).[9] Helgerson identifies Spenser as England's "first laureate poet" (1983, 100)

---

[7] To my knowledge, the phenomenon has never been studied. In a personal communication, Willy Maley writes, "Other critical forms and kinds of textual apparatus have been well-covered. Jacques Derrida has written on the preface, Anthony Grafton has written a history of the footnote, and Geoff Bennington has a fascinating essay on the index, but I'm not familiar with any critical work on chronologies" (5 February 2004).

[8] Mohl is particularly helpful here: "Greenblatt 1980 and Helgerson 1983, following Bradbrook 1960, reassess Spenser's life and poetry as a consciously shaped creation" (671). Two other major influences include the essays in Berger (1988), many of them emphasizing Spenser's self-reflexive language, thought, and representation; and the work of Goldberg (1981, 1989), who first offers a post-structuralist Spenser.

[9] A co-founder of career criticism is Lipking (1981), who does not discuss Spenser. On Lipking and Helgerson as pioneers of career criticism, see Cheney (2002a).

and emphasizes the laureate's defining feature: *his self-presentation to the nation*. Whereas "amateur" poets like Sidney see their art as an escape from national service, and professional writers like Shakespeare see their writing as a way to make a living, the laureate makes poetry his vital contribution to the state. For Helgerson, "the something of great constancy at the center of the laureate's work is...the poet himself" (40): "His laureate function requires that he speak from the center" (12). Helgerson's argument is also notable for its clear narrative about Spenser's final disillusionment: "In his last works... Spenser...comes home to the pastoral, the personal, and the amorous" (97).

Miller sounds a similar note: "it has become a commonplace...that the poet's attitude toward the historical world changes in his late work...[T]he central premise of his idealized vocation, the humanist faith in literature as a mode of persuasion, is repeatedly questioned" (215–16). By "vocation," Miller means the "ideal of the poet's cultural role"; by "career," "the rhetorical strategies by which the ideal is advocated" (199). Through this distinction, Miller argues, first, that "Spenser conceived of his 'laureate enterprise' as both visionary participation in the spiritual shaping of the material world and a rhetorical effort to extend that process in the making of community" (198); and second, that eventually Spenser creates a "split poetics" (213) when his "idealized vocation" becomes "problematical" under pressure from historical contingency (212).

Such a construction also informs Joseph Loewenstein (1986), who argues that *Epithalamion* is "the ripest fruit of meditations" on "canon and career" (298); that Spenser "introduces the marriage poem as an intrusion on a generic continuum" (299); that it "testifies to...the heterodoxy of his own career" (300); and that it "insists on binding...the heterodox to the orthodox career" (300). Like Miller and Helgerson, Loewenstein disrupts the idea of Spenser as a poet of harmony: "the *Epithalamion* is a poem particularly anxious for power" (287). For Loewenstein, "Spenser's choice of Orpheus' wedding song as the authoritative model for his own enterprise seems curiously reckless" (289). Thus, Loewenstein concludes that "Spenser's technique here is to inscribe...a half-superstitious poetics in which the poet descends into the fearful as an occult charm against the sources of fear" (291).

Patrick Cheney (1993) challenges the received wisdom about the shape, goal, and final character of Spenser's literary career. He argues that Spenser's idea of a literary career constitutes a Christian Renaissance revision of the Virgilian model of pastoral leading to epic. Influenced by Pertarch and the Protestant Reformation, Spenser reconceives the sonnet sequence and marriage ode as genres of epic renewal; and toward the end of his career he turns from courtly poetry to contemplative poetry, represented by *Fowre Hymnes*. In "October," Spenser prophesies this "Orphic" idea of a literary career, and by the end of 1596 he succeeds in completing its arc. As such, Spenser does not become disillusioned with his poetics; rather, he completes a bold progress that secures his status as England's Orphic poet. Curiously, Cheney's study ends up functioning as something of an endpoint to Greenblatt's thematics of self-fashioning.[10]

For little did Cheney know that a *new* model of "career" would emerge also in 1993. Richard Rambuss (1993) revolutionizes career criticism by distinguishing between Spenser's "literary" and "secretarial" careers. Showing that the full corpus of Spenser's poetry advertises himself as a keeper of state secrets, Rambuss argues that Spenser's secretarial career is not separate from but integral to his literary career.[11] In two subsequent essays, Rambuss consolidates the link between Spenser's two careers, effectively re-bridging biographical with career criticism. Rambuss (1996) argues that we need to supplant the "poetical Spenser" with a "colonial Spenser" (17)—the Spenser presented by Helgerson, Miller, Loewenstein, and Cheney with a new biographical criticism attentive to Spenser's dual role as "poet/bureaucrat" (12). As such, Rambuss calls for "decanonizing Spenser as poet's poet" to advocate "an author who produces literature in English from a position in the Empire outside England: Spenser, an early modern anglophone poet" (17). Perhaps, then, Rambuss (2001), in Andrew Hadfield's *Cambridge Companion to Spenser* (2001), is the best place to turn for a full view of the twin features of Spenser's professional identity. Rambuss includes a readable inventory of the facts of Spenser's life as both "a poet who presents himself as the nation's laureate" and "a colonial official and planter" (13). Yet Rambuss also offers a lucid criticism on Spenser's dual professional profile: "it is across…competing, shiftingly defined social placements and markers of identity that the life and career of this dually employed poet/bureaucrat took their extraordinary shape" (14).

Even so, critics continue to be interested in Spenser's literary career. Anne Lake Prescott (1996) foregrounds an important methodology for biographical and career criticism: the poet's own intertextual reading of other authors. She shows how Spenser's engagement with the works of du Bellay can help chart the shape and chronology of Spenser's development as an artist. Subsequently, Prescott (2000) moves her French intertextual project to Ronsard in order to introduce the principle of "intercareerism." She demonstrates how the fortunes of Ronsard provide Spenser with a model for the career of the national poet in the late sixteenth century.

The collection of Anderson, D. Cheney, and Richardson (1996) warrants a special place here because it forms the most sustained attempt since Judson to pursue the subject of Spenser's biography. In the "Foreword," Anderson raises "the most vexing question of all": "precisely what bearing might the poetry have on his biography?" (ix). She identifies the "rub" as "*what* the poetry means biographically" (x). She observes that her volume is no substitute for

---

[10] For other work on literary careers, see Cheney (1997).
[11] For my review of Rambuss, see Cheney (1994).

an updated biography, but hopes that it will inspire further research. Fundamentally, she suggests that her volume has "twin convictions": "that we must seriously question the problematics of biography and the biographical bases of Spenser's life before undertaking a major biography and that any credible biography of him will be characterized by openness and ambiguity rather than by closure" (x). In addition to Prescott and Rambuss, and an afterword by Donald Cheney, contributors include Jay Farness, Vincent P. Carey and Clare L. Carroll, Jean R. Brink, F. J. Levy, Jon A. Quitslund, Joseph Loewenstein, and David Lee Miller.

The essays by Miller and Loewenstein allow us to measure some changes from the previous decade. Miller (1996) relies on deconstruction to emphasize "why [Spenser's] . . . life cannot be written": the "indeterminacy of texts" precisely prohibits the long-standing Spenserian project to use the poet's fictions as the basis of his biography. For Miller, recent arguments about "Spenser as colonial oppressor" and "careerist" ignore the "indeterminacy of texts in favor of the imagined certainties of politics, presumed to be more important, determinable, and real" (162). Alternatively, he finds "an allegory of authorship under erasure" (169). In contrast, Loewenstein (1996) finds Spenser's authorship *printed*, and he offers "a bibliographical cultural poetics" as "a contribution to the intersecting historiographies of authorial subjectivity and the institutions of print": a "material history of [the poet's] autobiography" in printed books, especially the dedicatory sonnets to the 1590 *Faerie Queene* (99). Loewenstein warns against "career criticism" that represents each stage of the poet's generic cursus as inevitable: "In Spenser's case, the passage between works is high-strung, nervous, full of backward glances, anything but inevitable" (115). Although deconstruction remains largely a Derridean *trace* in current criticism, print culture and the materiality of the book form a cutting edge.[12]

In the same year as the publication of Anderson's volume, Kevin Pask (1996) slots a chapter on Spenser into his book *The Emergence of the English Author*. Placing Spenser between Chaucer and Sidney at one end and Donne and Milton at the other, Pask aims to demonstrate how "the life of the poet" contributes to this emergence, especially how "a speculative fascination with the relationship between Sidney and Spenser" stands in place of "a significant life-narrative in the early modern period" (83). The early narratives "increasingly turned the relationship of patron and client into one of 'intimate friendship' or familiarity between two *poets*," a "process which began with Spenser himself" (83; his emphasis) but ended with Spenser

---

[12] So much so that Loewenstein, Miller, Cheney, and Elizabeth Fowler are structuring their Oxford University Press revision of the Smith and de Sélincourt edition of the works on the chronology of Spenser's print career, not on the older rubric of major poem and minor poems.

becoming Sidney's teacher. For Pask, "Spenser's biographical status as the literary *teacher* of Sidney is thus an effect produced by the institutionalization within the school of an earlier and unofficial canonical organization of English literature as a patrimony in which Spenser, not Sidney, played the role of 'father' " (112; his emphasis).

About the same time, Colin Burrow (1993) and William Oram (1997) provide excellent overview studies accessible for generalist and specialist alike. Both include chapters on Spenser's life and literary career; they offer chronological chapters on Spenser's publications; and they seek to offer distinctive portraits of the man and writer in the context of his times.[13] In his opening chapter, "The Biographical Record" (1–10), Burrow provides a modern version of the earlier "life," emphasizing the darker narrative we have identified. This reading stresses Spenser's detachment from "centres of power": on Mount Acidale, "the poet is pointedly removed from a political environment: he is a poet of loss, exile, and solitude" (9). Thus the "chief quality that emerges from Spenser's life might be called... "edginess". He was a master at sitting on cultural boundaries" (10). Burrow's little book is as handy as it is modular for our time: *observation replaces interpretation*; we have become more interested in *what lies behind the verse* than *what lies within it.*

Oram's opening chapter, "Spenser's Career" (1–24), acknowledges Spenser's success in becoming "the most famous poet of his generation" but emphasizes "a less happy view of his career" (1): "If Spenser was England's Virgil, he became a Virgil speaking from the margins rather than from the center. For all its successes, his life is the biography of an outsider" (2). Structured very much like Hales' life, in discreet units with titles like "Early years: 1552–1569" (2), Oram's chapter presents an excellent recent version of the extant archival documents sifted through a judicious critical voice. At the close, he quotes lines 150–60 of *Prothalamion* to suggest something fresh and compelling: "Spenser was perhaps looking to start over again." In his last published poem, the poet thus uses the "idealizing chivalric rhetoric" to develop "for the last time the grand political vision of a laureate poet," with "Essex in the line of military Protestant patrons" (23).

The close of the twentieth century also saw the publication of Maley's *A Spenser Chronology* (1994), the most complete compilation of biographical

---

[13] Andrew Hadfield (1994, 1997, 2003) also deserves to be singled out; although not strictly either a biographer or a career critic, he has recuperated Spenser's exile in Ireland and the Irish dynamics of his poetry, foregrounding questions of politics and nationalism. Other critics who have written importantly about Spenser's role as a poet include Richard Mallette (1979), A. Leigh DeNeef (1982), David Shore (1985), Paul Alpers (1989), John Bernard (1989), Anthony Esolen (1990), Theresa M. Krier (1990), John Watkins (1995), Bart van Es (2002a), and Syrithe Pugh (2004).

information available. An updating of Frederic Ives Carpenter's *Reference Guide* (1923), Maley's research tool is especially useful for assembling the known facts of Spenser's life and work, with particular attention to Ireland. Mohl's (1990) article on Spenser's life in *The Spenser Encyclopedia* remains the most authoritative *short* biography in print. She includes in brief the full facts of Spenser's life, observing that "few new documents have been added to the biography since 1960, by which time Spenser's life was regarded as a 'work' within the context of changing social and literary patterns in Elizabethan England" (671).[14] Mohl also includes an especially useful list of scholarship.

Stump (1996) aims less to provide the facts than to "understand" Spenser's "place in the extraordinary literary renaissance"; he presents, in other words, a *literary* life. He does include the facts, but hangs them on the high points of Spenser's career, especially individual works, and he includes a useful unit on Spenser's reception from the seventeenth through the twentieth centuries (256–60). Stumps's essay includes a helpful bibliographical apparatus: a list of early Spenser editions (228–9); portraits, title pages, and other facsimile documents; and a bibliography (260–3).

Waller (1994) also writes a "literary life," and he follows the trend of hanging the life on Spenser's published poems. Deeply inflected by post-structuralist theory, his narrative already feels out of date. Spenser is not the poet of harmony but the poet of gaps and dissonances. The book does not advance our knowledge of Spenser's life, and it tends to offer interpretations of Spenser's works based on other critics, but it does offer a sustained reading of the poet in his works by an informed critic. Curiously, Waller foregrounds *The Faerie Queene* at the expense of the shorter poetry, limiting discussion of such shorter poems as *Fowre Hymnes* and *Prothalamion* to a single paragraph. For some, Waller's study may be broadly useful for its sympathetic summarizing of Spenser's historic achievement as an English author.

To conclude this section, we may turn to two critics who influentially pursue different national foci for Spenser, although their most recent work takes us into the new century. Louis Montrose (1986a, 1996, 2002) foregrounds Spenser's identity as an English author who fashions his relationship with Queen Elizabeth, who in turn fashions Spenser through historical pressures and agendas. Montrose's central idea of the "reciprocal" relation between poet and queen forms the center of what he comes to call "the Elizabethan political imaginary" (2002), "the collective repertoire of representational forms and figures—mythological, rhetorical, narrative, iconic—in which the beliefs and practices of Tudor political culture were pervasively articulated"

---

[14] Since Mohl's article, Brink (1994, 1996, 1997b) is noteworthy for adding to the biography.

(907). In this last essay, Montrose argues that Spenser's poetry does not merely engage with "literary history" but constitutes a significant "intervention into the Elizabethan public sphere": Spenser "further[s] the political agenda of limited monarchy" in "resistance to royal autocracy" (939). According to Montrose, "in his rhetorical bridling of the monarch, Spenser invented a gender-specific poetic equivalent of what the Elizabethan political nation understood as republicanism" (940).

In contrast, Richard McCabe (2002) foregrounds Spenser's identity as an English poet spending the main part of his professional career in Ireland. In fact, McCabe crowns the 1990s wave of "Irish" criticism with a stunning investigation into the Gaelic literary context for Spenser's poetry and prose. Presenting Spenser as a "poet of exile," McCabe examines the Spenser canon through two contexts: imperial aspiration and female "regiment." As a result of Elizabeth's policy in Ireland, settlers like Spenser became frustrated with their expansionist project and eventually were alienated from the queen's sovereignty. The result is the striking twinning of sexual with colonial enterprises in *The Faerie Queene*. Spenser's commitment to violence against the Irish ends up compromising the idealized moral vision at the heart of the national epic and thus threatens its attempt to fashion English national identity. Our most authoritative recent monograph on Spenser, McCabe's book continues to sound a dominant note: Spenser is the poet of exile who fashions Elizabethan England's greatest body of art out of alienation from the nation's imperial center.

The early twenty-first century

Since both McCabe's monograph and Montrose's last essay appear in the opening years of the twenty-first century, they at once crown the past century and inaugurate the new. Andrew Hadfield's *Cambridge Companion* (2001) formally functions in this pivotal role, as does the present guide. While it is still too early to make informed judgments about the new century, we might conclude with reference to a few recent works and events.

Serving as a kind of counter-complement to Anderson, D. Cheney, and Richardson on the "subject of biography," *European Literary Careers: The Author from Antiquity to the Renaissance*, edited by Patrick Cheney and Frederick A. de Armas (2002), takes "career criticism" out of its mooring in Spenser and the English Renaissance and extends it to classics, medieval studies, studies of the continental Renaissance, and women's studies. For instance, Joseph Farrell (2002) pioneers commentary on the origins of Virgil's career, while Mark Vessey (2002) and Robert R. Edwards (2002) both examine medieval literary careers. William J. Kennedy (2002) attends to the career of Petrarch, and Patrick Cheney (2002b) argues that we see Spenser's "Februarie" eclogue as a "career document" positioning the New

Poet between the careers of Virgil and Chaucer. Cheney's introduction to the volume (2002a) is the first attempt to theorize "career criticism" as a distinctive branch of literary methodology. He sees this branch aiming primarily to "delineate a writer's self-conscious inscription of a pattern of genres, which itself responds to the careers of other writers, in order to pursue literary, political, religious, and sometimes erotic goals" (12), even as he hopes the branch will break free from simplistic models of authorial agency and self-presentation.

In part inspired by this volume, Philip Hardie and Helen Moore directed the third Passmore Edwards Symposium on the topic of "Literary Careers" at the University of Oxford on 2–4 September 2004. The symposium brought together classicists and scholars from English, with primary reference to the careers of Virgil and Ovid, including their instantiation during the English Renaissance. The symposium was important in displaying the fruit that career criticism on Spenser is now bearing.

At the same time, career criticism has recently been giving way to *authorship criticism*. Most often, that is, critics are viewing Spenser as the primary inventor of the modern notion of authorship, and they see Jonson as Spenser's most important successor: "When Spenser and Jonson used the book format to generate the author's laureate status, ... they produced ... modern and familiar images of literary authority—classically authorized writers who serve as the origin and arbiter of a literary monument that exceeds its place in everyday cultural transactions" (Wall 2000, 86). As these terms indicate, our primary narrative about Spenser as the inventor of English authorship still relies on Helgerson's model of the laureate poet, but now reconfigures it in terms of more recent work on the materiality of the book and print culture. Thus the Spenser we value today is *the first laureate author who uses print and book to present himself as England's national poet*.

In these terms, the project that began with Camden and Hughes, of trying to relate Spenser's life to his literary career, continues vitally today. Since those early times, we have greatly expanded our knowledge of the facts of his life, and we have intertwined his literary with his secretarial career. Spenser's life and career(s) continue to be fascinating for their enigmatic relation between biography and fiction, the real and the imagined. As presented through four hundred years of commentary, we might say that Spenser's life and career construct a profound monument to a rather singular early modern individual: a diplomat, a treatise writer, a husband, a father, and a planter-subject of the English crown, Spenser is also a poet, an author, the creator of *The Faerie Queene*, and finally Elizabethan England's supremely sovereign singer.

Without question, the new century continues to be attentive to both biographical and career criticism. While the latter may have reached its peak in the mid-1990s, significant work still needs to be done in the area of biography. We might hope that before the first decade of the twenty-first century ends, we will have a new biography to complement and perhaps succeed Judson. Even now, sounds herald the life of this hope.[15]

Acknowledgement

Thanks to Bart van Es, Richard Frushell, and Richard McCabe for thorough readings of this essay; to Dustin Stegner for helping collect and assemble the materials; and to Joseph Loewenstein, Willy Maley, and David Lee Miller for their conversation.

Further reading

Anderson, J. H., D. Cheney, and D. A. Richardson. eds 1996. *Spenser's Life and the Subject of Biography*, Amherst: University of Massachusetts Press.

Burrow, C. 1996. "The Biographical Record", *Edmund Spenser*, Plymouth: Northcote House, 1–10.

Cheney, P. 1993. *Spenser's Famous Flight: A Renaissance Idea of a Literary Career*, Toronto: University of Toronto Press.

Cummings, R. M. ed. 1971. *Spenser: The Critical Heritage*, London: Routledge & Kegan Paul.

Helgerson, R. 1983. "The New Poet Presents Himself", *Self-Crowned Laureates: Spenser, Jonson, Milton, and the Literary System*, Berkeley: University of California Press, 55–100.

Judson, A. C. 1945. *The Life of Edmund Spenser*, Vol. 11, in *The Works of Edmund Spenser: A Variorum Edition*. 11 vols, eds Edwin Greenlaw, *et al*. Baltimore: Johns Hopkins Press, 1932–57.

Loewenstein, J. F. 1986. "Echo's Ring: Orpheus and Spenser's Career", *English Literary Renaissance*, 16: 287–302.

Maley, W. 1994. *A Spenser Chronology*, Lanham, MD: Barnes & Noble.

McCabe, R. A. 2002. *Spenser's Monstrous Regiment: Elizabethan Ireland and the Poetics of Difference*, Oxford: Oxford University Press.

Miller, D. L. 1983. "Spenser's Vocation, Spenser's Career", *ELH* 50: 197–231.

Mohl, R. 1990. "Spenser, Edmund", *The Spenser Encyclopedia*, Gen. ed. A. C. Hamilton. Toronto: University of Toronto Press.

Montrose, L. A. 1986. "The Elizabethan Subject and the Spenserian Text", Patricia Parker and David Quint, eds 1986. *Literary Theory/Renaissance Texts*. Baltimore: Johns Hopkins University Press, 303–40.

——. 1996. "Spenser's Domestic Domain: Poetry, Property and the Early Modern Subject", *in Subject and Object in Renaissance Culture*, eds Margreta de Grazia, Maureen Quilligan, Peter Stallybrass, Cambridge: Cambridge University Press, 83–122.

——. 2002. "Spenser and the Elizabethan Political Imaginary", *ELH* 69: 907–46.

---

[15] Readers might be interested to know that at least two Spenser scholars are known to be working on a new biography. Moreover, I have been asked by a well-known Renaissance biographer about the prospect of his/her writing one. And informally I have suggested to another senior biographer that among Renaissance authors Spenser is most in need of a life.

Oram, W. 1997. "Spenser's Career", *Edmund Spenser*, New York: Twayne, 1–24.

Prescott, A. L. 2000. "The Laurel and Myrtle: Spenser and Ronsard", Patrick Cheney and Lauren Silberman, eds, *Worldmaking Spenser: Explorations in the Early Modern Age*, Lexington: University Press of Kentucky, 63–78.

Rambuss, R. 1993. *Spenser's Secret Career*. Cambridge: Cambridge University Press.

——. 2001. "Spenser's Life and Career", *The Cambridge Companion to Spenser*, ed. Andrew Hadfield. Cambridge: Cambridge University Press, 13–36.

Stump, D. V. 1996. "Edmund Spenser", *Sixteenth-Century British Nondramatic Writers*, 3rd Series, ed. David A. Richardson, *Dictionary of Literary Biography*, Vol. 167. Detroit: Gale Research, 228–63.

Waller, G. F. 1994. *Edmund Spenser: A Literary Life*, New York: St. Martin's Press.

3
Politics

Andrew Hadfield

Spenser and Contemporary Political Readings

In 1648, fifty years after Spenser's death, a section of *The Faerie Queene* was published separately in a small quarto of eleven printed pages. The work consisted of twenty-five verses from Spenser's *magnum opus*, (V.ii.29–54), detailing Artegall's defeat of the Giant with the Scales, obviously recognised then as now, as one of the key political passages in the work (Patterson 1992; O'Connell 1990b). The extract was given the grand title, *The faerie leveller, or, King Charles his leveller descried and deciphered in Queene Elizabeths dayes by her poet laureat Edmond Spenser, in his unparaleld poeme entituled, The faerie qveene, a lively representation of our times*. The last phrase is the key to reading the text, an insight developed in the prefatory material which argues that 'the Prince of English Poets *Edmund Spenser*' wrote verses which 'then propheticall are now become historicall in our dayes' (3). Spenser's story of the knight of Justice arguing with the Giant who tries to impose universal equality by weighing everything in his scales, before throwing him off a cliff, is interpreted as a royalist fable. Artegall is King Charles; Talus is 'The Kings forces'; 'The Giant Leveller' is 'Col. Oliver Cromwell' (4).

The editor of the extract shows that he is a careful reader of *The Faerie Queene*, and he provides helpful information for the readers he wishes to persuade. He defends the use of extracts with a series of literate examples culminating in, 'here is meat out of the Eater, sweet hony to be found in the carkasse of a slaine Lyon'. He recognises that Spenser's poem is an allegory that needs to be decoded, and has clearly read the letter to Ralegh as a guide: 'the drift and intention of the Author in it, is to set forth a compleat Gentleman, accomplisht with all vertues adorning a truly noble Person'. And, in order to defend his belief that the poem is a prophecy of his times he provides some anagrams which prove Spenser's ability to see into the future. On the cover below the title is printed:

Anagram
Parliaments Army
Partie mar's al men.

After Cromwell is cast as the 'Giant Leveller', the editor notes 'the Letters of whose name fall into this Anagram. Oliver Cromwell. Com' our vil' Leveller'. The extract is to be read as a defence of true nobility against the evils and chaos caused by democracy, which leads only to the rule of the mob and, therefore, tyranny.[1] The text ends with the 'Lawlesse multitude' hounding Artegall, who 'ne wist what to doe, / For loath he was his noble hands t'embrew, / In the base blood of such a Rascall crew'. Eventually he sends Talus and his iron flail to impose order, and the poem concludes with an epic simile, giving the work a satisfying classical gloss for the royalist reader:

> As when a Faulcon hath with nimble-flight
> Flowne at a flush of Ducks fore-by the brooke:
> The trembling Fowle dismay'd with dreadull fight
> Of Death the which them allmost overtooke,
> Doe hide themselves from her astonying looke,
> Amongst the Flags, and covert round about:
> When Talus saw they all the field forsooke,
> And none appear'd of all that Raskall Rout:
> To Artegall he turnd, and went with him throughout.

A contemporary royal reader had a very different sense of the second edition of the poem when he read it in 1596. James VI of Scotland, by this time likely—but by no means certain—to become the next king of England, expressed outrage at the representation of the trial of his mother, Mary Stuart, in Book V, Canto ix of Spenser's poem. James refused to allow the second edition of *The Faerie Queene* to be sold in Scotland because of 'som dishonourable effects (as the King deems thereof) against himself and his mother deceased', later demanding 'that Edward [*sic*] Spenser for his fault be duly tried and punished' (Maley 1994, 68). James clearly felt that Spenser's poetic narration of the trial of Duessa was likely to hinder his chances of achieving his lifetime ambition of uniting the crowns of England and Scotland, by slandering Mary as guilty of 'vyld treasons, and outrageous shame' (40) in her attempts to overthrow Mercilla (Elizabeth) (McCabe 1987). The accusations made by the courtier, Zele, make Duessa's crimes public through a series of personifications:

> Then brought he forth, with griesly and grim aspect,
> Abhorred *Murder*, who with bloudie knyfe

---

[1] A commonplace of political argument: see Aristotle, 1946, 216.

> Yet dropping fresh in hand did her detect,
> And there with guiltie bloudshed charged ryfe:
> Then brought he forth *Sedition*, breeding stryfe
> In troublous wits, he forth *Incontinence* of lyfe,
> Euen foule *Adulterie* her face before,
> And lewd *Impietie*, that her accused sore.

(V.ix.48)

It is hardly surprising that James took umbrage at these lines. He may have had no personal affection for his mother, whom he had not seen since childhood, but they clearly reflected badly on the house of Stuart, already a tainted bloodline in many English eyes because of their association with the worst elements of Catholicism (McLaren 1999). Furthermore, Spenser's comments echo the savage criticisms of Mary's behaviour made by her Scottish detractors, many of whom, like George Buchanan, James's former tutor, wanted the monarchy to be as limited in its powers as possible (Buchanan 1571; Phillips 1964; Mason 1982). James certainly did not read Spenser as a strong supporter of the institution of monarchy.

These divergent readings show that Spenser was a controversial figure among his contemporaries and the political meaning of his work contested, perhaps something we might expect when passages are extracted from the whole and then hailed as the key to all mythologies. Perhaps we might define three political strains of Spenser criticism in the seventeenth century: there are those readers who emphasise the oppositional, Protestant nature of Spenser's writing, seeing him as hostile to the court and cultivating a pastoral internal exile among like-minded writers (see O'Callaghan 2000); those who saw him as the most important English poet and one who defined and upheld a central literary tradition (see Radcliffe 1996); and those who saw him as the spokesperson for the English in Ireland (see Henley 1928; Canny 1983).

Spenser and Elizabeth

James's reading is in line with the broad consensus of contemporary scholars of *The Faerie Queene*, who have tended to emphasise the work's increasing disillusionment with Elizabeth, despair at her vacillating policies, especially in Ireland, and flirtation with alternative forms of government (Cain 1978; Hadfield 1998; Canny 2000; Gregory 2000; Montrose 2002). Recent work has revised the once universally held position that Spenser was a poet who simply wanted to celebrate the virtues of his virgin queen, and was a political conservative (Jones 1930; Yates 1975; Wells 1983). As David Scott Wilson-Okamura has recently argued, 'The idea that Spenser's epic contains implicit criticism of Elizabeth, and especially of her decision not to marry, has now passed into the realm of critical orthodoxy...the question is no longer "whether Spenser criticises Elizabeth, but when he starts to do so"'

(Wilson-Okamura 2002, 63). This new understanding of Spenser as a disaffected critic of Elizabeth is in line with a new orthodoxy in Tudor historiography, which places a similar emphasis on the criticism voiced implicitly and explicitly throughout what is now called Elizabeth's 'second reign' (c. 1580–1603), a period that coincides neatly with Spenser's entire literary career. Historians routinely highlight the despair and disillusionment felt by many of the queen's articulate subjects at her failure to secure the succession; the fear at the growing power of Spain and the weakness of an embattled England, despite the fortunate success over the Armada in 1588; the feelings of vulnerability owing to the outbreak of the Nine Years War in Ireland (1594–1603); the growth of factionalism at court as the Essex circle fought with the Cecils for control of government policy; and the unrest caused by a series of poor harvests (Guy 1995).

It is probably no accident that what most critics agree must have been Spenser's last poem, 'Two Cantos of Mutabilitie', was not published in his lifetime, and only appeared in 1609. It was apparently discovered by the publisher, Matthew Lownes, who appended the cantos to *The Faerie Queene* in the first folio edition of the poem (Johnson 1933; Zitner 1968). In this work Spenser describes how the Titaness Mutability confronts Jove, conqueror of the universe and the ruling God of Cynthia (a figure for Elizabeth, as Spenser's letter to Ralegh makes clear (Hamilton 2001, 716)), and they meet on Arlo Hill, outside Spenser's house in Kilcolman, to determine who controls the universe. The judge, Nature, eventually awards victory to Jove, on the grounds that Mutability's claim that change is the determining principle in the universe means that she herself is subject to change and so cannot rule herself:

> I well consider all that ye haue sayd,
>> And find that all things stedfastnes doe hate
>> And changed be: yet being rightly wayd
>> They are not changed from their first estate;
>> But by their change their being doe dilate:
>> And turning to themsleves at length againe,
>> Doe worke their owne perfection so by fate:
>> Then ouer them Change doth not rule and raigne;
> But they raigne ouer change, and doe their states maintaine.

> (VII.vii.58)

This confidence in the eventual stability of matter is undercut by the setting of the debate, which takes place in Ireland, a land subject to catastrophic change both historically, in the form of the rebellion of Hugh O'Neill, which was to reach its climax soon after Spenser wrote the cantos, and within the poem itself. Spenser transposes Ovid's tale of Actaeon seeing Diana naked in Ireland, having the cheeky god Faunus persuade Molanna, one of Diana's handmaidens, to tell him where she bathes. He hides in the bushes and sees Diana. Feeling such 'great joy' at the sight of the naked goddess he cannot contain himself and 'breaking forth in laughter, loud profest / His foolish thought' (VII.vi.46). Understandably angry at this intrusion—and insult—she has her handmaidens dress him in a deerskin and they hunt him. Whereas Actaeon is torn to pieces, Faunus escapes and Molanna marries her beloved Fanchin, another one of Diana's handmaidens (Holahan 1976). Diana reacts with fury at this transgression and not only never visits Ireland again but 'an heauy haplesse curse did lay' on the island, so that it ceases to be the fairest of the British Isles and is made into a place

> that Wolues, where she was wont to space,
> Should harbour'd be, and all those Woods deface,
> And Thieues should rob and spoile that Coast around.
> Since which, those Woods, and all that goodly Chase,
> Doth to this day with Wolues and Thieues abound:
> Which too-too true that lands in-dwellers since haue found.

(VII.vi.55)

The myth is carefully rooted in contemporary reality, Spenser even making a joke about his home by asking the rhetorical question, 'Who knowes not *Arlo-hill*? (VII.vi.36.6) (Coughlan 1996). The answer would have been that many Irish readers would have known the location, but very few English readers, a sign that, as the future of the world is about to be decided, the English public remains ignorant of the cataclysmic events taking place in a land they are supposed to govern (Hadfield 1997, Ch. 6). It is hardly surprising that the cantos did not enter the public sphere during Elizabeth's realm as they cast Cynthia/Elizabeth as an ailing ruler subject to the ravages of time, who has lost control of her kingdom because she is always changing her mind:

> Then is she mortall borne, how-so ye crake;
> Besides, her face and countenance euery day
> We changed see, and sundry forms partake,
> Now hornd, now round, now bright, now brown and gray:
> So that *as changefull as the Moone* men use to say.

(VII.vii.50.5–9; cited Norbrook 1984, Ch. 5)

As the 'Two Cantos of Mutabilitie' make clear, Elizabeth is seen naked in Ireland. The cheeky Faunus—who may stand for Hugh O'Neill, or, even, the poet himself who acknowledged that he had effectively become Irish in *Colin Clouts come home againe* (1595) (Shire 1978, 187; Hadfield 1994c, Ch. 6)—exposes that the would-be empress has no clothes. Power is simply achieved through conquest, as Jove asserts in his defence of his right to rule (VII.vi.29–31), and Elizabeth is shown to be in danger of not being strong enough to protect her lands and her subjects. Furthermore, if we read Mutabilitie as a figure of Mary Stuart challenging the right of Cynthia/ Elizabeth to rule, then we can see that Spenser thought that his worst fears about the succession were about to be realised (Hadfield 2003, Ch. 8). The son of the daughter of chaos was about to become king, a man who had already demanded that the poet be punished for slandering his mother.

Coded criticism

It is indeed hard not to read these late works as critical of the queen and expressing the frustration that so many felt in the 1590s at their inability to control the future. The question is, how far back did Spenser's criticism go? And, who understood what he was trying to say? This is a complex problem, given the lack of surviving evidence of reading of Spenser's poetry. Spenser may well have coded his works carefully so that only the initiated could have read them carefully, his narratives developing meticulously and painstakingly, and requiring readers to go back and rethink earlier episodes in the light of new evidence. Certainly contemporary critics generally read *The Faerie Queene* as a coherent, integrated whole with a meticulously constructed overall design, often intended to make the reader reconsider and revise what he or she has assumed the poem meant at an earlier point in the narrative (Alpers 1967; McCaffrey 1976). Elizabeth awarded Spenser a pension of £50 a year in 1591, just after his lengthy visit to the court with Sir Walter Ralegh, a rare example of the queen's generosity to writers (Maley 1994, 56). If his work did attack the monarch then she appears not to have noticed from the narrative of *The Shepheardes Calender* and the first three books of *The Faerie Queene*. Furthermore, the evidence we have of the first reader of *The Faerie Queene*, John Dixon, who left extensive annotations to Book I in his copy, suggest that the poem could be read as a literal and straightforward historical allegory of recent events in 1597 (rather as James read Book V). He sees the book as a defence of the Elizabethan church settlement as the culmination of England's Protestant revolution, which will lead to an eventual triumph over her Catholic enemies (Dixon 1964; O'Connell 1990a).

But perhaps such issues should not concern us unduly, or force us to slavishly follow the limited evidence we have. After all, our understanding of early modern reading habits and practices is still fairly rudimentary (Raven, Small and Tadmor 1996; Sharpe and Zwicker 2003). It should also be noted that some books of a fairly radical nature were dedicated to the queen, including Richard Beacon's *Solon his Follie* (1594), a Machiavellian discussion of the problems of government in Ireland and England, which made explicit use of republican notions of government (Peltonen 1995). This might indicate that Elizabethan political debate was a lot livelier than many modern critics believe, and that getting to the heart of the nation was better than staying in the margins (McEachern 1996, Ch. 2).

The Shepheardes Calender

The publication of *The Shepheardes Calender* in 1579 was an event designed to draw attention to the arrival on the literary scene of a great new poet who wanted to assume the mantle of a national spokesman (Helgerson 1983). The format of the book itself—with its elaborate preface, extensive annotation, woodcuts, and pages carefully divided up into sections of text and notes—is clearly designed to mimic the appearance of a humanist edition of a rediscovered classic. The commentary of E. K., who is almost certainly a creation of Spenser and Gabriel Harvey, is one of a number of elaborate intellectual interventions that they pioneered in the late 1570s before Spenser went to Ireland severing the close partnership they were keen to advertise publicly. The evidence of this book should remind us that from the start of his career Spenser was interested in unsettling and baiting an audience, trying to make readers follow the twists and turns of his particular thoughts, and so enable his ideas and arguments to speak for a nation. Throughout the work Spenser drops a series of hints for those alert enough to read the text properly that he is at least as interested in questions of government and national politics as he is in the ostensible subject matter of the lives and loves of the shepherds he represents (something most readers of pastoral in the sixteenth century would have realised (Bernard 1989; Haber 1994)). The first eclogue shows a shepherd's boy, Colin Clout, lamenting that he is unable to take care of his flock properly because of his all-encompassing love for the unobtainable Rosalind. The name, 'Colin Clout', is borrowed from John Skelton, who invented Colin as a figure of homely English virtue to criticise the wealthy and powerful who were exploiting those they should have been looking after (Walker 1988, Ch. 4). Colin refers to his own inadequate performance of his duties as 'ill government' ('Januarye', l. 45), and a note to the use of the word 'couthe' at the bottom of the page refers the reader to Sir Thomas Smith's *De Republica Anglorum*, a work which had not yet been published (it appeared in 1583) but which circulated extensively in manuscript. E. K.'s note reads:

> couthe) commeth of the verbe Conne, that is, to know or to have skill. As well interpreteth the same the worthy Sir Thomas Smitth in his booke of gouernment: whereof I have a perfect copie in wryting, lent me by his kinesman, and my verye singular good friend, M. Gabriel Harvey: as also some other of his most grave and excellent writings. (McCabe 1999, 38)

These details provide the reader with enough information to know that the poem has grand ambitions to make political as well as poetic statements. Metaphors and allegorical passages can easily be reversed so that the vehicle and subject of the trope change places. Here, the shepherd guarding the flock is *like* government, but the inference we draw as readers may be that government is like the lives of the shepherds shown in the eclogues. And, as might be expected, this does prove to be the case. The note draws attention to Sir Thomas Smith's work, with E. K. letting the reader know that Gabriel Harvey possesses a copy of his writings which he circulates to his friends. Posing as a fiction, this is undoubtedly a piece of real information that the author wishes to pass on to the reader. Smith's *De Republica Anglorum* was the most influential description of the constitution and government of England available in Elizabeth's reign. It makes the case that England has a 'mixed' constitution that successfully combines the three political elements of monarchy, aristocracy and democracy, principally through the operation of parliament as the highest authority in the land which has the power to establish the laws that govern the country. The queen rules as 'king in parliament', not simply via her own authority (Smith 1583; McLaren 1999, Ch. 7; Collinson 2003, Ch. 1). Spenser is warning the reader that Smith's well-known description of government in England is centrally relevant to the poems that follow.

New Historicist critics writing in the 1980s found a renewed interest in *The Shepheardes Calender*, reading it as a 'pastoral of power', in Louis Montrose's words (Hadfield, ed., 1996b, Ch. 3). The allusions to contemporary events had already been exhaustively analysed by 'Old' Historicist scholars such as Paul McLane (McLane 1961), but they were now rediscovered by a new generation of critical readers who were keen to untangle the relationship between the aesthetic and the political significance of the poem, rather than read it simply as a literary work by a great writer.

One political event which haunts *The Shepheardes Calender* is the projected marriage of Elizabeth and the Duke of Alençon (McLane 1961). Sir Philip Sidney, a court figure with whom Spenser was keen to be associated, was banished from court for writing a letter to the queen urging her not to place the future of England in the hands of a foreign ruler (Duncan-Jones 1991, 148–52). Closer to home still, Hugh Singleton, the publisher of *The Shepheardes Calender*, had earlier published John Stubbes's *A Discovery of a Gaping Gulf* (1579), a scathing attack on the match, and had only just avoided the fate of the author, who had his right hand severed in public for sedition (Stubbes). The April eclogue, for example, is advertised as a poem that 'is purposely intended to the honor and prayse of our most gracious sovereigne, Queene Elizabeth'. However, the opening lines are startlingly at odds with any expectation the reader might reasonably have that the poem is one of happy celebration:

> THENOT Tell me good Hobbinoll, what garres thee greet?
> What? hath some Wolfe they tender Lambes ytorne?
> Or is thy Bagpype broke, that sounds so sweete?
> Or art thou of thy loved lasse forlorne?

> ('Aprill', ll. 1–4)

The question that the lines pose is, if all is well in Elizabeth's realm, then why are her loyal subjects so unhappy? The second line uses the familiar language of Reformation polemic, whereby Catholic wolves are seen to be devouring Protestant sheep, suggesting that religion is the key issue here, with the Catholics about to overwhelm the Protestants. The song in praise of the queen emphasises her virginity, a manipulative intervention for a woman who was planning to get married when the poem went to press, and one that, in Helen Hackett's words, 'served to establish an iconographic convention whereby virginity and fertility were not seen as opposites, but as complementary properties in the figure of Elizabeth' (Hackett 1995, 111). The attempt would appear to be to persuade the queen that virginity might be a better option for her people than a marriage to a foreigner, especially bearing in mind the experience of her older half-sister (Loades 1991). The fear is the same as that articulated in the 'Two Cantos of Mutabilitie', showing that some political issues remained constant throughout Spenser's writing career.

In the next eclogue, 'Maye', Piers and Palinode debate the merits of different forms of religion, Piers being a 'protestant' and Palinode a 'Catholic', as the 'Argument' informs the reader, a subject that dominates the subsequent eclogues (King 1990a, Ch. 1, Norbrook 1984, Ch. 3). It is not difficult to decide who gets the better of the argument here, and in the July eclogue the shepherds are represented as good servants of the church 'to the shame and disprayse of the proude and ambitious Pastours. Such as Morell is here imagined to be' (McCabe 1999, 95). This eclogue laments the house arrest of the puritan Edmund Grindall, Archbishop of Canterbury—here represented as Algrind—for his sponsorship of radical Protestants, an episode that, Patrick Collinson has argued, reveals 'Spenser's barely suppressed republicanism' (Collinson 2003, 44; McLane 1961). In short, *The Shepheardes Calender* provides numerous hints—only a small number of which have been noted here—that the monarch has been led astray and is not serving her people well, especially in matters of religion. The reference to *De Republica Anglorum* and the fact that it was circulating around the Spenser circle indicate that many were well aware that those in power were losing sight of the fact they were supposed to rule a realm in the interests of the people as well as themselves.

Lord Burghley

Spenser's opposition to powerful figures within the upper echelons of court circles defined the trajectory of his career as a writer and as a civil servant. It is possible that he felt it wise to make his way in Ireland as secretary to Lord Grey in 1580 because the circulation of a manuscript version of his satire, 'Prosopopoia, or Mother Hubberds Tale', offended William Cecil, 1st. Baron Burghley, her Lord Treasurer (1572–98) and one of the most powerful men who advised Elizabeth (Bradbrook 1960). The work certainly caused an outrage when it was published as one of the volume of *Complaints* in 1591, as recently discovered evidence has confirmed (Peterson 1998). The poem tells the story of the Ape and the Fox (the fox being Burghley), who practise a series of deceptions in order to improve their station in the world, culminating in them usurping the throne when they steal the scepter, crown and skin of a sleeping lion. It is not hard to see why Burghley might take offence at being portrayed as a devious creature who allowed a fake to 'tyrannize at will' (l. 1127), cramming his court with 'forreine beasts' (l. 1119). Burghley's animosity was evidently powerful enough to make Spenser despair that his poetry would never be read properly and he articulated this fear in the last verse published in his lifetime. The second edition of *The Faerie Queene* concludes with the Blatant Beast, the monster with a thousand tongues who attacks its targets without discrimination or purpose, escaping from the chains that briefly bound it to run riot:

> Ne may this homely verse, of many menaest,
> > Hope to escape his venemous despite,
> > More then my former writs, all were they clearest
> > From blamefull blot, and free from all that wite,
> > With which some wicked tongues did it backbite,
> > And bring into a mighty Peres displeasure,
> > That never so deserved to endite.

(VI.xii.41.1–7)

The Faerie Queene is submerged in a linguistic world of slander so that no one knows how to read properly, and the truth that the poet articulates is lost among a wealth of falsehoods (Kaplan 1997, Ch. 2). Spenser explicitly relates this failure of reading to a political vacuum at the very centre of the realm. No one can direct the people in the right direction as long as figures like the fox, Burghley, decide on the regime's policies, misleading the queen and stifling true religion.

Powerful women

Spenser's perception of political authority means that he concentrates his political analysis on the role of the queen (which does not mean that he supports everything that she does, or that he believes that her position is defined in exactly the right way). Louis Montrose, in an influential essay, has made the compelling case that, while poets were servants of the monarch, they often realised that they had the power to represent and so manipulate the image and, perhaps, the behaviour of their ruler (Montrose 1986a). John Foxe made a serious effort to force Elizabeth's hand in his *Actes and Monuments of the Christian Church* (1563, 1581) by representing her as more committed to a radical reform of the English church than she really was, and Spenser followed suit in *The Faerie Queene* (Yates 1975). Politics could not be separated from issues of gender during Elizabeth's reign. John Knox had written his inflammatory *The First Blast of the Trumpet against the Monstrous Regiment of Women* (1558) against Mary, but her death whilst the work was in press meant that his attack on women rulers was unfortunately re-directed towards the Protestant Elizabeth and, Knox was forced into a humiliating mixture of a defence of his position and backtracking. Knox argued, following a standard misogynist line of thought, that women should not be allowed to become monarchs because they were the weaker sex and it was an inversion of the natural order for them to rule over men. Elizabeth's right to rule was defended by John Aylmer, Bishop of London, in *An Harbourowe for Faithfull and True Subjects, against the late blowne Blaste, concerning the Government of Wemen* (1559), but only as an exception to the natural order, a compromised position that helped determine the way that Elizabeth had to behave throughout her reign (McLaren 1999, Ch. 2).

These debates are probably the most important context we need for understanding the political significance of *The Faerie Queene*. The poem contains a whole series of representations of powerful women, inviting the reader to imagine them as different manifestations of Elizabeth. The 'Letter to Ralegh' famously argues that

> In that Faery Queene I meane glory in my generall intention, but in my particular I conceive the most excellent and glorious person of our sove-raigne the Queene ... For considering she beareth two persons, the one of a most royall Queene or Empresse, the other of a most vertous and beautifull Lady, this latter part in some places I doe expresse in Belphoebe. (Hamilton, 2001, 716; Miller 1988)[2]

The poem also contains other figures that appear to be types of Elizabeth, both positive and negative: the vain Lucifera, who rules over the House of Pride; the wandering Serena, who causes chaos when she gets lost in the woods in Book VI; Britomart, the warrior heroine of Book III, who achieves all that Elizabeth would have wanted to achieve; Cynthia herself in 'Two Cantos of Mutabilitie' (McEachern 1996, Ch. 2; Hadfield 1997, Ch. 5; Suttie 1998). *The Faerie Queene* can be read as a mirror showing the varieties of real and possible behaviour of the queen and the effects each path she takes will have on her subjects.

Stephen Greenblatt has famously argued that '*The Faerie Queene* is ... wholly wedded to the autocratic ruler of the English state' (Greenblatt 1980, 174). This is why, according to Greenblatt, the poem produces the tense and explosive moments that characterise its most exciting poetic achievements,

---

[2] On the problematic relationship between the letter and the poem, see Gless, 1994, p. 48–51.

such as Guyon's destruction of the Bower of Bliss (II.xii). Louis Montrose has disagreed, arguing instead that 'Spenser's relationship to royal authority is more equivocal' than Greenblatt believes (Montrose 1986a, 329). The 'erotic appeal' of the Knight of Temperance's destruction of Acrasia's beautiful but delusive secret garden can also be read as the vengeance of a frustrated male subject forced to play female political games when he believes that masculine action is what is really required. If we read the episode in this light, then we might also want to read Radigund, the archenemy of Britomart in Book III, who binds and so emasculates Artegall, as a type of Elizabeth, with Britomart as the queen she could have been in a better world. Britomart, we know from the visions that Merlin conjures up for her, will marry Artegall and have children, thus establishing a long line of monarchs who will be extinguished by the virgin queen. Britomart's fictional triumphs over the Spanish in the Low Countries and the glorious rule of her phallic Protestant rod throughout Europe articulated in the first edition of the poem (III.iii.49.7) appear less as prophesies than as reminders of what could have been by the time the second edition appeared. All too often positive images of the monarch in *The Faerie Queene* appear as ironies lamenting a lost opportunity rather than celebrations of her triumphs in the name of the English people. Spenser might have wanted Elizabeth to be Britomart, but he was well aware that she would have appeared to many as the aimless Serena, the proud Lucifera or even the wanton Hellenore, who ends up as the blissed out 'quean' (slut rather than monarch) of the potent satyrs (III.x.47–8) when she is abandoned by Paridell. The images of happily married couples only serve to emphasise her barren nature. The ending of the first edition of *The Faerie Queene* showed Britomart observing the hermaphroditic union of Scudamore and Amoret:

> That *Britomart* halfe envying their blesse,
> Was much empassioned in her gentle sprite,
> And to her selfe oft wisht like happinesse,
> In vaine she wisht, that fate n'ould let her yet possesse.

> (III.xii.46. 6–9)

Britomart only 'halfe' envies their joy because she does not 'yet' have what they have. The reader knows that in 1590, at fifty-seven, Elizabeth will never have such happiness because she is well past the age of childbearing. The increasingly pornographic images of sexuality produced in the second half of the poem only serve to reinforce this sad fact, highlighting the voyeuristic envy (which, for Britomart, is only a temporary stage) of those without (Paglia 1990).

But if such examples become increasingly vitriolic as the poem continues, one should also note that they are already a prominent feature of the first edition. In Book I, Arthur tells Una of his dream of Gloriana, an episode that uncomfortably recalls Redcrosse's delusive dream of Una 'In wanton lust and leud embracement' (I.ii.5.5) with a knight in the House of Archimago (an event which led to their separation). Arthur recalls how a 'royall Mayd' appeared to be beside him when he fell asleep in the forest while on his quest for Gloriana (I.ix.13). His encounter is described in lush language that leaves it open for the reader to decide whether Arthur actually slept with Gloriana or was deluded (Lewis 1966, 158–9):

> Most goodly glee, and lovely blandishment
>> She to me made, and bad me love her deare,
>> For dearely sure her love was to me bent,
>> As when just time expired should appeare.
>> But whether dreames delude, or true it were,
>> Was never hart so ravisht with delight,
>> Ne living man like words did ever heare,
>> As she to me delivered all that night;
> And at her parting said, She Queene of Faeries hight.

> (I.ix.14)

But if anything tips the balance, it is the subsequent evidence of Gloriana's presence, the 'pressed grass' (15.2) that Arthur finds beside him when he awakes. Gloriana, identified as a type of Elizabeth, appears to be a sexual being in the poem that ostensibly celebrates her as a virgin queen. Feminist critics have not been slow to draw such issues to the reader's attention, often developing the insights of New Historicist critics to show how issues of politics and gender are related throughout Spenser's works (Silberman 1995; Hadfield, 1996b, Ch. 9).

The point is made more clear and explicit in the following book when we are introduced to Belphoebe, the other form of Elizabeth singled out in the letter, who is granted the longest physical description of any character in the poem (II.iii.21–31). Spenser employs the familiar Renaissance genre of the blazon, usually a physical description of a woman from the head down to the feet. When the lines reach her waist, Spenser omits a crucial half line that deliberately draws attention to what is not described, making that more important than what is actually there:

> [She] was yclad, for heat of scorching aire,
> All in a silken Camus lylly whight,
> Purfled vpon with many a folded plight,
> Which all aboue besprinckled was throughout,
> With golden aygulets, that glistred bright,
> Like twinckling starres, and all the skirt about
>> Was hemd with a golden fringe

Below her ham her weed did somewhat trayne,
And her streight legs...

(II.iii.26.3–27.2)

The apparent emphasis on the clothing of Belphoebe, a type of Diana, the goddess of hunting and chastity, only serves to demonstrate that what is really important about her is the absence of her organ of generation (Montrose 1986a, 326–8). This is clearly what interests Trompart, the cunning and sycophantic type of a servant, who sees her come out of the woods. But it is also what interests legitimate readers of the poem, anxious to know what their future might hold. Spenser is showing that in the land ruled by the ageing virgin queen, politics is reduced to what is between a woman's legs.

Politics by another means

The current emphasis in Spenser studies on political issues has not only allowed a more sophisticated understanding of the relationship between gender politics and national politics to develop, it has also rescued key sections of Spenser's writing from relative obscurity and made them central to our readings of his life and work. The most obvious example is *A View of the Present State of Ireland*, generated by the fascination with Spenser's role as a colonial official in Ireland. There has also been a renewed emphasis on Book V of *The Faerie Queene*, once dismissed as an empty and facile work precisely because it concentrated on historical and political issues.[3] Book V is now more likely to be read as a painful meditation on the problems of implementing proper justice in the harsh age of iron than crude propaganda for an absolutist regime (which is not, of course, to dispute its cruelty) (O'Connell 1977; Fowler 1995; Mallette 1997, 143–68). Artegall, as the knight of justice, is a 'salvage knight', a man with a savage nature who has been rescued. His singularly appropriate quest is to rescue the 'salvage island' (Ireland) from the foes who threaten to overwhelm it. Already we can see that Spenser is showing what a fine line separates good and evil, and, as often as not, it is hard to tell them apart in the age of stone (V.Proem.2). Artegall is abandoned by his mentor, the goddess Astraea, another type of Elizabeth, who cannot bear to stay on earth 'Mongst wicked men' (V.i.11.3). The implication is that Elizabeth has lost the desire and ability to deal with the world properly and leaves it to her knights to defend her realm. When she does intervene in Artegall's quest she only succeeds in making matters worse. As Radigund she unmans the knight and has him dress in women's clothes (V.v–vii), until slain by Britomart who should be the true type of

---

[3] Although, see the sophisticated work of Aptekar, 1969.

Elizabeth but who has become her anti-type. When she appears as Mercilla in canto ix, she is shown to be ruling over a chaotic court who simply do not know what service the knights perform for them, showing that the centre has failed to understand that the real work of civilisation is performed in the margins of the realm (V.ix.24). Spenser also presents us with the graphic image of the poet Bon Font, who has had his tongue nailed to a post for his supposed 'forged guyle' and blasphemy against Mercilla (25–6), and his name changed to Malfont. Given Spenser's complaints about the treatment of his poetry at the end of Book VI, this image of the disgraced poet must surely reflect on his own position, showing that in the iron age the difference between sound advice and treason is hard to establish. Mercilla's own reluctance to have Duessa (Mary Stuart) executed at the end of the canto (38–50) shows how much she needs her advisers, one of whom is, of course, the author of *The Faerie Queene*. The book ends with Elizabeth, once again, intervening to thwart the good service of her knights when Gloriana recalls Artegall from the 'salvage island' 'ere he could reforme it thoroughly' (V.xii.27.1). It may be too late for many of Elizabeth's errors to be corrected, but if she—or her close advisers—read some passages carefully enough, disaster may be averted in key areas. Books VI and VII show the British Isles overrun by savages—precisely what Artegall was supposed to prevent (Hadfield 1997, Chs. 5–6). In terms of its political thrust, *The Faerie Queene* concludes, like *A View of the Present State of Ireland*, as a plea for military intervention in Ireland to stem the tide of the apocalyptic advance of the combined forces of the enemies of Protestant England. The failure of women's rule, as Spenser saw it, would have to be met by that most masculine of endeavours, war, politics by another means (Fowler 1989, McCabe 2002).

Conclusion

Historical literary criticism of Spenser has returned with a vengeance after years when it was distinctly unfashionable. It is interesting to compare what was written in the 1920s and 1930 in America, by critics such as Edwin Greenlaw and Frederic Padleford, two of the leading lights behind the Variorum Edition of Spenser's Works (1932–48), with that written in the post-war period up to 1980, and that afterwards. Critics in the first and last periods are very obviously interested in the historical context of Spenser's writing; those writing between 1945 and 1980 are much less keen to stress the rooted nature of his work and more keen to read literature in terms of a more universal ideal of literature. However, while there was often a purist, philological motive at work in the pre-war period, more recent critical writing has often had a more overtly political thrust, a polemical desire to expose the reactionary nature of Renaissance humanism and its modern enthusiasts. Spenser, being the most prominent English poet who spent his life in Ireland, as well as one who represented the queen in such extensive and controversial terms, has served as a useful battleground between those who want to read literature as inherently political, and those who baulk at such links. There is clearly something of a reaction in literary studies generally to the apparent triumph of the former mode of reading, and many critics now want a return to less controversial topics and a clearer focus on questions of literary value. Other critics simply want readers to be more scholarly and to pay more attention to detail and less to arguments inspired by theoretical and political ideas. The chances are that Spenser's work will remain controversial within the academy for some years to come.

Further reading

Aptekar, J. 1969. *Icons of Justice: Iconography and Thematic Imagery in the 'Faerie Queene', Book V*, New York: Columbia University Press.

Cain, T. H. 1978. *Praise in 'The Faerie Queene'*, Lincoln, Neb.: University of Nebraska Press.

Canny, N. 2000. 'The Social and Political Thought of Spenser in His Maturity', in Jennifer Klein Morrison and Matthew Greenfield, eds, *Edmund Spenser: Essays on Culture and Allegory*, Aldershot: Ashgate, pp. 107–22.

Fowler, E. 1995. 'The Failure of Moral Philosophy in the Work of Edmund Spenser', *Representations* 51: 47–76.

Hackett, H. 1995. *Virgin Mother, Maiden Queen: Elizabeth I and the Cult of the Virgin Mary*, Basingstoke: Macmillan.

Hadfield, A. 1998. 'Was Spenser a Republican?', *English* 47: 169–82.

McCabe, R. A. 1987. 'The Masks of Duessa: Spenser, Mary Queen of Scots, and James VI', *ELR* 17: 224–42.

McLane, P. E. 1961. *Spenser's 'Shepheardes Calender': A Study in Elizabethan Allegory*, Notre Dame, Ind.: Notre Dame University Press.

Montrose, L. 2002. 'Spenser and the Elizabethan Political Imaginary', *ELH* 69: 907–46.

Norbrook, D. 2002. *Poetry and Politics in the English Renaissance*, rev. edn, Oxford: Oxford University Press.

O'Connell, M. 1977. *Mirror and Veil: The Historical Dimension of Spenser's Faerie Queene*, Chapel Hill: University of North Carolina Press.

Suttie, P. 1998. 'Edmund Spenser's Political Pragmatism', *Studies in Philology* 95: 56–76.

Wilson-Okamura, D. S. 2002. 'Spenser and the Two Queens', *ELR* 32: 62–84.

4
Religion

John N. King

Despite the commitment of C. S. Lewis to an essentialist view of human nature and an appreciative mode of criticism that have fallen out of favor with modern scholars, he captures many viewpoints that have prevailed in the interpretation of Edmund Spenser's religious allegory from the beginning through the present day.[1] During his career at the Universities of Oxford and Cambridge, this medieval and Renaissance scholar earned great renown during the middle of the twentieth century. Speaking of *The Faerie Queene*, he observes:

> Innumerable details come from the Bible, and specially from those books of the Bible which have meant much to Protestantism—the Pauline epistles and the Revelation. His anti-papal allegories strike the very note of popular, even of rustic, Protestant aversion; they can be understood and enjoyed by the modern reader (whatever his religion) only if he remembers that Roman Catholicism was in Spenser's day simply the most potent contemporary symbol for something more primitive—the sheer Bogey, who often changes his name but never wholly retires from the popular mind. Foxe's *Book of Martyrs*[2] was in every one's hands; horrible stories of the Inquisition and the galleys came from overseas; and every nervous child must have heard tales of a panel slid back at twilight in a seemingly innocent manor house to reveal the pale face and thin, black body of a Jesuit. (Lewis 1936, 311)

---

[1] For an overview concerning Spenser and religion, see King 2000. I gratefully acknowledge support for research from the American Council of Learned Societies and the College of Humanities at The Ohio State University. Steven Galbraith provided valuable assistance with research.

[2] From the outset, this was the popular title of Foxe's *Acts and Monuments of These Latter and Perilous Days* (originally published in 1563).

He thus describes the pro-Protestant, nationalistic fervor that gripped England from the late 1570s to the 1590s, the period of Spenser's active poetic career, when a Jesuit missionary effort and the Spanish Armada threatened the overthrow of Queen Elizabeth I.

Lewis's romanticized vignette exemplifies several enduring strands in Spenser criticism that emerge before the poet's death in 1599. This chapter will follow his lead in investigating connections between apocalypticism and antipapal allegory, which are evident as early as Spenser's translations of Du Bellay's poetic paraphrases of the Book of Revelation (or Apocalypse) in *The Theatre for Worldlings*. Ecclesiastical politics is an enduring concern, particularly in criticism on *The Shepheardes Calender*. Critics of *The Faerie Queene* have long investigated its engagement with the Reformation, especially in the historical allegories found in Books I and V. This essay also considers preoccupations of critics in the period since the publication of Lewis's *Allegory of Love*. They concern allegorization of theology, iconography, and iconoclasm, and Milton's imitation of Spenserian verse as exemplary English Protestant poetry.

Early context and reception

Whoever wrote the General Argument of the *Calender*, presumably the mysterious E. K. who initials the dedicatory Epistle, outlines the collection's engagement with ecclesiastical satire in a way that has framed critical approaches until the present day. (Regardless of whether E. K. is a fictional construction, as seems likely, the remarks attributed to him represent a functional part of this book as a material object.) These views are echoed, for example, in William Webbe's *Discourse of English Poetry* (1586) (Cummings, 58). E. K. identifies three pastoral eclogues on ecclesiastical affairs within the group of five poems "mixed with some Satyrical bitternesse, namely...the fift of coloured deceipt, the seuenth and ninth of dissolute shepheards and pastours" ("Generall Argument", ll. 30–3). If it is E. K. who provides the headnotes and annotations on the individual eclogues, he clarifies the objects of satirical attack by explaining that two interlocutors, Piers and Palinode, represent "two formes of pastoures or Ministers, or the protestant and the Catholique" ("Maye," Argument). A notation concerning "the shame and disprayse of proude and ambitious Pastours" ("Julye," Argument) identifies the impulse to climb high in the church hierarchy as a flaw embodied both in Morrell's pride and in the tragic fall of Algrind. The association between the latter figure and Edmund Grindal, the recently disgraced Archbishop of Canterbury, is palpable. He lost favor when he rejected a directive from Elizabeth I to suppress the prophesyings, in which Puritan clerics engaged in unauthorized interpretation of the Bible. Critics have generally associated hill-dwelling Morrell with John Aylmer, the conformist Bishop of London. The commentator goes a step further in attacking the wearing of elaborate ecclesiastical vestments, the issue that triggered the first outburst of Puritan protest in the 1560s, as a Roman Catholic vestige ("Glosse" on l. 173). The annotations on "September," in turn, attack the "loose living of Popish prelates" ("Argument") and "popish Exorcismes and practises" ("Glosse" on l. 92).

Readers have recognized that Revelation is the central model for religious allegory in Book I of *The Faerie Queene* from as early as 1597, when John Dixon entered handwritten notations into a copy of the 1596 edition (Hough 1964b). A committed Protestant patriot, Dixon interprets the "Legend of Holiness" as an allegory of the English Reformation. Even though his annotations were not discovered until the twentieth century, their existence lends credence to a critical line that endures in present-day criticism. Not only does Dixon liken both Archimago and Orgoglio to the Antichrist (1.12.24n, 1.8.2), whom many Protestants associated with the pope, he interprets Corceca with her rosary beads as "blind devotion" (1.1.29n). Observing that Una and Duessa are modeled respectively on the Woman Clothed with the Sun (Rev. 12) and Whore of Babylon (Rev. 17), Dixon identifies the former with the "true Church" (1.12.20n) and the latter as the "Romish harlot" (i.e., the Church of Rome) (1.7.1n). He sees Sans Loy's attempted rape of Una as "Idolatry, which is spiritual whoredom" (1.6.3n).

Dixon draws specific connections among characters and historical personages. Una accordingly typifies Elizabeth I as governor of the Church of England, whereas Duessa figures forth either Mary I, who was much hated for burning Protestants alive as heretics, or Mary, Queen of Scots, whom English nationalists vilified as a Catholic pretender to the throne of England (King 1990). Dixon was not the first to notice the allusion to the Scottish queen, because King James VI of Scotland (later James I of England) demanded that Spenser "may be duly tried and punished" for publishing "some dishonorable effects (as the King deemeth thereof) against himself and his mother deceased" (Heffner, 45). King James lodged this complaint against the trial at the court of Mercilla (V.ix.27–50), which affords a highly accessible allegory for the conviction and execution of Duessa (i.e., Mary, Queen of Scots).

Prior to the accession of Charles I in 1625 and the ascendancy of William Laud as Archbishop of Canterbury, which brought to an end a broad Protestant consensus that existed in the Church of England during the reigns of both Elizabeth I and James I, early readers tended to emphasize the presence of antipapal satire, rather than Puritan sentiment, in Spenser's verse. (*Puritan* is a highly flexible term that originally denoted an orthodox Protestant commitment to the complete eradication of religious practices not based on the Bible.) In the aftermath of the Gunpowder Plot, a Roman Catholic conspiracy to blow up James I and Parliament on 5 November 1605, the editor of the 1606 edition of *The Plowman's Tale* accordingly likens this beast fable, which features a Protestant Pelican and Roman Catholic Griffon, to Spenser's eclogues on religious affairs: "Of such shepherds speaks Master Spenser in his *Calender*" (Heffner, 108). These beasts respectively attack and defend clerical transgression. The employment of Spenserian poetry as a model for antipapal satire is apparent in Thomas Dekker's *The Whore of Babylon* (1607), an apocalyptic drama modeled on both *The Faerie Queene* and John Foxe's *Book of Martyrs*, a massive ecclesiastical history that won great renown among English Protestants. Indeed, Ben Jonson, the notable poet and self-proclaimed rival of William Shakespeare, declared in his *Conversations with William Drummond of Hawthornden* (1619) that "in that paper S[ir]. W[alter]. Ralegh had of the Allegories of his Fairy Queen, by the Blating [i.e., Blatant] Beast the Puritans were understood, by the false Duessa the Q[ueen] of Scots" (Cummings 1971, 136).

The Spenserian poets, a seventeenth-century school of academic imitators, looked to Spenser's *Calender* and *Faerie Queene* for models for nationalistic Protestant verse. In addition to Christopher Brooke, John Davies of Hereford, William Browne of Tavistock, and George Wither, this group included two brothers, Giles and Phineas Fletcher. In *The Locusts, or Apollyonists* (1627) by Phineas Fletcher, a Cambridge scholar who became a country parson, both the Gunpowder Plot and the onslaught of the Blatant Beast (VI.xii.23–5) supply models for virulently antipapal satire (Quint 1993; King 2000). We may note the endurance of this association between Spenserianism and nationalistic Protestant sentiment (Norbrook 1984) in *A Protestant Memorial: or, the Shepherd's Tale of the Powder Plot* (1713).[3]

During the heat of the successful presbyterian effort to disestablish the bishops, which heralded the English Civil Wars, John Milton broke away from previous interpreters when he appropriated the May Eclogue as antiprelatical prophecy. With the publication of *Paradise Lost* and *Paradise Regained*, he would eventually share with Spenser the distinction of writing the greatest English epic poems. In the preface to *Fables, Ancient and Modern* (1700), John Dryden records the well-known comment that "Milton has acknowledged to me, that Spenser was his original" (Hamilton 1990, 473).

Before Milton embarked on his career as an epic poet, he developed a reputation as a vitriolic pamphleteer. In one of his tracts against the bishops, *Animadversions Upon the Remonstrant's Defence Against Smectymnuus* (1641), he alleges that it is the

> false shepherd Palinode in the eclogue of May, under whom the poet lively personates our prelates, whose whole life is a recantation of their pastoral vow, and whose profession to forsake the world, as they use the

---

[3] Composed c. 1630–40 by an Irish bishop, the original manuscript is now lost.

matter, bogs them deeper into the world: those our admired Spenser inveighs against, not without some presage of these reforming times. (Cummings, 163)

We should recall that Milton employed "Maye" as a model for St Peter's attack on false shepherds (i.e., clerics) in his own pastoral elegy, *Lycidas* (1638). He also reinterpreted this poem as an attack on the bishops in *The Poems of Mr. John Milton* (1646). In *Eikonoklastes* (1649), he invokes *The Faerie Queene* in defense of the recent execution of Charles I:

If there were a man of iron, such as Talus, by our poet Spenser, is fained to be, the page of Justice, who with his iron flail could do all this, and expeditiously, without those deceitful forms and circumstances of law, worse than ceremonies in religion; I say God send it down, whether by one Talus, or by a thousand. (Cummings, 164)

This view did not go uncontested. In 1648 an anonymous royalist pamphleteer republished V.ii.29–54 interpreting the Giant with the Scales, whom Talus slaughters, as both an anti-monarchist and a sectarian radical.

During the Restoration, Henry More continued to emphasize how Revelation functions as a poetic model for Book I of *The Faerie Queene*. A contemporary of Milton, More was a fellow of Christ's Church, Cambridge, and a prominent Platonic scholar. Recognizing that Una's experience as a damsel in distress functions as a variation of the withdrawal into the wilderness of the Woman Clothed with the Sun, More declares in *An Explanation of the Grand Mystery of Godliness* (1660) that Una's "entertainment by satyrs in the desert does lively set out the condition of Christianity since the time that the Church of a garden became a wilderness." He declares that their insistence upon "external homages and observances" in place of the religious truths that she attempted "to impart to them" (I.vi.12–19) constitutes idolatry (Heffner, 249–50).

The eighteenth and nineteenth centuries

During the eighteenth century, the adoption of neoclassical canons of taste led to controversy concerning Spenser's imitation of the Bible, Revelation in particular, on the mistaken ground that this practice constituted a violation of poetic decorum. In *Polymetis* (1747), Joseph Spence thus enumerates among the "faults of Spenser" his "mixing the fables of heathenism, with the truths of Christianity" (*Variorum*, 1.363). Having lost touch with the importance of religious syncretism, Thomas Warton the Younger, usually a shrewd critic, also censured Spenser for "making Christian allegory subservient to the purposes of romantic fiction." A member of the famed literary circle of Samuel Johnson, Warton was the Poet Laureate of England, and

Camden Professor of Ancient History at the University of Oxford. In his *Observations on "The Faerie Queene"* (1762), he pronounces this judgment:

> This fault our author, through defect of judgment rather than a contempt of religion, has most glaringly committed throughout his first whole book, where the imaginary instruments and expedients of romance, are perpetually interwoven, with the mysteries contained in the Book of Revelations [*sic*]. Duessa, who is formed upon the idea of a romantic enchantress, is gorgeously arrayed in gold and purple, presented with a triple crown [i.e., a papal tiara] by the giant Orgoglio, and seated by him on a monstrous seven-headed dragon [I.viii.6–25].... This is the Scarlet Whore, and the Red Dragon in the Revelations [*sic*]." (*Variorum*, 1.368)

Warton's interpretation of VII.vii.35 follows along lines laid down by Ben Jonson, when he notes that Spenser "seems here to have intended a satirical stroke against the Puritans who were a prevailing party in the age of Queen Elizabeth; and, indeed, our author, from his profession, had some reason to declare himself their enemy, as poetry was what they particularly stigmatized, and bitterly inveighed against" (*Variorum*, 6.304).

In contrast to the views of both Spence and Warton, however, John Upton accepted Spenserian practice without hesitation in his edition of *The Faerie Queene* (1758), the earliest annotated text. A graduate of the University of Oxford, Upton held multiple clerical appointments that enabled him to dedicate his life to scholarship. Among the notes in which he diligently records allusions to Revelation, he lodges no complaint against the intermingling of biblical and classical imagery. For example, he makes this observation concerning the armor worn by the Red Cross Knight (I,i):

> Those old dints have been made by the fiery darts of the wicked, and this panoply has been worn by every Christian man in every age.... These too were the arms which Michael wore when he routed the great dragon, that dragon figuratively which our knight is going to attack (Revelation 12.9). (*Variorum*, 1.176)

He further indicates that when Duessa rides forth from Orgoglio's Castle atop the Seven-headed Beast, her golden cup, "replete with magick artes," alludes both to the golden cup carried by the Whore of Babylon (Rev. 17:2, 4; 18:3) and to the one borne by Circe, the sorceress who captivated the crew of Odysseus. In a note that approves of the apocalypticism evident throughout "The Legend of Holiness," this editor exclaims " 'tis very remarkable how our poet has varied the prophecy concerning the persecuted state of the church, exemplified in Una's parents, Una herself, and in this Christian knight [i.e., the Red Cross Knight].—This allegory might escape the ordinary reader" (Upton 1987, 269; 275).

Soon after the turn of the nineteenth century, Sir Walter Scott revived critical concern with historical allusion and identification of recognizable individuals in Spenserian allegory. In a review that appeared in the *Edinburgh Review* (1806), he criticizes H. J. Todd, editor of the eight-volume edition of the *Works of Edmund Spenser* (1805), for ignoring connections to sixteenth-century religion and politics. In keeping with Scott's romantic ideals, the novelist detects in Book I an alignment between "the adventures of St. George" and "the history of the Church of England as established by Queen Elizabeth." In the manner of readers going back to John Dixon, he discovers in "the imprisonment of the Red-Cross Knight in the Castle of Orgoglio, and in Duessa's assuming the trappings and seven-headed palfrey of the Whore of Babylon" a remote connection to the burning alive of Protestant heretics during "the persecution in the days of Queen Mary" (*Variorum*, 1.450).

In a related manner, John Wilson issued a rejoinder to "Tom Warton" when he defended Spenser's representation of the Whore of Babylon in the guise of "a romantic enchantress" in an essay in *Blackwood's Magazine* (1834). Rejecting Warton's imposition of neoclassical standards alien to the sixteenth century, Wilson has persuasive historical grounds for this riposte:

> And how does Warton support this accusation? He says Spenser has glaringly committed this fault "through a defect of judgment, rather than in contempt of religion," throughout his whole first book, where the imaginary instruments and expedients of romance are perpetually inter-woven with the mysteries contained in the Book of Revelation.... But we utterly deny that there is here either defect of judgment or contempt of religion. The aim of the poet was so high, that he was privileged to employ imagery from the apocalypse.... There is here no desecration of things holy, but effective worship. (*Variorum*, 1.369–70)

Among the Romantic poets, John Keats represented a departure from the norm in *The Eve of Saint Agnes* (1819), which contains the most successful imitation of the Spenserian stanza. He emphasized the sensuously romantic aspect of Spenserian verse when he fused religious and erotic themes in this pseudo-medieval fable. By contrast, post-Romantic critics tended to emphasize the moral and spiritual dimension of the religious allegory in Book I of *The Faerie Queene* more than its sensuously ornamental qualities or engagement with religious controversy. *The Stones of Venice* (1853) by John Ruskin, the Victorian artist and man of letters, thus offered a generalized interpretation that exerted considerable influence on his contemporaries and later critics. In his view, the entry into the Wandering Wood of the Red Cross Knight and Una represents an encounter with "Error in her universal form, the first enemy of Reverence and Holiness." Archimago, Sans Foy, Sans Loy, Sans Joy, and Duessa respectively allegorize Hypocrisy, Infidelity, Lawlessness ("the 'unrighteousness,' or 'adikia,' of St. Paul"), Despondency, and Falsehood

(*Variorum*, 1.422). Even the Lion and Kirkrapine (I.iii.5–22), who are key figures in a highly historical episode concerning the political Reformation under Henry VIII, which focused on an outburst of iconoclasm and the Dissolution of the Abbeys, represent for Ruskin a generalized encounter between Violence and Superstition.

Only when it comes to the defeat of the Red Cross Knight at Orgoglio's Castle does Ruskin open the door to topical allegory of the kind that Sir Walter Scott and his sixteenth- and seventeenth-century predecessors advocated. He acknowledges that the knight's imprisonment by Duessa's paramour is identified not only as the defeat of Holiness by "Orgueil, or carnal Pride," but also as

> a type of the captivity of true religion under the temporal power of corrupt churches, more especially of the Church of Rome.... That Spenser means, especially, the pride of the Papacy, is shown by the 16th stanza of the book [I,vii,16]; for there the giant Orgoglio is said to have taken Duessa, or Falsehood, for his "deare," and to have set upon her head a triple crown, and endowed her with royal majesty, and made her to ride upon a seven-headed beast.... Prince Arthur.... [as the] power of England, going forth with Truth, attacks Orgoglio, or the Pride of Papacy, [and] slays him." (*Variorum*, 1.423–4)

Other Victorian criticism, such as J. E. Whitney's "The Continued Allegory in the First Book of *The Faery Queene*" (1888), recognized the importance of historical allegory concerning the course of the English Reformation. Acknowledging the apocalyptic allegory whereby Una and Duessa are respectively likened to Elizabeth I and Mary, Queen of Scots, R. W. Church's volume on Spenser (1879) in *English Men of Letters* went on to compare Book I to John Bunyan's *Pilgrims Progress* as a more generalized allegory "that religion, purified from falsehood, superstition, and sin, is the foundation of all nobleness in man" (*Variorum*, 1.424).

Church also prepared the groundwork for a debate that played an enduring role in twentieth-century criticism. It concerns whether Spenser's verse is affiliated with the Puritan circles within the Church of England. He accordingly observes that even though the poet "hated with an Englishman's hatred all that he considered Roman superstition and tyranny, he had a sense of the poetical impressiveness of the old ceremonial, and the ideas which belong to it, its pomp, its beauty, its suggestiveness, very far removed from the iconoclastic temper of the Puritans" (*Variorum*, 7.601). (We should remember that Roman Catholics have always denied that they were disloyal subjects of England's Protestant monarchy.) This controversy finds its origin in the conflict between E. K.'s identification of the *Calender* with the views of "hot" Protestants versus Ben Jonson's belief that the poet attacked the Puritans.

The early twentieth century

Following the lead of Victorian scholars such as G. L. Craik, James Russell Lowell, and C. H. Herford, Lillian Winstanley argued that Spenser's ecclesiastical eclogues articulate Puritan values in "Spenser and Puritanism," *Modern Language Quarterly* (1900). This two-part article claims that the essential elements of Puritanism are Calvinistic theology, Calvinistic ecclesiastical polity, and "opposition to the Renaissance or pagan spirit." Making the tenuous claim that Piers, the rigorist speaker of the May Eclogue, is a mouthpiece for Spenser's personal views, she insists that the poet disapproved of the Elizabethan Compromise, a term applied to the 1559 religious settlement that combined thorough-going Protestant doctrine with a retention of Catholic practices such as the wearing of clerical vestments and use of religious art in churches (*Variorum*, 7.601–2). In her edition of Book I of *The Faerie Queene* (1915), she extends this line of argument in fanciful claims that characters represent personages such as Bishop Stephen Gardiner, Archbishop Thomas Cranmer, and Cardinal Reginald Pole (*Variorum*, 1.460–65). Arcane topical identifications were a common feature of early twentieth-century criticism.

Frederick M. Padelford extended this argument in a set of seminal studies including *The Political and Ecclesiastical Allegory of the First Book of "The Faerie Queene"* (1911), "Spenser and Puritan Propaganda" (1913), "Spenser and the Theology of Calvin" (1914), and "Spenser and the Spirit of Puritanism" (1916), all published in *Modern Philology*; and "The Spiritual Allegory of the *Faerie Queene* Book One," published in *JEGP* (1923). Based upon his study of contemporary documents, Padelford concludes that Spenser's ecclesiastical eclogues are devoid of anti-episcopal sentiment of the kind articulated by John Field and Thomas Wilcox, the leaders of the nascent presbyterian movement of the 1570s. Indeed, he makes note of the sympathetic characterization of Algrind in "Maye" and "Julye," whose name is a transparent anagram for Edmund Grindal (*Variorum*, 7.607–8). In the case of the "Legend of Holiness," he focuses not on historical identification, but on interpretation of the adventures of the Red Cross Knight as a Protestant spiritual progress indebted to Calvin's *Institutes*, in particular. As such, he emphasizes issues such as religious conversion and growth in grace. He places particular emphasis on divine mercy and the doctrine of justification by faith as it is embodied in the knight's encounter with Despair and the passage through the House of Holiness (*Variorum*, 1.431–40).

Largely due to Padelford's influence, the issue of Spenser's relationship to Puritanism was an important concern in American academic circles during the formative period when Ph. D. programs grew up on the model of German higher education. This concern corresponded to the dominant interest in Spenser's historical allegory, in the study of which scholars at Johns Hopkins University took the lead, notably Edwin Greenlaw, Ray

Heffner, and James McManaway. Those at other universities included Charles G. Osgood and Frederick Padelford. Their labor culminated in the eleven-volume *Variorum Spenser* (Spenser 1932–57) published by Johns Hopkins University Press in eleven volumes with assistance of subvention from the Rockefeller Foundation, Princeton University, the American Philosophical Society, and private donors. This massive edition constitutes a monument that dominated Spenser scholarship during the middle quarters of the twentieth century. It remains quite useful to the present day.

Edwin Greenlaw, the dean of American Spenserians during the early twentieth century, exerted a moderating force in an article published in *PMLA* (Greenlaw 1911). Referring to Spenser's imitation of Geoffrey Chaucer, he notes that the medieval poet developed a reputation as a religious satirist because of the inclusion of apocryphal writings within the Chaucer canon during the sixteenth century. Greenlaw accordingly cites the pseudo-Chaucerian *Plowman's Tale* as a model for satire on clerical abuses (e.g., pursuit of wealth and neglect of pastoral care) in Spenser's ecclesiastical eclogues. His identification of these poems with Puritanism is conventional, but the observation that Spenser's "Puritanism was not doctrinal but political" is forward-looking. He rightly notes that Spenser sought patronage from Robert Dudley, Earl of Leicester, and Sir Philip Sidney, to whom militant Protestants or moderate Puritans looked for leadership in their search for completion of unfinished Protestant reforms (*Variorum*, 7.i.602–5). He also resisted the efforts of Winstanley and others to interpret *The Faerie Queene* as consistent historical allegory (Greenlaw 1932).

During the period leading up to and following World War II, critics renewed long-standing concern with the apocalypticism of *The Faerie Queene*, Book I in particular. I can well recall the impact that this criticism had on my own studies at the undergraduate, graduate, and postgraduate levels. C. S. Lewis led the way with his observation that the downfall of the Red Cross Knight before Duessa and Orgoglio constitutes the "allegorical core" of the "Legend of Holiness" (Lewis 1936, 335). Although Josephine Waters Bennett's thesis concerning the order of composition of *The Faerie Queene* never won widespread acceptance, she made a seminal contribution in her study of the fusion of the legend of St George and the latter part of Revelation as structural models for Book I as a Reformation allegory (1942). Like other critics, she also made note of Virgil's *Aeneid* and Ariosto's *Orlando furioso* as narrative models. In applying the long-standing identification of the pope as Antichrist and both the Whore of Babylon and the Seven-headed Beast with the Church of Rome, she grounds her historical argument on a survey of Protestant interpretations of Revelation, including John Bale's *Image of Both Churches*, commentaries by Heinrich Bullinger and others, and glosses on the Geneva Bible. John Hankins then expanded and extended Bennett's findings in an article in *PMLA* that explores the relationship of

Revelation to a network of apocalyptic passages throughout the Bible as well as patristic and medieval commentaries on these materials (1945).

Post-war criticism

During and after the war years, Frances Yates investigated Spenser's apocalypticism from the vantage point of iconographical analysis of a labyrinthine network of symbolic meanings embedded in visual and textual imagery. She belonged to a school of thought that flourished at the Warburg Library, which moved from Hamburg to London just before the outbreak of the war in Europe. Her colleagues included notable emigrants from Germany, such as Erwin Panofsky, E. H. Gombrich, Edgar Wind, and Fritz Saxl. They placed considerable emphasis on the survival of the myths of classical antiquity in medieval and Renaissance culture. She took the further step of exploring the intermingling of Christian and classical symbolism in the iconography of Elizabeth I, who undergoes exaltation as a Protestant heroine in *The Faerie Queene*, Foxe's *Book of Martyrs*, and other propagandistic texts. Yates presented her findings in a seminal article, "Queen Elizabeth as Astraea" (1947), and an ensuing set of "Empire Lectures" delivered at London University in the early 1950s. In expanded form, these materials made up Yates's *Astrea: The Imperial Theme in the Sixteenth Century* (1975).

With reference to Spenser's poetry, Yates explored the representation of Elizabeth I as a manifestation of Astraea, the virgin goddess of justice whose return heralded the renewal of a golden age of peace and tranquility. She discovers traces of this symbolism in Una, whose link to the Virgin Queen of England received recognition from the beginning, but also in Gloriana, Belphoebe, and Britomart. I can recall the excitement with which I read this book during a train trip to the United Kingdom in 1977. This is not to deny that Yates often extended her arcane investigation in ways incapable of proof. Flaws in her work have undergone correction in the studies of feminist scholars and new historicists, who have criticized it on the ground that it embodies an "old" historicism based upon untenable idealistic and essentialist principles (Berry 1989, 62–7).

This critique extends to the work of Yates's student, Roy Strong, who shared her conviction that Spenserian verse bears the imprint of Elizabethan chivalry, and that an imperial "cult" of Elizabeth as a Virgin Queen filled a vacuum created when Protestant iconoclasts dismantled the symbolic system of the cult of the Virgin Mary (1977). Even more problematic is Robin H. Wells's (1983) extension of the Yates–Strong thesis. Building upon their contention that much Elizabethan iconography constitutes an adaptation of emblematic formulae once associated with the late medieval cult of the Virgin Mary as Queen of Heaven, he lodges the debatable case that Marian imagery survives in the romantic epic in a form that is more or less undiluted.

During the 1960s, Frank Kermode took exception to efforts by Northrup Frye (1957 and 1961) and A. C. Hamilton (1961) to subordinate historical allegory to ethical and mythic concerns. In an interlocking pair of essays, Kermode argues that a thick texture of allusions to Revelation and to Foxe's *Book of Martyrs* and other defenses of the Elizabethan Church of England demonstrate that Book I of *The Faerie Queene* functions as a "Tudor Apocalypse" within a consistent allegory concerning ecclesiastical history (1962). He sides with Yates in concluding that the "Legend of Holiness" celebrates an "Astraean Elizabeth," who functions as an imperial leader of the "true" Church of England versus the Church of Rome (1964). On Spenser's apocalypticism, also see Sandler 1984.

During the 1970s and early 1980s, a number of studies drew upon iconographical materials in their investigation of religious aspects of Spenser's historical allegory. D. Douglas Waters (1970) bases unnuanced claims concerning sacramental symbolism upon his study of sixteenth-century anti-Catholic propaganda. Although the blood sacrifices at Orgoglio's Castle and the golden cup borne by Duessa surely imply an attack on the Roman rite, his claims that Orgoglio personifies a prideful priest who officiates at the Mass personified both as a witch and as a whore are disputable. Thomas H. Cain's *Praise in "The Faerie Queene"* (1978) builds upon the seminal work of Frances Yates and O. B. Hardison, Jr (1962) in his analysis of Spenser's employment of epideictic *topoi* in the construction of Eliza in the April Eclogue and Una in the "Legend of Holiness" as "icons" that personify the dual nature of Elizabeth I as head of state and governor of the Church of England. Michael O'Connell fruitfully moves in the direction of a "new historicist" critique in *Mirror and Veil: The Historical Dimension of Spenser's Faerie Queene* (1977), a probing study that sustains Greenlaw's rejection of systematic historical allegory at the same time that it approaches Una as a personification of Elizabeth I and her embodiment of religious reform. For further investigations into iconographical representations of Elizabeth I as a "godly" monarch, see King 1989, 1990a, b.

As a counterpart to iconographical scholarship, the investigation of iconoclasm has played a major role in Spenser studies ever since the publication of the classic "new historicist" study: Stephen Greenblatt's *Renaissance Self-Fashioning: From More to Shakespeare* (1980). In a highly innovative interpretation of the Bower of Bliss, arguably the most problematic moment in *The Faerie Queene* (II.xii.38–87), he reconfigured the dialectic of Art and Nature that C. S. Lewis offered in explanation of the apparent paradox that the consummate artistry of this episode evinces "actual sensuality and theoretic austerity" (Lewis 1936, 324–33). In drawing a provocative analogy between Guyon's demolition of the Bower of Bliss and the Reformation attack on Roman Catholic devotional images, Greenblatt sees the seductive enchantress Acrasia as a parodic Madonna related to both Archimago and Duessa. Greenblatt discovers in the dismantling of her bower a "principle of regenerative violence" whereby "the act of tearing down is the act of fashioning" (188). He offers the following explanation for the paradox that Spenser flaunts artifice in poetry that condemns "demonic" art: "The answer lies in an art that constantly calls attention to its own processes, that includes within itself framing devices and signs of its own createdness" (190).

Ensuing studies have offered competing responses to Greenblatt's translation of iconoclasm from a historical phenomenon involving the actual destruction of material artifacts (e.g., stained glass windows, roods and rood screens, or statues of the Madonna and Child or saints) into a metaphorical reconstitution of allegedly "false" art. The ahistorical and largely non-iconographical approach of Kenneth Gross leads to disputable conclusions that English Renaissance literature lacks a strong commitment to Protestant ideology and that *The Faerie Queene* is a construction by a "post-Reformation poet" whose thinking is in line with "the displaced, diffused, demystified, ironic, and hyperbolized Protestantism we have learned to call Romanticism" (Gross 1985, 10, 116). By contrast, a thoroughly historicized iconographical investigation led Ernest Gilman to abstract an "iconoclastic poetics" out of the early modern controversy concerning the smashing of images. In *Iconoclasm and Poetry in the English Reformation: Down Went Dagon* (1986), he approaches Spenser as a counterpart to other paradigmatic poets (Quarles, Donne, and Milton) who resolved a collision between iconic and iconoclastic impulses in line with a general Protestant shift away from external visual images toward the internalized imagery of metaphor and poetic language.

In *Spenser's Poetry and the Reformation Tradition* (1990a), John N. King demonstrated how iconographical and iconoclastic impulses compete each other within *The Faerie Queene*. This book's discussion of "Spenserian iconoclasm" extended two preceding studies in which he demonstrated that Spenser (1) joined Foxe as a member of a long-standing Reformation cultural tradition (1982) and (2) accompanied Hans Holbein the Younger, Christopher Marlowe, William Shakespeare, and many less well-known writers and artists as contributors to and shapers of an iconographical network that praised Tudor monarchs as "godly" rulers (1989). Like those studies, his book on Spenser is attuned to the position of *The Faerie Queene* within distinctively Protestant cultural history. His consideration of "Spenserian iconoclasm" begins by identifying conventions of anti-monastic satire that we may identify in polemics written by John Bale and his contemporaries. King then demonstrates how the House of Holiness (I.x) provides an iconoclastic antidote to the religious practices associated with parodic monastics such as Archimago, Idleness, Corceca, and Abessa. The core of his case rests upon an examination of a dense sequence of iconoclastic episodes (e.g., Orgoglio's Castle, the Bower of Bliss, the Castle of Busirane, and Geryoneo's Church) in which destruction alternates with construction in a dialectical representation of the use and abuse of art.

This book also explores Spenser's employment and redefinition of artistic practices associated with Protestant poets and apologists. Acknowledging the richness of classical and Italian influences on Spenser's work, which have been subject to intense investigation, King demonstrates that the poet also transforms conventions, topoi, and iconographical devices from English Protestant literature and art. In his view, the ecclesiastical eclogues evince the powerful influence of English Protestant satirical tradition. His demonstration of the polyvalence of Spenserian allegory attends to the paradoxicality of Kirkrapine, for example, whose plundering of churches results in a two-sided portrayal of Protestant iconoclasm and monastic misappropriation of ecclesiastical wealth. His examination of the "Legend of Holiness" extends to Spenser's critique of the Renaissance hierarchy of genres, whereby he invokes romantic epic, hagiography, pastoral, tragedy, georgic, and comedy in the process of elevating them in line with Protestant ideology.

Over and beyond apocalypticism, iconography, and iconoclasm, scrutiny of Spenserian theology has constituted an enduring issue during the latter half of the twentieth century. We may note the highly contentious nature of this discussion as early as *The Religious Basis of Spenser's Thought* (1950) by Virgil Whitaker, who took issue with the findings of a host of preceding critics. Arguing against received opinions concerning Spenser's alleged Puritanism, he not only claims that the poet was a conservative Anglican, but that he was more sympathetic to Roman Catholic than reformist views. Although Whitaker rightly notes that Spenser never takes issue with episcopacy *per se*, he adopts the disputable assumption that the anti-Roman sentiments expressed by E. K. constitute nothing more than covert references to the Church of England. John N. Wall (1988) lodges a more recent claim concerning the existence of an Anglican poetics.

John N. King clarified how debate concerning Puritanism versus Anglicanism disregarded the findings of contemporary ecclesiastical historians. In "Was Spenser a Puritan?" (1986), he also replied to a contention that the poet of the *Calender* began as a Puritan, but ended up as a Protestant who composed *The Faerie Queene* (Hume 1984). The magisterial work of Patrick Collinson (1967, 1979, 1980, 1982) and scholarship by Peter Lake (1982) has demonstrated that attitudes once defined as "Puritan" fall into a broad consensus among progressive Protestants who considered themselves to be "godly" Christians dedicated to the complete implementation of the Elizabethan religious settlement. These issues include commitment to gospel preaching and reform of church discipline, eradication of vestiges of "papistry," and an ideal of evangelical ministry dedicated to pastoral care rather than clerical prerogative. In their view, application of the term "Anglican" to the early modern Church of England represents a back-formation from nineteenth-century Anglo-Catholicism that came into vogue during the era of the Oxford Movement.

Recent years

Recent years have witnessed lively debate concerning Spenser's religious and political allegory. David Norbrook led the way in *Poetry and Politics in the English Renaissance* (1984), a seminal study that demonstrates that a close continuity that existed between the prophetic poetry of radical Protestants active during the reign of Edward VI (King 1982) and compositions by Spenser and his contemporaries. "Maye," "Julye," and "September," in particular, represent a throwback to the harsh stridency of Edwardian ecclesiastical satire. In *The Faerie Queene*, Spenser adopts the guise of Colin Clout, who functions as a plain-speaking Protestant prophet. In response to the stubborn view that Spenser was a Puritan, Norbrook explains that radical Puritans favored the rhetoric of his ecclesiastical eclogues because it was at least superficially similar to their own propaganda.

Although Book V has traditionally lagged in popularity behind other books of *The Faerie Queene*, it has been the subject of renewed interest during the final decades of the twentieth century. Among studies engaged with religion, Kenneth Borris's *Spenser's Poetics of Prophecy in "The Faerie Queene"* V (1991) helpfully extends our knowledge of how prophetic poetry advanced the political agenda of patrons such as Sir Philip Sidney and Robert Dudley, Earl of Leicester (Norbrook 1984). In doing so, he demonstrates how Spenser reshapes scriptural and iconographical materials into a stirring representation of sixteenth-century history. In this way he deepens our understanding of the final cantos of the "Legend of Justice." He dedicates close examination to detailed allusions to Revelation and apocalyptic expectations of final victory over Antichrist that are embedded in the Belge and Irena episodes.

In the only book-length study of the "Legend of Holiness" of which I am aware, Darryl J. Gless addresses the critical problem that certain theologically charged passages have evoked utterly contradictory responses from critics who have variously interpreted the House of Holiness, for example, as an articulation of Roman Catholic, establishmentarian Church of England, Puritan, or militant Protestant religious principles. His richly rewarding book, *Interpretation and Theology in Spenser* (1994), concentrates on textual cruxes that intersect with theological problems with which reformed Protestant and post-Tridentine Catholic theologians wrestled. Ruling out delimitation of meaning by reference to the presumed ideology of readers, he denies that texts contain stable meanings that accord with authorial intention. In his view, the polysemousness of text affords rich opportunities for readers to construct interpretations determined by radically different critical axioms, principles, and assumptions.

Although Harold Weatherby's *Mirrors of Celestial Grace: Patristic Theology in Spenser's Allegory* (1994) bears some affinity to Roman Catholic readings of Spenserian texts, he has constructed an arcane interpretative model without precedent in existing scholarship. He argues that *The Faerie Queene* is indebted not to the theology of St Augustine, but to other Greek and Latin patristic authorities and to the Greek Orthodox liturgy. His highly debatable argument throws new light on old theological cruxes concerning Spenser's unorthodox choice of the legend of St George as a model for Book I and the Red Cross Knight's late baptism during the climactic battle with the Dragon (I.xi).

In *Spenser and the Discourses of Reformation England* (1997), Richard Mallette offers a valuable interrogation of religious discourses not by focusing on theology *per se*, but by stressing the psychological, political, social, and ethical dimensions of Protestant belief. In his seriatim reading of *The Faerie Queene*, he considers the importance of homiletic discourse (Book I), the body (Book II), sexuality and marriage (Books III and IV), apocalypticism (Book V), and the interrelationship of human will, providence, and fortune (Book VI).

Carol Kaske's *Spenser and Biblical Poetics* (1999) applies her mastery of biblical exegesis to contradictory passages that have baffled many critics of *The Faerie Queene*. In so doing, she investigates textual cruxes with reference to the operation of three hermeneutic modes: alternation of images *in bono* and *in malo*; prepositional contradictions; and the seemingly inappropriate representation of divine things. In the first instance, she traces alternating examples of "good" and "bad" images (e.g., the "true" and "false" beads borne by Corceca, Dame Cælia, and Contemplation, or the cups of Duessa and Fidelia) that invite antithetical theological interpretations from the varied theological perspectives. Her provocatively learned argument offers considerable insight into Spenserian dialectics.

Conclusion

In moving toward a conclusion, we may attend to C. S. Lewis's remark that "Spenser is the master of Milton in a far deeper sense than we had supposed" (Lewis 1936, 321). Harold Bloom and critics whom he has influenced have applied the insights of post-structuralist theory and feminist scholarship to their understanding of mimetic rivalry or transumptive (i.e., self-reflexive) allusion in Milton's misreading of *The Faerie Queene* in *Areopagitica* (Bloom 1973, Guillory 1983, Quilligan 1983). Like earlier critics, however, they ignore the shared commitment of Spenser and Milton to militantly Protestant politics and poetics. Of course, it is important to acknowledge that Milton differs from Spenser in taking the radical step of renouncing episcopal and monarchical governance of the Church of England.

More recent approaches to these issues include Linda Gregerson's *The Reformation of the Subject: Spenser, Milton, and the English Protestant Epic* (1995). In a study inflected with up-to-date critical theory and Lacanian psychology, she considers ideological, political, and gender-bound contradictions in England's greatest epic poems. Her approach to Spenserian iconoclasm investigates rhetorical strategies that the poet devised to inoculate poetic imagery against the charge that it constitutes a kind of "idolatry." In *Milton and Religious Controversy: Satire and Polemic in Paradise Lost* (2000), John N. King considers ways in which Milton's *Lycidas*, his antiprelatical pamphlets, and *Paradise Lost* are engaged in mimetic rivalry with Spenser's May Eclogue and *The Faerie Queene*. He demonstrates how writings by Milton reconfigure a Spenserian tradition of religious satire.

We may conclude this survey by taking note of a recent contributions to these debates. The 2002 issue of the journal *Reformation*, "Spenser's Theology: The Sacraments in *The Faerie Queene*", makes no effort to resolve contradictions inherent in the present state of criticism. Edited by Margaret Christian, this set of interlocking essays features contributions by Borris, Clinton Brand, Gless, Kaske, King, Anne Lake Prescott, James Schiavoni, and Weatherby. Their approaches include arguments for and against Spenser's Augustinianism, Catholicism, or Calvinism. Other essays attend less to theology than to particular sacramental allusions or allegories, or to semiotic issues that enliven sacramental allegory. Harry Berger, Jr moves in a different direction in his essay "Sexual and Religious Politics in Book I of Spenser's *Faerie Queene*" (2004). Grounding his reconsideration of religious allegory upon feminist theory and gender criticism, he argues that doctrinal theology is a peripheral concern in Spenser's problematic representation of religious truth in feminine form. He finds instead that the negative representation of Lucifera, for example, is imbued with "misogyny diffused across the Reformation continuum and through the archive of male discourse" (p. 242). In *Nationalism and Historical Loss in Renaissance England: Foxe, Dee, Spenser, Milton* (2004), Andrew Escobedo returns to apocalypticism in his argument that Spenser grapples with alienation from medieval society and religion by articulating a sense of English nationhood rooted in a historical past that is continuous with the present and immediate future.

The place of religion in Spenserian poetry has been a remarkably constant element in commentary stretching back to the initial point of publication. "Spenser's Theology" and the arguments by Berger and Escobedo provide an appropriate point of closure not least because, in their diversity, they accurately reflect the current "post-theoretical" and "interdisciplinary" nature of reading practice. New historicist and feminist criticism of the 1980s is often regarded as having neglected religion in its approach to early modern literature and culture. Yet, amongst today's scholars it is common to find feminist and new historicist inspired modes of interpretation directed at religious experience in Spenserian texts. In their different ways, the arguments of Berger, Escobedo, and the contributors to "Spenser's Theology" afford a valuable "snapshot" of the importance of religion in critical argument at the present moment. The absence of consensus attests to a vibrant critical economy driven by competing critical assumptions, ideas, and methods.

Further reading

Bennett, J. W. 1942. *The Evolution of The Faerie Queene*, Chicago: University of Chicago Press.

Borris, K. 1991. *Spenser's Poetics of Prophecy in The Faerie Queene V*, Victoria: University of Victoria.

Christian, M., G. Borris, K. Kaske, C. B. Weatherby, A. L. Prescott, and J. Schiavoni. 2001. "Spenser's Theology: The Sacraments in *The Faerie Queene*", *Reformation* 6: 103–77.

Gless, D. J. 1994. *Interpretation and Theology in Spenser*, Cambridge: Cambridge University Press.

Greenblatt, S. 1980. *Renaissance Self-Fashioning: From More to Shakespeare*, Chicago: University of Chicago Press.

Gregerson, L. 1995. *The Reformation of the Subject: Spenser, Milton, and the English Protestant Epic*, Cambridge: Cambridge University Press.

Hankins, J. E. 1945. "Spenser and the Revelation of St. John", *PMLA* 60: 364–81.

Kaske, C. 1999. *Spenser and Biblical Poetics*, Ithaca: Cornell University Press.

King, J. N. 1985. "Was Spenser a Puritan?", *Spenser Studies* 6: 1–31.

——. 1990. *Spenser's Poetry and the Reformation Tradition*, Princeton: Princeton University Press.

——. 2000. *Milton and Religious Controversy: Satire and Polemic in Paradise Lost*, Cambridge: Cambridge University Press.

Mallette, R. 1997. *Spenser and the Discourses of Reformation England*, Lincoln: University of Nebraska Press.

Norbrook, D. G. 1984. *Poetry and Politics in the English Renaissance*, London: Routledge & Kegan Paul.

Whitaker, V. K. 1950. *The Religious Basis of Spenser's Thought*, Stanford: Stanford University Press.

Yates, F. 1947. "Queen Elizabeth as Astraea", *Journal of the Warburg and Courtauld Institutes* 10: 27–82.

5

Gender

Elizabeth Jane Bellamy

In his "Letter to Ralegh," Spenser famously proclaims the goal of *The Faerie Queene* to "fashion a gentleman or noble person in vertuous and gentle discipline"; and, indeed, *The Faerie Queene*'s Virgilian opening line, "Lo I the man" (Proem I.i.1), identifies the voice of Spenser's epic as explicitly masculine. The poem's overarching epic purpose is to narrate the impending imperial marriage of Arthur and Gloriana and their joining forces to triumph over the "Paynim King." But four lines later, the poet also proclaims his Ariostan intention to narrate "Knights and Ladies gentle deeds." It is Spenser's Ariostan voice, not always happily accommodating "Ladies gentle deeds" within his epic goal of fashioning knights in "gentle discipline," that inserts the wedge of "gender trouble" into *The Faerie Queene*. Notoriously at odds with epic purposiveness are the aimless meanderings of romance narrative that entangle knights within the standard romance apparatus of abductions, seductions, strange castle customs, erotic dreams, demonic spells, and so on—labyrinthine impediments to epic closure often coded as "female." When the paths of "Knights and Ladies" intersect with increasing frequency in *The Faerie Queene*'s so-called "romance middle," Spenser's epic begins its indefinite delay of Arthur and Gloriana's imperial marriage. Though defeated early by Redcrosse, the monstrous Errour achieves the status of an allegorical pun, living on in the poem's many "errant" and inconclusive episodes. Put another way, Errour's "endlesse traine" (I.i.18.9) entangles *The Faerie Queene*, transforming Spenser's narrative into an "endlesse worke" (IV.xii.1.1). The point to emphasize here is that if we ponder the fact that Errour is a female, we can begin to appreciate the extent to which any interpretation of *The Faerie Queene*—despite its opening "Lo I the man"—must negotiate Spenser's complex mix of gender and genre.

The topos of praise for women resonates throughout *The Faerie Queene*, but the praise is often attenuated. At one point, the poet generously acknowledges women who "haue exceld in artes and pollicy" (III.ii.2.8). But later he curiously laments: "Where is the Antique glory now become, / That whilome wont in women to appeare?/Where be the braue atchieuements doen by some?" (III.iv.1.2–3). All of which is to say that feminist literary criticism of Spenser has been unable to determine definitively when the poet is in dialogue with female voices, or when he shades toward outright misogyny. Accordingly, feminist criticism has been unable to locate any kind of unified female subjectivity or stable representation of women in Spenser's poetry. For every steadfast emblem of truth like Una, there is a duplicitous False Una (or False Florimell). For every beautiful, goddess-like Belphoebe, there is a hag Ate or Occasion. For every gracious hostess like Medina there is a Hellenore, who openly flirts with her male guests. For every nurturing mother like Charissa, who maternally presides over the purification of Redcrosse, there is a Cymoent, suffocating her son Marinell with maternal overprotection. For every virtuous queen like Mercilla, there is a hellish queen like Lucifera. For every virgin, like Britomart, who militantly guards her chastity, there are virgins chronically vulnerable to abduction or rape (i.e., Amoret by Busyrane, Florimell by Proteus, Aemylia by the phallic Lust). For every temperate, harmonious body, as demonstrated in the structure of Alma's Castle, there are the "neather partes misshapen" of Duessa (I.ii.41.1). For every faithful instructional companion like Britomart's Glauce, there is an Astraea who, after teaching Arthegall the principles of justice, abruptly abandons earth for heaven, taking the Golden Age with her.

Over the last quarter-century, it has been the task of feminist and gender studies to confront the complexity of Spenser's representations of women with sustained analytical attention and detail. This chapter, tracing this critical history, is primarily organized around the emergence of key interpretive trends that have determined the direction of gender studies of Spenser's poetry. In its broadest scope, this chapter discusses gender studies of Spenser as emerging from some of the most influential trends within feminist theory in general: feminist reconfigurations of Foucault's "regimes" of power/knowledge (gender as not so much an "essence" as a social, cultural, and historical construct); feminist reworkings of psychoanalytic theory; and certain strands of queer theory, such as theories of the homoerotic, homosocial, or homosexual—as well as Judith Butler's landmark theory of gender as a "performance." This chapter demonstrates how *The Faerie Queene*, in particular, serves as an ideal core text for tracking the history of gender criticism itself.

More specifically, this chapter traces how gender studies of Spenser have emerged from some of the most influential trends in early modern literary studies over the last quarter-century: studies of the emergence of an early modern "subjectivity," or psychic interiority; the New Historicism's attention to the relationship between gender and the politics of early modern literary genres, such as the pastoral; studies of the complex interrelatedness of early modern patronage and courtship practices; studies of early modern hermaphrodites, Amazons, and cross-dressers; studies of early modern medical and anatomical discourses, especially on the reproductive body; and early modern discourses of maternal nurture, fosterage, and breast-feeding practices, and their relationship to discourses of national identity. Finally, this chapter demonstrates how gender criticism intersects with and enriches investigations of other key Spenserian rubrics, such as his imperial poetics, his narrative and allegorical structure, his deployment of Petrarchan erotic conventions, his shaping of his poetic career, the Irish context of his writings, and many others.

The emergence of gender study

Feminist studies of Spenser's poetry enable us to understand the extent to which gender was a significant blindspot in early critical receptions of the poet. In the early nineteenth century, Coleridge, though perceptively describing Spenser's Fairy Land as a "mental space" that invites a reading of the epic as an extended dream vision (Raysor 1936, 36), nevertheless overlooks the erotic undertones of such key "mental spaces" as Arthur's dream vision of Gloriana in Book I and Britomart's dream in Isis Church in Book V. Several decades later, the Victorian literary critic Edward Dowden, in his 1879 essay "Heroines of Spenser," did call attention to *The Faerie Queene*'s female characters. But his description of Una, for example, speaks volumes about Victorian preferences for the passive female. Dowden's Una is sweetly protective of Redcrosse, demonstrating a "gentle, fervid loyalty and trust" that "seems to imply no consciousness of superiority" (668). As Clare R. Kinney (2002) has recently argued, Una's allegorical scope as the True Church is effaced by Dowden's need to view her as a passive romance heroine, not as the embodiment of Truth for a theologically faltering knight. Dowden's essay is a prime example of a male Victorian critic's reluctance to locate women within the allegorical/intellectual terrain of Spenser's epic.

To identify an "original" work of feminist criticism of Spenser's poetry can only be arbitrary. Nevertheless, one could do worse than to single out Frances Yates's 1975 *Astraea: The Imperial Theme in the Sixteenth Century*, a book authored by a woman with a chapter on *the* key woman of *The Faerie Queene*. To attend to the general topic of gender in Spenser's poetry is, of course, to think immediately of Elizabeth Tudor, "Mirrour of grace and Maiestie diuine, / Great Lady of the greatest Isle" (Proem I.4.2–3). Central to the structure of the poem as a dynastic epic is Elizabeth, England's virgin "fairy queen," the Gloriana for whom Arthur searches. Accordingly, Yates's *Astraea*, though not explicitly informed by feminist perspectives, was among the first comprehensive attempts to investigate, in the author's words, the "complex tissue of Elizabethan imperialism" (50). Yates's study traced the elaborate iconography surrounding Elizabeth as Tudor England's imperial virgin of Trojan descent, a British version of Virgo-Astraea as a figure of justice. Her book immediately established itself as an indispensable backdrop for understanding the rich symbolism behind Spenser's depiction of Elizabeth-as-Gloriana. Coming from *Astraea*, readers of *The Faerie Queene* could more fully appreciate how Spenser's intention to write his poem for "that sacred Saint my soueraigne Queene, / In whose chast breast all bountie naturall, / And treasures of true loue enlocked beene" (Proem IV.4) celebrates Elizabeth as Tudor England's "triumph of chastity."

After Yates, a number of studies turned their attention to the majestic presence of Elizabeth in Spenser's poetry—studies which constituted what could be referred to as the first wave of feminist studies of Spenser. Isabel MacCaffrey, for example, depicted Gloriana neoplatonically as the "ingathering of feminine virtue" (274), also calling attention to the poem's other key avatars of chastity, such as the goddess-like Belphoebe who possesses "intuitive understanding" (96). Within the next decade, several studies, either implicitly or explicitly countering arguments, dating from the 1940s, that Spenser accepted Calvin's view that women could rule only if ordained by God, offered Elizabeth as Spenser's grand vision of female rule and authority—the Elizabethan era's most celebratory praise of the feminine and of a female monarch, defending the female order against male attempts to dominate and marginalize it. (See Woods 1985; Benson 1985, 1992.)

Feminism from the 1980s onwards

In feminist theory in general, by the early 1980s the term "gender" began replacing "sex" as an important new keyword. More than just the biological, essentialist term "sex," "gender" was conceived as a social, cultural, and historical construct—a crucial distinction that redefined much feminist criticism and, more specifically, opened up new directions in Spenser studies. Treatments of Elizabeth as *subject* began to shift to treatments of Elizabeth as *subject-position*. In 1983, Maureen Quilligan's influential *Milton's Spenser* inaugurated a second phase in gender studies of *The Faerie Queene*—a phase no longer predicated on the tacit assumption that Spenser's epic was addressed to a solely male readership. Focusing on the political power of the queen's virginity, Quilligan called attention to Spenser's strategies to accommodate within his poetry the intractable fact of the queen's gender; and she foregrounded Elizabeth as not just *The Faerie Queene*'s most powerful reader, but also as its most powerful *gendered* reader. In particular, *Milton's Spenser* introduced a new complexity into celebrations of Elizabeth as England's virgin queen. Moving beyond a focus on Elizabeth as an individual, Quilligan unpacked the sexual politics behind the queen's official cult of chastity, arguing for Elizabeth as implicated in an intricate web of gender, representation, and power.

Also in the 1980s, this interrelationship among gender, power, and the cult of Elizabeth was further pursued with the emergence of the New Historicism. Influenced by, among other theories, Foucault's "regimes" of power/knowledge, the New Historicism became a dominant discourse in early modern literary studies in general, and in Spenser studies in particular. Rejecting formalist and new critical readings of Spenser's poetry, four seminal essays by Louis A. Montrose (published from 1979 to 1986) investigated the close relationship between Elizabethan courtly pastorals and poetic ambition. For Montrose, pastorals such as Spenser's *The Shepheardes Calender* perform cultural *work*: they enhance not only the monarchy, but also—it is hoped—that of their literary creator. Montrose argued for Elizabeth's gender as socially and discursively "produced," a process culminating (in his resonant and now widely quoted phrase) in the pervasive cultural presence of the queen, that is "the collective discourse of Elizabethan power that we call 'Queen Elizabeth'" (1986a, 317). Though most fully useful when read in conjunction with studies of Spenser's career, Montrose's essays nevertheless epitomized the New Historicism's interest in the gender politics between poet and patron. His 1979 analysis of the "Aprill" eclogue of *The Shepheardes Calender*, for example, demonstrated how Spenser-as-Colin confidently fashions the pastoral "fayre *Elisa*, Queene of Shepheardes all," "[t]he flowre of Virgins," as his poetic subject (1979; 34, 48). The result is a fruitful reciprocity between Spenser and Elizabeth that impels his poetic voice: Spenser is the queen's subject even as the queen is "subject"-ed within his poetics.

By the late 1980s, however, a counter-trend in Spenser studies was less sanguine about the effect of Elizabeth's forty-five-year-long reign and her cult of chastity on the poet's literary production. In these studies, Elizabeth is no longer depicted as such an "ideal" subject of Spenser's poetry. An important precursor of this trend was a 1982 essay by Judith Anderson, who argued that Spenser, at certain critical moments throughout *The Faerie Queene*, seems to be distancing Elizabeth from the virtuous deeds of exemplary women in antiquity. Anderson argued that when, for instance, the poet describes Belphoebe as an "ensample dead" (III.v.54.9), he disturbingly implies that Elizabeth's virtue will not live on in her offspring. Subsequent studies of *The Faerie Queene* have asserted that Spenser's "masculinist" concept of chastity, threatened by Elizabeth's barrenness, necessarily entailed marriage and the subjugation of women. Other studies have contended that the very language Spenser uses to describe the queen serves only to underscore her elusiveness, further occasioning a kind of vocational crisis for the poet. The momentum of this scholarly trend has carried over into the twenty-first century, as evidenced by Katherine Eggert's 2000 study of how Spenser is both gratified and troubled by the prospect of "hanging an ambitious and innovative literary project upon techniques associated with effeminized writing" (14–15).

In recent years, much has been written about Elizabeth's manipulation of her many courtiers, her undermining of their attempts to dominate her. One consequence of less positive assessments of Elizabeth's reign has been changing perceptions of the role of Belphoebe as one of the poem's primary avatars of Elizabeth. At this point, a brief summary of Belphoebe's encounter in Books III and IV with Arthur's squire Timias (also a stand-in for Ralegh) is in order. The badly wounded Timias, nursed by Belphoebe, falls hopelessly in love with her: "So still his hart woxe sore, and health decayd" (III.v.43.2). But Belphoebe remains cruelly oblivious to his suffering; and in Book IV, when Belphoebe sees Timias with Amoret, she is "fild / With deepe disdaine" (IV.vii.36.2–3), abandoning Timias to "sad anguish" (IV.vii.38.4). The Belphoebe of several studies from the late 1980s and early 1990s has been taken to task for her cruel rejection of Timias. In contrast to MacCaffrey's 1976 Belphoebe as the neoplatonic embodiment of "intuitive understanding" and Timias's tutor in the Platonic ladder of love, David Miller's 1988 Belphoebe is nothing less than "a castrating Diana" (225). Like Elizabeth, a "dearest dred" (Proem I.iv) who both demands and forbids desire, Belphoebe has been portrayed by several studies as symptomatic of Spenser's anxiety about the queen's ability to emasculate her courtiers by resisting their desires. (See Anderson 1982; Bellamy 1987, 1991; P. Berry 1989; D. Miller 1988; Frye 1993; Eggert 2000a.)

Does the pervasive cultural presence of Elizabeth enable Spenser's poetry (as the early Montrose has argued)? Or, rather, does the cult of Elizabeth emasculate his creative energies as a male poet? In the last twenty years or so, in the wake of Montrose's seminal essays, studies of early modern patronage and courtship as complex literary and political practices have burgeoned; and Spenser's poetry has proven to be a particularly rich site for investigating the interrelatedness between courtship practices and the politics of Elizabethan England. Moreover, these studies have revealed a Spenser not always in control of how he feels about women as a subject for his poetry. A number of studies, focusing on Spenser's many allusions to the court and Elizabeth in *The Shepheardes Calender*, the *Amoretti*, the *Epithalamion*, as well as *The Faerie Queene*, have argued for Spenser's outright disillusionment with the Elizabethan courtly cult of the 1590s, offering a more negative view of the queen-as-patron than earlier New Historicist investigations of the power politics between poet and patron. Catherine Bates (1992), for example, has portrayed a conflicted and ambivalent Spenser—an ambivalence evident even in his sonnet sequence the *Amoretti*, which, unlike other Elizabethan sonnet sequences, commemorates a successful courtship of his bride-to-be Elizabeth Boyle. In Sonnet 75, the poet, writing to his beloved, affectionately announces that his verse will immortalize her: "My verse your virtues rare shall eternize, / And in the hevens wryte your glorious name" (75; 11–12). But earlier, in Sonnet 33, the poet confesses to Lodowick Bryskett his neglect of another Elizabeth—Elizabeth Tudor herself: "Great wrong I doe, I can it not deny, / To that most sacred Empresse my dear dred, / Not finishing her Queene of faery" (1–3). Thus, the two sonnets reveal a tension between his private wooing of Elizabeth Boyle (via the tidy confines of a sonnet) and his public courtship of Elizabeth Tudor (via a sprawling epic with no conclusion in sight). Similarly, some studies have perceived *The Shepheardes Calender*'s Colin (Colin-as-Spenser), mired in unrequited longing for Rosalind, as engaged not in a happy reciprocity between poet and queen, but rather in a struggle to escape from the burdensome shadow the queen casts over his poetic labor—"to overturn," quoting Jane Tylus, "what he perceived as the potentially threatening sterility of Elizabeth's court" (115)—a struggle that renders Spenser's prophetic, celebratory role as "England's Virgil" increasingly unrealizable. (See Bates 1992; Tylus 1993; Owens 2002.)

Investigations of the interrelatedness of gender and power overlap with another influential trend in early modern studies in general from the mid-1980s to the 1990s, that is investigations of Petrarchism as the sixteenth century's most formulaic, yet powerful discourse of male desire, as well as one of the sixteenth century's more complex interweavings of gender and genre. Spenser's *Amoretti* is, of course, the poet's most prominent experiment with Petrarchism. A stereotypical Petrarchan address to the lover can be found in Sonnet 7, where the poet writes:

> For when ye mildly looke with lovely hew,
> Then is my soule with life and love inspired:
> But when ye lower, or looke on me askew
> Then doe I die, as one with lightning fyred.
>
> (5–8)

Here, as in many of the *Amoretti*'s first twenty-two sonnets, the sonnet poet traffics in such stock Petrarchan images as the lover's suffering a paradoxical "living death." The poet struggles to overcome the isolation of Petrarchan eroticism, what A. Leigh DeNeef refers to as the "semantic traps" (67), the solipsistic tropes, that imprison him, like so many other Elizabethan sonneteers, in an endlessly unproductive cycle of hope and despair. And, as we have already seen, reading Sonnets 33 and 75 in tandem reveals a Spenser uncertain to what extent his Petrarchan poetics is merely a prison-house of unrealized epic ambitions.

In her influential 1982 essay "Diana Described," Nancy Vickers argued that the Petrarchan *blason* is, in effect, the male poet's aggressive fragmentation of the beloved's body. Accordingly, as feminist studies of Spenser have shown, the poet's entanglements within Petrarchan discourse are not without their perverse satisfaction. Although, again in Sonnet 7, the sonnet lover whom the poet addresses "looke[s] on me askew," thereby possessing the controlling gaze, in Sonnet 35, the poet shows he can masochistically return her gaze, calling attention to "My hungry eyes through greedy covetize,/Still to behold the object of their paine" (35, 1–2). Here the poet, trading gazes with his lover, actively revels in the decadent game of Petrarchism. Thus, an implicit debate emerging from studies of Spenser's Petrarchan discourse in the *Amoretti* has been whether it is Spenser-as-Petrarchan poet or whether it is the woman to whom/about whom he writes who is the eventual "winner" of this discursive game. (See J. Miller 1979; Vickers 1982; DeNeef 1982; Loewenstein 1986; Krier 1990; Wall 1993; Dubrow 1995; Bell 1998.)

The dangers of Petrarchan love are also evident in *The Faerie Queene*, particularly in Book VI (ironically, the Book of Courtesy), which features the alter egos Mirabella, as the epic's paradigmatic Cruel Fair and Petrarchan victimizer of men, and Serena, as the Petrarchan victim of male idolatry (lustily eyed by the cannibals). But undoubtedly the poem's most notorious Petrarchan victimizer is Book III's Busyrane, the tyrant who abducts the helpless virgin Amoret on her wedding night and imprisons her in his castle. Busyrane sadistically presides over her torture: Amoret, soaked in her own blood that streams from a wound "Entrenched deepe with knife accursed keene" (III.xii.20.6), suffers under his voyeuristic watch.

Long before the onset of feminist criticism, this memorable episode has enthralled readers of *The Faerie Queene*. Interestingly, Spenser scholarship has unearthed few significant literary historical sources for the Busyrane–Amoret episode. Hence, gender criticism of the last fifteen years or so has emerged as an especially productive discourse for understanding the complexities of Amoret's sado-erotic encounter with Busyrane. Some forty years ago, the ways in which Amoret's seemingly benign "wedded love" to Scudamour turns into a bloody nightmare in the House of Busyrane—and the critics' need to probe what, precisely, is being allegorized by the graphic pageantry of Busyrane's cruelty to Amoret—occasioned a lively debate between Thomas P. Roche, Jr (1961) and A. Kent Hieatt (1962). Their debate, as an intriguing precursor to more contemporary feminist analyses of this episode, merits a brief summary. Hieatt argued that Roche blamed Amoret for fearing sexual love in marriage. Roche, correcting Hieatt, insisted that he blamed not Amoret but Busyrane for *objectifying* her fear of sexual love, thereby insuring that her husband Scudamour would be unable to rescue her. The legacy of this earlier exchange has been gender critics' ongoing debate over the extent of Amoret's fear of sexuality and male aggressiveness in marriage. (Gender criticism has also argued that Spenser hints at a nuptial sexual violence in his *Epithalamion*, whose narrator often proclaims a kind of ownership of the bride.)

To return to this essay's earlier discussion of Spenser's Petrarchan discourse, when we read that Amoret's "trembling hart / Was drawne forth, and in siluer basin layd" (III.xii.21.1–2), we begin to realize that Busyrane is not just a torturer, but an explicitly *Petrarchan* torturer:

> And her before the vile Enchaunter sate,
>   Figuring straunge characters of his art;
>   With liuing bloud he those characters wrate,
>   Dreadfully dropping from her dying hart.

(III.xii.31.1–4)

Since the mid-1980s, critiques of Spenser's Petrarchism have seized on this painfully vivid episode, raising the interest-level of Busyrane's troubling dominance over Amoret to a new intensity, and arguing that Busyrane's "Figuring straunge characters" in Amoret's "Dreadfully dropping" blood is nothing less than a horrifying literalization of Petrarchan poetry itself. A number of critics, influenced by Maureen Quilligan's pithy summary of Busyrane as a "sadistic sonneteer" (1983; 198), and focusing on Scudamour's description of Amoret as "cruelly pend" by Busyrane (III.xi.11.1), have teased out a crucial play on words in this episode. They argue for "penning" as not just Busyrane's imprisoning of Amoret, but also his aggressive *writing* of/to her—a writing that literalizes the dangers of Petrarchism's dominance over the woman: Busyrane "textualizes" Amoret (what Lauren Silberman has termed Busyrane's "forcible troping" (1986; 266)). In the process, these critics have suggested uneasy parallels between Spenser as poet and Busyrane as would-be poet and rapist.

Amoret is rescued by *The Faerie Queene*'s heroine of chastity Britomart, who reverses Busyrane's cursed enchantments, permitting Amoret's "wyde wound" to close up into a miraculous "perfect hole" (III.xii.38.3,9). But again, since the mid-1980s, a recurrent critical impulse—originating with Jonathan Goldberg (1981)—has been to tease out yet another possible play on words with Amoret's "perfect hole": does her "perfect hole" become perfectly "whole," that is fully healed? Or does her "perfect hole" constitute a void—a "hole" in her subjectivity that serves as an icon of her alarming vulnerability to rape and male domination? (We are well reminded here that in Book IV Amoret is also captured by the phallic Lust, "a wilde and saluage man.../All ouergrowne with haire" (IV.vii.5.1,4).) By the mid-1990s, the Amoret—Busyrane episode had achieved emblematic status in Spenser studies as virtually every study of Book III attended to the speed with which Spenser's Petrarchan erotics could spiral out of control to become a poetics of outright sexual violence. (See Goldberg 1981; Quilligan 1983; Gross 1985; Wofford 1988, 1992; Fumerton 1991; Frye 1993; Silberman 1995; Eggert 1996; Teskey 1996; Bellamy 1997.)

The lyrical enactments of male desire for and power over the female that constitute Petarchan conventions are highly stylized. But they can all too easily threaten to deteriorate into a vulgar misogyny. In addition to the aforementioned studies of Spenser's anxieties about Elizabeth's female power and authority, a significant trend in Spenser studies over the last thirty years or so has been to confront the anxiety about masculinity that haunts the narrative of *The Faerie Queene* itself: its attendant crises of fears of emasculation (by the likes of Acrasia and Phaedria), castration anxieties, gynephobia, and compensatory demonizings of women. A quarter-century ago, Stephen Greenblatt, in a powerful—though, at times, controversial—chapter in his landmark *Renaissance Self-Fashioning*, called attention to the otherwise temperate Guyon's excessively violent destruction of the Bower of Bliss, the locus of Acrasia's seductive female dominance, as less the fulfillment of an epic quest than an extreme, antierotic renunciation of the threats of sexual pleasure. At key moments throughout *The Faerie Queene*, readers witness infantilized, unmanned knights separated from their armor: an unarmed Redcrosse, in an erotic dalliance with Duessa, is "Pourd out in loosnesse on the grassy grownd" (I.vii.7.2); Verdant dallies with Acrasia while his "warlike Armes, the ydle instruments / Of sleeping praise, . . . hong vpon a tree" (II.xii.80.1–2); Arthegall, emasculated by the Amazon Radigund, is "disarmed quight, / Of all the ornaments of knightly name" (V.v.20.3–4). These and other moments of knightly emasculation signal *The Faerie Queene's* misogynistic anxieties about, as Patricia Parker (1987) has noted, the poem's ongoing interrelationship between martial and sexual impotence. By the mid-1990s, Sheila Cavanagh (one of the first critics, it bears mentioning, to write a book-length study of Spenser and gender) had argued that what passes as "chivalric adventure" in the poem is, in fact, an unending series of pursuits, abductions, rapes, and other demonstrations of male dominance that have the effect of colliding with Elizabeth's defense of the female order against male attempts to dominate it— against, in David Miller's words, "male desire [as it] seeks restlessly to cross the threshold of the feminine 'Other' [and] to domesticate it" (217). (See Greenblatt 1980; Berger 1983; Parker 1987; D. Miller 1988; Cavanagh 1994.)

In 1990, Thomas Laqueur published his landmark study *Making Sex: Body and Gender from the Greeks to Freud*, generating a powerful, far-ranging medical discourse on the early modern reproductive body. Accordingly, scholars began turning their attention to Renaissance physiology and embryology, and the extent to which the Renaissance male consciousness, as mirrored in Ambroise Paré's 1573 *Des Monstres et prodiges*, was haunted by a fear of grotesque female bodies, monstrous births, and degenerative maternity. This scholarly trend has had a major impact on studies of Spenserian misogyny. A precursor essay of this interest in *The Faerie Queene's* monstrous wombs is Judith Anderson's 1988 "Arthur, Argante, and the Ideal Vision," bringing to light such previously unexamined figures as Argante and her twin brother Ollyphant, who mingle "In fleshly lust" in their mother's womb (III.vii.48.8), and even interpreting Argante's incestuous sexuality as Spenser's monstrous parody of the Elizabethan body politic itself. More explicitly gender-based studies have argued that in *The Faerie Queene*, such horror of the monstrous female body is emblematized by the figure of Errour (Redcrosse's first nemesis) whose "womans shape" is described as "Most lothsom, filthie, foule, and full of vile disdaine" (I.i.14.8–9)—or Duessa, the "Whore of Babylon" whose exterior beauty hides her "neather partes, misshapen, monstruous" (I.ii.41.1). As David Miller has argued, Errour's monstrous womb is "the antithetical form . . . of the poet's form-giving creativity" (254). In the wake of these studies, Errour, allegorically speaking, should be interpreted as more than just the enemy of the Protestant Church: she is the allegory of female monstrosity itself. Critics have also turned their attention to *The Faerie Queene*'s demonic/demonized females—the grotesque female genitalia of its many witches, succubi, and hags (Ate, Envy, Detraction, etc.)—as vivid projections of the poet's own male psyche, his own presumed fear and loathing of the female body. (See D. Miller 1988; Anderson 1988; Berger 1991, 1998; Cavanagh 1994; Silberman 1995.)

But *The Faerie Queene* offers good mothers, too—figures inspiring in Spenser's readers something other than fear and revulsion of the womb. Within early modern studies in general, a significant counter-discourse to a focus on the monstrous womb and degenerative maternity has once again emerged from the archives. This scholarly trend, turning to domestic guidebooks as primary sources for investigating early modern conceptions of the role of maternal nurture and breast-feeding practices, have offered considerably more positive views of early modern mother-hood. Consequently, a small but growing number of studies, theoretically informed and/or archivally based, have begun to explore the maternal world of *The Faerie Queene*. As early as the mid-1970s, Jungian-inflected critics such as James Nohrnberg began calling attention to the "fruitfull soyle" (III.vi.31.1) of the Garden of Adonis as the poem's *locus amoenus* of maternal procreation. In the 1980s, Maureen Quilligan and Lauren Silberman also focused on the Garden of Adonis as sites of maternal fecundity. More recently, Theresa Krier, deploying feminist psychoana-lytic perspectives to reject traditional Oedipal models of phallic fatherhood, has focused on the epic's mother–child dyads, and its rich array of mothers, ranging from the nurturing mother of Amoret and Belphoebe, Chrysogone and her "wombe of Morning dew" (III.vi.3.1), to Cymoent, Marinell's protective mother. Taking their cue from the early modern domestic guidebooks' accounts of wet nurses, several studies have redeemed Spenser's representations of the maternal breast. In opposition to Sheila Cavanagh's reading of the maternal aspects of Charissa (in effect Redcrosse's wet nurse in the House of Holinesse) as "desexualized" and "distanc[ing] sexuality" in the epic (32), Caroline McManus interprets Charissa's "euer open bare" (I.x.30.7) breasts as emblematic of Redcrosse's spiritual regeneration. In such a scheme, Charissa's maternity stands in opposition to the bad mother Errour, whose "poisonous dugs" (I.i.15.6) symbolize the abuse of the mother's power to give her children moral instruction. (See Goldberg 1975; Quilligan 1983; Silberman 1986; Cavanagh 1994; D. Miller 1988; Paster 1993; McManus 1997; Krier 2001.)

From *The Faerie Queene*'s wombs and mothers, we move to Spenser's allegory of Chastity as particularly embodied by the female warrior Britomart (who, speaking of mothers, is also Troynovant's dynastic mother-to-be). Harking back to the Amoret–Busyrane episode, we are well reminded that the only one who can see through the horrors of Busyrane's castle to rescue Amoret from the prison-house of Petrarchan love is Britomart, Book III's heroine of chastity. In the last thirty years, a major trend in Spenser studies, concerned with how the unmarried chastity of the childless, *not*-mother Elizabeth generated the anxiety that informs the prophetic structure of *The Faerie Queene*, has focused more sharply on Britomart's role as Tudor empire's dynastic spouse-to-be and the extent to which this role both fulfills and critiques Elizabeth as a chaste queen under pressure to marry. These studies have tended to shift the focus from the historical Elizabeth's female authority to the complexities of the fictional Britomart's female desire, where erotic self-consciousness and chastity are in constant tension.

In stark contrast to the prelapsarian world of Milton's *Paradise Lost*, where the "two great sexes animate the world" (8.151), the characters in *The Faerie Queene's* Book III continually suffer gender crises. Harry Berger, Jr, much of whose work on Spenser in the last two decades or so has explicitly focused on gender, cogently observed a number of years ago that Book III's many narrative crises "arise from one's being a masculine or feminine creature" (1969, 234). The character of Britomart particularly bears out this observation. Though *The Faerie Queene* is most prominent allegory of chastity, Britomart is also the epic's most psychologically complex, contradictory figure, not always comfortably fitting into the confines of allegory. She is a virgin, but she is also a woman warrior (largely modeled on the *Orlando furioso's* Bradamante), reveling in her martial prowess by unhorsing Guyon (III.1.6), wounding Marinell (III.iv.16), and defeating Paridell (III.ix.16) in armed combat. Though embroiled in frequent combat with men, she is also destined to marry Arthegall and become a dynastic spouse for England's version of the *imperium sine fine*, or empire without end. According to the magician Merlin's imperial prophecy, Britomart is also a mother-to-be, destined (unlike Elizabeth) to give birth to "fruitfull Ofspring" (III.iii.23.2) and insure Britain's genealogical continuity. Not surprisingly, at least a decade before the first wave of gender criticism, Thomas P. Roche, Jr's *The Kindly Flame* (1964) astutely identified Britomart, oscillating between male and female perspectives, as the poem's most dramatic characterization.

Throughout the 1980s, such prominent early modern critics as Stephen Greenblatt (1980), Francis Barker (1984), Catherine Belsey (1985), and Joel Fineman (1986) were instrumental in theorizing the nature of early modern selfhood, or subjectivity. Thus in the last twenty years, a significant trend in Spenser scholarship, investigating the psychological complexities of Britomart's contradictory roles, has attempted to tease out her psychic interiority. Several critics have focused on Book III's so-called "mirror episode" as nothing less than Britomart's struggle to move beyond allegory to achieve a fully realized selfhood. By way of a brief overview of this episode, the young Britomart discovers in her father's closet a "looking glasse," given to him by Merlin:

> when she had espyde that mirrhour fayre,
> Her selfe a while therein she vewd in vaine;
> Tho her auizing of the virtues rare,
> Which thereof spoken were, she gain againe
> Her to bethink of, that mote to her selfe pertaine.
>
> (III.ii.22.5–9)

Sorting through the complexities of Britomart's pondering of her reflection—the oddities of "Her selfe a while therein vew[ing] in vaine"—is difficult enough. But added to this complexity is the momentary appearance of a second image: also "presented to her eye" is the image of a "comely knight, all arm'd in complete wize" (III.ii.24.1–2). This image of a "comely knight" is Britomart's first glimpse of Arthegall, her dynastic spouse-to-be for whom she must now search. Intriguingly, Britomart scarcely reacts to this image: although she "well did vew his personage, / And liked well, [she] ne further fastned not" (III.ii.26.1–2). All of which is to say that, as gender-based studies of this episode have variously argued, she does not yet understand her *own* reflected "selfe"—much less a feminine "selfe" that must love and marry a masculine "selfe." Throughout much of Book III, Britomart's lack of self-understanding takes its psychic toll. Soon after gazing at her and Arthegall's reflection,

> Sad, solemne, sowre, and full of fancies fraile
> She woxe; yet wist she neither how, nor why,
> She wist not, silly Mayd, and she did aile,
> Yet wist, she was not well at ease perdy,
> Yet thought it was not loue, but some melancholy.
>
> (III.ii.27.5–9)

Kathleen Williams (1966), though pre-dating feminist criticism as such, was among the first critics to offer an extended account of Britomart's troubled encounter with her mirror reflection. And in the mid-1970s, Isabel MacCaffrey, elegantly describing Britomart as yielding to "the impulse to seal off the psyche in a self-created world of love, a dark glass" (312), paved the way for evolving accounts of the extent to which Britomart could be said to possess the traces of a psychic interiority. In 1988, Susanne Wofford, commenting on the multiple meanings of "closet" (where Britomart discovers the mirror) as a private room, heart, or mind, suggested an interiority in her character. By the mid-1990s, it was almost inevitable that studies of the mirror episode would turn to psychoanalytic theory—particularly Lacan's landmark account of the infant's "mirror stage"—to complicate Britomart's self-gazing as both, in Elizabeth Jane Bellamy's 1992 conception, an act of (mis)recognition or rupture on the precarious threshold of self-consciousness, and, in Linda Gregerson's 1993 conception, an act of narcissistic self-absorption.

Attempting to sort through the turbulences of Britomart's inner life, these studies have prompted readers to rethink Book III not just as the "legend" of Chastity, but also as "legend" of psychosexual angst. (Timias and Marinell, both of whom suffer wounds deeply connected with sexual desires, are among a number of characters in Book III whose actions also reward psychoanalytic explication.) These studies have highlighted Britomart not simply as an avatar of chastity or as an agent of English imperial identity, but also as an individual ego, struggling throughout Book III with her newly emerging sexual fears and desires—perhaps most vividly depicted when Britomart, "sighing softly sore," flees to the rocky seacoast to work through her waves of "tempestuous griefe" that mime the crashing waves (III.iv.8–11). This group of studies has set the standard for future treatments of Britomart, which will first have to negotiate the following questions, still under debate: when Britomart glimpses herself in Merlin's mirror of epic destiny, is she an avatar of chastity or an embodiment of erotic self-consciousness? When she glimpses herself in the magic mirror, does she see a happy reflection of her "selfe"—or does she rather experience nothing less than the psychic trauma of becoming gendered? Does Britomart, later in the epic, move beyond self-absorption to a sense of self based on differentiation and individuation? Or has Spenser denied Britomart, embodying Elizabeth's struggles with her own contradictory roles, any kind of harmonious internal life? (See Berger 1971; Silberman 1986; Wofford 1988; Krier 1990; Bellamy 1992; Benson 1992; Cavanagh 1994; Gregerson 1993, 1995; Walker 1998.)

These studies of Britomart's psychic complexities have logically led to a burgeoning scholarly interest in *The Faerie Queene*'s other female warrior, Radigund, Book V's provocative Amazon queen—a scholarly trend also much indebted to such broader, more sustained investigations of early modern representations of the Amazon as Lillian Robinson's 1985 *Monstrous Regiment: The Lady Knight in Sixteenth-Century Epic*. This trend in Spenser studies, contributing greatly to recently renewed interest in the allegory of Chastity and Justice in Book V, has convincingly argued that no consideration of Britomart can be complete without also taking into account Radigund as Britomart's possible alter ego. Spurned by her lover Bellodant, the angry Radigund founds an Amazon city-state, where unmanned knights languish in abject bondage under her female rule—among other things, a vivid example of Spenser's ambivalence toward female authority in Book V. Radigund emasculates Arthegall, stripping his armor, clothing him "In womans weedes, that is to manhood shame," and forcing him to do women's work, that is to "spin both flax and tow" (V.v.23.3). In a violent, grisly combat, Radigund is eventually decapitated by Britomart, who "hauing force increast through furious paine, / She her so rudely on the helmet smit, / That it empierced to the very braine" (V.vii.33.6–8):

> She with one stroke both head and helmet cleft.
> Which dreadfull sight, when all her warlike traine
> There present saw, each one of sence bereft,
> Fled fast into the towne, and her sole victor left.
>
> (V.vii.34.6–9)

As recent gender-based studies have shown, the sadistic violence of this episode should give us pause. On the one hand, critics such as Susanne Woods have interpreted Britomart's brutal defeat of Radigund and the reconstitution of her city-state as the former's restoration of her husband-to-be Arthegall's phallic power: Britomart relinquishes her female authority and, in so doing, overturns Radigund's usurpation of patriarchal authority. These studies have interpreted Britomart's decapitation of Radigund as her subduing of the monstrous part of female power that threatens male empowerment. But by the late 1980s, critics such as Mihoko Suzuki began warning against the temptation to interpret Britomart as the "good" Amazon and Radigund as the "bad" Amazon. Noting the seemingly inter-changeable pronoun antecedents of the above passage's "she" and "her," Suzuki has pointed to the difficulties of maintaining any such distinction. Britomart's vengeful defeat of Radigund ironically reveals unsettling resemblances between her and her victim; and Britomart's ferocity suggests that she may share more significant parallels with Radigund than with the virtuous virgins Florimell and Amoret. By 1994, Sheila Cavanagh rendered it virtually axiomatic that there were significant parallels between Britomart's militant chastity and Radigund's sexual excess (i.e., the fury of her reaction to Bellodant's rejection). Still other studies have contended that Arthegall's effeminate captivity by Radigund serves as a figure for the poet himself—that is, the dangerous parallels between Arthegall's emasculation and Spenser's own subordinate role in serving Queen Elizabeth. (See Woods 1985, 1991; Quilligan 1987; P. Berry 1989; Suzuki 1989; Harvey 1992; Cavanagh 1994; Eggert 1996; Walker 1998; Schwarz 2000.)

The many ways in which Britomart's defense of chastity conflicts with her masculine role as warrior, culminating in her combat with the Amazon Radigund (herself Arthegall's cross-dresser), productively overlap with another pathbreaking trend in gender-based studies of *The Faerie Queene*, that is an insistence on gender in Spenser's epic as not an "essence" but rather a construct. In the 1980s Maureen Quilligan, as we have seen, was perhaps the first Spenserian to shift the focus from "sex" to "gender." More recent feminist approaches, making use of what Judith Butler has recently termed "gender-as-performance" carry with them a more explosive sexual charge as they configure new ways of defining a Spenserian erotics that cannot be contained within the confines of heteroeroticism. Kathryn Schwarz's recent *Tough Love* (2000), acknowledging the specific influence of Butler, has investigated how Spenser's Amazons disrupt the homosocial order of his poem. Despite Spenser's positing of the Britomart–Arthegall pairing as English empire's ideal union, Schwarz has chosen to focus on *The Faerie Queene*'s significant transgressions of gender roles—not the least of which are Britomart's marked confusions as to her gender identity. In the mid-1980s, Lillian Robinson was content to refer to the Amazons of early modern epic as "lady knights." But studies such as Schwarz's have exposed this term as hopelessly quaint. Spenser's "lady knights" are, in fact, enmeshed in "tough love": a complex—and sometimes deadly—web of transvestism, gender subversion, and gender excess.

A prime locus of this gender confusion is Britomart's erotic encounter with Malecasta (or "evil chastity") early in Book III. Apparently enamored by Britomart's appearance as a "male" knight, Malecasta sneaks into the sleeping Britomart's bed in the hope of being seduced by him/her, and "softly felt, if any member mooued" (III.1.60–1). Though her female body lacks a phallic "moou[ing] member," Britomart does wield her phallic lance in alarmed defiance of the transgression of Malecasta, who she mistakenly believes to be male. As recent gender-based studies have argued, the pseudo-comic tone of this episode should not distract the reader from the more serious task of considering just how permeable the boundaries can be between male and female. The martial Britomart's disguise as a male, at once concealing and inviting sex, unsettles sexual identity, challenging patriarchal notions of biological "maleness." In sum, this episode—where Malecasta and Britomart become, to quote Dorothy Stephens, "strange bedfellows" (1998, 74)—may be one of early modern literature's most significant anticipations of Judith Butler's contention that gender, never just simply an "essence," is more often a performance: Britomart's female sexuality, successfully performing masculinity, points to no less than the collapse of sexual difference itself.

Book III's ongoing confusions as to whether gender is an essence or a construct culminates in the book's conclusion, which encapsulates the gendered dimension of Spenser's increasingly futile efforts to achieve narrative closure for his epic as a whole. In the original conclusion to the 1590 *Faerie Queene*, Book III ends happily with Scudamour and Amoret, reunited after Amoret's rescue from the House of Busyrane, intertwined in loving embrace:

> No word they spake, nor earthly thing they felt,
> But like two senceles stocks in long embracement dwelt.

> Had ye then seene, ye would haue surely thought,
>   That they had been that fair *Hermaphrodite*,
>   Which that rich *Romane* of white marble wrought.

> (III.xii.45.8–46.3)

Meanwhile Britomart, envying their bliss, "to her selfe oft wisht like happinesse" (III.xii.49.8). But Spenser retracted this original conclusion for the poem's 1596 edition. In his revised version, Scudamour, despairing that Britomart will not be able to free Amoret from Busyrane's prison, "depart[s] for further aide t'enquire" (III.xii.45.8), inadvertently abandoning Amoret to Britomart's female protection, as well as denying closure to Book III. Gender-based critics have enabled us to identify this 1596 ending, canceling Scudamour and Amoret's hermaphroditic embrace, as the point at which gender and the narrative structure of *The Faerie Queene* intersect with the greatest complexity.

In 1972, Donald Cheney was among the first critics to point out that the 1590 conclusion is indebted to a rich iconographic tradition of the hermaphrodite as synthesis; and for years, it was customary to interpret Scudamour and Amoret's loving "long embracement" as harmoniously embodying the emblem of Ovid's hermaphroditus—the miracle of male and female merging in one body. More recently, studies have moved away from these earlier "redemptive" readings of the 1590 conclusion. These studies of what Lauren Silberman has termed *The Faerie Queene*'s "androgynous discourse" (1986) have interpreted the hermaphroditic image as the poet's way of deconstructing gender as an "essence." Moreover, focusing on Britomart's fragmented distance from Scudamour and Amoret's heterosexual embrace, critics, most notably Silberman, have read Britomart against the grain of Ovid's myth of the hermaphrodite as *effacing* sexual difference, concluding that, at this point, Britomart's chastity represents both sexual identity and sexual difference. Thus, Spenser's retraction of his 1590 ending must be read alongside *The Faerie Queene*'s other failed attempts to build its narrative on the seemingly secure bedrock of sexual difference.

Recent developments

Most recently, gender-based criticism has inserted the 1590 conclusion into the broader historical context of early modern anxieties about women's friendships. Dorothy Stephens (1998) has argued that Spenser's hermaphrodite image fails to offer any kind of positive fulfillment for Amoret. Stephens calls for a new discourse of Spenserian erotics, that is a specifically *feminine* desire that emerges when Spenser transports Amoret from Scudamour's embrace to Britomart's protection. This new erotics implicitly critiques Busyrane for positing heterosexual union as the only possible alliance for women. (See Goldberg 1981; Silberman 1986, 1987, 1995; Stephens 1991, 1998; Bellamy 1992; Schwarz 2000.)

The Faerie Queene's deployments of the discourse of androgyny and its many serio-comic confusions between "sex" and "gender" have, in the last twenty years or so, prompted investigations of explicitly homosocial and/or homosexual themes in Spenser's poetry, studies that have benefited from the burgeoning field of cultural histories of homosexuality. This critical trend toward investigating male–male relationships reflects a central inadequacy in strictly feminist readings of Spenser's poetry. A key founder of this critical trend is Jonathan Goldberg who, in the early 1990s, argued that homosexual currents are the "open secret" of *The Shepheardes Calender*, particularly Hobbinol's suffering from unrequited love for Colin, despite the latter's infatuation with Rosalind. Examining Spenser's correspondence with Gabriel Harvey, Goldberg suggested strong parallels between the friendships of Colin and Hobbinol and the homosocial friendship of Spenser and Harvey. Turning to *The Faerie Queene*, a number of recent studies, highlighting Spenser's critiques of institutionalized gender norms, have argued that homosexuality and heterosexuality in Spenser's epic are not opposed but occupy the same narrative space—with the homosocial nature of Arthur's relationship to Timias serving as a prime example. In addition, gender critics such as Sheila Cavanagh, influenced by Gayle Rubin's concept of "the traffic in women," have examined the poem's kinship networks, that is the many episodes in which women are simply interchangeable with one another (i.e., Florimell and the False Florimell). Analyzing Satyrane's tournament in Book IV as a fight over a pseudo-woman, the False Florimell, whom the combatants do not even want, Cavanagh has contended that homosocial bonds between men are the real meaning of Spenser's epic. Most recently Kathryn Schwarz, focusing, as we have seen, on the transvestite nature of Spenser's female warriors, conducts a more explicit "outing" of some of the lesbian undercurrents that are occasionally alluded to in gender studies dating from the mid-1990s. (See Berger 1989; Stephens 1991; Goldberg 1992; Cavanagh 1994; Silberman 1995; Schwarz 2000.)

As has been earlier noted, gender-based studies of Spenser, dating from the early 1980s, often focused on the sexual politics of Elizabeth's cult of chastity. A quarter-century later, these studies, though fully gender-informed, can now be read as dependent on specifically Anglocentric perspectives. A highly influential recent direction in Spenser studies—one that, early in the twenty-first century, is still playing itself out and is perhaps the most rigorously historicist-based of recent trends in Spenser studies—is a focus on Spenser's career as an Irish civil servant, introducing the complex wedge of Ireland into his trajectory as an English Virgil. Current studies of the political implications of Spenser's colonial experiences in Ireland and his plans for Irish reform are having a significant impact on gender studies of Spenser. This trend, productively combining feminist and New Historicist perspectives, has begun to explore the particular relationship between gender and Spenser's Ireland (allegorized in *The Faerie Queene*, it should be noted, by the female figure of Irena). A number of critics have revisited Spenser's *View of the Present State of Ireland* in the context of sixteenth-century English descriptions of Ireland that depict political and military problems posed by the presumably "effeminate" Irish in need of masculine guidance.

Clare Carroll (1990), for example, has argued that Britomart's defeat of Radigund allegorizes Spenser's agenda for subduing the Irish, and that Arthegall's humiliating imprisonment by Radigund embodies Spenser's protest of Elizabeth's "womanish" policies toward Ireland, his targeting of Elizabeth's "feminine" compassion as partly to blame for Ireland's ongoing rebellion. Richard McCabe (2002) has called attention to Elizabeth's frustrations with the military aspirations of Grey (Book V's Arthegall), Leicester, and Ralegh, prompting a rereading of Book V as a particularly fraught mix of colonial and sexual anxieties. Jacqueline T. Miller (1997), reading the *View*'s perception of a barbarous, "salvage" Ireland in tandem with English anxieties about the possible danger of Irish wet nurses as purveyors of cultural contagion, has called attention to E. K.'s blaming Irish wet nurses for causing the English "mother tongue" to become barren by giving English infants doses of a degenerate Irish language along with their Irish milk. These and other studies have been instrumental in shifting a gender-based focus from a devoted Spenser celebrating Elizabeth Tudor to a disappointed Spenser exposing the "monstrous regiment" of Elizabethan Ireland. These studies are rendering it increasingly untenable to investigate Spenser and the "Irish question" without also accommodating gender perspectives. (See Carroll 1990; J. Miller 1997; J. Craig 2001; McCabe 2002.)

A long-standing debate—a philosophical divide, if you will—within feminist literary criticism in general has been whether feminist critics should remain focused on male authors' representations of women, or whether they should abandon the canonical male author altogether as part of a coordinated effort to recover the all too often underread or lost voices of women writers. Not surprisingly, the last decade or so has witnessed a burgeoning interest in early modern women writers; and a number of new anthologies introducing readers to the literary achievements of early modern women writers are being published. Accordingly, a number of recent feminist studies have shifted the focus from Spenser to his importance for such key seventeenth-century women writers as Aemilia Lanyer and Lady Mary Wroth. As these studies have shown, Lanyer's 1611 *Salve Deus Rex Judaeorum* and Wroth's 1621 *Urania*, not just passively "influenced" by Spenser, constitute significant reworkings of his poetry, particularly the Amoret–Busyrane and Britomart–Radigund episodes—revisions that are significantly gendered. Critics have argued that Wroth's many revisions of the Amoret–Busyrane episode in her *Urania* represent her repeated attempts to bring closure to Spenser's provisional endings to Book III. Other critics have turned their attention to Aemilia Lanyer, who, in addition to being indebted to Spenser's *Fowre Hymnes*, found in *The Faerie Queene* significant models for, in Susanne Woods's conception, "interject[ing] the active authority of female figures, who come into the picture at key times to warn or affect the actions of men" (108). A recent critical impulse, initiated by Shannon Miller (2000), has demonstrated how Spenser's influence on Wroth and Lanyer is class-determined: the aristocratic Wroth is drawn to Spenserian romance, while the middle-class Lanyer models her addresses to her patrons on Spenser's invocations of Elizabeth. Overall, these studies have been instrumental in demonstrating how Lanyer and Wroth, not content with simply drawing on Spenser, resolutely seek to distance themselves from him. (See Beilin 1987; Quilligan 1990; Roberts 1990; Hannay 1999; Woods 1999, 2000; J. Miller 2000; S. Miller 2000.)

This recent move to consider Spenser's reception at the hands of early modern women writers marks a significant shift from the focus on Spenser's Elizabeth with which this survey began. By way of an overview, the first wave of feminist literary criticism in Spenser studies focused on *The Faerie Queene*'s many celebrations of Elizabeth as the poet's "soueraigne Queene." Maureen Quilligan's 1983 *Milton's Spenser*, however, ushered in a powerful second wave of feminist criticism of Spenser, influenced by the general trend in feminism to shift from the category of "sex" to the category of "gender." Quilligan's study, articulating the cultural and political power of the queen's virginity, shifted the focus from essentialist studies of Elizabeth as a female subject to a focus on Elizabeth as a *subject-position*. After Quilligan's book, this second wave of feminist criticism, often shedding a less benign, more ambivalent light on Elizabeth (as well as Belphoebe), gave rise to a key question still under debate: did Elizabeth, as Spenser's chief patron, enable his poetry? Or did Spenser resent having to praise her in the shadow of her power?

The mid-1980s to the mid-1990s marked a third wave of theoretically informed approaches to Spenser's poetry. Phrased broadly, this temporal span could also be termed the "Amoret–Busyrane decade" in feminist studies of Spenser, the years when the feminist focus on Amoret's virginal vulnerability to Busyrane's sadism raised the interest-level in this episode to a new intensity and urgency. Because few literary historical sources for the episode had been discovered, gender studies of this episode emerged as the most comprehensive means of analyzing Busyrane's "cruell penning" of Amoret. This focus on the peculiarly literary nature of Amoret's torture also occasioned important reassessments of Spenser's Petrarchist impulses in the *Amoretti*, particularly as they related to Spenser's ambivalence toward Queen Elizabeth. By the late 1980s, a number of studies, several of them psychoanalytically informed, began to focus on Britomart's encounter with her reflection in Merlin's mirror in order to explore the complexities of Britomart's subjectivity—or selfhood—and its relationship to Book III as less about Chastity than erotic self-consciousness. These studies gave rise to a still-debated question: is Book III indeed the "legend" of Chastity? Or is it better read as the "legend" of psychosexual angst?

By the mid-to-late 1990s, a number of feminist critics, continuing the theoretical sophistication of earlier feminist studies of Amoret and Britomart, made cogent use of Judith Butler's landmark concept of gender as "performance" to successfully unearth *The Faerie Queene*'s many episodes of cross-dressing, transvestitism, gender confusion, gender subversion, and gender excess, necessitating key revisitings of the sexuality of Britomart and Amoret, as well as the less scrutinized Radigund and Malecasta. Also in the 1990s, studies of Spenser's homosocial/sexual imaginary investigated male same-sex desire not only in *The Faerie Queene* but also in *The Shepheardes Calender*. These studies have highlighted the central inadequacy of strictly feminist readings of Spenser's poetry, as well as demonstrating the appropriateness of replacing the term "feminist literary criticism" with the more comprehensive term "gender criticism."

Alongside, these theoretically informed studies (making extensive use of the New Historicism, psychoanalytic theory, genre theory, etc.), a number of studies in the 1990s turned to the archives to understand Spenser's representations of the female body. Turning to primary sources in Renaissance embryology and anatomy, several studies ask whether the female womb in Spenser's poetry is monstrous or redemptive. Turning to early modern manuals on wet nursing and fosterage practices, others debate the related question of whether Spenser represents maternity as loathsome or regenerative? Heading into the twenty-first century, a vital trend in Spenser studies is for rigorously historicized investigations of Spenser's colonial experiences in Ireland. Recent feminist criticism on Spenser and the "Irish question" has shown that gender perspectives are indispensable to this area of scholarly inquiry that remains one of the most prominent in Spenser studies.

Whether theoretical or historicist—or both—what gender studies of Spenser's poetry have in common are the many ways they have successfully exposed his primary ambition to "fashion a gentleman" as gendered in ways he could not have imagined or predicted. Though gender critics will no doubt continue their practice of favoring one theoretical and/or historical perspective over another, gender criticism itself will never be displaced from the critical terrain of Spenser studies.

Further reading

Boehrer, B. T. 1988. " 'Careless Modestee': Chastity as Politics in Book 3 of *The Faerie Queene*," *ELH* 55: 555–73.

Bowman, M. R. 1990. " 'she there as princess rained': Spenser's Figure of Elizabeth", *Renaissance Quarterly* 43: 509–28.

Champagne, C. M. 1990. "Wounding the Body of Woman in Book III of *The Faerie Queene*", *LIT: Literature/Interpretation/Theory* 2: 95–115.

Cohee, G. E. 2000. " 'To Fashion a Noble Person': Spenser's Readers and the Politics of Gender," *SSt* 14: 83–105.

Deitch, J. 2001. "The Girl He Left Behind: Ovidian *imitatio* and the Body of Echo in Spenser's *Epithalamion*", in *Ovid and the Renaissance Body*, ed. Goran V. Stauivukovic, Toronto: University of Toronto Press, 224–38.

King, J. N. 1990. "Queen Elizabeth: Representations of the Virgin Queen," *Renaissance Quarterly* 43: 30–74.

Kinney, C. R. 1992. *Strategies of Poetic Narrative: Chaucer, Spenser, Milton, Eliot*, Cambridge: Cambridge University Press.

Klein, L. M. 1989. "Protestant Marriage and the Revision of Petrarchan Loving in Spenser's, *Amoretti*," *SSt* 10: 109–38.

Lamb, M. E. 2000. "Gloriana, Acrasia, and the House of Busirane: Gendered Fictions in *The Faerie Queene* as Fairy Tale," in *Worldmaking Spenser: Explorations in the Early Modern Age*, ed. Patrick Cheney and Lauren Silberman, Lexington, KY: University of Kentucky Press, 81–100.

Mazzola, E. 1992. "Marrying Medusa: Spenser's *Epithalamion* and Renaissance Reconstructions of Female Privacy," *Genre* 25, 3: 193–210.

———. 2000. "'O unifying confounding': Elizabeth I, Mary Stuart, and the Matrix of Renaissance Gender," *Exemplaria* 12, 2: 385–416.

Sedinger, T. 2000. "Women's Friendship and the Refusal of Lesbian Desire in *The Faerie Queene*," *Criticism* 42: 91–113.

Shaver, A. 1988. "Rereading Mirabella," *SSt* 9: 211–26.

Stump, D. 1999. "A Slow Return to Eden: Spenser on Women's Rule," *ELR* 29: 401–21.

6
Sources

Anne Lake Prescott

Renaissance humanists were not alone in their fascination with sources, with moving upriver to see where the tributaries of a literary river might diverge or where some originating fountain might be located.[1] Renaissance antiquarians thought the same way about history: "My thirst compeld mee always seeke the *Fountaines*," wrote John Selden.[2] Similarly, Renaissance rulers were often obsessed with dynastic origins—and hence in need of dynastic epics. If less compelled to search out—or even to believe in— literary fountains, modern readers can also find tracing sources useful or entertaining. Locating minor ones in Spenser's textual geography can reveal his methods, while noticing the major ones configures a "horizon of expectation," in Jauss's still useful phrase. In most current criticism, though, flowing water and half-hidden springs have given way to fibers and looms: fingering the warp and woof of intertextuality arouses more excitement than stumbling upon yet one more rivulet of "influence" or dribbling "source." An intertext is something that writers usually hope we notice.

We need, perhaps, another metaphor to indicate a *complex* of intertexts and sources—a "magnetic field," maybe, of recollection. When Redcrosse and Una enter the Wood of Error in Book I of *The Faerie Queene*, for example, they enter just such a dynamic of voices and memories. The forest is a textually mobile catalogue of trees with origins (notes *The Spenser Encyclopedia*) in Virgil (*Aeneid* 6.179–82), Ovid (*Met* 10: 86–105), Statius (*Thebaid* 6.98–106), Claudian (*Rape of Proserpina* 2.107–11), Boccaccio (*Teseida* II. 22–4), Chaucer (*Parliament of Fowls* 176–82), and possibly Dante, whose *Convito*

---

[1] On Renaissance writers and predecessors see T. Greene 1982 and Quint 1983; the study of "sources" overlaps with that of *imitation* and *translation*.

[2] From Selden's introduction to Michael Drayton's *Poly-Olbion*, quoted in Prescott 1991.

4.24.12 refers to "selva erronea di questa vita." The multiple trees, the chaotic world in which Una/ity became the Many and humanity left Eden to wander, are identified by name and function, so that Error's wood is at once a collective and a group of named individuals. In this it has a striking parallel in the multiplicity of sources, a parallel reinforced by Error's vomiting books and ink (cf. Vaught 2001). This "wandering wood" embodies the bustle of human activity indicated by the adjectives that Spenser applies to the trees and also the mental jostle and buzz of books in part remembered diachronically as unique voices with a history and in part merged synchronically in the mind.

In this essay, I will note some, although hardly all, of Spenser's known sources or intertexts, for the most part moving forward from the most ancient and observing complications on the way. One immediate complication is that Spenser's books would often have had commentary that chattered opinions or information, for Renaissance printers and readers did not think margins sacred white space; what was printed there affected how Spenser read and, sometimes, how we should read him (Kennedy 2000). Nor do we know much about his books, although we know of a few he owned (Piepho 2002, 2003), or what he had with him in Ireland. Many sources are visual— Spenser's description of Tantalus in Book II of *The Faerie Queene*, for example, seems to come from a picture in Alciato's *Emblemata* or its copy in Geffrey Whitney's *Choice of Emblemes* (1586). Other sources could be bedtime stories, tavern songs, jests, wall hangings, school lessons, or letters from friends. The fastest way to trace Spenser's known *literary* sources is to check the possibilities in *The Spenser Encyclopedia*, consult the multi-volume Variorum edition of Spenser (including its separate index) for anything *Encyclopedia* ignores, and then do relevant searches in the Modern Language Association database (see Zurcher, p. 265 in this book.)

Religious texts

The Bible is everywhere in Spenser's poetry, sometimes indicating a larger meaning or structure: that Una's parents are Adam and Eve indicates the historical sweep of St George's task in defeating a Satanic dragon; that creatures in the Garden of Adonis can still hear God's "mightie word" telling "them to increase and multiply" (III.vi.34; Gen 1:22) proves the value of sex in chaste love; and that Book V points so insistently to the book of Revelation but then trails off with Justice's task unfinished implies an ironic, resigned, or ambivalent takes on apocalyptic expectation. Spenser knew the Geneva Bible (1560) and its often militant annotations, although in church he would hear other versions, and he could adopt for a secular poem methods by which commentators read scripture, for example, taking an image *in bono* (altars can be good) or *in malo* (altars can be bad), revisiting an earlier motif to read it and its meaning from a new angle.[3] The Book of Common Prayer, too, offered Spenser texts and prayers, as well as a concept of communal, not only individual, holiness (Wall 1988). It also offered him a structure, for many perceive in *Amoretti* a pattern based on the liturgical year, further evidence that Spenser wanted to reconcile earthly love poetry with divine love in ways earlier love poets could not do because they were clerics or loved married women and also to affirm a primarily Protestant conviction that faithful marriage is holier than celibacy.[4]

There can be little doubt about Spenser's Protestantism, however defined. Book I of *The Faerie Queene* borrows from Tudor anti-Catholic propaganda that, for example, allegorized the Catholic mass as a whore (Waters 1970; J. King 1990a). And yet Catholic religious texts are among his likely sources. These include printed calendars or books of hours (their illustrations, it is true, sometimes reused in Bibles authorized by the Elizabethan church) and also the liturgically rich Catholic prayer book, the Sarum Missal (Prescott 2001). The betrothal of Una and St George at the end of Book I has details, such as the blessing of candles, that resemble those in Sarum's Easter Saturday baptismal rite, an elaborate ritual with traces of its origin as a sacrament for adults (Weatherby 1984). In the Book of Common Prayer, baptism entails foreswearing the Devil, but Sarum's rite virtually turns the ceremony into something like an exorcism. George needs one, for he is not done with the magician Archimago, who arrives, disguised, with a message from Duessa claiming to be George's betrothed. The saint and Duessa have in fact been more than good friends, but then Easter Saturday is a time of cleansing and demon-explusion, not of claiming moral perfection. In Sarum the priest says, for example, "I exorcise thee, filthy spirit, . . . that thou leavest this thy servant," and prays that the catechumen hold to "firm hope, right counsel, and holy doctrine." And again: "Begone every wicked spirit, and every iniquity of diabolical fraud." That should care of the likes of Archimago.[5]

---

[3] Kaske 1999; Shaheen 1976 lists Spenser's biblical allusions. *Epithalamion*'s imitation of the Song of Songs in stanza 10 also ties human to divine love, as do the marriage service and the Geneva Bible's headnote to Song.

[4] See Dunlop 1980; Prescott 1985; Johnson 1990; Larsen 1997. Spenser was not, though, the first poet to write lyrics and an epithalamion for his wife; Jean Salmon-Macrin, a Catholic, did the same in his *Livre des épithalames* (1528–31)—and wrote a poem on the resulting baby.

[5] Maskell ed., *Monumenta Ritualia*, "Exorcizo te, immunde spiritus, per Patrem, et Filium, et Spiritum Sanctum: ut exeas et recedas ab hac famula Dei" (I, 9); "firmam spem, consilium rectum, doctrinam sanctam, et aptus *vel* apta sit ad percipiendam gratiam Baptizmi tui" (I, 10); "Procul ergo hinc jubente te, Domine, omnis spiritus immundus abscedat: procul tota nequitia diabolicae fraudis assistat" (I.11). Note the inclusion of both genders.

Epithalamion, too, may owe something to Sarum. It is in Sarum, not in the Book of Common Prayer, that the priest declares the service performed "in the sight of angels and saints." Spenser includes the angels (although not the saints), perhaps thinking that they are his "little loves" revealed as angels of *agape*.[6] At last in the marriage chamber, furthermore, he prays for "gentle sleep" free from, among other noxious forces, "deluding dreames," "evill sprights," and other "things that be not" (ll. 334–50). Sarum has an intriguingly analogous prayer: "Bless this bed," the priest asks, "and all who inhabit it, that they remain in thy peace and endure in thy will.... Who keepest Israel, keep thy servants in this bed untroubled by all phantasmagoric illusory demons...."[7]

Even if a source, is Sarum an intertext? Does Spenser expect his first readers—including a queen who, although battling a Catholic Church that denied her right to reign, retained some nostalgia for older forms of worship—to recognize it? Is the effect irenic or ironic? At the very least it is interesting to see Spenser mixing Catholic holy water with his other sources; perhaps he thought that there is nothing doctrinally or politically offensive in these passages. Something similar must be at work behind the ease with which he borrows material for his St George (and Guyon's name) from Jacopus Voraigne's Medieval *Golden Legend* despite Protestants' and Renaissance humanists' scorn for the work's improbabilities. Spenser, though, allows *his* St George a betrothal to the lady; in Voraigne, the saint kills the dragon then rides off into martyrdom, celibacy preserved.

Greece and Rome

That Spenser's poetry has many classical sources hardly needs saying. He must have read some Aristotle, although the list of virtues he explores is not the philosopher's. Homer was famous—but how much actually read is unclear. Especially if Spenser is the translator of the pseudo-Platonic dialogue, *Axiochus*, he would have had good Greek, and in any case 1583 saw a Latin translation with commentary by the French humanist and lyric poet, Jean de Sponde.[8] Certainly Guyon's voyage to the Bower of Bliss is filled with images that trace back to the Odyssey, and its resident witch is another Circe, complete with once human animals. Hog-minded

---

[6] I.42: "coram Deo, et Angelis, et omnibus Sanctis eius, in facie Ecclesiae."

[7] I.63: "Benedic, Domine, thalamum istum et omnes habibantes in eo: ut in tua pace consistant et in tua voluntate permaneant." And "Benedic Domine hoc cubiculum...Qui custodis Israel, custodi famulos tuos in hoc lecto quiescentes ab omnibus phantasmaticis daemonum illusionibus."

[8] Burrow 2001 believes Spenser knew Homer.

Grill, though, has trotted in from Plutarch's *Moralia* or an imitator.[9] And
Plato? E. K. alludes to the *Symposium* in his notes to "Januarye," but the
modified Platonism of *Amoretti* and *Fowre Hymnes* is more likely to derive
from such Neoplatonists as Italy's Ficino or Pontus de Tyard in France.[10]
Among the Romans, Spenser found Virgil and Ovid most vivid in his
imagination. For him, these sources are no secret springs but great rushing
rivers: the challenge was as much to dam or divert as to drink from them.[11]
The two sources, moreover, were not entirely compatible in that Virgil had
served and ostensibly celebrated the same emperor, Augustus, who exiled
Ovid for reasons that remain mysterious but that Spenser's generation
usually thought must have involved disreputable poetry. Ovid's *Metamorphoses*, one of the best-known poems in Spenser's day and much annotated or consulted by the mythographers Spenser read, is in some ways a
counter to or sendup of the *Aeneid*, although to make a neat division
between the work and the careers of the two poets entails ignoring Virgil's
political ambivalence and minimizing what is luxuriant and erotic in his
epic. Ovid in fact made some show of his *not* writing an epic, explaining
mischievously in *Amores* I.i that he would have written epic dactylic
hexameters had not Cupid flown by and stolen a syllable, thus forcing
him to write elegiacs. This tension between epic and Eros haunted
Renaissance poets who, like Pierre de Ronsard struggling to finish his
Franciade or Spenser diverted from *The Faerie Queene* to write of Elizabeth
Boyle, thought they should imitate Virgil but found themselves imitating
Ovid (or Petrarch, of course).[12] Indeed, to imitate Ovid could signal that
the writer was consciously choosing not to be a laureate celebrator of
imperial power but was instead turning to a more inward or private world.
Following Eros is not always admirable, as witness the corrupt Paridell,
seducer of Helenore (the names signal that this moment of fabliau is also

---

[9] Plutarch, *Moralia* 986B. Spenser would have found good material on Isis and Osiris
(Book V) in *De Iside et Osiride* (*Moralia* 351c), and *De sera numinis vindicta* (*Moralia*
548A, "On the delays of divine justice") is relevant to Books V and VII.

[10] Quitslund 2001 is the fullest recent study of Spenser's Platonism.

[11] Echoes of the major Roman writers are audible throughout Spenser's verse even in
small details. For example, the aged oak in Lucan's *Pharsalia* contributed to Spenser's
various oaks (Prescott 1996), while Horace's injunction not to judge Tantalus because
we too are guilty (Satires I.i.69–70) makes Guyon's condemnation look glib. Some
borrowings are more extensive: Lucretius' *De Natura Rerum* probably affected
Spenser's Garden of Adonis (III.vi) and certainly the hymn to Venus in IV.x.44–7 (if
merged with Chaucer's version in the Knight's Tale).

[12] See Quint 1993, Cheney 1997. For Ronsard, see Prescott 2000. Helfer 2003 argues
that Spenser shared Augustine's skepticism concerning endless empire in this world.
Typical of Spenser, however, the tags at the end of "Aprill," which figures Elizabeth as
a private lady, are in *Aeneid* I.327–8 applied to Venus.

mock-epic), whose suggestive scribbles in spilled wine recall those of his ancestor Paris in Ovid's *Heroides* 17.[13]

A turn to the private, however, is also Spenserian, although the scene (VI.x) in which Spenser's Colin sings alone to his beloved (alone, that is, except for three graces and a hundred naked dancing ladies) owes more to Italian Neoplatonists than to Ovid. One of Spenser's favorite Renaissance poets, moreover, was Joachim Du Bellay, who had with some paradox thought himself an exile when in Rome, the very city for which Ovid had longed, and had with some irony incorporated lines from Ovid's *Tristia* in his similarly titled *Regrets*. Did Spenser consider himself in some sense an exile because living in Ireland? Probably not—he had steady work and nice acreage—but if in some moods he did, then Ovid's poetry, written to a deaf ruler while amongst alien people who knew no Latin, would have carried particular resonance.

When thinking about Virgil as a source or object of imitation, Spenser would also have pondered the shape of Virgil's career from pastoral to georgic to epic. Virgil was model for ambitious poets in search of fame, laurels, and patrons in high places. (Christians could, however, think the trajectory better aimed at poetry celebrating the true God, which could mean writing biblical poetry like the French Huguenot poet Guillaume Du Bartas or hymns like Ronsard; true, it was thought that Homer had also done so, if as a pagan, which may be one more reason Spenser wrote his *Fowre Hymnes*.)[14] Spenser's first adult publication, *The Shepheardes Calender*, then, is a Virgilian move, first turn of the famous *rota Virgilii*, if also a modernization of the calendrical *horae*, with their illustrations of human activity and accompanying little monitory verses linking the months to the stages of a human life (and individual eclogues of course have varied sources). Spenser makes sure we grasp this by having the illustration for "Januarye" show a shepherd staring at the ruins of the Coliseum and by borrowing from Virgil's second eclogue. There is more to this choice, however, for in both eclogues a male shepherd laments that another male shepherd spurns his advances ("Januarye" 55–60, *Eclogues* 2.54–6). E. K. calls this noble preference for boys over women, not "forbidden and unlawfull fleshlinesse." But to deny is to mention. Renaissance imitations of classical writers sometimes evoke the homosocial world of humanist education (perpetuated, often, in the largely all-male world of secretaryships). For a flirtation with homoerotic discourse, whatever its motive, antique authority is good cover—if more often a veil than a fig leaf.

Spenser moved on to the epic, apparently skipping Virgil's intermediary *Georgics*, but, in a wonderful coincidence of motives, by way of a hero

---

[13] Cf. *Amores* I.4.20, II.5.17. For other Ovidian sources see *Encyclopedia*.
[14] Donnelly 2003 points out that in the biographical material available in Spenser's day Virgil's career was advisory, hence political as well as literary.

named "George." Indeed, the name of a hero found in plowed field and duty-bound to leave his fiancée to labor for Gloriana shows that in spite of its distrust of good works the Book of Holiness is a georgic in more than one sense. The "Ge" in "George" means earth, like "Adam" in Hebrew, but it also suggests Virgilian labor (and Adam's curse) and the need for self-cultivation and self-control. Echoes of the *Aeneid* itself are frequent in Spenser's poetry.[15] Just as important, though, are the opening lines of the Proem to *Faerie Queene* Book I: "Lo I the man, whose Muse whylome did maske, / As time her taught, in lowly Shephards weeds; / Am now enforst a farre unfitter taske, / For trumpets sterne to chaunge mine Oaten reeds." This is not the opening of the *Aeneid* as we have it, but readers would have known the lines as those with which tradition said Virgil had begun his epic before canceling them. "I am he," says Virgil, "who once tuned by song on a slender reed, then, leaving the woodland, constrained the neighbouring fields to serve the husbandman, however grasping—a work welcome to farmers: but now of Mar's bristling..." (241). The next line, however, relocates the horizon of expectation, for at least some readers in 1590 would recognize "And sing of Knights and Ladies gentle deeds" as the start of Ariosto's *Orlando Furioso*: "Of dames, of knights, of arms, of love's delight, / Of courtesies, of high attempts I speak."[16] Now we can look forward to battles, if not ones based on the author's personal expertise (the task is "unfit" for him), and also to romance, ladies, and perhaps, for those who remember Ariosto, exotic Saracens and all they represent. The shift in tone may be limited, however, by the culture's fascination with Dido, Aeneas' wife (or so thinks the goddess Juno, who should know), whom the fate-driven hero deserts and leaves to suicidal despair. Moreover, since the Medieval *Aeneid*, especially when allegorized as the soul's voyage, was halfway to being a romance, Spenser's intertextual gesture here may not *juxtapose* epic and romance so much as continue their interweaving (Fichter 1982). This epic/romance will also be a pilgrimage and quest.

The middle ages

Spenser would have read some of the Church Fathers, either as individual texts or in the excerpts and quotations found everywhere in the Renaissance, and doubtless some other early Christian works as well, such as Boethius'

---

[15] See *Encyclopedia*. The funniest echoes are the first and last lines of *Muiopotmos*, which parody the opening and closing passages of the *Aeneid*. *Virgils Gnat* is based on the *Culex*, once thought Virgil's, and Spenser takes from *Ciris*, also thought Virgil's, the conversation between Britomart and her nurse in Book III; Spenser makes the lovesick lady chaste, though, and gives her a name that in *Ciris* belongs to the nurse's daughter.

[16] I quote John Harington's translation (1591).

Consolation of Philosophy, parts of which the queen herself translated. In Book III, for instance, it is clear that the lady knight Britomart's exploits on behalf of endangered chastity against the heart-wounding magician Busirane have a number of analogues; one more may be the battle of an armored Lady Chastity, unfazed by Lust's fire, in Prudentius' *Psychomachia*. Among later medieval writers, though, it is Chaucer to whom Spenser most often turned and whom he praises in watery metaphors. In the *Calender*, where Chaucer appears as "Tityrus," the shepherd/poet Colin hopes that "on me some little drops would flowe, / Of that the spring was in his learned hedde" ("June," 93–4), while in *The Faerie Queene*, Chaucer is a "well of English undefyled" (IV.2.32) in whom "The pure well head of Poesie did dwell" (VII.vii.9). True, in Spenser's day this "learned hedde" was considered the author of some proto-Protestant verse and love complaints that have since disappeared from his canon.[17] Spenser's Chaucer is not our Chaucer.

Spenser's most obvious sources are in Chaucer's works are the *Book of the Duchess*, which lies behind the lugubrious elegy *Daphnaida*; the unfinished Squire's Tale that Book IV.ii–iii completes; the parodic Tale of Sir Thopas in which, against all probability and with how much of the humor retained is hard to judge, Spenser found the name of his incestuous giant "Ollyphant" (III.xi.3–6) as well as a model for Arthur's poignant dream of Gloriana (I.ix.12–15); and the *Parliament of Fowls*, explicitly acknowledged as a model for the description of Nature in the Mutabilitie Cantos.[18]

There are plenty of other Chaucerian moments. Few could read how Helenore cuckolded her elderly, rich, half-blind, and jealous husband Malbecco without remembering Chaucer's fabliaux, even if Spenser has other analogues (Kennedy 2000) and even if tale veers into personification allegory as the husband dwindles into the mere noun "Gealosie" (III.x.60; losing substance, he becomes a substantive). More curious is the parallel between the narrator's claim in The Franklin's Tale that "Whan maistrie comth, the God of Love anon / Beteth his wynges, and farewell, he is gone!" and the insistence in Book IV.i.46 that "Loue is free, and led with selfe delight, / Ne will enforced be with maisterdome or might." These lines are said by the diabolical Duessa, who apparently can quote Chaucer for her purpose, yet despite risks inherent in "selfe delight" Spenser does seem to have believed something like this, as is clear from his love poetry and from Scudamour's missteps in pursuing Amoret (cf. Hieatt 1975). Just as important are set pieces such as Chaucer's descriptions of temples in The Knight's Tale, the palace of Venus *Parliament*, or the House of Fame.

---

[17] Spenser's Chaucer has had much attention; for a recent array, see Anderson, Berry, Hieatt, and Steinberg in Krier 1998.

[18] VII.vii.9 says to see Alanus' *De planctu naturae*, which, as Spenser notes, Chaucer cites, but the phrasing suggests that he did not know it at first hand.

Spenser's technique of alternating labyrinthine wanderings with buildings or scenes that permit us to examine allegorical details in some leisure (see Fletcher 1971) is not peculiar to him, but he may have found it particularly congenial in Chaucer. It was Chaucer, moreover, who offered English poets the happy knowledge that in him, more gloriously than in Langland, Lydgate, or Gower, they had a vernacular tradition that let them hold their heads up when contemplating Continental literatures. Chaucer is not just a wellhead of good poetry but of good *English* poetry—and had the further advantage of being a wellhead of good *older* English poetry: in Chaucer, Spenser found somebody whose very language he could imitate (to the puzzled irritation of some readers), yet not somebody so close in time as to threaten rivalry or overshadowing. It can be easier to love a grandfather poet than a father poet.

No educated reader in 1590 could have seen Arthur's name without thinking of a chronicle tradition that included Geoffrey of Monmouth's *History of the Kings of Britain*, a model for "Briton Moniments" and (II.x) and Merlin's dynastic prophecies (III.iii), and also of Malory's *Morte d'Arthur*, printed in Caxton's version five times between 1498 and 1585. How and if Malory is an actual source is harder to say, although Spenser's St George resembles Malory's Sir Gareth in being initially rustic and inexperienced.[19] The traditional St George, England's patron whose feast day survived the Reformation's purge of saints and who was associated with the Order of the Garter, comes from elsewhere: *The Golden Legend*; Alexander Barclay's *Life of St George* (?1551); folklore and seasonal ceremony (Lamb 2003); title pages in some editions of the Sarum Missal that show the knight with a lady and lamb, royal parents peering anxiously over castle battlements, a dragon, and—significant in the Anglicization of George—a hovering royal coat of arms.

Malory has only a little to say about Arthur's earlier life, whereas Spenser only hints at his kingship—in the poem we have. Even if it seems absurd to speculate about the sources of books Spenser never wrote, attempting to see where the allegory was going in before Spenser died can be irresistible. One detail in Malory and the chronicler John Hardying hints at how the epic might have ended: their Arthur fights his way to Rome itself and is crowned. Spenser alludes to this when Arthur reads in *Briton Moniments* that "this land was tributarie made / T'ambitious *Rome*, and did their rule obay, / Till *Arthur* all that reckoning defrayd" (II.x.49). Kent Hieatt has suggested that this refers not only to Arthur's ironic delivery of a Roman general's body to Rome as "tribute" but also to his coronation there, which in turn allows us

---

[19] Summers 1997, who notes, citing Nohrnberg 1976 (p. 7), the similar dynamic of loss (Arthur is gone) and hope (Arthur will return). On Spenser and Malory see also Rovang 1996 and, on Spenser and medieval romance generally and generically, A. King 2000. Millican 1932 has good illustrations.

to imagine that Spenser planned to close with an imperial Arthur ending Rome's oppression and figuring the spread of the Gospel and Reform into the very lair of the Anti-Christ.[20]

This Roman coronation, says Hieatt, is not found in other stories of Arthur, yet there is a less notable text that Spenser probably knew and that may be yet another "source" without being an "intertext": John Derricke's *Image of Irelande* (1581). Dedicated to Sidney, it contains annotated encomia to major English rulers, including Arthur (not one of the English, Derricke confesses, but beloved by them). Famed for "Magnanimitie,"

> Prince Arthure is that noble kyng,
> whose fame and greate reporte:
> Stirde up the Nobles of the worlde,
> to seeke unto his Courte....
> This is the knight whose bloodie blade,
> Obtained *Caesars* Croune:
> This is the man that brought at laste,
> The haughtie Romanes doune.

Although Derricke does not explicitly connect "Prince" Arthur's ancient Roman exploit and the future collapse of papal Rome, his praise of Edward III several pages later is a dithyramb of anti-Catholicism in which Edward's shaming of a cowardly and drunken Pope should teach other kings how to handle the papacy so that "the beaste would beware how he entermedled with Princes matters impertinent to his calling."[21] It is hard to believe that Spenser, recently arrived in Ireland, did not read Derricke as homework for his new job. Is Derricke, then, a "source"? His doggerel probably figured somewhere in Spenser's mind and he could assume readers such as Ralegh and any Sidneys alive in 1590 would also have read it. Remembering Derricke would reinforce the thought of Arthur's Roman conquest and its allegorical potential. It seems unlikely, however, that Spenser expected most readers to remember this poem and let it shape their expectations.

The romance tradition in which Arthur stars has a cousin in pilgrimage allegory, some of it indebted to St Bernard's allegorization of the Prodigal Son parable in which a young man on a feisty horse named Desire deviates into Error, then into Pride, then into Despair, and recovers himself in a holy house. Spenser is likely to have seen an illustrated Protestant version of the

---

[20] Hieatt 1987; in the same issue T. P. Roche calls Tasso a better model. There may be a quiet pun when *Moniments* breaks off without even a "Cesure" (II.x.68)—Arthur will defeat a "Caesar." Spenser's interest in and use of chronicle and history have drawn much attention. See van Es 2002, who cites earlier scholarship.

[21] Sig. A4; for a rare notice of Derricke's Arthur, see Moroney 1999.

parable by Stephen Bateman (1569). Although it has no dragon fight, it and Jean de Cartigny's related (and several times reprinted) *Voyage of the Wandering Knight* (1581) provide one way to understand Book I's narrative. Spenser's Continental sources include some big names. Cornelius Agrippa's *De Incertitudine et Vanitate scientiarum et artium* (trans. 1569, Chapter 68) anticipates Spenser's anti-court satire in *Mother Hubberds Tale*, and the astute advice on Christian pilgrimage in Erasmus' *Enchiridion* helps explain, for example, St George's escape from one sort of pride only to fall into another.[22] Spenser doubtless read around in Protestant theologians too (he might have found the Englishman's William Tyndale's *Parable of the Wicked Mammon* interesting when thinking about Guyon in the House of Mammon). The most important of his Continental sources, though, are Italian and French.[23]

Renaissance love poets could not escape Petrarch's *Rime Sparse* even when they tried. Spenser's boyhood translation of *Rime Sparse* 323 on the death of Laura (recycled for *Complaints* as *The Visions of Petrarch*) comes close by being transmuted into anti-Catholic allegory (and indeed Petrarch, although Catholic, had written angrily on Rome's corruption). But when Britomart's love melts into lament in III.iv.8–10, her words appropriately recall *Rime*'s sonnet 189, and Petrarch or his followers are models for both imitation and avoidance in *Amoretti*. More interesting than discerning this or that source, such as Desportes for *Am* 15, for example, or Tasso for *Am* 43 is watching Spenser evoke Petrarchan motifs that he exploits to signal his ability to go beyond all those blocked and failed Continental lovers. *Amoretti* ends with moping and chilly solitude, but readers have only to turn a page or two to find *Epithalamion*. How unlike poor Petrarch, Ronsard, and Sidney! Petrarch cannot catch his deer in *Rime* 190 because it belongs to Caesar, whom commentators read as Augustus (advocate of family values) or God, and whom Wyatt, who translated the poem as "Whoso list to hunt," probably imagined as Henry VIII. But in *Amoretti* 67 Spenser's lover ties her up. Petrarch's ship in *Rime* 189 is tempest-tossed, but in *Amoretti* 63 the lover can "descry the happy shore." As usual, though, Spenser's mingled sources complicate the picture. To capture his deer is to triumph over female refusal and Petrarch, but the sonnet also recalls Tasso's hopeful "Questa fera

---

[22] *Encyclopedia* mentions Agrippa's crafty fox and scoffing ape, but apish imitation would be more relevant. Spenser probably read Castiglione's *Courtier*, although his view of courtiership could be skeptical. Schoolboys read Erasmus' *Adagia*, collection of classical proverbs (see also Smith 1970), and everybody read *The Praise of Folly*. At the end of "Februarie" E. K. jokingly calls Erasmus foolish, and *Encyclopedia* notes (citing Thomas Warton) a passage in *Lingua* which has slander run, as will the Blattant Beast in VI.xii.23–5, "per domos privatas, per collegia, per monasteria, per alulas principum, per civitates, per regna." See also Cullen 1974 and Wells 1979.

[23] See, however, Greene 2001 on the Portuguese and Spanish.

gentil" (Dasenbrock 1985). Petrarch is an object of poetic gesture. Is Tasso? He was much read, so maybe. But there is a better parallel to Spenser's narrative—a deer's self-surrender after the exhausted hunter rests with his hounds near water—in a poem from Marguerite de Navarre's *Chansons spirituals* (Prescott 1985). The deer is Christ and the hunter wins by giving up, which makes the poem relevant to Spenser's liturgical pattern, but unless Marguerite was more widely read than seems the case, her *chanson* is not an intertext. Spenser may well remember Marguerite, but he points at Petrarch/Tasso.

If Petrarch is the object of pointing, Spenser's swerve away from him (or attempted swerve, a sort of bend in the river) is the point. The ambivalence— imitation and effort to break free—shows in *The Faerie Queene* as well. If the knight of chastity, Britomart, has taken some of her love complaint from Petrarch (III.iv.8–10; cf. *Rime* 189), young Amoret, engaged or possibly even just married, has a harder time of it in the House of Busirane (III.xii) when surrounded by personified clichés from Petrarchism (and the *Romance of the Rose*). So too, Petrarch haunts the temptingly sensuous Bower of Bliss (II.xii), enemy of Temperance and place of excess, for it is amidst its artifice, not in the healthily natural Garden of Adonis (III.vi), that laurel grows: poets win more fame from craft and at least the appearance of being in love than they do from good moral health.

Ludivico Ariosto's *Orlando Furioso* (1532) and Torquato Tasso's *Gerusa-lemme Liberata* (1580) both weigh heavily on *The Faerie Queene* (so may Matteo Boiardo's *Orlando Innamorato* by way of Ariosto). As with Ovid and Virgil, though, the two poets came to Spenser with different tones and politics. To simplify one subtle argument, Tasso values a noble monarch who guides his warriors toward a definitive and noble end, whereas Ariosto's world is feudal, its power dispersed.[24] In generic terms, Ariosto offered Spenser more romance, and Tasso offered him more epic. His own interlaced narrative with its errant knights and relaxed attitude toward closure resembles the feudal world of *Orlando*, although one can imagine, in some alternative universe in which Spenser survived to dedicate Book XII to James I, Arthur and Gloriana presiding over a centralized and ordered kingdom.

According to Spenser's friend Gabriel Harvey, Spenser hoped to "ouergo" Ariosto (*Prose* 471), but to overgo is not to foreswear indebtedness. Whatever her other ancestors, Britomart is largely a version of Ariosto's Bradamante, and Ariosto, sometimes accompanied by other writers, is behind a number of other episodes or characters. The talking tree Fradubio (I.ii), for instance, who tells the naively uncomprehending Redcrosse knight early in Book I

---

[24] Helgerson 1992. Summers 1997 finds in Malory a similar a tension between wandering knights on individual quests and a settled central figure serving a community.

that he was transformed into his current arboreal shape thanks to misplaced love for the witch Duessa—who is standing right there, disguised as the holy "Fidessa"—derives from the enchanted Astolfo (*OF* 6.26–53; Fradubio also recalls Virgil's arborified Polydorus in *Aeneid* 3.27–42, who bleeds when a branch is torn off; on this particularly crowded *topos*; cf. Scott 1986).

In the scene with Fradubio, memories of Ariosto encourage the reader to recall the frequency with which the incautious fall victim to enticing illusion. In other scenes, however, what can seem to come from Ariosto or other poets well known to modern scholars may have other significant sources that are now largely forgotten but were once famous. Thus *Encyclopedia* notes under "Ariosto" that the thieving toll-keeper Pollente (V.ii) is based on the Saracen loudmouth Rodomonte, who demands a fight before anybody can cross his bridge (*OF* 29, 31, 35) and that Munera, Pollente's corrupt and golden-handed daughter, is modeled on Lady Mede in Langland's *Piers Plowman*, which quotes psalm 26.10: "In quorum manibus iniquitates sunt, dextera eorum repleta est muneribus" ("in whose hands are iniquities, their right hands full of reward/meed/pay"). All this is doubtless true. Even if remembering Rodomonte, though, and even while bearing Ariosto and Langland in mind, many of Spenser's first readers would also have remembered Antwerp's famed giant Druon Antigonus, whose effigy still sits in that city (*Encyclopedia* under "Belge"). A toll-keeper like Pollente, Antigonus would demand money of those crossing the Scheldt and cut off their hands if unsatisfied. One day a champion cut off Antigonus' own hands, which is why the city's coat of arms shows two hands above a castle. Since "Pollente" means "mighty man," and since that is regularly a term for "giant" in the Bible, he has the feel of a giant.

Antigonus has become Pollente, his hands have become Munera's extremities, which Artegall nails high on the castle, and his first name, Druon, is now the name of a knight in Book IV. Does this matter? Yes. Book V is among other things a Book of Foreign Policy and includes, toward the end, an idealized version of Elizabeth's attempted rescue of the Low Countries from Spain. Her decision to intervene had been precipitated by Spain's successful siege of Antwerp in 1585, and so that city had been much on English minds. To sense Antigonus as well as Ariosto so early in Book V is to see Spenser not waiting until the final cantos to think about war in the Netherlands and Ireland. Geopolitics comes earlier in Book V than might now appear if we ignore Pollente's full genealogy.

Spenser's treatment of Ariosto is thus complicated, and understanding it is no mere matter of identifying which of his lines or scenes owe something to the Italian poet. He not only adds to the complexity by merging recollections of *Orlando Furioso* with those of other texts, but twists what he takes in ways that seem to beg for but resist easy interpretation. A notorious instance is Prince Arthur's diamond shield, modern scholarly readings of it shifting, just as fashions shift from observing debt and transformation to seeing active resistance to predecessor poets. Arthur's illusion-destroying shield has its primary parallel in the illusion-*producing* shield (and read thus by contemporary commentators) belonging to Ariosto's magician Atlante. Does this only seemingly "perverse" imitation "by reversal" show Spenser's "constant determination to make story the servant of invention," as William Nelson thinks? Is Paul Alpers right that Spenser hopes to convert a magical object to more inward and psychological uses? Or is the shield's dazzle meant to outshine Ariosto and distract us from the extent of Spenser's debt to the Italian poet? Is Spenser's move bold appropriation, meaningful transformation, or literary aggression?[25] The deeper mystery, one might argue, and something that source study is not always adroit at solving, is Spenser's tone. Ariosto is funny, although detecting allegories can nudge him closer to sobriety, and so it has long been thought that whatever Spenser borrowed from him, he made even more allegorical and much more sage and serious. In recent years, though, as many scholars have come to find Spenser's poetry less interested in illustrating moral ideals than in interrogating them, Spenser has seemed more urbane, even comic. It is possible that he sobered up Ariosto because he thought him in need of moral improvement; that is one way to "overgo" a source. It is just as possible that he thought the memory of Ariosto's comedy would lighten his own poetry.[26]

Echoes of Tasso are if anything even more often to be heard in Spenser's poetry than are those of Ariosto. Some have been mentioned above. Spenser's Fradubio, for example, has yet another tree-cousin in *Gerusa-lemme*: Tancred meets a tree from which emanates the spirit of his beloved Clorinda, whom he had killed by error. The two texts have some telling differences, though. Tasso's scene is crowded, whereas Spenser's is an allegorized internal struggle that has public—because ecclesiastical and geopolitical—significance but that as a literal narrative involves merely one future saint (Redcrosse), one whore of Babylon (Duessa), and one talking tree. (Fradubio's wife Fraelissa, also a tree, is present but silent; maybe frail flesh, which is what her name seems to mean, is wordless, although it might be instructive to imagine one or two stanzas of what *she* might say about Duessa's seduction of her husband.) In Tasso a whole forest has been subjected to pagan spells so that legions of arboreal demons are present when Godfrey sends workmen to fell the woods. They and others who come are greeted by flames and monsters in a scene that anticipates both the encounter with Fradubio and Britomart's passage through the flames around Busirane's house (typically, Spenser takes a source and parts its stream into two directions). Tancred knows that this is all illusory, whereas

[25] Wiggins 1991 discusses these readings by Nelson (1963) and Alpers (1967); the third is his own.

[26] Silberman 1995 argues for comedy in Spenser as well as in Ariosto.

we have no reason to disbelieve Fradubio. Or does the recollection that Tasso's forest voices are really demonic illusion, not real, cast doubt on Fradubio's story of his seduction by a witch? Eventually the Tassoean woods (and together with them, romance) will fall to epic heroism, whereas in Spenser, Redcrosse simply goes on his way, truly deluded. Far from felling the forest, he buries the bit of Fradubio that he cut off before he realized that the tree was human.

Then there is the hero Rinaldo's imprisonment on the witch Armida's island. This "source" is clear, its diversion into the Bower of Bliss less so. In Tasso the plan is to rescue the knight by showing him to himself in a sobering diamond shield (XIV.77; compare a picture in Bateman's *Pylgrime* that shows Reason holding up a mirror to a protagonist beguiled by fleshly delight). The rescue itself in cantos XV–XVI has many close parallels in Spenser including two naked girls playing in the water that make the rescuers' self-control waver before they pass on in manly meditation, fancy free. And the seductive song in XVI.4–16 is the source of the one that Guyon hears in the Bower. Indeed, the closeness of the translation suits an episode that comments negatively on imitation—where seeming ivy is gold with green enamel. Is this, like the presence of laurel, wry self-mockery, a poet's version of the liar paradox?

There is more to be said on Spenser's Tasso, but also more on how noting imitations of a major figure need not exhaust the possibilities. When, at the closing stages of Book I, canto x, St George is taken up a mountain by the hermit Contemplation he sees from afar a celestial city. What does Spenser want us to remember? The Apocalypse, of course, and St John on a mountain gazing rapturously at new Heaven and new Earth. Other memories deepen the perspective. In *Gerusalemme liberata* Book XVIII, after advice from a hermit who reminds him of his errors, Tasso's Rinaldo ascends Mount Olivet, where the dew turns his clothes white (St 16). He has no vision, but as David Quint says (*Encyclopedia* under Tasso), in Book XIV Godfrey learns of his future task and accomplishment. Spenser combines these. Yet he possibly knew of other, minor models. One is an illustration of Faith in Stephen Bateman's *Christall glasse of christian reformation* (1569): a knight, a cross on his shield, stands over a supine demon and looks across water at a high city. The sun shows God's name in Hebrew and the text says: "The man in armour signifieth all stedfast belevers of the veritie, being armed with constant zeale of Christianitie, and weaponed with the shielde of lively faith, the spere of continuaunce, and the sworde of the word of God: The Devil under him is temptation, being overcome by faith in Christ Jesus" (sig. M4). The knight *looks* like Redcrosse, if without a hermit; he is not, however, on a hill.

A hill does figure in Guy Le Fèvre de la Boderie's *Galliade* (1578, 1582), a treasure house of excited commentary on the cosmic dance, the body, musical intervals, and much more. Did Spenser read it? Granted his knowledge of French poetry it seems possible. If so, he would have read that David, drunk with divinity, climbs the "mont de Contemplation," where his soul hears songs that excel those of Helicon and Parnassus just as "Eternité stable"—steadfast Eternity—surpasses the "Temps qui fuit"—fleeting Time (460–1). St George's vision and the author's final prayer for the "Sabaoths sight" of a city set on eternal pillars have many sources. The phrase "mount of Contemplation," the mention of Parnassus, and the contrast of steadfast Eternity and slippery time make one wonder if this passage did not haunt Spenser early and late.

Boderie is a minor writer. Two of Spenser's undeniable French sources are more famous and identified by name. Pastorals by Clément Marot are the models for "November" and "December" in *The Shepheardes Calendar*, even if E. K. is unimpressed by the Frenchman, perhaps because Marot was a court poet with more charm than laureate ambition, one whose psalms, although immensely influential, got him into troubles that the English seem to have read less as martyrdom than as imprudence (Prescott 1978; Patterson 1986 takes a different view). Spenser went on reading Marot, for two of the Anacreontics in *Amoretti and Epithalamion* translate his lyrics; in context, and despite their provenance in the court of François I, they sound like something from the now fashionable Greek *Anthology*, which may be why Spenser liked them.

The other poet Spenser names as a source is Joachim Du Bellay.[27] Spenser had reworked his early translation of Du Bellay's *Songe* as *The Visions of Bellay* and translated the *Antiquitez de Rome* as *The Ruines of Rome*, publishing both in *Complaints*. There is more than this to Du Bellay's impact on Spenser, however, for these texts are a major source of the discourse of ruination that so affected him and then a number of English poets, including Shakespeare (Hieatt 1983). Even before 1591 some had deployed this discourse, but it was Spenser's Du Bellay who gave it faster cultural energy. Traces are found elsewhere in *Complaints*, most notably in the *Ruines of Time*, and intermittently throughout *The Faerie Queene*. There is not much of Du Bellay's Petrarchan *Olive*, although its structure anticipates the liturgical foundation of *Amoretti*. At the end of his short career Du Bellay was turning to satire; it would be good to know if Spenser read the end of "Le poète courtesan" advising the sage ("saige") court poet to strive to please ("plaire") and so win treasure ("riches benefices"). Compare the bitter conclusion of Book VI.

Spenser called Du Bellay "first garland of free Poësie" (*Ruines of Rome* 33.1) but in the same sonnet he also praised Du Bartas, whose biblical poetry was for a while enormously admired in England. It is hard to find lines in Spenser, though, for which he is a source. Perhaps Spenser thought biblical

---

[27] Prescott 1978, 1996; for a more theoretical perspective see Coldiron 2002.

poetry too true—not "right" poetry in Philip Sidney's terms because it is not fiction. Spenser found Ronsard more useful here and there (Prescott 1978, 2000) but he never mentions him. True, most of his sources go unnamed. The silence on Ronsard remains intriguing. If Spenser wanted a role model, a behavioral source, he could have done worse than Ronsard, still productive after *Calender* saw print. When a shepherd claims in the October eclogue that the fittest place for "pierlesse Poesye" is in "Princes pallace," Spenser would have known that Ronsard had published sonnets, odes, satires, epistles, elegies, Anacreontics, an essay on poetry, and the start of an epic, had lived in the Louvre, and had exchanged verses with the king. Ronsard enjoyed self-pity, but from across the Channel his career must have looked both glorious and disconcertingly nearby. Du Bellay was closer to Spenser in spirit—and less intimidating.

Spenser is among our most original poets—and also among our most derivative. His poetry is proof, if proof were needed, that to mix old ingredients— some of them from way back on the shelf and some with very strange points of origin—is one way to make something strikingly new. And Spenser can mix and (un)match. In the Book of Holiness, for example, we have a modified Virgilian opening that seems to foretell dynastic epic and laureate authorship; a sequence of episodes eventually from Bernard; a hero and heroine from folklore, *The Golden Legend*, and Tudor ceremony; a pair of villains from Tudor anti-Catholic polemic; a dragon who may have one forebear in a poem by Stephen Hawes (Kaske 1989); romance material from Tasso and Ariosto; a forest from Ovid, Chaucer, Tasso, and others; a princely hero from Geoffrey, Malory, and Tudor propaganda; details that recall the Sarum Missal; and, providing a cosmic structure from the Fall to the New Jerusalem, the Bible. And yet the end is not.... The word "eclectic" hardly begins to describe Spenser.

In scholars' attempts to locate the materials that Spenser used, challenged, modified, and intermingled, the stress has broadened from notice of *a* source, one that the person who notices it could add to an all too often inert list of background materials (as in the Variorum edition of Spenser), to observations of a syncretic artist at work putting such materials, especially when readers may be expected to identify and remember them, into a dynamic juxtaposition that contributes to the poetry's effect and even meaning. Older source study remains valuable; indeed, recent years have brought more finds and it is doubtless such excavation will continue. Criticism like that of Helgerson and Kaske, however, gives us a Spenser who certainly collects bits and pieces of the recent or remote past but who also, in one way or another, exploits the intellectual and cultural energy such fragments generate when strategically positioned inside the host text. Some "sources," that is, remain mere droplets, not fully "intertextual" (or interfluvial), even though finding them allows us the pleasure of watching Spenser at work. Others such as texts by Virgil, Ovid, Chaucer, Malory, or Tasso, to say nothing of the Bible or Book of Common Prayer, demand notice because what Spenser does with and to them are visibly crucial to his own performance and the significance of his poetry. Even when the source seems minor or peripheral, recent criticism is inclined to stress why locating the prior text matters to Spenser's larger agenda. The mock-heroic butterfly hero of Spenser's *Muiopotmos*, for example, has obvious Virgilian and Ovidian connections, ones long duly noted by editors, but a recent short essay by James Morey has argued for the relevance of a famous sermon preached in 1548 by Hugh Latimer that recalls how an earlier preacher had called members of Parliament "butterflies" and for this and other offenses had been executed as a heretic by Henry VIII.[28] Morey's point, however, is not to find yet another source for Spenser's poem, although of course he does that too, but further to map the religious forcefield that helps us to clarify Spenser's poem and to recover more of its original electricity. Even Spenserian butterflies, let alone Spenserian knights and villains, have their genealogies, and that ancestry, like a set of cultural or literary chromosomes, affects how Spenser's creations live in our minds.

Further reading

Anderson, H. 1976. *The Growth of a Personal Voice: "Piers Plowman" and "The Faerie Queene"*, New Haven: Yale University Press.

Coldiron, A. E. B. 2002. "How Spenser Excavates Du Bellay's *Antiquitez*: Or, the Role of the Poet, Lyric, Historiography, and the English sonnet", *JEGP* 101: 41–67.

Fichter, A. 1982. *Poets Historical, Dynastic Epic in the Renaissance*, Yale: Yale University Press.

King, J. N. 1990. *Spenser's Poetry and the Reformation Tradition*, Princeton, NJ: Princeton University Press.

Prescott, A. L. 1978. *French Poets and the English Renaissance: Studies in Fame and Transformation*, New Haven: Yale University Press.

——. 1996. "Spenser (Re)Reading du Bellay: Chronology and Literary Response", in *Spenser's Life and the Subject of Biography*, ed. Judith H. Anderson, Donald Cheney, and David A. Richardson Amherst: University of Massachusetts Press, 131–45.

——. 2000. "The Laurel and the Myrtle: Spenser and Ronsard", in *Worldmaking Spenser: Explorations in the Early Modern Age*, ed. Patrick Cheney and Lauren Silberman, Lexington: University Press of Kentucky, 63–78.

Rovang, P. R. 1996. *Refashioning "Knights and Ladies Gentle Deeds": The Intertextuality of Spenser's "Faerie Queene" and Malory's "Morte Darthur"*, Cranbury, NJ: Associated University Presses.

van Es, Bart. 2002. *Spenser's Forms of History*, Oxford: Oxford University Press.

Watkins, J. 1995. *The Specter of Dido: Spenser and Virgilian Epic*, New Haven: Yale University Press.

Wiggins, P. DeSa "Spenser's Use of Ariosto: Imitation and Allusion in Book I of the *Faerie Queene*", *Renaissance Quarterly* 45: 257–79.

---

[28] James H. Morey, "Latimer's 'Sermon on the Plough' and Spenser's *Muiopotmos*," *Notes and Queries* 42.3 (September 1995), 286–8.

7
Works Published Before 1589
Bart van Es

Early modern texts and contexts

A Theatre for Voluptuous Worldlings (1569), *The Shepheardes Calender* (1579) and the two sets of Spenser/Harvey *Letters* (1580) present very different pictures of a young English writer. In the first we find an unacknowledged translator in a collection of continental Renaissance verse. In the second a 'New Poet' is heralded as the equal of the best of those writers. In the third we encounter a 'University Man' full of the concerns of London and Cambridge intellectual life. In each case, the author himself remains anonymous. In the persona of '*Immeritô*' Spenser writes at the opening of *The Shepheardes Calender*:

> Goe little booke: thy selfe present,
> As child whose parent is vnkent...
> And when thou art past ieopardee,
> Come tell me, what was sayd of mee.

(ll. 1–2; 16–17)

The works published before 1589 all show a deep and explicit concern with the response of their readers. In each case prose commentary is pre-applied to the author's verse. The *Theatre* has its (lengthy) 'Brief Declaration' explaining the visions of the sonnets as Protestant allegory. The *Calender* includes E. K.'s 'Epistle', 'Argument', and 'Gloss'. The *Letters* feature still more commentary, setting snippets of poetry within a dense framework of debate. From the first, these works anticipate their own 'critical history'. Academic writing today has become suspicious of any simple division between 'primary' and 'secondary' material in these texts. Their verse and prose are now widely seen as existing in historically specific interdependence. Much recent academic work is focused on the artful balance between the two and

116

this survey will therefore—like the *Calender* itself—come full circle: beginning and ending with the physical books produced in 1569, 1579, and 1580.

Right from the start it is *The Shepheardes Calender* that stands at the heart of the tradition of commentary. Even after the publication of his epic Spenser continued to be associated very strongly with the rustic persona of Colin Clout presented in this work. Indeed, by returning to this pastoral figure in *Colin Clouts Come Home Againe* and the 1596 instalment of *The Faerie Queene* the author cemented the significance of the *Calender* and invited a stronger biographical reading of its central character. Whereas the translator of the *Theatre* and the uncertain young writer of the *Letters* did not attract significant attention until the end of the nineteenth century, the shepherd of the *Calender* was a consistent presence for at least a century and a half. E. K.'s judgements on the *Calender* (its literary status, sources, archaism, morality, and religious politics) were all echoed amongst Spenser's early readership. That readership was clearly large and attentive. The *Calender* went through five editions in the poet's lifetime and Blenerhasset, Vallans, Peele, and Lodge all produced work that alluded to the poem within the first decade of its publication (Wells 1971–72, 5–13).

The most controversial feature of the *Calender* was its language. Here, as elsewhere, E. K. anticipated the response of Spenser's readership. The issue takes up a prominent part of the Epistle as that 'which of the many thinges which in him be straunge, I know will seeme the straungest' (ll. 22–4). Gabriel Harvey, who is addressed by the Epistle, himself focused on archaism in his early discussion of the poem (Wells 1971–72, 4). Harvey's justification of the revival of old words, on the grounds of poetical licence, reflects E. K.'s in its defensive edge. It was certainly this aspect of the poem that drew the most negative comment from early writers; something spurred, no doubt, by Sidney's parenthetical rejection of the *Calender*'s 'framing of his style to an old rustic language' (Wells 1971–72, 54). The criticism was to be echoed in Jonson's memorable claim that 'Spencer, in affecting the Ancients writ no Language' (Wells 1971–72, 206). Yet, for some, the connection with those ancients was successfully established. Francis Beaumont, in an epistle attached to Speght's edition of Chaucer (1597), claimed that 'his much frequenting of *Chaucers* antient speeches causeth many to allow farre better of him, then otherwise they would' (Wells 1971–72, 53).

While Sidney features prominently in the *Letters* and is the dedicatee of the *Calender*, his *Defence of Poesy* gives no open acknowledgement of Spenser's authorship. In this it is in line with other early commentators and here too, E. K. may be said to provoke and anticipate this response. The gloss of the January eclogue repeatedly hints at the biographical: Colin Clout is the name under which 'this Poete secretly shadoweth himself', in Hobinnol 'seemeth to be hidden the person of some very speciall and most familiar freend' and Rosalinde 'is also a feigned name, which being wel ordered, wil bewray the very name of hys loue and mistresse'. Few, it seems, were prepared to order the *Calender*'s hints in such a way as to connect the poem to its author. George Whetstone attributed the work to Sidney, and Puttenham offered praise in passing only to 'that other Gentleman who wrate the late shepheardes Callender' (Wells 1971–72, 9, 13). Webbe's lengthy consideration of the poem in *A Discourse of English Poetry* (1586), however, suggests that artfully feigned ignorance on this matter is not the preserve of E. K. alone. Early on, his commentary only edges towards an attribution to 'Master *Sp.*', but subsequent discussion shows he has little doubt on the matter. As recent studies, such as Goldberg's of 1986, have observed, anonymity and authorial presence are an artful game within the *Calender*. It seems reasonable to suppose that this game was pursued with equal vigour among the coterie of writers who first received the work in 1579.

Webbe's *Discourse* exemplifies the success of E. K.'s commentary in establishing the critical norms through which to examine Spenser's work. Spenser is compared with Virgil and Theocritus, commended for his attempt to civilise the English language, for his religious satire, and for moral teaching. Webbe also echoes E. K.'s hints about the political content of the volume: 'There is also much matter uttered somewhat couertly, especially the abuses of some [with] whom he would not be too playne withall' (Wells 1971–72, 9). More marginal (but likewise of significance for late twentieth-century critics, such as Goldberg, 1992) is Webbe's qualified uneasiness about the 'unsauery love' between male shepherds in the January eclogue. Like E. K. (who also detects 'some sauour of disorderly loue' in the eclogue) Webbe first forwards and then retracts an accusation about the presence of homosexual desire in Spenser's composition.

With the exception of this one expression of unease, the overwhelming response of Webbe and his contemporaries was to see the *Calender* as a treasure house of moral and literary example. Most strikingly, Abraham Fraunce mined the work for educational passages useful for his *Lawyers Logike* and (unpublished) *Shepheardes Logike*. Such texts were produced to give their readers easy access to quotations and stylistic models, and they give perhaps the most representative picture of the response of the *Calender*'s first audience. Robert Allot's *England's Parnassus* (1600), which frequently refers to the *Calender*, offers another instance of such reading practice. The large number of quotations from the *Calender* reflect its significance as a literary text. Still more, the encyclopaedic structure of Allot's work reflects the critical culture under which Spenser's poem flourished: a culture that valued thematic inclusiveness and stylistic variety. The *Calender*—itemising not just the months of the year but also a series of moral, political, emotional, and literary topics—spoke directly to the reader envisaged by such a text.

As is apparent from *England's Parnassus*, in the early modern period the work of analysing texts is almost inseparable from that of creating new ones. It is through the practice of imitation, therefore, that we get the strongest sense of the influence of the *Calender* in the first half-century of its existence. In the assessment of Chaudhuri (1989, 5) 'the *Calender* virtually inaugurates

English Renaissance pastoral' and sets it on 'a completely different course from the continental'. The English Spenserians Drayton, Wither, and Browne are foremost in this tradition (see Grundy (1969); O'Callaghan (2000)). As Michelle O'Callaghan has shown, these writers presented the pastoral community as a unified body (minimising internal conflict, and taking Colin clout as a direct figure for the poet). The mutually supportive debate of the October eclogue thus became a model for the Spenserian pastoral of these writers. That sense of community was itself already there to be discovered in the *Calender* as printed text: E. K.'s commentary on the eclogues setting up a model for dialogue in which 'meaning is produced collectively through such acts of collaboration' (O'Callaghan, 11). Spenserian pastoral, as opposed to the Royalist anacreontics of men like Lovelace and Cowley, could thus be understood to have an oppositional politics. Milton too found political sympathies with the *Calender*, although not focused on a united community. Writing on the May eclogue in 1641 he found in Palinode a presentation of 'our Prelates, whoose whole life is a recantation of their pastorall vow, and whose profession to forsake the world, as they use the matter, boggs them deeper into the world' (Wells 1971–72, 208). Milton's *Lycidas* (1637), the most subtle and inclusive of all pastorals in the Spenserian tradition, holds in suspension almost all aspects highlighted by the *Calender*'s first readers. In important ways, in its concluding act of distancing from 'the uncouth swain' and onward movement to 'pastures new' (*Lycidas*, ll. 186, 193) the poem also marks a break in the reception history of the *Calender*. As the literary climate changed in the years that followed, it became impossible to respond to Spenser's early poetry in quite the same way again.

The late-sixteenth to nineteenth century: Neo-classical to romantic criticism

For Milton, writing before the outbreak of the Civil War, it was still possible to praise the politics of the *Calender* without finding their inclusion inappropriate to the genre of pastoral. By the time of the Restoration this would become much more difficult. While it is nowhere coherently articulated in these terms, the period before 1660 evinces a widespread receptivity to the generic breadth of the *Calender*. As Webbe describes it, the poem successfully imitates Virgil and Theocritus, and also persuasively directs religious allegory against 'popish prelates'. He sees no incompatibility in these objectives. Webbe's reading celebrates the *Calender*'s diversity. If Chaudhuri (1989) is right in believing that much in the spectrum of early seventeenth-century pastoral (from romance and drama to the independent lyric of poets such as Wither) takes inspiration from the *Calender*, then such openness in the understanding of the form must have been widespread. Placed in the context of Sidney's pastoral *Arcadia*, and the wider eclecticism of the medieval and renaissance tradition (see Cullen 1970; Cooper 1977) it is possible to understand Spenser's 1579 publication as a supremely inclusive text.

With the Restoration there comes a more discriminating neo-classicism much less sympathetic to such generic innovation. The major treatments of the poem—while overwhelmingly appreciative—all find fault with its openness to non-classical influences. The fate of the *Calender* in critical discussion over the following decades is very closely tied to the shifting understanding and valuation of pastoral itself (a critical history that is closely tied to the rise and fall of neo-classical aesthetics). In the period from the seventeenth to the eighteenth century we find the *Calender* buffeted by the rapidly shifting winds of criticism. In the first instance, it is little damaged (and even benefits) through a development in polite taste under which *The Faerie Queene* suffers considerably. For Thomas Rhymer (Wells 1971–72, 266) and others, the *Calender* even becomes a kind of weapon against *The Faerie Queene*. The poem's pleasing proportions (a circularity and unity of design that Rhymer compares favourably even with the works of Virgil) give it a classical quality to be set against the 'barbarous' romance of *The Faerie Queene*. In the longer poem Spenser was misled by the slipshod poetics of Ariosto, but in the earlier work he largely escaped that influence. Dryden's verdict was comparable, although vastly more generous in its account of Spenser's genius. Spenser was 'England's prime pastoralist' (Wells 1971–72, 153) and thus a pervasive influence on Dryden's translation of the *Eclogues*. For him the author of the *Calender* was the third great pastoral innovator in the tradition of Theocritus and Virgil.

John Hughes, as editor of the 1715 *Works*, produced the most sustained critical analysis in the spirit of Dryden's verdict. His 'Remarks' on the poem famously declared that 'there seems to be the same difference between the *Fairy Queen* and the *Shepherd's Calendar*, as between a Royal Palace and a little Country Seat... the first strikes the Eye with more Magnificence but the latter may perhaps give the greatest pleasure' (xcvii–xcviii). In the *Calender* Spenser had not been 'misled by the Italians' but guided instead by inner and outer nature. It was the simple 'Theocritan' quality of the poem that most struck Hughes. Rather than the elevated example of Virgil, Spenser took his inspiration from his personal passion for Rosalind. In this biographical reading of the *Calender*, incidentally, Hughes followed a general trend in post-Restoration commentary. As the 'Life' emerged as a literary category the clues left by the *Calender* and *Letters* became increasingly important: Aubrey goes so far as to identify Rosalind as 'a kindswoman of Sir Erasmus's lady' (Wells 1971–72, 276).

Hughes admitted that by including a satirical element in the *Calender* Spenser had transgressed 'the strict Rules of Criticism' (civ). The 'Excellency of the Moral', however, went a long way in excusing this shortcoming. The neo-classical spotlight of Alexander Pope exposed such flaws more starkly. In the *Pastorals* there is again a generous acknowledgement of influence. Pope opens 'summer' with a close imitation of the first line of the *Calender*. Yet where early readers rejoiced in the expansion of the genre, Pope opens his 'Discourse on Pastoral Poetry' (1717) with the brilliantly assertive observation that 'there are not, I believe, a greater number of any sort of verses than of those which are called Pastorals, nor a smaller, than of those which are truly so' (23). As Heninger (1961) has observed, early eighteenth-century writers like Pope spotted in Renaissance verse a 'perversion' of true pastoral form. Pope found the *Calender* too long, too allegorical, and too low in its dialect. Under the influence of Fontenelle, who argued for a pastoral rooted in the tranquillity of rural life, Pope also found Spenser too much situated in a fallen world. The calendar structure itself was Spenser's great innovation, although Pope believed he had bettered its twelve months with his more economical four seasons.

Having risen in the wake of a new understanding of pastoral, the *Calender* paid the price when a reaction against prescriptive classicism proved a critical disaster for the genre. Samuel Johnson's predominantly negative account of pastoral left the form punctured beyond repair for centuries to come. A critical mindset that had made room for an appreciation of something as apparently shapeless and true to life as the novel inevitably found it hard to retain a space for a form as artificial and formulaic as pastoral seemed to be. Johnson found it a 'narrow' species of literature in which it would be difficult to make an advance on what antiquity had achieved. He mocked the 'learned' justification for Spenser's 'studied barbarity' in crafting the *Calender*'s language. Quoting the opening of the anti-Catholic September Eclogue—'Diggon Dauie, I bidde her god day'—Johnson muses with devastating aloofness that 'surely, at the same time that a shepherd learns theology, he may gain some acquaintance with his native language' (*Rambler*, 1750).

By the mid-eighteenth century the balance of critical interest (always, of course, on the side of *The Faerie Queene*) swung decisively in favour of Spenser's epic. The literary allusiveness of the *Calender* did not appeal to the Romantics and they were at best equivocal about its historically specific allegory. The nature of that allegory was newly accessible through Todd's variorum *Works* (1805), which for the first time added a second comprehensive 'gloss' to the *Calender*. If E. K.'s annotations were designed to anticipate the poem's arrival as a canonical text it was here, finally, that this process was completed. Not for the last time, however, a move towards the historical grounding of Spenser's text was followed by a reaction in the opposite direction. Wordsworth (1805, repr. 1967) was unhappy with the character of Todd's (highly scholarly) annotation. Here, as elsewhere, Romantic readers tended to emphasise what Leigh Hunt (1833, repr. 1952, 420) termed the '*merely* poetical' character of Spenser's verse. Although Hunt's perspective on Spenser changed considerably over the years, his emphasis remained on the pictorial. His vision was dominated by *The Faerie Queene* but the essay on Spenser's 'Gallery of Pictures' concluded on Cupid 'with spotted winges like Peacocks trayne' depicted in the March Eclogue (l. 80). Lowell (1875, repr. 1890) was writing in the same tradition when he argued that 'The "Shepherd's

Calendar" contains perhaps the most picturesque verse which Spenser has written' (303). 'The poem itself' was 'of little interest' but in its imagery it marked a watershed after the fallow years of post-Chaucerian verse (299). Its allegory 'could be reasonably left on one side' (326).

The Romantic poets themselves wrote little about the *Calender*. Yet their vision of nature, and of the role of poet, had a profound effect on readings of Spenser's pastoral. Alexander Grosart's edition of the *Complete Works* (1882–84) gives us an intriguing picture of Victorian criticism as a development of the Romantic mindset. The edition opens with a new 'Life of Spenser' and four critical essays. In important ways they present Spenser as a proto-Romantic artist. The edition is striking in its frequent comparison of Wordsworth and Spenser, and in Grosart's 'Life' Lancashire becomes a kind of Spenserian Lake District. Although the poet's urban upbringing is acknowledged, Grosart offers circumstantial evidence for Spenser's northern roots in the dialect words of the *Calender*. For him the poem reveals a youthful communion with nature (illustrated in the 'Life' through some splendidly craggy etchings) and an unrequited passion for a real-life Rosalind (identified in a supplementary essay). While studious in its awareness of literary precedent, Gosse's 'Essay on English Pastoral Poetry' thinks about the *Calender* along similar lines. It praises Spenser for returning to the spirit of Theocritus, and for the first time attempting 'to bring upon his pastoral stage the actual rustics of his native country, using their own peasant dialect' (III, xvi) as part of a movement of 'protest against what is artificial' (III, xlviii; plus Grossart's 'Rider', III, liii).

There are, however, limits to the extent that the 1882–84 *Works* endorse this vision. Hubbard's essay on 'Introspection and Outlook' argues that Spenser did not in fact feel himself called upon 'to act as Nature's interpreter' and that in this he differed fundamentally from Wordsworth (I, 373). For Hubbard, Spenser 'used Nature to image and make himself intelligible' (373). It is this 'power of *self-projection*' (375) that he finds comparable to the poets of the nineteenth century. Looking at both the beginning and the ending of the *Calender*, Hubbard finds it suffused with this quality of '*intellectual self-consciousness*' (378). The January eclogue, he argues, begins with Colin finding in nature a 'mirror' of his inner self, and the poem concludes with extraordinary audacity about the poet's vatic aspiration: 'Loe I have made a Calender for euery yeare, / That steele in strength, and time in durance shall outweare' (I, 381; *Calender*, 156, ll. 1–2).

Hubbard's essay, although not focused on the *Calender*, represents a watershed in the appreciation of Spenser's first masterpiece. Under the broad critical influence of Schlegel, Coleridge, and Hazlitt, amongst others, Hubbard was able to give a new kind of attention to the combination of form and vision in literary art. In fixing on Colin's use of the mirror as emblematic of a wider concern within the work as a whole he offers scrutiny of a sort that had not previously been directed at this verse. Spenser's lines 'Thou barrein ground, whome winters wrath has wasted, / Art made a myrrhour, to behold my plight' simultaneously anthropomorphise nature and turn it into an inanimate instrument to behold the speaker. The double meaning of 'Art' here—whether intentional or not—beautifully captures the way in which nature is at once a picture and a feeling entity. This 'Mirror Stage of Colin Clout' was to be subject of a celebrated essay by Harry Berger (1988, 325–46). Yet it is fair to say that such insights have their intellectual origins in Hubbard's work.

Hubbard learnt much from Romantic criticism, including an awareness of the cult of the artist that allowed him to discover in Spenser a literary self-consciousness that has been the subject of more recent critical interest (Helgerson 1978; Miller 1983; Montrose 1979; Cheney 1993). Yet in various ways the essays in the 1882–84 *Works* also move beyond Romantic concerns and towards the specific historical context of literature. Hunt (1857, repr. 1956) had already used biographical material in the February Eclogue to present Spenser as the stoical victim of court politics, but Dowden (addressing 'The Poet and Teacher' in Grosart's volume) made more complex claims for the *Calender*'s engagement with society. He rejected Lowell's dreamy image-maker and argued instead for Milton's 'sage' moralist. The *Calender*, in this light, becomes a small-scale version of *The Faerie Queene*: 'it is now gay and sportive, now staid and serious; sensuous ardour and moral wisdom are united in it; the allegorical form in miniature is already employed; it exhibits a mode of idealized treatment of contemporary public affairs not dissimilar in essentials from that afterwards put to use in his romantic epic' (1882–84, I, 313). In its emphasis on complexity, allegory, and the specific politics of the time, Dowden's praise of the *Calender* is almost the reverse of that offered by neo-classicists like Hughes. Where Hughes emphasised the simplicity and balance of the poem, Dowden sees it as a gothic masterpiece.

The contributors to Grosart's volume are all more willing than their predecessors to set Spenser in a defined historical milieu. Grosart's efforts to reconstruct a full life of the artist thus also return the *Theatre* and *Letters* to the Spenser canon. Although Todd had long since made the case for their inclusion, Grosart delivers a more coherent account of Spenser's authorship of the visions, and stresses their importance in Spenser's development. In all this there is a deep confidence in the recoverability and literary relevance of the events of Spenser's life: even Jan van der Noot is, in Grosart's opinion, to be discovered in the *Calender*'s allegory as Diggon Davie of the September Eclogue.

From 1900 to the 1960s: Old Historicism and the New Critics

The 1582–84 *Works*, produced largely by gentleman scholars, is both a precursor and a contrast to the *Variorum* that began to appear half a century later (1932–49). Dowden was one of the first professors of English literature;

the long list of contributors to the 1932–49 edition shows how rapidly that profession grew. The scholarship of the *Variorum* was the product of a new kind of literary study that made progress through footnoted editions, journal articles, and monographs. The annotated texts of the *Theatre, Letters*, and *Calender* provide easy access to that work. One of the earliest Spenser monographs, that of W. L. Renwick (1925), might be said to provide a synthesis of the discoveries made by this generation of academic writers. It sets the *Calender* in its historical and cultural context and offers carefully supported verdicts on such questions as the identity of E. K., the politics of the 1570s, and the national debate about langauge. Looking carefully at the evidence of the *Letters* it speaks with a different kind of authority about the development of Spenser's poetry. We have here a balanced overview that is not radically different from the current scholarly consensus.

Yet, within a decade, Renwick's 'old' historicism was already looking outdated, and the new modes of reading proved generally unsympathetic to the *Calender* and uninterested in the *Theatre* and *Letters*. Spenser failed to feature significantly in the reassessments of the literary canon undertaken by T. S. Eliot, F. R. Leavis, and the *Scrutiny* critics. The New Critical school could do little with Spenser and still less with the work published before 1589. D. A. Traversi, writing in *Scrutiny* 5 (1936), contrasted the 'immediacy' and 'power' of Langland with *The Shepheardes Calender*, whose words 'are fastidiously chosen to present to the court a courtly picture of the country-side' and 'set in a rhythm which acts as a decorative border to the whole'. Spenser's artificial lexicon is seen to have had a deeply negative ethical dimension: in a spirit of life-denying puritanism it was dedicated to crushing 'the true poetic tradition of England' (285).

Even C. S. Lewis (1954)—who had something of the same reverence for the medieval influence—did not attempt a defence of the *Calender*. To some extent he presented it a transitional work between the 'Drab' and the 'Golden' ages of English literature. Lewis was, however, uneasy with even that implied compliment. Indeed, he deliberately avoided placing the *Calender* in its chronological sequence before the work of Sidney because such a position would help 'to maintain the importance—in my opinion, mistaken—which critical tradition has come to give it' (324). Lewis stands alongside Dr Johnson as one of the great detractors of the *Calender*. Not for the first time, the comparison between it and *The Faerie Queene* functioned as a way of articulating a critical position on the work of Spenser as a whole. What Lewis values in Spenser (his romance inclusiveness, his pictorial imagination) are exactly the qualities that he misses in Spenser's first published poem. Conversely, Spenser's enduring faults (his prosaic Protestantism, his quotidian political concerns) are those he finds at their height in this work. Lewis's overall defence of Spenser puts him in the unusual position of distancing the poet from E. K. The closeness of E. K. and Spenser had been set out with historical exactitude by Renwick, who provided a catalogue of reasons for the editor's presence: marking the *Calender* as 'an experiment', 'a manifesto', and 'a declaration of allegiance to a school' (34). If, for Lewis, it was all these things, each was fundamentally misconceived. For him E. K. represents a clique of scholarly ideologues attempting to push the young Spenser in precisely the wrong direction: 'it seems to me certain that E. K., far from being Spenser, is a very good specimen of the friendly, yet in the long run wholly uncongenial, *coterie* who patronized Spenser in his nonage but from whose principles he departed as widely and easily as the duckling from the hen that mothered it' (Lewis, 354–5). The distance between E. K. and Spenser was never greater than in this assessment; greater than ever, too, is the distance between the 'minor' *Calender* and the great work of *The Faerie Queene*. Lewis's judgement of the poem was unprecedented, although, he claimed, rooted in popular sentiment: 'of the *Shepherd's Calender* as poetry we must frankly confess that it commits the one sin for which, in literature, no merits can compensate; it is rather dull...I have never in my life met anyone who spoke of it in the tones that betray real enjoyment' (363).

Probably the strongest of Lewis's objections to the *Calender* fixes on its historical particularity. The years that followed his study continued to be marked by a backbeat of studies on the *Calender*'s historical concerns. Most prominent among these was McLane's account of 'the complete allegory of the *Calender*' (1961, xi). McLane's assessment is intensely historical: linking the content of the poem very closely to the Elizabeth–Alençon courtship at its height in 1579. His readings, although speculative, continue to be central to accounts of the *Calender*'s politics. Yet the principal effort of the first generation of post-war critics of the *Calender* was to distance it from the history which pre-war critics had discovered. Hamilton's influential article on its 'argument', for example, began with an attack on the 'perverse' scholarly effort to 'identify historical allusions that Spenser has laboured so carefully to conceal' (Hamilton 1956, 171). In Hamilton's vision, Spenser's poem is one of transcendence charting a movement away from the quotidian world whose details the historicists had worked so hard to uncover. As Hubbard had observed, the January eclogue begins with an extraordinary act of self-projection: Colin Clout makes the natural world a 'mirror' for his inner state. In Hubbard's view this fixation on the self is a consistent (and fascinating) Spenserian quality. In the arguments of Hamilton and (later) Isabel MacCaffrey, however, this 'mirror stage' (to quote Berger's term again) is one that Colin Clout must learn to move beyond. In October, November, and—finally—December, these critics see the shepherd moving away from the false gods of romantic love and pagan poetry and ascending to a higher realm.

Hamilton and MacCaffrey's arguments offered an entirely new way of approaching the structure of *The Shepheardes Calender*. Earlier criticism had tended to treat the work almost as an anthology—rarely looking for developments across the volume. Other pastoral works were not felt to make such a progression and there seemed no immediate reason to look for it in the *Calender*. Yet while the poem alludes to almost all its pastoral predecessors (whether classical, biblical, medieval, or Renaissance) it is not *like* any of them. Its unique structural quality had previously been recognised. Pope had praised this as Spenser's great contribution to the pastoral form. Yet where, for Pope, the circular succession of months was simply a device for offering pleasing variety, for Hamilton that structure is directly related to the meaning of the text.

If Lewis had seen the *Calender* and *The Faerie Queene* as poles apart, Hamilton and MacCaffrey brought them much closer together. Dowden, in the 1880s, had attempted to do the same, seeing both as profoundly moral texts engaged with the realities of everyday life. These later critics, however, were informed by new thinking on structure and the nature of allegory (as well as a new resistance to the historical 'everyday'). In Hamilton's vision the *Calender* has a kind of architectural quality, with the eclogues moving elegantly through 'plaintive' to 'moral' to 'recreative' modes. At the heart of this reading sits the 'October' Eclogue on which Dowden too had fixed. The argument of *The Shepheardes Calender* is, then, 'the rejection of the pastoral life for the truly dedicated life in the world' (Hamilton, 181). In the October Eclogue we learn that this life is that of the heroic poet 'whose high religious calling is to serve the Queen by inspiring her people to all virtuous action' (181). In November we begin to see its place within the great cycle involving the Fall and Nativity in which man must reject 'the pastoral Paradise' for the promise of rebirth (181–2).

While Hamilton acknowledges the *Calender's* place in Spenser's compositional history, the tenor of his argument is a shift towards universal significance. MacCaffrey, whose structural understanding of the *Calender* is very close to that of Hamilton (see also Heninger 1962), modifies his conclusions a little:

> Spenser's analysis of human life involves neither an ascetic disdain for the pleasures of the temporal world, nor a 'rejection' of pastoral. Rather, those pleasures are defined and confirmed with relation to an ultimately religious sanction; and the power of the pastoral paradigm is reaffirmed as having *metaphorical* validity. (MacCaffrey 1969, 100)

Hamilton had already brought the *Calender* closer to *The Faerie Queene*, but in MacCaffrey's account the two works become almost inseparable. In a conclusion that thrills with its sense of a holistic Renaissance world picture, she argues for the *Calender* as 'an ambitious, encyclopedic allegory' that forms 'an essential prologue to the bold inventions of *The Faerie Queene*' (105).

The 1970s and genre criticism

The work of the 1970s drew on the thinking typified by MacCaffrey and Hamilton—like them it tended to make strong claims for the self-sufficiency and coherence of the *Calender* as a work of art. (As a result, the *Theatre* and the *Letters*, which had drawn some attention from 'old' historicist critics, remained of minimal literary interest.) The dominant discourse of the 1970s, however, was much less characterised by the tone of philosophical evangelism so prevalent a decade before. Critics influenced by New Criticism and Formalism (and by Fowler and Frye rather than F. R. Leavis) wrote instead much more clinically of 'genres', 'modes', and 'kinds'. As far as the *Calender* was concerned, this line of thinking fixed especially on various 'forms' of pastoral. The pastoral had long been recognised as an underdetermined genre. Dryden, for one, regretted that the ancients had left no prescriptive judgements on the matter. As Pope's 'Discourse' on the subject had made clear, pastoral could be considered as a subject (the idyllic rural life) or as a mode of delivery (the eclogues of Theocritus and Virgil) or as a combination of the two. Pope's strict insistence on the last of these definitions made the pastoral canon very small indeed (even the ancients were not consistently true to the form). Yet if Pope's efforts were directed at reducing the body 'of those which are called Pastorals' the combined effect of twentieth-century criticism has worked in the opposite direction. Most spectacular in this respect was Empson's *Some Versions of the Pastoral* (1935). Although not specifically concerned with the *Calender* itself, the work's definition of 'pastoral process' as the work 'of putting the complex into the simple' (23) was to make a lasting impression on the discussion of Spenser's text.

It is clearly a simplification to describe a chronological movement from the 'transcendence' model of Hamilton to the 'generic complexity' of the next generation. Empson wrote in the 1930s, and as early as 1906 Greg had produced an encyclopaedic study which acknowledged Spenser's unique position as a mediator between pastoral traditions. Greg, however, provided little beyond a summary of the *Calender's* constituent parts. A number of important works, from the late 1960s on, put the *Calender's* generic diversity at the heart of its value as a literary text. Unlike Hamilton and MacCaffrey these readers embraced the *Calender's* artificiality—emphasising allusive playfulness and tension above the notion of philosophical transcendence.

Patrick Cullen's work on Renaissance pastoral (1970) is seminal here. As his starting point, Cullen identifies two opposing pastoral visions: the Arcadian and the Mantuanesque. The former, rooted in Theocritus (fl. 270 BC), takes as its model the life of the *pastor felix* and the soft life of *otium*. It celebrates (and sometimes contemplates threats to) the idealised landscape of Arcadia. The latter, taking its name from the eclogues of Baptista Spagnuoli of Mantua (1447–1516), instead forwards the ideal of the Judaeo-Christian *pastor bonus*, the shepherd unwaveringly committed to the flock and to the requirements for eternal salvation. This shepherd exists in a harsher world and is largely opposed to the self-indulgence of the shepherd of worldly felicity. The two, of course, are never entirely distinct: the Mantuanesque is a later development and prominent only during the Renaissance. It is the conflict of these positions, however, that drives the 'multiform ambivalence' (Cullen, 18) of *The Shepheardes Calender*. In fixing on uncertainty as a primary virtue Cullen sets up a literary ideal very different from that of earlier critics of the *Calender*. He made it possible to express enthusiasm for a generic instability that had often been held up as a fault of Spenser's composition. As late as 1961, it was possible for S. K. Heninger to complain that in the Renaissance 'pastoral was perverted to satire, moral allegory, and sentimental narrative; it assumed modish, superficial forms' (261). That clash of forms is precisely what interested Cullen:

> To pastoral had gravitated many of the crucial and unresolved conflicts of Renaissance thinking: nature and art, ortherworldliness and secularism, Christianity and paganism, reason and emotion. Not only was pastoral a vehicle for these divisions in thinking, it was itself marked by that division. This division in pastoral is, I believe, the proper starting point for any analysis of the *Calender*. (Cullen 1970, 261)

If 'transcendent' readings focus most on the concluding section of Spenser's poem, 'conflicting' ones unsurprisingly concentrate on the work's centre. For Cullen, June and July are thus companion pieces: each subtly poised between ambition and retreat, self-fulfilment and self-denial, celebration and complaint. On the surface, June (featuring Colin's complaint over the loss of his love Rosalind) is Arcadian, and July (in which the 'low church' shepherd Thomalin debates with an 'ambitious' pastor of the high hill named Morrell) is Mantuanesque. Yet within each eclogue we have same debate about the place of literary ambition: a debate which complicates the simple opposition of 'pleasure' and 'duty'. The combined eclogues speak to the poet's uncertainty as to the place of his own endeavour. Is poetry a vocation or an escape? Should it be concerned with private romantic love or national greatness? Colin, in his concluding song of the June Eclogue, expresses a solipsistic credo that has its roots in Theocritus: 'I neuer lyst presume to *Parnasse* hyll, / But pyping lowe in shade of lowly groue, / I play to plase my selfe, all be it ill' (ll. 70–3). Such sentiment has little place in Humanist poetics, and it is at odds with the sentiments of E. K. and Hobbinoll in the June Eclogue. But the independent spirit of the pastoral poet is not abandoned by Spenser. Rather, the adaptability of the 'Arcadian' and 'Mantuanesque' perspectives gives the author space in which to explore and set in tension a diversity of literary visions. Pastoral becomes the ideal locale in which to debate the nature of poetry.

Cullen is not alone in addressing the multiform nature of pastoral, or in discovering the virtue of inclusiveness. The late 1960s and 1970s saw string of important studies that attempted to encapsulate the genre: Cody (1969), Rosenmeyer (1969), Marinelli (1971), Tolliver (1971), Lerner (1972), and Poggioli (1975) all produced monographs that help explain the qualities of Spenserian pastoral. Of particular relevance to the *Calender* is Helen Cooper's *Pastoral: Medieval into Renaissance* (1977). The two strains identified by Cullen are here given a less schematic, more historically specific, account. The Mantuanesque is characterised as just one influence alongside a broader medieval tradition. Cooper is the first to take Spenser's Chaucerianism seriously, to see the importance of the *Calender's* allusion to Skelton, and to explain the reasons for its adoption of a title with a medieval pedigree. In her assessment 'Spenser's pastoral is the supreme example of the fusion of the mediaeval and Renaissance forms' (153). Above all, Cooper argues that the moral function of the Shepherd has strong medieval roots. Thus, the February Eclogue with its fable of the Oak and Briar, if not authentically Chaucerian in its theme or language, is nevertheless deeply medieval in what Cooper calls 'one of Spenser's most remarkable achievements: to make allegory subservient to poetry' (155).

Cooper's book is characteristic of many that lay particular stress on the *Calender's* generic complexity. This tradition is at its strongest in the 1970s, but it also stretches into the 1980s and beyond. Notable contributors include Hoffman (1977), Rosenberg (1981), Mallette (1981), King (1986), Bernard (1989), and Snyder (1998). Although not the last, Chaudhuri's comprehensive survey, *Renaissance Pastoral and its English Developments* (1989), provides a logical endpoint to these studies when it claims that the *Calender* contains '*all* the possibilities of pastoral' (156). In her assessment, not only does it draw together elements from its many predecessors, it is also a profoundly original work in is own right. In particular, it contains aspects of two distinctive English traditions: the 'non-allusive, independent pastoralism in the Elizabethan lyric' and the 'vein of philosophic pastoral developed in romance and drama' (156). The *Calender*, by expanding pastoral as a *genre* effectively made room for it to function as a *mode*: most notably in the poet's own work in Book VI of *The Faerie Queene*.

There are two important late flowerings of what might be characterised as a school of 'generic' criticism: books by Harry Berger and Paul Alpers. Both had their first beginnings in articles published decades earlier, but each also bears the influence of the work of the 1980s discussed below. The second half of Berger's *Revisionary Play* (1988) is effectively a monograph on *The Shepheardes Calender*. It is a kind of critical palimpsest. The earliest sections were first written in the 1950s, yet in its eventual published form the book is a testament to the critical re-readings of over three decades. At the core of the book sits a transcendence argument that bears comparison with Hamilton's: the notion that Spenser critiques pastoral and expects his reader to move beyond it. The bulk of Berger's work, however, is concerned with the complexities of genre (with Cullen a key influence) and its concluding section has a 1980s deconstructionist edge. On top of this, *Revisionary Play* has an E. K. figure in the New Historicist Louis Montrose who wrote the work's introduction. Berger, one suspects, relishes the way his text mirrors the structure of its subject. Certainly, the combination of modish and outmoded criticism in Berger's work has much in common with the 'play' of the old and new he has so expertly described in Spenser's compositions. Spenser, Berger argues, has a habit of re-visiting his own work and that of others with a sense of its 'datedness'; it is a habit that the poet has passed on to his reader.

Revisionary Play is remarkable in its combination of critical voices and its awareness of its own reading practice. It is noteworthy too for its sustained engagement with the *Calender*'s individual eclogues (the lack of close reading is one aspect of 1980s criticism to which Berger objects). A glance at 'Februarie', where the aged Thenot disputes with the young Herdsman's boy Cuddie, offers a revealing instance of Berger's argument and reading practice. At a basic level the eclogue offers a debate between youth and age. Berger connects this with the false 'paradise principle' which is his theme throughout: Cuddie's misguided belief in the earthly joy of youth thus fits in with a wider 'metapastoral' discourse in which 'the pastoral critique is first and foremost a critique of pastoral' (289). Yet the texture of the eclogue is more complex. This is evident at its conclusion, where Thenot offers 'a tale of truth, Which I cond of *Tityrus* in my youth' (ll. 91–2). By Tityrus, E. K.'s note tells us, 'I suppose he meane Chaucer' (49). But as the annotator observes, the tale we hear has few convincing Chaucerian aspects. In fact, what Cuddie describes as Thenot's '*nouells* of his devise' (l. 95, emphasis mine) contain the eclogue's most obvious contemporary allusions—connecting the Oak and Briar with the court politics of the 1570s. *Old* Thenot's *youthful* memory of a *would-be ancient* tale with *present day* application exposes the difficulty of separating old and new in the *Calender*—a poem whose archaism is itself a very modern trick. The same is true of the balance of old and new in Berger's writing, which veers from strident New Criticism to a deconstructive rootlessness.

The 'rootlessness' of this work (its lack of engagement with context) has come under attack from a number of critics, not least Paul Alpers (whose book, like Berger's, is the product of several decades of developing thinking on the pastoral).[1] Alpers's *What is Pastoral?* (1996) answers its titular question with perfect clarity: it is literature based on the 'representative anecdote' of the shepherd and his flocks. If Berger has absorbed critical voices, Alpers has reacted against them. His work is valuable, amongst other things, for its rigorous critique of what he characterises as Romantic readings of the

---

[1] See, for example, McCabe (1993) and Montrose's introduction to Berger (1988).

Calender that see in the work a desire to move *beyond* its own genre. Alpers's picture of a gentler pastoral irony operating across the *Calender* provides a useful corrective to much post-war criticism. More than this, however, it is also a subtle account of Spenser's work. For Alpers the poem is *brilliantly* conventional. Its poetry is not 'strong' (in the sense of being innovative, individual, and combative, as Berger would have it) but 'weak' (in accepting the influence of earlier forms) in a way that is endlessly subtle.

The 1980s: New Historicism, Deconstruction, and gender criticism

Although published in the 1980s and 1990s, the work of Berger and Alpers distils many of the insights of earlier criticism of the *Calender*. At the end of the 1970s one may speak of a consensus that the poem's energy resides in the productive tension between the Classical and the Christian models. The 'Virgilian wheel' predicting a progression into the epic is felt to fit relatively harmoniously into this pattern. In various ways the criticism of the 1980s and 1990s moved beyond these concerns (although, as we have seen, it also continued to refine these long-standing questions). A watershed is to be found in the year 1979. At a conference held at this date (its papers published two years later) Montrose acted as respondent to Ronald Bond's talk on the 'Februarie' Eclogue. The subject of the eclogue is, of course, a debate between youth and age. Montrose, to seize on this motif of generational change, may be said to have taken the role of Cuddie: a combative young man challenging the tired assumptions of an older generation. His piece (one of four seminal articles on Renaissance pastoral) transformed the critical landscape. Bond had written of 'Februarie' in comfortable old historical and generic terms. He saw Spenser as an objective moral arbiter making good use of an established literary form to criticise the 'vying for position at court' and presenting 'a case for accepting one's lot, even in adversity' (1981, 66). Montrose was later to criticise such writing as a kind of academic escapism: itself a 'metapastoral' form of retreat from the material realities of Elizabethan politics (1983, 415). His response to Bond's paper, restricting itself to pretty much the same material, offered a very different approach. The wise poet of Bond's account thus becomes—in Montrose's version—a political agent for whom genres, and even individual rhetorical figures, have a functional aspect. Montrose picked up on Puttenham's *Arte of English Poesie* (1586), which characterised pastoral as the covert mode of the courtier, and also on the Marxist cultural criticism of twentieth-century thinkers such as Raymond Williams, which showed that 'the country' was not simply a place but also an ideological construct. This new intellectual framework allowed him to see the debate between Cuddie and Thenot not as a detached moral lesson, but rather as a complex act of self-representation. Instead of simply observing that Thenot is allowed to win the argument in favour of stable old age, Montrose teases out the contradictions that face Spenser as part of a new generation of would-be courtiers. The argument of 'Februarie' is thus produced under considerable strain. The poet himself, in terms of his cultural and political status, is a 'youth' attempting to ventriloquise the establishment stance to which he aspires. He is, as Montrose puts it, 'exceedingly ambitious to achieve something conservative' (68). The drama of the eclogue thus resides in a succession of politically motivated narratives about youth and age in which the rhetoric of the briar to the husbandman, the interpretation of Thenot, and the interpretation of E. K. all play a part (70). These voices, alongside those of 'Immerito', 'the New Poet', and 'Colin Clout' all express aspects of the self-representation of Spenser.

Montrose's article on the 'Februarie' eclogue is the least ambitious of his pieces on Elizabethan pastoral. A more expansive piece on Spenser's laureate aspirations (1979) had already shown the Cuddie/Thenot debate to be but one of many pictures of the negotiation between youthful ambition and literary precedent to be found in the *Calender*. Montrose saw that negotiation as present not only in formal dialogues but also in the blending of literary modes (such as Petrarchan love lyric and pastoral allegory). Above all, it is the female figures in the *Calender* that become the nexus for the (sometimes conflicting) demands of political praise and literary self-assertion. For Montrose, the iconic presence of the Queen is crucial to the *Calender*'s 'poetics of courtship' even where she is not directly represented. The personal/erotic Rosalind, the public/political Elisa, and the historical/transcendent Dido of whom Colin sings are thus all to be understood as versions or inversions of Elizabeth.

Montrose's approach was perhaps especially satisfying because it fused two distinct currents of response to the *Calender*: thinking about genre, and a long and troublesome acknowledgement of the work's political and personal references. Reflecting on his own writing, Montrose described it as based on the belief that literature is not only 'socially produced' but also 'socially productive' (1986a, 303). It would be unreasonable to claim (as some have done) that such a view presents a monolithic picture of Elizabeth's power: Spenser is understood as the Queen's 'subject', but the monarch is also seen to be the 'subject' of the poet's radically transformative literary text. Accusations that the 'Pastoral of Power' constitutes what Alan Sinfield (1992, 8) terms a 'totalising system' might be closer to the mark. There are certainly dangers in Montrose's rather grim insistence on the correspondence between 'form' and 'function' (1980, 153) in the Spenserian text.

The work of Richard Helgerson (1978, 1983), which developed at the same time along separate if similar lines, provides one qualification of Montrose's position.[2] Like Montrose, Helgerson is interested in Spenser's desire to create

---

[2] *Self-Crowned Laureates* (1983); the chapter on the *Calender* appeared first in 1978. A comparable argument was also developed independently by Miller (1979).

a new 'author function' and sees the *Calender* as a central document in this narrative. *Self-Crowned Laureates*, however, offers a very different picture of Elizabethan national culture: one in which poetry plays a much less central role than that suggested by Montrose's work. In place of Montrose's description of a poetics which works to 'sanctify political power' (1980, 168) Helgerson presents a world in which neither 'amateurs' (such as Sir Philip Sidney) nor 'professionals' (such as Robert Greene) are able to make serious moral or political claims for the role of poetry. It was Spenser's unique ambition to carve out such a role, but the *Calender* is a testament as much to the difficulty of such a project as it is to its success. Where Montrose sees the personal/erotic and national/vatic aspects of the poem as part of a brilliant fusion, Helgerson sees them as intrinsically opposed. In some ways Helgerson returns to the 'transcendence' paradigm forwarded by Hamilton. The *Calender*, he argues, 'contains a forceful critique of the conventional poet-as-lover, revealing that poetry written under such a guise is solipsistic, self-indulgent, and fruitless—that it leads inevitably to its own renunciation' (1983, 72). Yet for him the path beyond this Sidneian 'recreational' form of poetry is still uncharted, so that the *Calender* shows a man sure of his great ability and mission, but profoundly uncertain of the direction it should take (69). Rather than uniting form and function, it offers numerous versions of the conflict between the two.

Montrose and Helgerson see the 'New Poet' presented by *The Shepheardes Calender* as the product of a complex combination of cultural, material, and generic influences. Other critics, however, went still further in deconstructing what E. K. calls 'the Author selfe'. Miller (1979) argued along comparable lines to Montrose and Helgerson, but placed a greater emphasis on the work's status as an 'orphan' text. This argument was later developed along Derridean lines by Jonathan Goldberg (1986), who wrote brilliantly on the *Calender*'s multiform anonymity. Immerito, E. K., Colin, and the shepherds who repeat his songs are thus all part of a chain of deferred meaning leading ultimately to a disembodied voice. That paradigm is already to be discovered in the *Calender*'s opening verse address 'To His Booke', quoted at the opening of this chapter. Fixing on an untraceable author ('Immeritô') and uncertain dedicatee (Sidney? Harvey? the book itself?) Goldberg confronts us with a text in which:

> this new poet has no name of his own, no beginning except as he is received and as he receives, no story to tell until he has been taken under another's wing, unless the text is consumed. (Goldberg 1986, 38)

The echoes of that opening act of self-deferral reverberate endlessly through the 'unfathered' gloss and poetry of the *Calender* (66).

Such close attention to the interplay between the *Calender*'s editorial apparatus and poetry is also a characteristic of Goldberg's later engagement with the poem. *Sodometries* (1992) examines the sexual politics of the eclogues and the texts that surround them (not only E. K.'s commentaries but also the exchanges of the Spenser/Harvey *Letters*). Whereas *Voice Terminal Echo* had been shaped by the influence of Derrida, this later work is more Foucauldian. Goldberg is careful to avoid claiming essentialist labels (such as 'homosexual') or physical acts (such as 'sodomy'). He does, however, argue for the existence of a sexual drama centred on the relationship between Colin and Spenser and Hobbinol and Harvey—a relationship mediated by classical as much as biographical allusions. One of the things that makes this reading more than simply provocative is its correspondence with early commentaries. It is not just E. K. who had spoken of the poem's 'sauour of disorderly loue, which the learned call pæderastice' ('Januarie'); as we have seen, one of its earliest readers (Webbe in 1586) had reacted violently to its 'loathsome beastlines' only to withdraw that accusation in the following sentence. It is in response to such uneasy half-suggestions that Goldberg makes his subtlest discoveries.

Like Goldberg's, Helgerson's later work also moved towards a more inter-textual understanding of the *Calender* and the *Letters*. Such a shift reflects a more widespread movement questioning the exclusivity of the category 'literature' as well as a new interest in the material history of the printed text. In this climate the *Theatre* and *Letters*—hitherto regarded largely as 'background' material—became valuable texts in the close-reading of cultural phenomena ranging from imperialism to gender identity. *Forms of Nationhood* (Helgerson 1992) opens with an exploration of the Spenser/Harvey *Letters* and the *Calender* that expands on its author's earlier analysis of the status of literature in the Elizabethan period. But Helgerson's focus is no longer exclusively literary, and it is unsurprising that the 'cultural document' of the Spenser/Harvey *Letters* should now be seized upon as a much richer subject for critical enquiry. Specifically, he is interested in the 'two versions of the gothic' that are latent in the debate between the two men: the gothic as barbarous and outdated, to be swept aside by classicism; and the gothic as a form of freedom, a 'natural' form that opposed the dictates of cultural and political authority. Casting new light on the dispute about 'quantitative verse' that had long seemed simply a literary blind alley, Helgerson was able to show how Spenser and Harvey's arguments on this topic were emblem-atic of much wider debates about 'form' and 'nationhood' in English poetry. In his attention to the overlapping concerns of theology, politics, and patronage Helgerson set a tone that is still perceptible in much contempo-rary debate on Spenser.

The current state of criticism

The readings of the *Calender* and *Letters* published in the 1980s opened up subjects for debate in court politics, the literary career, and the elusiveness of the author. By the end of the decade they were supplemented by a new interest in nationalism and gender. On all these topics there was also a growing awareness of the overlap between the personal, political, and literary. Allusions, generic shifts, and marginal commentaries were now routinely seen as tools in the presentation of the authorial persona. This way of approaching these texts was to some degree the product of New Historicism. Yet, although the influence is widespread, there are few, if any, Spenserians to whom that label can be applied without qualification—even Louis Montrose (1986b) began at an early stage to reflect upon the short-comings of the new critical practice.

The various 'strong' critical schools of the 1980s—New Historicism, Deconstruction, and work focused on gender—tended to paint with a broad brush. Writing of the last decade or so has often been more *particular* in its focus. Literary allusions, religious disputes, political actions, and physical texts themselves have all been the subject of precise attention. We are, in this sense, moving closer to the individual publications with which this survey began.

In a number of areas there have been moves to make subtler the paradigms forwarded by a previous generation of critics. In response to earlier arguments about the 'laureate' ambition envisaged in the *Calender*, for example, Rambuss (1993, 1996) and Cheney (1993, 2001) have offered new contexts through which to understand Spenser's career. Arguing that Helgerson had neglected Spenser's work as a secretary, Rambuss looks at both the *Calender* and the *Letters* as bids for professional preferment. He compares E. K.'s editorial practice with the work of an amanuensis and argues 'that the secret designs of *The Shepheardes Calender* have more to do with Spenser's *employability'* than with actual political intrigue (1993, 57). Cheney, in contrast, retains the centrality of Spenser's poetic ambition but feels that the Virgilian trajectory (of progress from pastoral, through georgic, to epic) is too simplistic a model to accommodate the *Calender's* authorial strategy. Cheney sees a more complex 'flight' (involving epic, love poetry, and a restorative return to pastoral) that is foreshadowed in the symbolic codes of the *Calender's* eclogues. In different ways these critics move outside the literary world envisaged by Helgerson (Rambuss by emphasising the material need for patronage; Cheney by looking at a wider European picture including Ovid, Petrarch, and Tasso). What connects these discussions to the long tradition of twentieth-century commentary, however, is a belief in Spenser's unique position in the self-conscious fashioning of his personal history: a process in which the *Calender* takes a defining role.

Rambuss and Cheney present a goal-centred Spenser best understood by the role that he occupied. Other critics—reacting against a historicism that had found it difficult to account for change over time—are insistent on a broader canvas. David Norbrook's *Poetry and Politics* (1984) offered an account of Spenser's work that was grounded in the religious and cultural conflicts of Tudor England.[3] His concern was with intellectual and political history as much as with literary criticism: one key theme being the confluence of Protestant and Humanist thinking that occurred in the long build-up to the English Civil War. Because Norbrook's questions are as much about history as they are about the literary qualities of individual texts, it is unsurprising that works like van der Noot's *Theatre* should find a more prominent place in his study. The *Theatre*'s balance of Renaissance poetics and apocalyptic Protestantism thus provides a precedent for the *Calender*: a work whose measured independent Puritanism is partly at odds with the Queen's own convictions. The blazon of Eliza in the 'Aprill' Eclogue—which Montrose (1980) had seen as a panegyric on royal power—is shown by Norbrook to have a more oppositional politics. As he points out, a monarch contemplating marriage to the Duke of Alençon would by no means have welcomed the foundation of a Protestant cult of royal virginity (76).

Norbrook's work is characteristic of a range of what might be called 'new historical' (as opposed to New Historicist) work on Spenser. This cautious specificity (characterised by detailed reference to early modern politics) is also found in the work of King (1982, 1986, 1990) who sees the *Calender* as operating in a Reformation tradition dating back to the time of Edward VI. The *Theatre*, with its illustrations and commentary, is part of that tradition and therefore valuable in understanding the allusive strategies of Spenser's later poems. Norbrook and King (in contrast to a New Historicist tendency to minimise individual autonomy in the face of a wider 'cultural poetics') see the *Calender* as operating in a fluid political environment. In the work of Annabel Patterson this resistance to a totalising perspective on Elizabethan politics is given a more polemical edge. *Pastoral and Ideology* (1988) attacks Montrose's caricature of an exclusively courtly 'semantics of power relations' (130) that leaves no room for the expression of popular feeling. In *Reading Between the Lines* (1992) the author goes further still in opposing Montrose's reading of the *Calender*—arguing that the 'mission' of the poem is to 'broaden the audience for poetry' by blending popular and learned culture (49). If New Historicists can be accused of projecting their own political consciousness onto the Tudor period they find a determined apposing counterpart in Patterson.

New Historicism thus continues to act as a spur to 'corrective' readings. Yet, along with other approaches, the movement has also been assimilated with wider critical practice. Recent writing on the *Theatre, Calender,* and *Letters* thus routinely combines 'literary' and 'historical' material while acknowledging the indeterminate boundaries between the two. Earlier thinking on genre, source, biography, gender, and politics all informs the debate. If anything,

---

[3] For an account of the development of Norbrook's methods see the 'Afterword' of the revised edition (2002).

what distinguishes current critical practice is a focus on the physical text and the circumstances of its interpretation.[4] The interpretative practices of the Early Modern reader have become a primary concern. Illustrations, dedications, typesetting, and, most of all, the position of commentary are thus all seen as integral to the meaning of Spenser's early work. Its objectives are often discovered in the interstices between the literary text and critical frame. Quitslund—writing in a collection that contains some of the best contemporary material on these texts—expresses something close to a critical consensus when he says that 'in *The Shepheardes Calender* and the *Letters*, everything is dialogical and intertextual, and to isolate an individual (to settle the identity of E. K., for example) would be to take a fish out of water' (1997, 84). There is an obvious sense in which such readings (like those before them) reflect the values of their time. Judith Anderson—introducing the collection in which Quitslund's article appears—speaks of Spenser as 'an author whose decentered lineaments look persuasively postmodern'. 'Our own eyes', she suggests, 'always meet us in the mirror' (1997, x). Even strongly historical work like that of Richard McCabe reflects a contemporary aesthetic when it characterises these texts as 'aggressively inter-textual' (1999, xix) and 'obsessively self-reflexive' (2000, 35).

Recent work has thus carefully intertwined the textual and the historical—fixing, for example, on the 'questionable evidence' of biography (Quitslund 1997) or on the political function of anonymity (McCabe 2000). Such criticism emphasises the aspects of the early texts that make them ceaselessly puzzling, but does so without sacrificing the idea of an author who thinks strategically and has definable personal aims. It seems appropriate, therefore, to close this survey with the last gloss of *The Shepheardes Calender*: a commentary that illustrates the enduringly productive gap between verse and criticism in this text. Like the preceding eclogue, 'December' looks set to conclude on an 'emblem' (a short set of verses summing up the character of its principal speaker). Yet in this case the words 'Colins Embleme' are followed simply by blank space and, eventually, the 'glosse' of the annotator. The lines that ought, finally, to pin down the credo of Colin Clout are missing.[5] They have a kind of presence, however, in the last note offered by E. K. Commenting on an 'emblem' that is invisible to the reader this note explains that the meaning thereof 'is that all thinges perish and come to theyr last end, but works of learned wits and monuments of Poetry abide for

---

[4] The roots of this approach may be said to lie in pioneering bibliographic work of Luborsky (1980, 1981). Recent studies that focus their arguments on the layout of these texts include Quitslund (1997), Donald Cheney (1997), McCabe (1995, 2000), van Es (2002a, 179–86) and Owens (2002, 38–68).

[5] The missing lines were first supplied by Hughes (1715) as 'vivitur ingenio, caetera mortis erunt'—a well-known pseudo-Virgilian tag that would, very likely, have come to the mind of many contemporary readers.

euer'. After this gloss comes one last set of verses that famously proclaim 'Loe I haue made a Calender for euery yeare, / That steele in strength, and time in durance shall outweare...'. The relationship between these three elements (the missing emblem and the present gloss and verse) is inherently unstable. Is the absence here simply a printing error? Should another set of verses asserting the immortality of poetry have stood where there is now blank space? Or is E. K.'s gloss designed to be richly ironic (giving voice to the silence of Colin's mutable text)? Does it get to the heart of Spenser's intention, or is it spectacularly wide of the mark? More than four hundred years on we are no better at answering such questions, but we are, perhaps, better at asking them.

Acknowledgement

As with the introduction, I would like to thank Andrew Zurcher for his generosity in commenting on this chapter at length in its first draft. For the section on Romantic criticism especially, I also acknowledge the influence of John Lee's very helpful survey, 'Spenser and his Critics', appended to his edition of Spenser's *Shorter Poems* (1998).

Further reading

Alpers, P. 1996. *What is Pastoral?*, Chicago: University of Chicago Press.

Chaudhuri, S. 1989. *Renaissance Pastoral and its English Developments*, Oxford: Clarendon Press.

Cheney, P. 2001. 'Spenser's Pastorals: *The Shepheardes Calender* and *Colin Clouts Come Home Againe*', *The Cambridge Companion to Spenser*, ed. Andrew Hadfield, Cambridge: Cambridge University Press.

Cullen, P. 1970. *Spenser, Marvell, and Renaissance Pastoral*, Cambridge, MA: Harvard University Press.

Dorsten, Jan van. 1997. '*A Theatre For Worldings*', in A. C. Hamilton, ed., *The Spenser Encyclopedia*, Toronto: University of Toronto Press.

Goldberg, J. 1986. 'Consuming Texts: Spenser and the Poet's Economy', in *Voice Terminal Echo: Postmodernism and English Renaissance Texts*, New York: Menthuen, 38–67.

Hamilton, A. C. 1956. 'The Argument of Spenser's *Shepheardes Calender*', *English Literary History*, 23: 171–82.

McCabe, R. A. 'Annotating Anonymity, or putting a gloss on *The Shepheardes Calender*', in Joe Bray, Miriam Handley, and Anne C. Henry eds, *Ma(r)king the Text: The Presentation of Meaning on the Literary Page*, Aldershot: Ashgate, 35–54.

McLane, P. E. 1961. *Spenser's Shepheardes Calender: A Study in Elizabethan Allegory*, Notre Dame, Indiana: University of Notre Dame Press.

Montrose, L. A. 1980. ' "Eliza, Queen of Shepheardes", and the Pastoral of Power', *ELR* 10: 153–82.

Woudhuysen, H. R. 1997. 'Letters, Spenser's and Harvey's', in A. C. Hamilton, ed., *The Spenser Encyclopedia*, Toronto: University of Toronto Press.

8

The Faerie Queene (1590)

David Lee Miller

"All suddeinly I saw the Faery Queene"

Sometime early in 1590, John Wolfe's London print shop started a job for the stationer William Ponsonby, turning out sheets that would later be folded twice and bound into quarto-sized volumes of more than six hundred pages. Proof was read while the presses worked, with corrections made on the fly. Sheets already printed off were used at random (waste not, want not), with the result that "existing copies exhibit an entirely haphazard combination of revised and unrevised readings, and it is quite possible that there are no two copies whose readings agree throughout" (Johnson 1933, 13). This is not unusual; on the contrary, it is the way early modern books were typically made.

Such "stop-press" corrections would be more likely if the author himself were present in the shop, eagerly scanning the sheets on which his words, for so long turned over in the mind or scratched with a goose quill onto loose pages, now came back to him in the mechanical form of print. The author of the present manuscript was an English civil servant back from Ireland, a learned man with a Cambridge degree and connections at court. A later poem reveals that he read before the queen (*Colin Clout*, ll. 358–67); we do not know whether this took place before or after the manuscript went to press, but a commendatory poem by "H. B." does mention that the queen "biddes" the poet to "bow downe his brow unto her sacred hand," suggesting that he has already obtained royal favor (Hamilton 2001, 723).

He probably did visit the print shop as well, and this may have presented Wolfe and his men with more complications than any other aspect of the job. Chances are that he brought the manuscript over from Ireland personally, and with it he "seems to have carried a manuscriptive disposition right into the printshop" (Loewenstein 1996, 100). How could he not? This was to be his great work. He had been composing it, off and on, for ten years—changing, rearranging, adding, polishing, sending drafts to friends. Now suddenly he had to surrender his words, first to an industrial workshop and then to the world at large. He must have found time foreshortened by the demands of the production schedule even as anticipation heightened his anxieties about public reception.

While this was going on he added a preface, composed as a letter to Sir Walter Ralegh—his neighbor in Ireland and sponsor at court—explaining the plan and purpose of the work. The letter, dated 23 January of the previous year (Brink 1994b), was "annexed" to the volume oddly, for it appears not at the front, as a preface normally would, but at the end, like an afterthought. So too do the commendatory poems contributed by the author's friends and the series of dedicatory sonnets addressed to ten notable figures in Elizabeth's court. That is, in some copies there are ten; in others, fifteen or seventeen; still other copies have both the original ten *and* the expanded group. The confusions created by these discrepancies seem especially telling, for if the placement of the series at the back of the book makes it look like an afterthought, the addition of seven new sonnets— along with the loss of two from the first group of ten—looks like an after-thought to the afterthought compounded by mistakes. Decorum clearly mattered, for the sonnets are sequenced according to the rules of precedence (Stillman 1985), but their printing and binding seems as rushed and indecorous as Lady Macbeth's farewell to her dinner guests: "Stand not upon the order of your going."

The author of these confusions is not named on the book's title page. His name appears instead on the reverse, where a fulsome dedication to Queen Elizabeth is signed "Ed. Spenser." Throughout the book, too, eminent names and titles are flourished while the author's name is hidden or abbre-viated. In the end matter, for example, "A Letter of the Authors" is addressed "To the Right noble, and Valorous, Sir Walter Ralegh knight, Lo. Wardein of the Stanneryes, and her Maiesties liefetenaunt of the County of Cornewayll," but it is signed, like the dedication to the queen, with the shortened form of the poet's name. The dedicatory sonnets are subscribed under names accoutered, like Ralegh's, with titles and adjectives, but only a few are even so much as initialed "E. S." The author's name appears wittily disguised at II.ix.27 and xii.42, and again in the commendatory poem by "H. B.," addressed to the Muses, which refers to the poet as "this rare dispenser of your graces." It is even, after a fashion, announced in the poem's opening flourish, although it does not appear there: "Lo I the man, whose Muse whilome did maske, / As time her taught, in lowly Shephards weeds...." This opening recalls the concluding *envoi* to his earlier poem *The Shepheardes Calender*: "Lo I have made a calendar for every year." But since the *Calendar* was published anonymously, the reference is oddly circular, identifying the author of each poem as the "I" who writes the other, but without naming either. Indeed, the movement from "Lo I have made" to "Lo I the man" suggests that the author *as* author is as much an effect of his poems as he is their source or cause (Miller 1990, 1993); they originate with his Muse and belong to the patrons who sustain him. They are "named" rather after these patrons than after their maker, in a gesture that, as Stephen Orgel observes, distinguishes sharply between the text's *invention*, proper to the poet, and its *authority*, which resides elsewhere (2002, 3, 80–1). *The Faerie Queene*, published in 1590, is named for the patron to whom it was presented.

Because *The Faerie Queene* is the first recognizably epic poem in English, its initial publication belongs to many histories, some of them literary. What must it have been like for the poets of London during the late 1580s, as parts of the poem circulated in manuscript, or still more in 1590, when Spenser's astonishing volume appeared in the bookstalls? How does its impact register in the work of Marlowe, Shakespeare, Jonson, and Donne? Despite interesting work on specific texts and authors (see especially Gross 2004), there has been no systematic attempt to address such questions; we know more, relatively speaking, about the poem's influence on early seventeenth-century "Spenserians" like Samuel Daniel and Phineas Fletcher, or on still later writers, than we do about its immediate impact on Spenser's contemporaries. Perhaps the first of Ralegh's two commendatory sonnets, with its suggestive mingling of visionary awe and envy, evokes some sense of what it was like to read *The Faerie Queene* for the first time:

> ME thought I saw the graue, where *Laura* lay,
> Within that Temple, where the vestall flame
> Was wont to burne, and passing by that way,
> To see that buried dust of liuing fame,
> Whose tumbe faire loue, and fairer vertue kept,
> All suddeinly I saw the Faery Queene:
> At whose approch the soule of *Petrarke* wept,
> And from thenceforth those graces were not seene.
> For they this Queene attended, in whose steed
> Obliuion laid him downe on *Lauras* herse:
> Hereat the hardest stones were seene to bleed,
> And grones of buried ghostes the heuens did perse.
> > Where *Homers* spright did tremble all for griefe,
> > And curst th'accesse of that celestiall theife.

> (Hamilton 2001, 721)

Presumably it is not only the souls of Petrarch and Homer who may fear the Promethean "accesse" of a poet so clearly determined to rewrite literary history. At the same time, rivalry is not the whole story. Great work may be enabling as well as preemptive; female authors and readers such as Mary Sidney and Lady Mary Wroth found openings for their own work—for inspiration as well as resistance—in the radical experiments Sidney and Spenser were making with versification, lyric form, allegory, and romance narrative.

The framework of events

Spenser's poem is immersed in the religious and political history of early modern England, but its concerns can be difficult to pin down. The poem approaches but also avoids contemporary history, an ambivalence not surprising in an author who identifies himself with "all the antique Poets historicall" at the same time as he seeks to ward off "gealous opinions and misconstructions" along with "the daunger of enuy, and suspition of present time" (Hamilton 2001, 714–15).

We may locate the moment of publication within what one historian calls "the framework of events" during the late sixteenth century in England (Smith 1997, 101–6, 223–34). Spenser's poem appeared not long after the defeat of the Spanish Armada. During the decade in which it was composed, Queen Elizabeth's resistance to the "war party" among her privy council finally gave way to a prolonged military conflict with Spain; the Earl of Leicester led an expedition to the Netherlands in support of Protestant resistance there. A Spanish invasion of England had been anticipated for years; when it finally came in 1588 the decisive English victory created a short-lived wave of euphoria. During the 1580s, the growing threat of invasion was accompanied by plots to depose or assassinate the queen—the Throckmorton plot in 1583, the Babington plot in 1586—and by the infiltration of Catholic priests from a seminary founded at Douai in 1568 and moved to Rheims ten years later. In 1587 Mary Queen of Scots was finally executed for her part in conspiracies to supplant Elizabeth. This combination of threats intensified English patriotism, but nationalistic zeal was always in tension with the internationalism of the Protestant cause. This ambivalence was embodied in the queen, who from the beginning of her reign had been a powerful symbol of Reformed religion but who was also the principal icon of English nationhood.

The 1580s were also a decade of mounting conflict over church governance. The Elizabethan settlement initially sought a precarious balance among contending forces, but as the Church of England established itself on a more secure footing, the Anglican hierarchy, led by Archbishop Whitgift, began to assert its authority more aggressively. By the time *The Faerie Queene* appeared in 1590, Whitgift was in the midst of a concerted and eventually successful campaign to root out Presbyterianism, which favored decentralized governance. At about the same time (1589), the first of the Martin Marprelate tracts appeared, trashing the bishops with an exuberance that stands out even in an age saturated by religious invective. These broadsides provoked virulent counter-attacks by hired pamphleteers such as Thomas Nashe. Caught the crossfire, an advocate of moderation like Spenser's friend

Gabriel Harvey found himself denounced along with the Puritan radicals (Huffman 1988, 104–5).

By the time the poem appeared, then, both the "cult" of Elizabeth that emerged in the 1570s and the militant patriotism of the 1580s were already receding, while resistance to the increasingly authoritarian character of the church was building rapidly. Sidney and Leicester, key members of the Puritan faction at court, were both dead—Walsingham, another Puritan leader, died in 1590—while Lord Burghley, their chief opponent, was more powerful than ever. By the mid-1590s the situation had changed even more drastically. Ralegh, Spenser's chief sponsor at court, was imprisoned in 1592 for secretly marrying Elizabeth Throckmorton. In 1593 the plague struck; a year later England suffered the first of four successive crop failures, leading to widespread famine. By 1596, when the second installment of the poem appeared, England was drastically altered. It was especially so for Spenser, as his reference to "my freendless case" in "Prothalamion" (1595) suggests.

It is traditional to contrast the poem's first and second parts in terms that mirror the changing mood of the 1590s. Books IV–VI have been seen as darker than I–III, and sometimes as less inspired. There are obvious reasons for this: one need to look no further than the opening and closing attacks on Burghley to see why the second part of the poem has been read as combative and discouraged. But it is worth bearing in mind that *The Faerie Queene*, although occasionally topical, is also creatively out of synch with "the framework of events" surrounding its publication. Major developments of the 1580s, such as Lord Grey's recall from Ireland or the execution of Mary Stuart, do not appear as allusions until the 1596 installment, while those in the 1590 text reach back to the Ridolfi plot and the St Bartholomew's Day Massacre in the early 1570s, to Elizabeth's accession and coronation pageant in the late 1550s, and perhaps even to the reign of Mary Tudor (McCabe 1987; Miller 1988, 120–64; Hough 1964a,b, 9–11).

It would be revealing if we could correlate the poem's composition with contemporary developments. Did Spenser's general conception change significantly between 1579, when an early draft was underway, and 1599, when he left the poem unfinished at his death? We know little of his plans. The major work to have addressed this issue, Josephine Waters Bennett's *The Evolution of "The Faerie Queene"* (1942), demonstrates both the interest of the topic and the difficulty of its pursuit. Bennett develops an elaborate but almost entirely hypothetical account of the stages through which the poem "evolved." Subsequent critics tended to dismiss the argument too quickly. In part this was because formalist doctrines in the post-war years decreed the finished artifact, not the process of composition or the intentions of the poet, to be the proper object of critical concern. But it was also in part because Bennett makes uncritical use of aesthetic judgments: passages she considers inferior are simply assumed to have been written earlier. More recent accounts take stylistic contrasts among different sections of the poem to be significant rather than inadvertent. Spenser probably did work much of the time by arranging previously drafted fragments, but the final revision and disposition of such mosaic pieces is just as deliberate a creative act as their initial composition.

We should read Bennett with caution, but this does not mean her work can be ignored. *The Evolution of the Faerie Queene* abounds in closely researched historical argument. Chapters 5 and 6, for example, trace fluctuations in the climate of skepticism surrounding chronicle accounts of Arthur; Chapter 7 delineates with some precision Spenser's use of names and heraldic symbols associated with the Leicester genealogy. Moreover, Bennett's hypothesis—that the poem began as an imitation of Ariosto and then developed in other directions—remains plausible in broad outline. And her description of the narrative structure contains a striking insight:

> It would have been easy enough to make [Arthur] the hero-in-chief. By all the rights of allegory and legend, the twelve exemplary knights belong in his court or train rather than in that of the Faery Queen. As virtues they are the parts of which Arthur is the sum, and as knights of romance Arthur is their natural lord. But the poet had begun by substituting the Faery Queen for Arthur in order to pay homage to a feminine sovereign, and he could not thereafter find a suitable place for Arthur in his poem (54).

We have learned since Bennett's day to give more weight to an allegorical and analogical structure in which Arthur's role is every bit as central as it is incidental to the narrative. In fact most criticism now takes the tension between these roles to be highly significant, not a defect or failure. But Bennett's perception of the way Gloriana displaces Arthur from Camelot in Spenser's version of the story rings as true now as it did in 1942.

The form of the poem

However *The Faerie Queene* evolved, its form is a remarkable invention, reminiscent of almost every major work and genre in the history of European literature without really resembling any of them. Virgil divided the *Aeneid* into twelve books, while Ariosto organized the *Orlando Furioso* into forty-six cantos. Spenser's title page announces a poem in twelve books, like the *Aeneid* (although the first installment contains only 1–3). But each book is further divided into twelve cantos, a hybrid structure that resembles neither of his originals. Cantos are further divided into stanzas, following Italian practice, but in place of the eight-line stanza common to Ariosto and Tasso, Spenser creates a nine-line stanza with an intricate rhyme scheme, adding an extra metrical foot to prolong the final line. The result is a verse form so original that it goes by the poet's name and so versatile that it lends itself equally to rapid narrative movement, lush description, song, lament, sententious generalization, buffoonery, oration, epic catalogue, extended simile, and every other variation necessary to a long poem. Its sheer difficulty is such that successful use by later poets is taken as a sign of technical mastery.

Across this grid Spenser lays out a storyline more diffuse than anything that came before, unless we look to romance cycles rather than individual poems. He says "the history of King Arthure" is his subject, but each book of *The Faerie Queene* introduces a new protagonist, and while Arthur appears in every book he is, on the level of story, central to none. Nor is he the mythic king "made famous by many mens former workes," for Spenser chooses "to pourtraict in Arthure, before he was king, the image of a braue knight" (Hamilton 2001, 715). In this version the king's legendary exploits give way to a borrowed story that seems, on the face of it, the most inappropriate material imaginable for the ancestor of the Tudor dynasty: Chaucer's "Tale of Sir Thopas," narrated in *The Canterbury Tales* by Dan Geoffrey—a ballad so inept, the host breaks it off with the objection that "thy drasty rhyming is nat woorth a turd." Spenser resumes the tale of Sir Thopas as that of Prince Arthur questing for the queen of Fairyland, who visited him in a dream. Like Chaucer, Spenser leaves the tale unfinished, but in every other respect it is changed, changed utterly. In his hands Chaucer's elaborate joke turns into a narrative marked by high pathos and ethical idealism, and it generates the allegorical structure through which Spenser purports to gather his far-flung narrative into a unified *ethos*.

Arthur's counterpart in this allegorical structure is Gloriana, the queen of Fairyland. In the Letter to Ralegh, Spenser identifies these characters with the virtue of magnificence and its reward, glory. In doing so he puts a number of contradictions into play. Ordinary inhabitants of Fairyland journey to Gloriana's court without difficulty: even a farm boy like Redcrosse can find his way. Yet Arthur searches endlessly and in vain; so far as we know, he never finds the fairy queen. Spenser describes his projected twelfth book not as the ending but the beginning of his story—not the marriage of Arthur with Gloriana, but the twelve-day feast that launches the quests of Holiness, Temperance, and the rest. As an elusive and mysterious symbol of transcendence, Gloriana occupies a place in Spenser's narrative analogous to that of the Grail in the *Morte D'Arthur*.

She also represents Elizabeth Tudor, and her realm stands for the kingdom of England (Hamilton 2001, 716). The historical allusions that let us read through Fairyland to sixteenth-century England have generated a long tradition of commentary, but so far as *form* is concerned the crucial point would seem to be that Arthur cannot find Gloriana without collapsing the structure of a metaphor. For his quest to end, Fairyland must become England so that Elizabeth I can be joined in matrimony to the fifth-century ancestor who has dreamed of her. Spenser never says that this will happen, leaving us to speculate that Arthur's quest may be not only unfinished but also, even on the literal level of the narrative, structurally incapable of conclusion.

Spenser hints that Gloriana does not exist in quite the same way as other characters. When Arthur first describes his dream of her, he says "So fayre a creature yet saw neuer sunny day" (I.ix.13.9). This means, as Hamilton's gloss puts it, that "either she is fairer than any other woman in this world; or, since he is dreaming, she does not exist in this world"—that is, Arthur's world (2001). But if Gloriana does not exist by daylight, then the "fiction" of Arthur's quest is no less ridiculous than that of Sir Thopas, though it is considerably more serious. Both the narrative and the imagined world in which it unfolds would have to be understood, radically and from the start, as figurative, and the figure would have to be understood as provocatively broken: if Arthur's errancy begins with an error about the essential nature of his experience, then *even within the terms of the story* it can never quite make sense.

Spenser's first readers

An admirable body of scholarship has been devoted to the first installment of *The Faerie Queene*. Hayden Carruth, an American modernist poet writing in the late 1960s, expressed his surprise on discovering "that Spenser, from a time well before his death until the present moment, has been the object of a vast critical attention, perhaps vaster, more varied, and more intelligent than that paid to any other poet in English. . . . I do not see how anyone who looks into even a little of it (which is as much as I have done) can fail to be struck by the human splendor of this love that only intelligence can display: so much warmth of heart engendered by great words on a printed page" (1983, 21–2). The attention paid to Spenser is certainly too vast for one essay. What follows is a glance at some early highlights (a sampling, not an overview) capped by a look at trends in the twentieth century that is "partial" in both senses.

Critical discussion of Spenser's poem began ten years before it was published. Not long after Spenser left for Ireland in 1580, Gabriel Harvey published a selection of their correspondence that includes remarks on an early draft of *The Faerie Queene*. Harvey's tone is bantering and a bit disparaging: he prefers other manuscript works his friend has shown him and thinks Spenser's desire to rival Ariosto has let "Hobgoblin runne away with the Garland from Apollo" (Cummings 1971, 51–2). It is hard to know what to make of this assessment. Bennett (1942) took it as evidence that Harvey was reading parts of Book III which seem closer in style to Ariosto than most of Books I and II; she concluded from this that the earlier books were in fact written later. Like speculation as to what became of various manuscript works mentioned in the correspondence but never published (or not, at any rate, under the titles given), this hypothesis remains tempting but unprovable.

We do not know which parts of the poem Harvey had seen in manuscript by 1580, nor how Spenser may have revised them in the years that followed. All we can say with certainty is that by 1590 Harvey was willing to commend the first installment of *The Faerie Queene* in language as lofty as that he reserved in 1580 for Spenser's *Dreames* (whatever they were): "Collyn," he writes, "I see by thy new taken taske, / some sacred fury hath enricht thy braynes" (Hamilton 2001, 722).

Early published references tend to be brief and generic: Spenser's name appears in lists of poets whose work is admired, and the terms chosen to praise him typically reflect one of three conceptions. There is Spenser the love-poet, Spenser the poet of heroic virtue, and Spenser the occult poet, repository of the Muses' mysteries. For a detailed sense of how readers actually responded to a specific text, the study of early marginalia has more to offer. Such comments are essentially private, however, and for the most part do not enter the critical tradition until they are recovered and discussed in twentieth-century scholarship. This is true of the earliest known example, a copy whose margins record the thoughts of one John Dixon residing near Tonbridge, in Kent (Hough 1964a and b). Dixon, his modern editor reports,

> has very little interest in the narrative line of *The Faerie Queene*, which indeed he often misunderstands. He is...interested in Book I almost entirely as an allegory of the English reformation....He has a close interest in the details of British history and Spenser's two long sections of chronicle-history in II.x and III.iii are minutely glossed.... The delicacies of Spenser's pictorial imagination and the subtleties of his love-psychology apparently leave our annotator cold, but he has a field-day with Guyon's attack on the Bower of Bliss, on which he comments with some fullness and evident relish.... [he] is indifferent to the courtly and romantic aspects of *The Faerie Queene*; it is the Protestant divinity, the ascetic morality and the national history that concern him.... Indeed it is to be observed that Dixon has a far clearer idea of the allegorical significance than he has of the actual story. (Hough 1964a)

In such marginalia we confront the traces of a unique event. Dixon is the historical aboriginal, a reader contemporary with the author himself, and is thus the living answer to a question most often posed rhetorically: how would an Elizabethan reader have understood this poem? To study his comments verbatim, or better yet to touch the page where they appear, to see the old-fashioned penmanship and the quaint abbreviations in ink long since faded to brown, is to be struck by the sheer reality of the past: no, we did not just imagine this. One day in 1597 a man sat at a table or a desk, and by daylight or candlelight he read the words we are reading.

Other early copies have been found with marginalia left by readers both obscure and illustrious—from the early seventeenth-century Puritan who was scandalized by Spenser's fairies (does not he know that they are all really demons?) to Ben Jonson himself, whose annotations in the margins of a copy of the 1617 folio testify to a lively engagement with Spenser's work (Orgel 2000; Riddell and Stewart 1995). Jonson's Spenser is by far the most important of such discoveries. Riddell and Stewart fully transcribe the annotations (161–92). Their critical use of this material is best approached with a combination of skepticism and strong coffee, but one important conclusion is supported by Jonson's notes to the celebrated "mathematical stanza" that begins Spenser's description of the House of Alma in Book II.

As one of its modern critics observes, "since the early seventeenth century, this stanza has attracted more commentary than any other in the poem" (Fowler 1964, 260):

> The frame thereof seemd partly circulare,
>> And part triangulare, O worke diuine;
>> Those two the first and last proportions are,
>> The one imperfect, mortall, foeminine;
>> Th'other immortal, perfect, masculine,
>> And twixt them both a quadrate was the base,
>> Proportioned equally by seuen and nine;
>> Nine was the circle set in heauens place,
> All which compacted made a goodly diapase.

(II.ix.22)

The stanza invites comment because in a highly compressed way it alludes to a broad range of popular and recondite concepts in the traditions of philosophy, architecture, mathematics, and numerology—"all which compacted" represent (in the words of Fowler again) "a *tour de force* of ambiguity." The lines "can be approached either as an architectural description of Alma's castle or as a geometrical description of the human body, or as generally allusive arithmology, or as step-by-step instructions for a specific geometrical construction or arithmetical operation" (Fowler 1964, 260). Even this list is incomplete; another critic subsequently discovered that the chronicle histories of England and Fairyland, which Arthur and Guyon read in the turret of the castle, are proportioned in multiples of seven and nine (as are subsequent installments of the chronicle material in Book III; Mills 1976). The stanza thus points us not only toward "a generally allusive arithmology," then, but also toward a specific set of numerical patterns implying that English history itself seeks to imitate the mysterious coherence of the human body.

Although no longer quite current, Fowler 1964 still offers the best account of this stanza and the commentaries it has elicited (260–88). Critical discussion was long thought to have begun with Sir Kenelm Digby, whose *Observations on the 22. Stanza in the 9th Canto of the 2d. Booke of Spencers Faery Queen*, published in 1643 and excerpted both in the *Variorum* and in Cummings

1971, is unusual in an age typified more by passing references than by sustained textual analysis. Digby reads the stanza (at some length) as a compressed allegory of "the body of a man inform'd with a rationall soul." He sees the circle and triangle as soul and body respectively, with the quadrate as "the foure principall humors" proportioned by the influence of the seven planets and the nine orders of angels (Cummings 1971, 152–7). But Digby's long-held reputation as "one of Spenser's earliest and best expositors" (Fowler 1964, 266) probably will not survive the discovery of Jonson's marginal notes, where the essential elements of his interpretation appear in suspicious detail. Opposite stanza 22, Jonson writes: "the circular signe represents th<e> Soule the triangular the body <of> man"; "By this Quadrat is meant <the> principall Humours in man<s> body"; and "*By seven and 9 are ment <the> Planetes and the Angells which ar<e> distributed into a Hierarch<y> which governe the body" (Riddell and Stewart 1995, 176–7). The explanation for this coincidence is apparently that Digby, as Jonson's literary executor, had privileged access to the annotations (Riddell and Stewart 1995, 107). As circumstantial evidence goes, this looks like enough to convict.

Whatever the provenance of the interpretation, though, it does suggest the appeal of Spenser as a poet of deep and extensive learning, as well as the precision an early reader might bring to glossing the allegory. William Austin, a barrister and author of religious treatises, affords another example in *Haec Homo* (1637; Cummings 1971, 172–3). After four paragraphs on the shape and proportions of the human body Austin notes, "All which discourse concerning the severall proportions of the body, are very elegantly and briefly contracted, by the late dead Spencer, in his everliving Fairy Queen; where, coming to describe the house of Alma (which, indeed, is no other but the body; the habitation of the Soule), he saith"—and then Austin quotes stanza 22. This use of Spenser as a learned authority is generically similar to the Digby amplification of Jonson's notes, but Austin does differ in a crucial respect. For Jonson/Digby the stanza is an allegory of the body "inform'd with a rationall soul," whereas for Austin it is an allegory of the body as "the habitation of the Soule." The phrases may sound similar, but Austin does not read the circle as an emblem of the soul in its perfection, opposed to the imperfect triangle of the body; instead he sees both shapes, and indeed "all Numbers and proportions," as "derived from the members, and dimensions of the humane body." He goes on to explain how the body in different postures may be seen to figure forth "a perfect Square," "a just Triangle," "a just circle," and so on. These shapes do, of course, have their spiritual analogs—the square, for example, being "the form of the Temple, and of the mysticall Church, in the Revelation," and the triangle "a figure of the Trinitie." But these allegories are not, like Digby's, based on conventional associations between geometric shapes and metaphysical values derived from Platonic and Aristotelian tradition. Instead, Austin's mystical allegories are figured in bodily postures concrete enough to be visualized—indeed, diagrammed (Fowler 1964, 261).

Milton, the most influential reader of Spenser during these years, left no marginalia. Instead the record of his responses must be gathered from references scattered in prose treatises and inferred from the texture of allusion and emulation in his poetry, notably *Lycidas, Comus,* and *Paradise Lost.* Indeed, Milton's first idea for an English epic was to take up the Arthurian legend once again. Dryden would later describe Milton as "the Poetical Son of Spenser," adding, "Milton has acknowledged to me, that Spencer was his Original" (1700, repr. Cummings 1971, 205).

Milton's most interesting reference to *The Faerie Queene* comes in *Areopagitica* (1644). Arguing against prior restraint on publication, Milton asserts that virtue needs to be tested against evil:

> That vertue therefore which is but a youngling in the contemplation of evill, and knows not the utmost that vice promises to her followers, and rejects it, is but a blank vertue, not a pure; her whiteness is but an excrementall whiteness; Which is the reason why our sage and serious poet *Spencer,* whom I dare be known to think a better teacher than *Scotus* or *Aquinas,* describing true temperance under the person of *Guion,* brings him in with his palmer through the cave of Mammon, and the bowr of earthly blisse that he might see and know, and yet abstain. (repr. Cummings 1971, 163–4)

Two features of this passage have drawn attention. First is Milton's sense that the best teaching does not mirror doctrine passively but shows it embattled. This has become a keynote in modern criticism of both poets, as for instance in the opening chapter of Fish's landmark study *Surprised by Sin.* Fish quotes Milton on the words of Christ—"not so much a teaching, as an intangling"—to characterize the poetic technique of *Paradise Lost,* but he also traces this technique back to the seduction of Redcrosse by Despair in Spenser (1967, 20–1). Alpers 1990 makes comparable use of Milton's argument about teaching, measuring the dissatisfaction of later readers against Milton's sense of the Bower episode as a deliberate provocation (105).

The second feature of the passage to have drawn attention is, of course, Milton's error about the Palmer, who does not accompany Guyon into Mammon's cave. Quilligan, building on the work of Fish and Alpers, relates this error to the self-critical reading strategies demanded by Spenserian allegory. In effect, we must always have the Palmer with us, internalized as a way of engaging the text (1983, 41–78). Quilligan's study also places the passage from *Areopagitica* in the wider context of Milton's poetic entanglement with Spenser.

Restoration and eighteenth century

By mid-century, comments on Spenser show his work fading into the past. D'Avenant could already refer to Spenser's "obsolete language" as "the most vulgar accusation that is lay'd to his charge." Along with references to the "ill" or "unlucky choise of his Stanza," this quickly becomes a critical commonplace (Cummings 1971, 188, 203, 207). Critics like Dryden and Rhymer were laying the foundations of English literary history. They sought for the first time to build a sustained account of how genre and versification had developed, and they sought to establish canons of taste and decorum as a basis for judging writers like Shakespeare and Spenser. The prevalence of such questions indicates that a historical gap has opened between these authors and their readers. Poets on the far side of this gap were increasingly seen as the primitive classics of a national tradition, one that was now moving on to the sophistications of Reformation comedy and the refinements of the heroic couplet.

These beginnings of the critical tradition were followed in the eighteenth century by the first serious editorial work on the text. In 1715, John Hughes brought out a six-volume edition of Spenser; it was reprinted in 1750, with three other editions following over the next decade. By 1805, Todd was able to consolidate the work of these predecessors in the first variorum-style edition.

No comprehensive treatment of the critical and editorial tradition from Milton to Keats has been written, and the topic is too vast to be covered here. A strong basis for further work may be found in Wurtsbaugh (1936), Mueller (1959), Kucich (1991), and especially Frushell (1999), which centers on the early eighteenth century but looks back to Milton and forward to Keats. Frushell's scrupulous inventory of archival materials and close attention to specific paths of transmission offer an invaluable resource (and model) for future work.

Dan Edmund meets the romantics

Spenser's peculiar sensibility has eluded many readers over the centuries. His use of Sir Thopas, for example—at once sublime and ridiculous—has moved critics to suggest that Spenser missed the humor of Chaucer's burlesque, that he had no gift for narrative, or that he worked somehow inadvertently, which is rather like saying that Renoir became an impressionist because he could not draw lines. This tendency to underestimate the sophistication of the poem's design goes hand in hand with a tendency to identify the narrative voice as the author's, and consequently to assume that everything the narrator says should be taken at face value. The "Spenser" created by such assumptions was earnest, idealistic, sentimental, and learned but not very clever; a lover of beauty and old books so carried away by his own music he was apt to lose track of the story. In short, he was "Dan Edmund": the comically inept figure Chaucer always pretended to be, though gifted with special powers of song.

This picture of Spenser made the poem easier to read. Without Dan Edmund to take us by the hand, it is a lot harder to know which meanings we can trust. The opening of Book I, Canto iii, is a case in point. After Redcrosse abandons

Una at the start of Canto ii, the story follows his exploits with Sansfoy, Duessa, and Fradubio before returning to the wanderings of Una. Spenser marks the transition back to Una by opening Canto iii in his standard manner, for as editors since Upton (1758) have observed, he "usually begins his canto with some moral reflection, agreeable to his subject" (*Var.* 1.206):

> Nought is there vnder heau'ns wide hollownesse,
>   That moues more deare compassion of mind,
>   Then beautie brought t'vnworthie wretchednesse
>   Through enuies snares or fortunes freakes vnkind:
>   I, whether lately through her brightnes blynd,
>   Or through alleageance and fast fealty,
>   Which I do owe vnto all womankynd,
>   Feele my hart perst with so great agony,
> When such I see, that all for pitty I could dy.

(I.iii.1)

Like Chaucer's Dan Geoffrey, the narrator in these lines casts himself as a humble servant of women—too humble indeed to put himself forward as a lover, but deeply susceptible to beauty in distress. What seems to be missing, when we look through the eyes of Romantic and Victorian readers, is a sense of comedy, a feel for some ironic distance between the poet and the earnest naivety of his narrator. The opening line offers a keynote for this response, since heaven will seem hollow either to the "Forsaken, wofull, solitarie mayd...in exile" (I.iii.3.2–3) or to the reader who finds his empathy quickened by her distress. This pathos, reinforced by the music of the phrase "heau'ns wide hollowness," would be sharply qualified by ironic distancing of the sort we associate with Chaucer.

As the *Variorum* shows, readers of this passage from Coleridge to the early twentieth century respond to the "plenilune loveliness" of the "tender stanzas" that open Canto iii much as Dan Edmund responds to Una's beauty in distress (Cory 1917, cited in *Var.* 1.206). Leigh Hunt (1844, Cited in *Var.* 1.206–7) offers a note of dissent: quoting Coleridge on "the indescribable sweetness and fluent projections" of Spenser's verse as illustrated in Stanza 3, Hunt objects that there are better examples to be found. He is right. What distinguishes the passage is not its sheer beauty (though it is beautiful) but its pathos—and, more specifically, its gender politics. Romantic critics typically rhapsodize over three qualities in Spenser: his imagery, his verbal music, and his heroines. Emile Legouis (1924, Cited in *Var.* 3.392) illustrates the first tendency—"fortune made him a painter in verse"—while Edward Dowden (1888, Cited in *Var.* 3.384) illustrates the last: "They rejoice, they sorrow; fears and hopes play through the life blood in their cheeks; they are tender, indignant, pensive, ardent; they know the pain the bliss of love; they are wise with the lore of purity, and loyalty, and fortitude."

None of these critics notices the equivocation in lines 5–6 of the stanza quoted: the narrator is pierced with agony, he tells us, either because of the allegiance he owes to "all womankynd," or because "her brightness" (beauty's?) has blinded him. This blurring of motives repeats a key feature of Redcrosse's response in the previous canto to Duessa, who simulates Una's pathos as well as her virtue:

> In this sad plight, friendlesse, vnfortunate,
>> Now miserable I *Fidessa* dwell,
>> Crauing of you in pitty of my state,
>> To do none ill, if please ye not do well.

(II.ii.26.1–4)

Line four with its singsong rhythm sounds just a little too pat, but Redcrosse hears no warning bell. Instead he responds like a Romantic critic:

> He in great passion al this while did dwell,
>> More busying his quick eies, her face to view,
>> Then his dull eares, to heare what shee did tell,
>> And said, Faire Lady hart of flint would rew
> The vndeserued woes and sorrowes, which ye shew.

(I.ii.26.5–9)

The conventional masculine response to imperiled beauty thrives on the bad faith of disavowed egotism and imperfectly repressed sexual desire. Duessa knows this, and uses her knowledge repeatedly to manipulate Redcrosse. In the closing stanza of Canto ii she distracts him from Fradubio's warning by pretending to faint: "Her vp he tooke, too simple and too trew, / And oft her kist" (45.7–8). As commentators always notice, the phrase "too simple and too trew" is adroitly suspended between the knight and his lady, applying to each in very different senses.

This stanza directly precedes the opening of Canto iii, already quoted. Since Una is not actually mentioned until the *second* stanza, Duessa/Fidessa remains tantalizingly available in stanza one as a point of reference for beauty brought to wretchedness—a gambit that extends the ambiguity already in play at the close of Canto ii. This possibility makes the narrator's equivocation in lines 5–6 seem less innocuous, and may even turn our sense of the stanza on its head. In place of clichéd sentiment embroidered with hyperbole, we find a passage that tempts us to recreate the Redcrosse Knight's error as part of the reading process. And the alternatives are not just different. As the critic Paul de Man writes in another context, "The two readings have to engage each other in direct confrontation, for the one reading is precisely the error denounced by the other and has to be undone by it" (1979, 12). The Romantic reading, here, is denounced and undone by an ironic reading.

The difference between these responses depends on our sense of the narrator. The ironic possibility is subdued, not emphasized by any pointed stylistic device: indeed, the most attention-getting flourish of the stanza is probably the sonorous music of its opening line, which (as we have seen) cues a sentimental identification with suffering beauty. By contrast, the signals for a more ironic reading include a juxtaposition we might ignore, since it spans the break between cantos, and a skeptical take on line 5, with its hint that the narrator's response to beauty may inhibit his powers of perception. The ironic reading also borrows an assumption from reader-response criticism, the idea that if a text invites misunderstandings, even momentarily, these misunderstandings are meaningful as part of the reading process.

Modern criticism recognizes such mixed signals as a pervasive element of *The Faerie Queene.* The text offers a profusion of cues, often muted, that invite incompatible responses. Many other questions are therefore bound up with our sense of the narrative voice: What values does the poem convey? How deliberate are its effects? How deep do its ironies go, and how frequent are they? The best answer to such questions was provided by critic and poet William Empson in remarks directed not to the character of the narrator but to the stylistic qualities of the Spenserian stanza—specifically its "use of diffuseness as an alternative to, or peculiar branch of, ambiguity." In the course of what must be the finest page and a half ever written on Spenser's style, Empson remarks that

> you have to yield yourself to [the stanza] very completely to take in the variety of its movement, and, at the same time, there is no need to concentrate the elements of the situation into a judgment as if for action. As a result of this, when there are ambiguities of idea, it is whole civilizations rather than details of the moment which are their elements; he can pour into the even dreamwork of his fairyland Christian, classical, and chivalrous materials with an air, not of ignoring their differences, but of holding all their systems of value floating as if at a distance, so as not to interfere with one another, in the prolonged and diffused energies of his mind. (1930, 34)

If we shift this evocation of the author's mind back in the direction of the text, we may wish to add that differences among systems of value are often experienced precisely in and through details of the moment. We may even want to insist that concentrating elements into a judgment can be productive because it activates what is latent in the text, bringing floating systems of value into contact to reveal that they *do* sometimes interfere with one another. Thus in the passage we have examined, an Augustinian warning against carnal understanding interferes with the chivalric ethos of fealty to womankind. Activating this latent conflict of values lets us see in the poem a prophetic critique of the neo-chivalric sexual politics of Romantic and Victorian critics.

Now a skeptical reader might object that in the process I am describing it is we, not the poet or the text, who trigger the clash of values. This is true: readers activate or repress what is latent. But as I mentioned earlier, a distinctive feature of Spenserian authorship is its separation of *invention* from *authority*. That authority, ceded in the first instance to Elizabeth, necessarily passes to each new reader who picks up a copy of *The Faerie Queene*. When Spenser "defers" the meaning of his text, he is deferring *to us*. I have argued elsewhere that he does so quite self-consciously, going so far as to build into the poem an allegory of the way readers construct his authorship (1996).

This deferral of authority has as its corollary the openness, the suspension of judgment, that Empson finds in Spenser. The term "dreamwork" is particularly suggestive of this uncensored ease with which radically incompatible networks of value and feeling pass into the text. This is not only a quality of mind, however; it is also a formal feature of the allegory. Perhaps I may dream of a librarian. She has my sister's name, with long hair braided like my first wife's, but she is saying things that remind me of a particularly scary colleague, and wearing a dress the color of ripe watermelon, like one I saw once on my babysitter when I was very small. Such a fusion of recent and archaic memories would be the result of what Freud calls dreamwork, a signifying process that evades conscious censorship through displacement and that produces texts marked by condensation and overdetermination. Something similar happens when I read of a hero who bears a saint's name but does not know it, who wears metaphoric armor from the Book of Ephesians but thinks he is an elf, and who has embarked on a quest that resembles both the exploits of Perseus and events in the Book of Revelation, though along the way he will encounter figures from pagan myth, classical epic, folklore, *The Canterbury Tales*, and chivalric as well as Italian romance, many of whom will behave like figures in a morality play. Lewis Carroll was that kind of allegorist.

We rationalize allegories by tracking correspondences among the registers from which their elements come: the adventures of Redcrosse recapitulate the salvation of Everyman, which resembles the history of the early church, which parallels the fortunes of the reformed church in England, which corresponds to events in the Book of Revelation, and so on. These analogies are marked by "the telling substitution that we call the 'allegorical interpolant,' the sign that gives allegory away" (Nohrnberg 1976, ix)—a special form of allusion. They are virtually innumerable, since each new allusion opens yet another set of potential correspondences; and they are theoretically open-ended, since in principle each new set is infinitely extensible, although sooner or later it will always break down in practice. In this way the text continually invites *and* frustrates the tracing of its "continued Allegory, or darke conceit" (Hamilton 2001, 714).

Modern Spenser studies

Spenser criticism changed dramatically in the late nineteenth and early twentieth centuries as the study of modern language and literature was institutionalized within the universities. The transformation of literary study into an academic specialization produced two related developments, for as the amount and variety of published research expanded, the focus of individual books and articles narrowed. Topics grew more sharply defined, and arguments were more clearly thesis-driven as scholars self-consciously built on the work of their predecessors. Among the most popular subjects were the quest for literary sources and elaborations of the historical allegory that equated characters in the poem with prominent Elizabethans. These lines of argument suffer from a common methodological problem, for whether they link the text to a literary source or to a historical personage, their evidence consists of resemblances. Without criteria as to what makes one resemblance probable or as to how many specific resemblances establish a connection, it was inevitable that much of this work would go to extremes; the *Variorum* selections on sources and historical allegory contain much that now seems tendentious and trivial.

But the increasing specialization of academic study did advance the state of critical, historical, textual, and bibliographical knowledge. By 1930 most of the major topics in twentieth-century criticism had received their first sustained treatment. Thus, for example, W. P. Ker's *Epic and Romance* (1897) paves the way for more focused studies such as Greene (1963) (which centers its discussion on episodes of a celestial messenger's "descent from heaven"), Giamatti (1966) (on the "earthly paradise"), Bellamy (1992) (which follows the topos of *translatio imperii*, or the "translation of empire"), Wofford (1992) (which explores the tension between figurative language and the ideological programs inherent in the epic celebration of imperial dynasties), and Burrow (1993). In a similar way, Pauline Henley's *Spenser in Ireland* (1928) looks forward to a wave of studies in the 1990s that take their immediate cue from post-colonial cultural theorists like Homi Babha and Edward Said. (Much of this work focuses on Spenser's later poetry and his prose treatise, but its implications for the 1590 *Faerie Queene* are brought home by a number of studies, including Rambuss 1993, 64–78 and McCabe 2002, 101–41.) Other studies from the period before 1930 trace Spenser's use of classical and medieval literary traditions, classical and popular mythology, biblical material, Italian romances, or chronicle histories; they explore theological and philosophical definitions of the virtues, and find the seeds of Spenser's allegory in the devices of royal and civic pageantry— all topics that prove central to later work. The lasting value of the best work from this period may be suggested by an example: Padelford and O'Connor in 1926 trace the St George legend Spenser uses in Book I of *The Faerie Queene* back to earlier re-tellings of the Perseus and Andromeda legend, demonstrating that older versions were already stories of religious "reforma-tion" in which the sacrificing community delivered from the sea-beast is converted to Christianity. This insight still offers an excellent point of entry for the beginning students of the poem.

The period 1930–60 saw the publication of the Spenser *Variorum*, beginning with the first three books of *The Faerie Queene*. Work by the editors and their students, both in the Variorum itself and in a long list of books and articles, not only synthesized the critical tradition from the eighteenth century forward but also refocused study of such formal properties as narrative and allegory. Greenlaw (1932), for example, marks a significant departure in the understanding of historical allegory with the contention Spenser invites "a general rather than a minute application" (*Variorum* I.494). Throughout the 1940s and 1950s, terms of critical discussion were set by essays that reflect the methods and assumptions of the Variorium school: Hankins (1945), for example, traces Spenser's use of imagery from the Book of Revelation in Book I of *The Faerie Queene* with such scholarly care that this essay is still the starting point for study of the subject; while Woodhouse's magisterial essay of 1949 set off a debate on the relation between realms of "nature" and "grace" that stimulated thinking about the overall structure of the six-book *Faerie Queene* and still reverberates in critical studies of the poem's theological dimension.

The grand exception to these trends was C. S. Lewis, whose chapter on *The Faerie Queene* in *Allegories of Love* (1936) bears little resemblance to *Variorum*-style scholarship. Most of his specific interpretations of *The Faerie Queene*—his assertions about art and nature, for instance—have been challenged, corrected, and superseded by subsequent critics. Yet somehow Lewis's genial blend of Christianity, Platonism, humanism, and common-sense moralizing, with its rhetoric of spiritual "health" and "maturity," retains a broad and immediate appeal that no academic discussion has rivaled. Lewis writes out of an immediate sympathy with his author; as Alpers puts it, he "treats Spenser as a living poet" (1990, 106). Wearing his considerable learning lightly, avoiding the tone and diction of academic prose in favor of a conversational style, Lewis brings the text to life even for nonacademic readers.

The late 1950s and early 1960s mark a watershed in Spenser studies. A new generation was coming to maturity: Harry Berger, Jr (1957, 1988), Northrop Frye (1961), A. C. Hamilton (1961), Kathleen Williams (1961, 1966), Thomas Roche (1961, 1964), Donald Cheney (1966), Paul Alpers (1967), and others were reading the poem more closely, bringing to it a more sophisticated critical vocabulary, and finding in it more varieties of coherence than previous generations imagined. As formal and thematic analysis came into its own, critical studies tended more and more to isolate individual books of the poem, whether treating them at monograph or chapter length. This burst of critical activity was sustained in the 1970s by ambitious critical treatments of the *Faerie Queene* (Nohrnberg 1976; MacCaffrey 1976) and by scores of more specific books and essays. Although it did not appear until 1990, *The Spenser Encyclopedia*, edited by Hamilton *et al.* is in many ways the culmination of this generational project; its articles on the poem's legends, characters, virtues, places, and other topics synthesize the best scholarship on all things Spenserian through the late 1970s. Hamilton's *Essential Articles* (1972) brings together a number of influential essays from Lewis to the 1960s, and enables readers to trace the progress of specific critical debates.

The 1960s and 1970s were a period of increasingly close textual analysis, but it was also during these decades that critics developed a clearer sense of Spenser's allegory as a unifying force in the poem. We have seen how allegory moves us constantly out and away from the text, into related fields of discourse—moral philosophy, theology, chronicle history, law, medicine, cosmology, literary history, Tudor politics, royal and civic pageantry, emblem books, and so on. But the movement outward is less important finally than the return: what matters most is not that a particular object in the narrative refers us to theological concepts, but that these concepts find their way into a particular object, through which they are called out of theology to appear in the text of the poem. This movement of return takes the poem itself as the most important context for any of its parts, and for this reason it gives more weight to analogies among those parts.

Spenser represents these analogies through narrative and symbolic means. His most explicit symbol for the unity of the poem is given at the opening of Book I, Canto ix, following Arthur's rescue of the Redcrosse knight:

> O Goodly golden chayne, wherewith yfere
> The vertues linked are in louely wize:
> And noble mindes of yore allyed were,
> In braue poursuitt of cheualrous emprize....

(I.ix.1.1–4)

In this passage Spenser appropriates a familiar symbol of cosmic harmony to signify the ideal unity of holiness, temperance, and the rest as they are perfected in the crowning virtue of magnificence, which "conteineth in it them all" (see the Letter to Ralegh and the gloss on this stanza in Hamilton 2001, 716, and 113). These lines also associate the golden chain with specific episodes in the narrative that establish alliances among the patron knights of the virtues, episodes that include not only Arthur's appearance in support of each knight except Britomart, but also "linking" incidents found in the first canto of each book, where the knight whose quest is beginning encounters the knight whose quest has just ended.

One set of analogies unifies the poem by treating its legends in successive pairs: Book II is clearly modeled on Book I, Book IV is closely joined to Book

III, and Books V–VI too may be seen as complementary. Another set takes the installments of 1590 and 1596 as parallel in a concentric or chiasmic pattern, matching Books I and VI, II and V, and—here overlapping with the first set—III and IV. (For a clear summary of these and other supplementary correspondences, see Roche 1964, 200–201). The poem affords much evidence in favor of these analogies, which have inspired a great deal of commentary—notably Northrop Frye (1961) elaborated in Nohrnberg's *The Analogy of the Faerie Queene* (1976), a monumental work organized according to the parallel between the two installments. Nohrnberg traces the poem's archetypes outward into European literary culture from the classics to the sixteenth century while analyzing the internal correspondences that organize its form. At 870 pages, his study demonstrates that both the poem's archetypal range of reference and its formal coherence are potentially infinite.

Discussions that emphasize the overarching unity of *The Faerie Queene* do confront minor embarrassments—stubborn details that remain unassimilated by any notion of the poem as a single entity. The most obvious of these are the different endings to Book III, one published in 1590 and the other replacing it in 1596. No modern editor wants to jettison the four stanzas Spenser struck out in 1596, so they are typically printed along with the three stanzas that replaced them, one or the other passage marked—with asterisks, a headnote, or an added border—as a kind of supplement, both there and not there at the same time. Critics usually have it both ways, referring to either or both endings as it suits them. But a larger problem is signaled by this minor disturbance, for in retrospect the new ending to Book III and the continuation of the narrative in Book IV radically transform the story of Scudamore and Amoret. In Book III and in the Letter to Ralegh, Scudamore is Amoret's lover; nowhere are they spoken of as man and wife. Book IV begins not with their marriage, which could easily have followed their reunion in the 1590 ending to Book III, but with the delayed revelation that they had already been married *before* Amoret's kidnapping at the hands of Busirane; in fact this kidnapping (we are now told) took place during the wedding festivities between the blessing of the priest and the bedding of the bride. Along with further retrospective elaboration in Canto x of Book IV, this radically transforms the story. In effect, it "rewrites" not just the last four stanzas of Book III but also the broad outline of its titular quest. Readings of Scudamore and Amoret that take them as married from the start complete this revision, in effect forgetting that although the poet backdates it, the marriage of Scudamore and Amoret did not really happen until 1596.

The 1980s were the decade of "New Historicism" in Spenser studies. Once again a generation of critics seem joined, in spite of many individual differences, by a common project, but this time the generation is post-Vietnam and the project is to give literary study a political edge seen as missing from the work of the previous two decades. Greenblatt (1980), Helgerson (1983), Norbrook (1984), and Montrose (1986a) were among the most influential practitioners of a mode of reading that connected the political and the literary in a new way. One example of its effects may be seen in renewed attention to the analysis of authorship—the topic of a considerable body of work across many fields since Roland Barthes, Michel Foucault, and Edward Said, among others, inspired a wholesale rethinking of the history and theory that inform the concept. Spenser provides an excellent opportunity for studying these matters because the 1590 *Faerie Queene* is so deeply engaged with the modes and conditions of literary authorship in its own historical moment. Work on this topic during the 1980s tended to be both historicist (after Foucault) and post-structuralist (after Barthes), but generally one influence or the other was uppermost. Goldberg (1981) offers a *tour de force* that draws synthetically on Barthes and Foucault along with Derrida and Lacan (the leading practitioners, respectively, of deconstruction and continental psychoanalysis). Although its focus is ostensibly limited to Book IV of *The Faerie Queene*, Goldberg's study has had a lasting influence on the way criticism conceives of the entire poem, both of the text and of its "authority." Orgel, for example, in the essay already cited, is making his point with reference to Goldberg, whose influence may be traced, with differing emphasis, in new historicist studies (Rambuss 1993) and in deconstructive approaches (Miller 1990, 1996).

Helgerson develops an influential account of Spenser in the broader context of what he calls the Elizabethan "literary system," concentrating first on its models of authorship (1976, 1983) and later on its engagement with the project of defining English nationhood (1992). Helgerson's Spenser played an important role in shaping both a version of "laureate" authorship and a literary politics of resistance to absolute monarchy. Among the studies that build on Helgerson's work are books by Patrick Cheney (1993, 1997, 2004b) that take Spenser, Marlowe, and Shakespeare, respectively, to exemplify differing notions of what it might mean to be England's "national poet," the one who shapes a lasting model of English nationhood. The 1590 *Faerie Queene* figures centrally in such studies as the poem that most fully realizes Spenser's laureate ambition.

Another strong presence during the 1980s were deconstructive and psychoanalytic approaches based on theoretical work from the late 1960s and early 1970s; following Goldberg (1980) in this vein were Guillory (1983), Gross (1985), Miller (1988), Bellamy (1992), Gregerson (1995), and Grossman (1998). Awareness of feminism and gender studies grew more slowly. Quilligan 1983 pointed the way for much that followed; momentum built in the work of Suzuki (1989), Krier (1990), Benson (1992), Susan Frye (1993), and Cavanagh (1994). Recent studies that carry this work forward include Berger (1994) and (1998), Stephens (1998), Eggert (2000a,b), McManus (2002), and Krier (2003).

As we have seen already, the 1990s were marked by renewed concern with the colonization of Ireland as a context for reading Spenser's poetry, and by growing interest in issues of gender and sexuality. This decade also saw a return to the long-unfashionable concerns of editorial theory. These became interesting all over again as the expansion of digital technologies opened new opportunities for hypertext editions, and in doing so brought "the book" and "the library" into perspective as cultural objects whose histories should be studied. Meanwhile 1980s interest in authorship prompted scholarly attention to the way this concept is caught up in the histories of print, book design, editing, censorship, and intellectual property (Loewenstein 1996, 2002), as I tried to suggest in the opening paragraphs of this chapter.

A "place" picked out

Any reader of literary criticism knows how much it depends on nuanced perceptions, on complexities of argument and qualities of attention to the text that no overview can adequately represent. In closing this thumbnail sketch of modern approaches to the *Faerie Queene*'s first installment, I want to look at examples of work on a single episode to suggest in slightly more detail the trajectory criticism has followed over the past seventy years. In *The Allegory of Love*, discussed above, C. S. Lewis unforgettably describes the Bower of Bliss at the close of Book II as "a picture, one of the most powerful ever painted, of the whole sexual nature in disease" (1936, 332). At times his eloquence drifts into overstatement, but Lewis offers a powerful response to the previous century's sympathy for the "voluptuous pathos, and languid brilliancy of fancy" (Hazlitt, quoted in Alpers 1990) that were seen as Spenser's special talent, fostering "the wide acceptance of the notion that he was at heart of Acrasia's party" (Durling 1954, in Hamilton 1972, 113). (Alpers situates Lewis in the critical tradition very astutely; students with access to *The Spenser Encyclopedia* should read his 1990 article in conjunction with the present discussion.) Even Lewis's overstatements proved stimulating, as critics weighing in to correct his influential account were pushed to analyze the poem with greater subtlety (see, for instance, Brooke, Durling, and Maclure, anthologized in Hamilton 1972).

Among later critics who challenge Lewis's remarks on the Bower is Stephen Greenblatt. By now his chapter on Spenser in *Renaissance Self-Fashioning* (1980) has been challenged and corrected about as often as Lewis, but like *The Allegory of Love* it retains a strong influence despite its overstatements. With a political edge characteristic of New Historicism (and its English counterpart, Cultural Materialism), Greenblatt asserts flatly that "Spenser was an agent of and an apologist for massacre" (186). He says much the same about the poem: "Spenser's art does not lead us to perceive ideology criti- cally, but rather affirms the existence and inescapable moral power of ideology as that principle of truth toward which art forever yearns" (192). This leap from the poet to the text parallels the conflation of poet and narrator that we saw earlier in Romantic responses to the opening of Book I,

Canto iii. Here the conflation goes even further: notice, for example, that art *yearns* for truth, as if the text were a conscious being filled with desire. The poem "forever yearns" in this way because, like the subject in Lacanian psychoanalysis, it finds within itself only lack. The self-conscious fictiveness of Shakespeare and Marlowe, says Greenblatt, serves "paradoxically to question the status of everything outside" their art, but Spenser's sustained questioning of his own fictions "opens up an internal distance within art itself." Through this self-disabling gesture, "art is questioned precisely to spare ideology," which "always lies safely outside the bounds of art."

But of course Greenblatt has already found ideology everywhere inside the text, where it reinscribes cultural narratives of colonial domination and religious iconclasm. Nevertheless, in seeking to bring the argument home he takes at face value the conventional deference of the proem, which claims that the poet's art can only "shadow" the queen's blinding brightness (II.Proem.5). Rather than put pressure on the term "shadow," Greenblatt uses this one stanza to characterize the text as a whole in relation to all of Tudor ideology, as if what Spenser *says* here about his relation to the queen were the truth, the whole truth, and nothing but the truth about his poem's relation to the world. Even if the stanza did not employ the obligatory mode of address to a monarch this would be a questionable procedure, because Greenblatt is extracting from this address a description of the text's relation to ideology that his own argument has already disproven. Ideology cannot be sustained in a realm beyond representation. It inheres precisely in the images, narratives, and discourses that the text imitates from the surrounding culture—images from which Spenser's text does indeed internally distance itself.

Nevertheless, the impetus and assumptions of Greenblatt's Spenser are alive and well in recent work, particularly feminist and Irish-colonialist approaches. These arguments read the text as a faithful expression of its author's intentions that embodies and transmits his agency as a subject. Cavanagh (1994) and Norbrook (1984), for example, both initially concede the ambiguity of the text, but they do so in a perfunctory way, as if acknowledging textual indeterminacy meant one could then ignore it. Such arguments do sometimes recognize that the values and assumptions they are foregrounding inhere not in the author's personal agency but in the conventions of established modes of discourse—narrative, moral, philosophical, or political. Susan Frye's 1993 discussion of chastity, for example, shows how the sexual power struggles of the court pass into the poem by way of discourses in which they are embedded. But Frye still sees the poet as taking up and using these discourses in the same way political agents used them. More recently, McManus (2002) acknowledges that Spenser's heroines are "suspended between the moralistic codes of courtesy literature and the easygoing conventions of the romance" (183), but does not take what might be seen as the logical next step—that is, to describe the text as staging and exploring the disjunctions between these and other conventions.

The critic who most decisively takes this step is Harry Berger, Jr. In seven essays on Books I–III of *The Faerie Queene* published since 1990, Berger engages three generations of critics, quoting at length to adjust and assimilate their insights. In the first of these essays Berger remarks that the convergence he is orchestrating suggests an emerging consensus. It is by no means, though, a neutral or easy synthesis, for his argument cuts against the practice of much historicist and cultural criticism. It regards Spenser not as exemplifying established modes of discourse, employing them instrumentally, or advocating their values, but rather as *imitating* them in a way that opens their assumptions and characteristic rhetorical maneuvers to critique.

Applied to the Bower of Bliss, this argument first of all insists on Acrasia's wandering island as specifically *textual* "place" (Berger 2003a, 85). If they agree on anything, discussions from Lewis to Greenblatt concur in reading the description of the Bower—"A place pickt out by choyce of best alyue / That natures worke by art can imitate" (II.xii.42.3–4)—to mean that it is "an actual place which has been chosen, as it were, by a committee of experts, as most suited to their purposes" (Durling 1954, in Hamilton 1972, 121). But those who use art to imitate nature's work include poets as well as magicians, and the word "place," as the *OED* reminds us, has a specifically rhetorical sense: it can be used to mean either "a particular part, page, or other point in a book or writing" (7.a) or "a subject, a topic: esp. in Logic and Rhet" (7.c). In other words, a place is also a commonplace, a literary topos—as Berger puts it, "a Tasso place, for example, or a Chaucer place, or a Homer place." It is also, of course, a Spenser place. If we think only of material space we will indeed find "The art, which all that wrought" appearing, as the narrator teasingly informs us, "in no *place*" (58.9, emphasis added). But if we attend to its literariness we will find that art everywhere, for as Alpers 1990 notes, it is "in some sense [Spenser's] own" (107). Indeed we may say that Spenser precedes Alpers on this point, for the same stanza that describes the Bower as "a place pickt out by choyce of best alyue" goes on to inform us that its pleasures are "poured forth with plentifull dispence" (42.8). As we saw earlier, the pun on Spenser's name functions as a kind of open secret both in his text and in references to him by contemporaries. Here, it serves as an authorial signature, hidden in plain sight, and even as a playful boast: we know who is the "best alyue, / That nature's work by art can imitate." We are reading him.

Berger's interpretation forges an alliance between this textual turn and the sharp awareness of sexual politics fostered by three decades of feminism and gender theory. Earlier discussions of the Bower betray an unconscious chauvinism, as when Lewis (combining class and gender prejudice) remarks of the maidens in Acrasia's fountain that "their names are obviously Cissie and Flossie," adding complacently that "a man does not have to go to fairie land to meet them" (331). Berger, in detailed readings of key passages, shows how the poem "imitates" the antifeminist topos of the seductive sorceress in order to reveal it as an anxious and defensive masculine projection (2003a, 98–104).

Berger's latest essays on *The Faerie Queene* I–III, gathered into a forthcoming book from Fordham University Press, bring the present account to its close. I am acutely aware of how much has been omitted, due both to my own limitations and to those of space. (I take consolation from the knowledge that Theresa Krier, in the essay on Books IV–VI, gives more attention to Northrop Frye, Paul Alpers, Angus Fletcher, and their influence.) I conclude with Berger not only because he was a harbinger of (and a major figure in) the Spenser renaissance in the 1960s, but also because he has never stopped intensely reading and rereading the poem and its critics, citing generously from and arguing shrewdly with peers and predecessors as well as younger scholars. The result is a half-century of work that in my judgment comprises the most sustained and impressive body of commentary in the history of Spenser criticism.

Further reading

Note: for the 1590 *Faerie Queene*, as for almost any topic, *The Spenser Encyclopedia* is an excellent place to begin: see articles on the various legends, places, protagonists, weapons, monsters, and magicians.

Alpers, P. 1967. *The Poetry of* The Faerie Queene, Princeton: Princeton University Press.
Berger, H, Jr. 1991. "Narrative as Rhetoric in *The Faerie Queene*", *ELR* 21: 3–48.
——. 1994. "Actaeon at the Hinder Gate: The Stag Party in Spenser's Gardens of Adonis", in *Desire in the Renaissance: Psychoanalysis and Literature*, ed. Valeria Funucci and Regina Schwarz. Princeton: Princeton University Press, 91–119.
——. 1998. "Displacing Autophobia in *Faerie Queene* I: Ethics, Gender, and Oppositional Reading in the Spenserian Text", *ELR* 28: 163–82.
——. 2003b. "Archimago: Between Text and Countertext", *SEL* 43.1: 20–32.
——. 2003a. "Wring Out the Old: Squeezing the Text, 1951–2001", *SSt* 18: 81–121.
——. 2004. "Sexual and Religious Politics in Book 1 of Spenser's *Faerie Queene*", *ELR* 34: 201–42.
——. 2005. "Resisting Translation: Britomart in Book 3 of Spenser's Faerie Queene", in *Translating Desire in Medieval and Early Modern Literature*, ed. Heather Hayton and Craig A. Berry. Tempe, Ariz: Medieval & Renaissance Texts & Studies Press.
Carruth, H. 1983. "Spenser and His Modern Critics", in *Effluences from the Sacred Caves: More Selected Essays and Reviews*, Ann Arbor: The University of Michigan Press.
Cheney, P and L. Silberman, eds 2000. *Worldmaking Spenser: Explorations in the Early Modern Age*, Lexington, KY: University Press of Kentucky.
Gregerson, L. 1995. *The Reformation of the Subject: Spenser, Milton, and the English Protestant Epic*, Cambridge: Cambridge University Press.
Hamilton, A. C. 1972. *Essential Articles for the Study of Edmund Spenser*. Hamden, Conn.: Archon. See especially articles by Baybak *et al.*, Frye, Hankins, Roche, K. Williams, and Woodhouse.

Krier, T. M. 1990. *Gazing on Secret Sights: Spenser, Classical Imitation, and the Decorums of Vision*, Ithaca: Cornell University Press.

——. 2003. "Mother's Sorrow, Mother's Joy: Mourning Birth in Edmund Spenser's Garden of Adonis", in *Grief and Gender, 700–1700*, ed. Jennifer C. Vaught with Lynne Dickson Bruckner. New York: Palgrave.

Lewis, C. S. 1936. *Allegories of Love*, Oxford: Clarendon.

McCabe, R. 2002. *Spenser's Monstrous Regiment: Elizabethan Ireland and the Poetics of Difference*, Oxford: Oxford University Press.

Miller, D. L. 1988. *The Poem's Two Bodies: The Poetics of the 1590* Faerie Queene, Princeton: Princeton University Press.

Nohrnberg, J. 1976. *The Analogy of* The Faerie Queene, Princeton: Princeton University Press.

Roche, Jr, T. P. 1964. *The Kindly Flame: A Study of the Third and Fourth Books of Spenser's "Faerie Queene"*, Princeton: Princeton University Press.

Padelford, F. M. and M. O'Connor. 1926. "Spenser's Use of the St. George Legend", *SP* 23: 142–56.

Silberman, L. 1995. *Transforming Desire: Erotic Knowledge in Books III and IV of* The Faerie Queene, Berkeley: University of California Press.

Stephens, D. 1998. *Limits of Eroticism in Post-Petrarchan Narrative: Conditional Pleasure from Spenser to Marvell*, Cambridge: Cambridge University Press.

9
Shorter Verse Published 1590–95

Richard A. McCabe

'*Spencer* is ruined' remarked John Weever in 1599 in an epigram lamenting the poet's death. The full text was quoted by H. S. V. Jones in 1930 in *A Spenser Handbook* in the short chapter entitled 'Complaints' (74):

> *Colin*'s gone home, the glorie of his clime,
> The Muses Mirrour, and the Shepheards Saint;
> *Spencer* is ruined, of our latter time
> The fairest ruine, Faëries foulest want:
> Then his *Time-ruines* did our ruine show,
> Which by his ruine we untimely know:
> *Spencer* therfore thy Ruines were cal'd in,
> Too soone to sorrow least we should begin.

Jones's purpose in quoting Weever is indicative of the prevailing critical concerns of the day, concerns that were heavily informed by the historicist methodology of Edwin Greenlaw's *Studies in Spenser's Historical Allegory* (1932) and the bibliographical and generic suppositions of Harold Stein's *Studies in Spenser's Complaints* (1934)—the latter being the first, and by 1947 still the only, monograph wholly devoted to the *Complaints* (Radcliffe 1996, 163–8). Jones was primarily concerned with corroborating the traditional allegation that the volume was 'cal'd in'; its wider cultural implications scarcely concern him. As a result, Weever's witty elision of the political motivation for the censorship passes unremarked, as do such complex issues as the relationship between 'Colin' (who has finally 'gone home') and 'Spenser' (who is disastrously 'ruined'), between creativity and patronage and, perhaps most important of all, between the literary 'architectonics' of a canon so anxious to emulate the grand structures of classical verse and the innumerable varieties of 'ruin' that lend it imaginative homogeneity (Ferguson, 1982). The critical journey from Greenlaw to Greenblatt has done much to shift commentators' attentions in such directions.

Complaints (1591)

According to its publisher, William Ponsonby, Spenser's *Complaints* is a collection of fugitive pieces gathered together in the poet's absence in order to satisfy (or capitalise upon) the demands of the reading public for more works by the now famous author of *The Faerie Queene*:

> Since my late setting foorth of the *Faerie Queene*, finding that it hath found a favourable passage amongst you; I have sithence endevoured by all good meanes (for the better encrease and accomplishment of your delights,) to get into my handes such smale Poemes of the same Authors; as I heard were disperst abroad in sundrie hands, and not easie to bee come by, by himselfe; some of them having bene diverslie imbeziled and purloyned from him, since his departure over Sea.

At least one modern commentator is disposed to take this at face value (Brink 1991), but it is both disingenuous and ingenious. *The Shepheardes Calender* (1579), containing dangerous political matter, was published anonymously. The *Complaints*, containing equally dangerous matter, contrives to name the author but simultaneously distance him—geographically and, by implication, politically—from the act of publication. In fact, in a remarkable retrospective allusion to the *Calender*, Ponsonby may be seen to adopt the role of E. K. when he asks his readers 'gentlie to accept of these, and graciouslie to entertaine the new Poet'. The collection he offers is somehow both authored and anonymous, allegedly gathered together from the hands of unnamed keepers and thieves and associated after the fashion of the commonplace book, 'for that they al seeme to containe like matter of argument in them: being all complaints and meditations of the worlds vanitie'. The reason for the adoption of such a circumspect strategy is not far to seek. If *The Faerie Queene* engages (at least overtly) in the public celebration of the monarch, the *Complaints* engage in the covert (but transparently public) degradation of the man who was, by 1591, unquestionably her chief minister, William Cecil, Lord Burghley. The immediate reaction, one of stringent official censorship, more than justified the elaborate mystification cast over the volume's appearance. Contemporary witnesses supply us with some sense of the *frisson* that the incident engendered. Writing in 1592 in *Foure Letters and Certaine Sonnets*, Gabriel Harvey, Spenser's friend and mentor, asserted that 'Mother Hubbard in the heat of choller, forgetting the pure sanguine of her sweete *Faery Queene*, wilfully over-shott her malcontented selfe' (Wells 1971–72, I. 24). Judging from Thomas Nashe's sharp response in *Pierce Penilesse His Supplication to the Divell* (1592) the matter was best forgotten in the interests of all parties concerned: 'if any man were unde- servedly touchd in it, thou hast revived his disgrace that so toucht in it

[sic], by renaming it, when it was worn out of al mens mouths and minds' (Wells 1971–72, I.27). That the matter had been something of a cause célèbre is demonstrated by Richard S. Peterson's discovery of further contemporary allusions in the papers of Sir Thomas Tresham: 'He that writ this discourse', Tresham remarks,

> is a Cantabrigian and of the blood of the Spencers. Yt is nott yett a yeare sence he writt his booke in the prayse of the Quene...which was so well liked, that her maiestie gave him ane hundred marks pencion forthe of the Exchequer: and so clerklie was yt penned, that he beareth the name of a Poett Laurell. But nowe in medlinge with his apes tayle he is gott into Ireland; also in hazard to loose his forsayd annuall reward: and fynallie hereby proove himselfe a Poett Lorrell. (Peterson 1998, 8)

According to this view of events, the publication of *Mother Hubberds Tale* has had a potentially devastating effect upon Spenser's public career, transforming the newly celebrated (if unofficial) poet laureate into a 'lorrell' or fool. It is a serious allegation, as Spenser knew: Morrell is accused of speaking like 'a lewde lorrell' in *The Shepheardes Calender* ('Julye', 93). As Tresham sees it, Spenser has acted in his own worst interests, hazarding the benefits derived from the publication of *The Faerie Queene* by a politically maladroit attack upon one of the queen's most trusted ministers. Ireland is now regarded not as his land of opportunity but as his place of refuge or even exile. That Mother Hubberd's target was Lord Burghley appears to have been widely known (Hadfield 2003), and it is especially noteworthy in this regard that passages critical of Burghley and his family in *The Ruines of Time* (ll. 216–17, 447–53) were tacitly altered in the folio of 1611, while *Mother Hubberds Tale* was omitted in its entirety. It reappeared only after the death of Robert Cecil, Burghley's son and political heir, in the folio edition of 1617.

Perhaps the single most important change in critical emphasis since the era of Jones's *Handbook* has been the growing awareness of the centrality to the Spenserian canon of what both de Selincourt (1910) and the editors of the *Variorum* were content to describe as 'minor poems'. It is indicative of the change in attitude that the Yale (1989), Longman (1995) and Penguin (1999) editions have all independently opted for 'shorter poems'. During the previous decades the 'minor poems' were regarded, at least implicitly, as marginal to the Virgilian template that was held to inform Spenser's career—even though an Ovidian pattern is equally evident, as Syrithe Pugh's recent monograph, *Spenser and Ovid* (2004) brilliantly demonstrates. They were mined by philologically oriented scholars for biographical information and literary allusions, and were frequently castigated for their 'obvious' poetic 'defects' (Jones 1947, 84; Nelson 1963). Since then our perception of the complexity of Renaissance literary career structures has been transformed by the work of Patrick Cheney who

provides one of the best overviews of the intricate, intertextual relationship between the shorter poems and *The Faerie Queene*. Although the
Complaints 'do not belong to the generic progression organizing the
fiction of the New Poet's career' in which Cheney is primarily interested,
he suggestively presents them as a modulation of tragedy, 'a genre vital
to the national poet's career' and one intimately associated with epic
(1993, 3, 257). More recently, however, Katherine Craik has asserted that
the volume's 'main preoccupations are scarcely identifiable in laureate
terms'. In particular, she argues, poems such as *Virgil's Gnat* and the
Visions 'announce Spenser's allegiance, in 1591, to the minor voice'
(2001, 65). But the matter is not quite that simple. Matters of 'allegiance'
seldom are. Ben Jonson, one of Spenser's earliest and acutest readers, had
no doubt that poems such as *The Ruines of Time* and *The Teares of the
Muses* were deeply concerned with the fate of the 'major voice', with the
'ultimate place of poetry in relation to a society that nurtures or fails to
nurture poets' (Riddell and Stewart 1995, 71). One needs to attend
to Richard Rambuss's cautionary observation that the 'auto-anthology'
of the *Complaints* 'resists assimilation to overly streamlined accounts of
Spenser's Virgilian laureateship and is consequently often ignored or
minimized in those accounts' (1993, 84). Our view of the 'Virgilian rota'
is not infrequently at odds with that of renaissance editors. As Colin
Burrow has astutely reminded us, the very title of *Virgils Gnat* proclaims
its association with the Virgilian canon as the Elizabethans constructed
it, and the work itself, as David Lee Miller has demonstrated, is no less
concerned with the issue of Spenser's 'vocation' than is *The Shepheardes
Calender* (Burrow 2001, 220; D. L. Miller 1983). Its dedicatory sonnet
serves the dual purpose of introducing the English reading public to
what would become known as the 'Spenserian' form (with its distinctive,
interlocking rhyming pattern *ababbcbcdcdee*) *and* of engineering a tense
tonal contrast with the opening of Virgil's *Culex* (Spiller 1992, 142–9;
Philmus 1999). A latter day 'Virgil' somehow betrayed by his 'Augustus'
translates into an anthology of political, social and personal complaint
the poem in which his Roman counterpart invites the young Octavius to
'come sliding soft, / And favour my beginnings graciously (37–8)' [from
'meis adlabere coeptis, / sancte puer']. Although the nature of the injury
remains uncertain (Brink 1996), *pace* Greenlaw's unsubstantiated assertion that it related to Spenser's banishment to the 'Siberia' of Ireland
(1932, 124–30), the notion of injured artistic merit is totally in keeping
with the ethos of the collection as a whole.

The first four poems of the *Complaints* volume—*The Ruins of Time*,
The Teares of the Muses, *Virgils Gnat* and *Mother Hubberds Tale*—are now
generally seen to be pervaded by the anxieties of failed patronage, neglected
arts and declining public standards (Fox 1995; Snare 1969; Rasmussen 1981),
and haunting the entire collection are the spectres of a fallen and a failing

empire, Rome and England (Cartmell 1986). Although, as Hugh Maclean has demonstrated, continuities with *The Shepheardes Calender* are manifold (1978), it is little exaggeration to say that the *Complaints* are as preoccupied with the *issue* of epic—with the relationship of Humanist poetic and political aspiration to its problematical classical templates—as is *The Faerie Queene* with the matter of complaint. The frequent recurrence of epic topoi, such as the descent of Mercury in *Mother Hubberds Tale*, in a series of ironic or even mock-heroic contexts seems designed to 'hazard' the idealism of *The Faerie Queene* in a very deliberate and calculated way (T. M. Greene 1963, 294–311). The notion of epic seems to function throughout the *Complaints* as a sort of subtextual reproach to satire, a constant reminder of the way things should be, the ghost of an abortive ideal.

The note of authorial absence and neglect struck in Ponsonby's prefatory letter echoes particularly (and highly appropriately for an ill-used *epic* poet) through the epyllia of *Virgil's Gnat* and *Muiopotmos* (Hulse 1981). In the first half of the twentieth century, readers were apt to view Spenser's poetics of metamorphosis (and particularly the wonderfully wrought episode of Pallas and Arachne in *Muiopotmos*) as dark political allegories detailing the antagonism between Ralegh and Essex (Lyons 1916), or Burghley and Leicester (Grierson 1922), or Essex and Burghley (Harris 1944). Later criticism has largely abandoned the pursuit of roman á clef to concentrate instead upon the poetry's engagement with the wider power structures of the Elizabethan court and its mechanisms of censorship and control (Brinkley 1981; Bernard 1989), or upon the even more generalised, if closely associated, relationship between art and public life (Dundas 1975; Macfie 1990; Rustice 1999; Mazzola 2000). Yet the overriding question must be why, as the recipient of a rare royal pension and author of one of the most well-received works of Elizabethan literary history, Spenser wished to 'complain' at all in 1591 (Goldberg 1981, 171). It was the very question that perplexed Sir Thomas Tresham, but much of the difficulty arises from the notion that Spenserian self-promotion, or 'self-fashioning', was the aim that superseded all others, and this is an assumption that should not be accepted uncritically. As the circumstances of the anonymous publication of *The Shepheardes Calender* demonstrate, Spenser did not shy away from political controversy. Although the *Calender* praises 'fayre *Elisa*' as 'Queene of shepheardes all' it does not hesitate to condemn the state of the church of which she was the supreme governor nor to praise Archbishop Grindal, her chief ecclesiastical antagonist (McLane 1961; McCabe 1995).

Similarly, while *The Teares of the Muses* lauds 'divine *Eliza*' as a 'peereles Poëtresse' and singles her out as the 'onelie' living person who 'supports the praise of noble Poësie' (ll. 571–82), the poem as a whole deplores the marked lack of poetic patronage that characterises her kingdom. Calliope, the muse of epic verse, raises the possibility that *The Faerie Queene* has been published in a land unfit for heroes: 'Ne doo they care to have the auncestrie/Of th'old Heroës memorizde anew' (ll. 439–40). These generalised complaints are lent immediate personal application by *Virgil's Gnat* which follows directly without separate titlepage. Its dedicatory sonnet, written 'in clowdie teares', contributes to the 'store of teares' wept by the very muse who praises Elizabeth (l. 595). If the effect is contradictory, it would appear to be consciously so. Nothing gives the lie to Ponsonby's disingenuous preface more surely than the volume's carefully crafted, and even more carefully gendered, authorial dedications. As in *The Faerie Queene*, where the monarch's virtues and vices are 'unfolded' in her various surrogates, it would appear that the volume's many voices of female complaint similarly unfold the contradictions of Eliza's polity: 'Where', asks Thalia, 'be the sweete delights of learnings treasure...In which I late was wont to raine as Queene?' (ll. 175, 179). The four dedications, by contrast, serve to 'unfold' the qualities of literary patronage (and, on the poet's part, reciprocal service) that define a civil nation: *The Ruines of Time* appeared with a dedication to the Countess of Pembroke, sister to Sir Philip Sidney who is here characterised as 'the Patron of my young Muses'—presumably the same Muses who are now weeping; *The Teares of the Muses*, *Mother Hubberds Tale* and *Muiopotmos* are prefaced by dedications to (respectively) the Ladies Strange, Compton and Mountegle, and Carey, the three daughters of Sir John Spencer of Althorp who guarantee the poet's personal gentility by acknowledging his claims to blood kinship.

Writing in 1934, Stein was generally disposed to accept the generic identity of the *Complaints* more or less at face value. Writing in 1999, however, Richard Danson Brown concluded that 'the major *Complaints* show Spenser transforming traditional complaint from stylised lament into a complex, self-reflexive meditation on the lament form' (Brown 1999, 256). Not surprisingly, our growing awareness of the intricacy of the *Complaints* has diverted critical attention from source-hunting to more complex issues of intertextuality. Emerging from this is a deepening sense of the conflicted 'role of literary culture in the structure of power' (Manley 1982, 203). The self-reflexive effects of which Brown speaks range from the subtle interplay of divergent voices within a single poem, such as *The Ruines of Time* (Rasmussen 1981), to the juxtaposing within the overall scheme of the collection of Virgil, Ovid, Petrarch, Chaucer, Du Bellay, Du Bartas, Marot, the Psalms, Ecclesiastes and Revelation—not to mention the revised, and revoiced, versions of Spenser's boyhood works. Most obviously, *Virgils Gnat* is translated, or rather adapted, from the *Culex*; *The Ruines of Rome* from Joachim Du Bellay's *Les Antiquitez de Rome contenant une generale description de sa grandeur, et comme une deploration de sa ruine* (1558); and *The Visions of Bellay* from the *Songe ou Vision sur le mesme subject* that had originally accompanied Du Bellay's *Antiquitez*. *The Visions of Petrarch* are taken from *Rime Sparse*

323, probably by way of Clement Marot's French version but evidently with some knowledge of the original (Bondanella 1978).

The Visions of Bellay and *The Visions of Petrarch* had originally appeared in Jan van der Noot's *A Theatre for Voluptuous Worldlings* (1569) where they served to illustrate an anti-papal, and anti-Hapsburg, commentary upon Revelation. Spenser's 1569 version of Du Bellay's *Songe*, the first instance of a blank verse sonnet sequence in English, had omitted four of the French sonnets (6, 8, 13 and 14) but these were restored in the *Complaints* and recast in the traditional English sonnet form (Bath 1988). The four 'Apocalyptic' sonnets that had originally concluded the sequence were now wholly omitted and the overall effect is to create a very different work: the sense of impending catastrophe is implied rather than expressed and is all the more disturbing for that (Tucker 1990; Prescott 1996). Similarly, in 1569 *The Visions of Petrarch* had appeared as six 'Epigrams' (two taking the form of English sonnets) and a four-line coda. In the *Complaints* the seven sections appear as seven English sonnets, and the expansion of the coda allows the volume to conclude with an address to one of Spenser's female patrons, the 'faire Ladie' who is most likely to be Lady Carey but may possibly be the Countess of Pembroke. These changes are highly significant for the design of the collection. As both Wayne A. Rebhorn and Leonard Barkan have argued, Du Bellay appears to have expressed his ambivalent response to Rome, both ancient and modern, through the guise of a disappointed Petrarchan lover (Rebhorn 1980; Barkan 2000). In Spenser's first version the Petrarchan poems had preceded those of Du Bellay, but now the order is reversed in keeping with the aesthetic concerns of the volume as a whole. In the version of 1591 it is as though the Petrarchan speaker adopts the guise of a disappointed Du Bellay lamenting not just Laura but the laureate status of poetry itself, the vulnerability of poetic reputations in 'this tickle trustles state'—Eliza's England and Spenser's world.

From what has been said in the preceding paragraphs it may be seen that the trajectory of modern criticism is towards an ever-increased awareness of the centrality of satire to Spenserian poetic vision, a movement reflected in the inclusion of 270 lines from *Mother Hubberds Tale* in Emrys Jones's *New Oxford Book of Sixteenth-Century Verse* (1991). Its predecessor, E. K. Chambers's *Oxford Book of Sixteenth-Century Verse*, contained nothing from *Complaints* (1932). In recent decades the volume has come to be seen less as a loose collection of occasional pieces, than as a structured articulation of social and aesthetic complaint, a crucial text for any serious discussion of Elizabethan literary culture (Brown 1999). In particular, it is now seen to occupy a pivotal place in what Judith Owens terms 'the poetics of patronage' through its unremitting and often pained exploration of the tensions that arise between the need to create a popular (and paying) reading public and simultaneously to elicit the sort of aristocratic patronage that would afford some form of 'laureate' status—the sort of status that might obliterate 'the stigma of print' even as it enhanced the commercial benefits of publication (Owens 2002, 30–8).

Daphnaïda (1591)

Published in the same year as the *Complaints*, *Daphnaïda* takes the form of a pastoral elegy on the death of Douglas Howard, late wife to Spenser's friend and fellow poet Sir Arthur Gorges. That, at least, is its ostensible theme but modern readings of the work have detected wider psychological and artistic concerns. Recent studies of the Renaissance elegy have tended to concentrate on the poetics of consolation, on the difficult relationship between the psychology of bereavement and the literary forms that struggle to contain or appease it (Sacks 1985; Pigman 1985; Kay 1990). Particularly to the fore in such readings are the various methods whereby the elegists, to use Dennis Kay's words, 'make themselves their own subject' (1990, 8). Gorges's marriage to Howard was legally contested by her father but the whole tangled history of familial discord is notable by its exclusion from the poem (Sandison 1928). Instead, the intensity of focus upon Alcyon's grief for 'Daphne'—the latter being the poetic name under which Gorges had sometimes addressed his wife (see Gorges's *Poems*)—is unremitting. So unremitting, in fact, that William A. Oram has read the poem as an admonition against excessive complaint (1981). Investigations into Spenser's handling of Chaucer's *Book of the Duchess*, upon which *Daphnaïda* is broadly modelled, have tended to lend weight to such readings (Harris and Steffen 1978). Amongst many other changes, Spenser dispenses with the element of dream-vision in order to establish a more immediate encounter between the two speakers. The narrator's melancholy demeanour suggests that he too may be bereaved and Oram has speculated that his attitude may reflect Spenser's reaction to the death of his first wife (1981, 158). Effectively this would mean that Spenser was struggling vicariously with a very private grief. It is noteworthy in this regard that *both* of Spenser's speakers are poets and their interview inevitably entails consideration of the relationship between the passions and the poetics of bereavement (Pigman 1985; Martin 1987). According to Patrick Cheney this eventually takes Spenser 'beyond the poetics of Christian redemption' into 'the danger zone of early modern fatality' in a movement that anticipates the darkly sceptical ethos of Renaissance Tragedy (2004a, 145).

The complaint assigned to Alcyon moves in seven sections of seven stanzas apiece and the poem's central stanza records his wife's resignation, not to say joy, in the face of death (ll. 281–7). Although this notable essay in the art of dying well is paraphrased within Alcyon's complaint, he hears only the 'deadly accents' (l. 297) of his dying spouse and has, therefore, been seen to fall short, and to be presented as falling short, of Christian assurance (DeNeef 1982, 41–50). Approaching the work from a numerological viewpoint, Marie-Sofen Røstvig has called attention to the poem's highly formalised structure: 28 stanzas of introduction (4×7), 49 stanzas of lament (7×7) and 4 stanzas of conclusion (4×7 lines). She regards the emphasis on the number seven as gesturing towards the consolation of the eternal Sabbath and Daphne's reception into divine grace (Røstvig 1963, 83–7). It would therefore serve an equivalent thematic function to, say, Dante's insistence upon the number nine in *La Vita Nuova*. However, Røstvig's supplementary suggestion that Alcyon finally overcomes his despair has generally been disputed. Rather, it would appear that he remains trapped within self-perpetuating rituals of social and poetic lament, deaf to the elements of elevating hymn within his wife's last words. Unlike the Alcyon of Ovid's *Metamorphoses* (ll. 384–748)—a source for both Chaucer and Spenser—he is not transformed into a bird but shuffles out of ken 'with staggring pace and dismall lookes dismay' (l. 564). In *Colin Clouts Come Home Againe* the pastoral narrator directly invites Gorges, again under the name of Alcyon, to forsake the 'endlesse plaints of pittie' arising from Daphne's death and 'lift up thy notes vnto their wonted height' (385–91). In effect, he calls for a transformed poetics. Ultimately Gorges responded by incorporating elements of the lament attributed to him in *Daphnaïda* into *The Olympian Catastrophe*, an elegy on the death of Prince Henry (compare ll. 1060–88 with *Daphnaïda* ll. 215–492). This strange act of alter-ego quotation serves to exemplify the intricate relationship between biographical fact and poetic fiction that Donald Cheney identifies as characteristic of the Spenserian canon during this period (1984). The contrast between the attitudes and emphases discernible in Cheney and those of, say, Greenlaw (1932) exemplify a growing awareness of the 'auto-biographical' as a literary trope, as, ironically, a species of the pseudonymous. This perception is related not only to the influence of Greenblatt's theories of 'self-fashioning' (Greenblatt 1980), but to the perceived pressures of shaping, and even justifying, a literary career at a time when aristocratic patronage appeared to be in decline and market forces threatened to vulgarise Humanist idealism (Helgerson 1978, 1983; Fox 1995). Instead of attempting to find biographical 'fact' at the expense of fiction, we have learned to appreciate the role of fictionality in the concept of the 'self'. We have learned to apply to supposedly 'auto-biographical' fictions Sir Philip Sidney's dictum that, in one very important sense, the poet 'never lyeth' (Smith 1904, I, 184).

Colin Clouts Come Home Againe (1595)

The reappearance of Spenser's own 'alter ego' in *Colin Clouts Come Home Againe* may best be viewed in a similar context. Colin Clout was originally the name 'under which', according to E. K., 'this Poete secretly shadoweth himself, as sometime did Virgil under the name of Tityrus'. In other words 'Colin Clout' was the pastoral persona of an aspiring epic poet. By 1595, however, *The Shepheardes Calender* had gone through four editions (with a fifth to come in 1597), and Spenser was widely celebrated under the name of Colin even in relation to *The Faerie Queene*. According to the opening lines of *Colin Clouts Come Home Againe* 'the shepheards boy...That after *Tityrus* first sung his lay' is now 'best knowen by that name' (ll. 1–2). Yet the persona had subtly altered. The aspiring epic poet had now staked his claim to fame. Commenting in 1715 on Colin's second incarnation, John Hughes perceptively asserted that 'we find him less a Shepherd than at first: He had then been drawn out of his Retirement, had appear'd at Court, and been engag'd in an Employment which brought him into a Variety of Business and Acquaintance, and gave him a quite different Sett of Ideas' (Cummings 1971, 272). 'Colin' had developed to embrace his creator's changing experience and was, in Hughes' view, far less suited to pastoral on that account. Hughes' shrewd observation set the tone for much of the succeeding debate. Despite detailed analyses of its rhetoric (Meyer 1969) and structure (Burchmore 1977), the genre of *Colin Clouts Come Home Againe* remains remarkably difficult to specify. Patrick Cheney, for example, regards it as a wholly new and consciously hybrid form, a minor epic in the pastoral mode (2001, 97–101). There can be no doubt that the poem's generic uncertainty reflects equivalent uncertainties of theme and attitude. Here was a self-proclaimed (or at least self-insinuated) 'Virgil' apparently defying the Virgilian rota by returning to his pastoral persona, a persona that would reappear even more daringly just one year later in *The Faerie Queene* itself. What, if anything, was Spenser trying to say about the relationship between pastoral and epic verse, or the role of the heroic poet in Elizabethan England? The thinly disguised introduction of Walter Ralegh (to whom the poem is dedicated) as 'the Shepheard of the Ocean' led early generations of scholars to scour the text for biographical information about both poets (Edwards 1868; Sandison 1934; Adamson and Holland 1969), but it is now generally agreed that what is primarily at issue is the social and political role of the poet and the nature of aristocratic and royal patronage (Mallette 1979; Shore 1985, 105). Jerome S. Dees has recently argued that we should regard Spenser's poem as engaging in 'dialogue' with Ralegh's *Ocean to Scinthia* on these issues (2001).

As I have argued elsewhere, the persona of Colin Clout is less autobiographical than autoreferential, a vehicle for exploring the poet's various concerns rather than a self-portrait (McCabe 1999, xvii). The 'Shepheard of the Ocean' is introduced *as a poet*, but a poet with an ambivalent relationship to the court, at once an insider and an exile. By depicting him in such a way Spenser allows himself to explore Ralegh's many roles—as courtier, colonist and writer—and their complex interrelationship (Greenblatt 1973, 60–2; Oram 1990). This is highly appropriate since Ralegh is also the figure to whom Spenser addressed his only public exposition of the aims and intentions of *The Faerie Queene* (Erickson 1989). His introduction into a poem in which 'Colin' arrives at the court of 'Cynthia' only to find that it can never be 'home', even with such illustrious patronage, is very telling (Comito, 1972). But where then was 'home'? Writing in 1954 C. S. Lewis believed it was Ireland on the grounds that Spenser 'may, as a poet, have needed the very country' (Lewis 1966, 125–6). But this is to confound two quite separate issues. Ovid, as a poet, may have needed Pontus, but Pontus was never his home. The poetics of exile require a distant 'home' and an alien domicile. The centrality of Ireland to the poetic vision of *Colin Clouts* is paradoxically located in its geographical marginality (McCabe 1993, 89–94). Although it has recently been argued that the depiction of Colin's pastoral community evinces Spenser's 'appropriation of a [Gaelic] bardic persona' (Highley 1997, 36; Starke 1998, 137), such claims are undermined by their lack of attention to sixteenth-century bardic verse. Spenser struggled against the formidable social and political power of the 'bardic persona' in *A View of the Present State of Ireland* where he presents the Gaelic 'bard' as the antithesis of the civil English 'poet' even though, or perhaps especially because, 'an undertone of uncertainty struggles through the vocabulary of condemnation' (McCabe 2002, 47). The closed bardic community—highly patronised, professionally assured, politically antagonistic, linguistically alien and socially dangerous—comprised yet another society, another 'centre', from which Colin was perpetually excluded. His experience of Irish society could never be that of a Gaelic bard. The poets with whom he empathises most deeply are those who, like William Alabaster, are unaccountably neglected by the court although deeply engaged in the creation of court myth: 'yet were he knowne to *Cynthia* as he ought, / His Eliseis would be redde anew' (*Colin Clout*, ll. 402–3).

Colin's response, Nancy Jo Hoffman has argued, is to retreat into the world of verse, to compensate for his perceived exclusion 'by exiling others from his private psychological world' (1977, 141). Alternatively, John Bernard regards him as rejecting 'the pastoral of courtly service to Gloriana in favour of one centring on love and personal devotion to a transcendent source of moral and poetic values' (1989, 110). But neither is quite Colin's response. The poem is by no means lacking in the apprehension of transcendence. Colin's eulogies of Gloriana and Cupid, stylistically too 'hie' for pastoral verse ('Such loftie flight, base shepheard seemeth not', l. 618), point forward to the lofty Neo-Platonism of the *Four Hymns*, but the context is radically different. In comparing Ireland with England, Colin contrasts experience with potential rather than achievement: 'For God his gifts there plenteously bestowes, / But gracelesse men them greatly do abuse' (*Colin Clout*, ll. 326–7). The emphasis on 'grace' here and in the preceding lines serves to link the passage, and the poem, to Colin's vision of the Graces in the sixth book of *The Faerie Queene*. What is demonstrated in both works is the acute vulnerability of poets and poetic visions to the wider world. It should not be forgotten that Colin's account of Ireland was published during the Nine Years War as the armies of O'Neill and O'Donnell threatened to pour south. *Colin Clouts Come Home Againe* ends on an ominous note as 'glooming skies', 'warn' the shepherds to 'draw their bleating flocks to rest' (ll. 954–5), a conclusion that echoes that of Virgil's tenth eclogue but significantly excises its reference to homecoming ('ite domum').

Published together with *Colin Clout*, and complementary to its themes of dislocation and loss, was *Astrophel. A Pastorall Elegie upon the Death of the Most Noble and Valorous Knight, Sir Philip Sidney*. The elegy concludes with 'The Doleful Lay of Clorinda' which in turn serves to introduce a further five elegies by Lodowick Bryskett (the 'Thestylis' of *Colin Clout*), Matthew Roydon, Sir Walter Ralegh and Sir Edward Dyer (or possibly Fulke Greville). The first of Bryskett's two contributions was entered in the Stationers' Register as early as 22 August 1587, but there are reasons for believing that the second may have been written in response to *Astrophel* (Tromly 1986). The other three pieces had already appeared in *The Phoenix Nest* (1593) but their republication under the auspices, so to speak, of Colin Clout lends them a new perspective and reflects upon Spenser's own literary and social endeavours (Rollins 1931, 115–32). While it was quite common in earlier editions of Spenser to include the entire collection of poems irrespective of authorship (from the 1611 folio to the 1910 de Selincourt edition, for example), it is only in the relatively recent past that serious attention has been paid to the design and purpose of the collection as a whole. Richard Falco has argued, for instance, that the appearance of *Astrophel* and its companion pieces represents a crucial stage in the evolution of Sidney's personal mythology (1992), and Dennis Kay has suggested that it exercised an even more enduring influence upon the development of the elegiac anthology (1990, 53–66). However, while Kay has argued for Spenser's development of the 'public' genre of elegy into a more introspective and even self-reflexive form, his work has been criticised for concentrating too heavily on literary conventions to the exclusion of wider contextual issues (Kay 1990; Strickland 1992). Spenser's first great pastoral elegy, the November eclogue of *The Shepheardes Calender*, was based upon Clément Marot's *Eglogue sur le Trépas de ma Dame Loyse de Savoye* (1531) and is, therefore, very much in the tradition of the elegy of state. The juxtaposing of *Astrophel* with *Colin Clout* would suggest a similarly public, and political, dimension. We are told that Astrophel 'grew vp fast in goodnesse and in grace' (l. 17) and his loss is consequently emblematic of the graceless condition of contemporary England of which Colin complains. In adapting Ronsard's *L'Adonis* (1563) to the circumstances of Sidney's untimely, and possibly futile, death during Leicester's abortive campaign in the Netherlands, Spenser seems to cast doubt on the wisdom of choosing a military over a literary career (P. E. Bondanella and J. C. Bondanella 1971; Steinberg 1990) while at the same time proffering himself as Sidney's true poetic heir (Falco 1993; Sacks 1985, 51–63). Yet both *Colin Clout* and *Astrophel* implicitly acknowledge the necessity for martial action since 'the pastoral world can neither cure itself nor defend itself against the violence of history' (Sacks 1985, 56).

The title of *Astrophel* seems designed to beg the question of the work's relationship to *Astrophil and Stella*, a work in which, ironically, Sidney complains of being distracted from public policy—including 'How *Ulster* likes of that same golden bit, / Wherewith my father once made it halfe tame' (Sonnet 30)—by amorous verse writing. The issue was difficult and potentially embarrassing. The 'Stella' of Spenser's *Astrophel* is Sidney's widow, Frances Walsingham, but the 'Stella' of the sonnet sequence was Penelope Devereux, wife to Lord Rich and sister to the Earl of Essex, Frances Walsingham's second husband. That is to say, the two 'Stellas' were sisters-in law at the time of publication—and neither had died for the love of Astrophel as the poem suggests. Spenser may be trying to imply (as apparently do most of the other elegists) that Sidney's wife replaced his former lady as his 'guiding star' but, even so, he appears to have engineered another startling conflict between ideal and real situations. It is perhaps significant in this regard that such resolution as the poem affords is attributed to neither of Astrophel's Stellas but to his sister 'Clorinda'. The authorship of her 'Doleful Lay' has sometimes been attributed to Mary Sidney even though there is no external evidence to support this (Herbert 1977, 56; D. Clarke 2000). I favour Spenser's claim in view of his evident skill at ventriloquizing the female voice in the *Complaints* but, whatever the truth of matter, it remains undeniable that the lay is clearly designed, both in theme and in structure, as a counterpart to *Astrophel* which it follows without separate heading or titlepage. It employs the same stanza form (rhyming *ababcc*) and is exactly half the length of the preceding work (108 lines in 18 stanzas to 216 lines in 36 stanzas)—a structural proportion of 2:1 commonly found in epideictic poems and implying, in this instance, a resolution of complaint in the perception of apotheosis (O'Connell 1971). As Alistair Fowler has argued, the number 108 may also constitute an allusion to the number of sonnets in the full text of Sidney's own *Astrophil and Stella* (1970, 174–80). If so, both the perception of such a coincidence, and our sense of its significance serve to illustrate one of the major trends in the modern criticism of the *Colin Clouts* volume: the growing concern with the agency of the author within his works, with the manner in which he employs his various *personae* to locate himself within the traditions in which he believes himself to be writing and to establish an authorial identity through a form of literary 'genealogy' (Falco 1993).

Amoretti and Epithalamion (1595)

Published in the same year as the *Colin Clouts* volume was the *Amoretti and Epithalamion: Written not long since by Edmunde Spenser* (1595), and it is remarkable how consistently the two volumes represent their author. The dedicatory letter to the first volume is addressed from 'my house of *Kilcolman*', and a major concern of the opening poem is Colin's sojourn in Ireland where, according to the Shepeard of the Ocean, 'I was quite forgot' (l. 183). The Irish landscape figures large both in Colin's description of contemporary conditions and in the elaborate etiological fable of the River Mulla (actually the Awbeg). In *Astrophel* the narrator compares the 'forrest' in which Sidney died to Ireland's 'fowle Arlo', the densely wooded Glen of Aherloo in which many colonists had perished, and 'Thestylis' (Bryskett) composes his first elegy for Sidney 'to gurgling sound / Of Liffies tumbling streames' (3–4). The *Amoretti* volume seems to be at pains to cultivate the same sense of distance and dislocation. The dedicatory letter to Sir Robert Needham, recently knighted for his service in Ireland, is signed not by the author but by the publisher William Ponsonby in a gesture that seems to be intended to recall the circumstances under which the *Complaints* had appeared. On this occasion Ponsonby writes 'to gratulate' Needham's 'safe return from Ireland' and judges the dedication to be appropriate because 'this gentle Muse for her former perfection long wished for in Englande, nowe at length crossing the seas in your happy companye...seemeth to make choice of you'. This is to suggest that the *Amoretti* volume has made the same journey in Needham's company that 'Colin' had made in the company of Ralegh. The first of the two commendatory sonnets (probably written by Geoffrey Witney Sr) develops such associations further by lamenting the 'author's' stay in 'forraine landes' and urges him to 'hie thee home'. Sonnet 33 of the *Amoretti* addresses Bryskett (Colin's 'Thestylis') on the incompletion of *The Faerie Queene*, and the *Epithalamion* is set in the same location as Colin's fable of the troubled marriage of Mulla and Bregog. The 'Nymphes of Mulla' are duly called upon to attend the bride (l. 56). This is love in a cold climate and that, I believe, is the point of the Irish setting. Of the various dangers that threaten the marriage bed many may be reckoned amongst the traditional terrors of the night, but others are of a different nature: 'Let no false treason seeke us to entrap' (l. 323). The echoes of *Colin Clouts Come Home Againe* high-light the anxieties of marrying, and writing about marrying, in 'forraine landes' (Fleming 2001).

The *Amoretti* volume ('written', according to its titlepage, 'not long since') has long been interpreted as commemorating Spenser's marriage to his second wife, first identified in 1882 by A. B. Grosart as Elizabeth Boyle, a member of Ireland's New English community and a close relative of Richard Boyle, first Earl of Cork (1882–84, I, 197–202). The sonnet sequence that it contains is remarkable for its time in leading not to despair, irresolution or spiritual sublimation but to the fulfilment and legitimisation of sexual desire in matrimony. Though multi-generic in design, the volume profits from being read as a unity. Its structure is tripartite: eighty-nine sonnets, followed by four mythological 'Anacreontics' and a concluding (if also deliberately inconclusive) *Epithalamion* (Kaske 1978). The central section seems to be designed to explore the nature of the relationship between love and desire through the medium of mythology, reflecting back over the problems of the sonnets and looking forwards to the joy of the *Epithalamion* (Hester 1993). The tripartite structure of the volume may have influenced the presentation of Shakespeare's sonnets (Kerrigan 1991).

A new approach towards the structure and unity of the *Amoretti* volume was signalled in 1960 with the publication of A. Kent Hieatt's *Short Time's Endless Monument: The Symbolism of the Numbers in Edmund Spenser's 'Epithalamion'*. As practised by Hieatt and his successors, numerological criticism is premised upon the centrality of number symbolism to the perceived order and regularity of the created universe in the Platonic, Neo-Platonic, Pythagorean, Hebraic and Christian systems of belief (to mention but the central areas of concern). Such symbolism is self-evidently essential to the Renaissance understanding of alchemy, magic, astrology, music, medicine, scriptural exegesis and architecture, yet its relevance to literature remains highly problematic although it has been argued to pervade a wide range of Elizabethan writings (Røstvig 1963; Roche 1989). As modern numerologists see it, the twenty-four sections of the *Epithalamion* represent the twenty-four hours of Spenser's wedding day, being 11 June 1594 or St Barnabas' Day. The onset of darkness at line 300, 'Now night is come' (at the opening of the fifth line of stanza 17), is held to correspond to the sixteen and a fraction hours of daylight calculated for this date in contemporary almanacs. Similarly, the poem's 365 'long' lines (the sum total of its pentameters and alexandrines) are held to allude to the annual cycle in which the wedding day is contained. The curtailment of the poem's twenty-fourth section into a seven-line envoy has been argued to compensate for the sun's accomplishment of a mere 359 days (corresponding to the number of 'long' lines in the twenty-three full sections) in the time it takes the sphere of fixed stars to complete a full revolution of 360 degrees (Hieatt 1960, 1961; Wickert 1968; Eade 1972; Fowler 1970; Gleason 1994).

Detection of such numerological patterns in the *Epithalamion* led to the extension of the same hermeneutic to the preceding sonnets which were seen to shadow the movements of the ecclesiastical year. The forty-seven sonnets that fall between Sonnet 22 (Ash Wednesday) and Sonnet 68 (Easter Sunday) are seen to correspond to the 47 days that elapse between these two feasts in the liturgical calendar. By the same calculation Sonnet 62 (which concerns the beginning of a new year) falls quite accurately on 25 March (New Year's Day in the old English calendar) thereby affording an accurate date of 31 March for Easter Sunday 1594 (Dunlop 1969, 1970; Hieatt 1973; W. C. Johnson 1974, 1976; Prescott 1986). It has recently been postulated that similar patterns inform the entire volume, serving to unite all three of its sections, but the calculations involved are formidably complex and remain controversial (C. Thompson 1985; Fukuda 1991). Indeed the very precision of such patterns seems to conflict with the elusive quality of the verse and, indeed, of time itself. As the 'moving image of eternity' (in Plato's words), time often defies calibration, and Spenser's representation of its passage typically involves mood, memory and uncertainty (McCabe 1989, 23). The 'holy day' of his marriage involves an intersection of the sacred and the secular, the temporal and the eternal. The 'hours' of the *Epithalamion* are, therefore, of uneven poetic length and their Italianate stanza structures, rhythms and rhyme patterns are constantly varying (McPeek 1936; Warkentin 1990).

I have referred in the paragraphs above to 'Spenser's second marriage' but the phrase raises serious issues about the autobiographical qualities of the *Amoretti* volume and of the nature of the speaker's fictive engagement with it. It has been argued, for example, that we should view the *Amoretti and Epithalamion* as a public rather than a private work (Wells 1984), or that we are in the presence of an elaborate 'persona' distinct from Spenser (Gibbs 1990), or that Spenser is trying to refashion himself as a 'Protestant poet' through the 'reform' of Petrarchan poetics (Klein 1992), or that he is employing amatory courtship to comment upon the politics of courtly advancement (Bates 1992). What is certain, however, is that Sonnets 33 and 80 unmistakably identify the lover as the author of *The Faerie Queene* and use that identification to reflect upon the relationship between epic and amatory verse, a theme that was to be further explored the following year in the proem to the fourth book. Sonnet 33 casts doubt upon Spenser's ability (and also, perhaps, his resolution) to complete his epic project, yet sonnet 80 slyly hints at the imminent publication of the second instalment by referring to 'six books' at a time when the reading public knew only three. Sonnet 33 presents love as an impediment to the poet's ability to endure the 'tædious toyle' of heroic verse, but sonnet 80 suggests that it may renew his vigour to such an extent 'that as a steed refreshed after toyle,/out of my prison I will breake anew'. Patrick Cheney regards this as no less than a reconfiguration of the Petrarchan tradition from one that impedes to one that promotes epic endeavour (1993, 182–4). The proem to 'The Legend of Friendship' similarly seeks to reconcile love and heroism through the popular etymological association of 'eros' and 'heros' (IV Proem.3). In its insistence upon the culmination of courtship in marriage, its recognition that chastity is no less compatible with sexual fulfilment than virginity, and its frank acknowledgement of the cost of heroism in all of its forms, the *Amoretti and Epithalamion* explore many of the major themes of books III–VI of *The Faerie Queene* from Britomart's quest for a husband to Calidore's temptation to forsake heroic quest for amatory pastoral.

Precisely what Spenser is saying in engineering such transgeneric echoes remains a matter of debate. Donald Cheney, for example, has argued for a growing perception on the poet's part that private happiness may be possible only at the cost of public fame (1984), while Catherine Bates detects a more anxious correlation of courtly and amatory aspirations

(1992). It is certainly true, as Arthur Marotti has argued, that themes of 'love' often encode a multitude of public aspirations and discontents (1982). For example, the use of dolphin imagery in Sonnet 38 has plausibly been interpreted as an appeal for patronage encrypted in an appeal for love (Wells 1984). Comparison between the proem to the fourth book of *The Faerie Queene* and the opening of the *Amoretti* yields provocative comparisons in this regard. In the proem Spenser rejects his critics and turns instead to the one reader he professes to value: 'to such therefore I do not sing at all,/But to that sacred Saint my soveraigne Queene…To her I sing of love'. The opening sonnet of the *Amoretti* adopts a similar strategy: 'Leaves, lines, and rymes, seeke her to please alone,/whom if ye please, I care for other none'. The third sonnet apostrophises 'the soverayne beauty which I doo adore' just as the proem addresses the monarch as 'the Queene of love'. Sonnet 74 invites comparison between the 'three Elizabeths'—mother, queen and lover—who comprise Spenser's 'three…graces'. They are discrete figures yet, as the mythological comparison implies, also oddly interchangeable. The proem expresses the hope that Cupid may dispel the queen's 'awfull Maiestie…that she may hearke to love, and read this lesson often', but the speaker of the *Epithalamion* hopes that his wedding night will resemble that on which Jove and Night 'begot Maiesty' (l. 331). In this manner the line between the public and the private is constantly crossed and recrossed. In the *Epithalamion* Cynthia 'peepes' through the newly weds' window and is asked not to 'envy' what she sees but rather, in her role as patron of 'generation', to help 'informe' the 'chast wombe' with 'timely seed'. It is an uneasy moment, this appeal to a goddess of virginity who 'likewise didst love, though now unthought' and was, in fact, once seduced by Endymion (ll. 372–86). There is perhaps more of the complex, contradictory personality of the queen in this stanza than anywhere else in the Spenserian canon: the chaste yet voluptuous virgin goddess, the childless mother of the nation, sublimely solitary yet absurdly envious.

None of this is to detract from the central concerns of love, desire and wedlock. On the contrary, the situation of the barren queen, 'now unthought' in the context of love (in a dizzying multiplicity of senses), only serves to exacerbate the 'unquiet thought' that is 'bred' like a viper in the male speaker's 'wombe' in Sonnet 2. Reed Way Dasenbrock (1985) has argued that the *Amoretti* is conceived as a critique of the 'egotism' of Petrarchan love (as, ironically, was the *Canzoniere*), but that is to underestimate the persistence of the problem. The Petrarchan influence, though strong, is mediated through that of Ronsard, Desportes and Tasso, to name but the most significant (Kastner 1908–09; Kostic 1959). The repetition of Sonnet 35 (comparing the lover's 'hungry eyes' to those of Narcissus) as Sonnet 83 underscores the speaker's difficulty in moving from possessiveness to mutuality, despite the shift from 'I' to 'we' in the concluding stanzas of the *Epithalamion* (Copeland 1988; W. C. Johnson 1993). Throughout the sequence the imagery of hunger and wildness struggles with that of contentment and domestication (Turner 1988). And the Narcissus device is self-reflexive in more senses than one. Narcissus's motto 'so plenty makes me poor' (Sonnets 35 and 83) also supplies Diggon's 'emblem' to the 'September' eclogue of *The Shepheardes Calender*. E. K. comments that 'this poesie I knowe, to haue bene much vsed of the author, and to suche like effecte, as fyrste Narcissus spake it' (p. 127). But the problem is by no means confined to the speaker. The lady too experiences equivalent difficulties: Sonnet 58, 'By her that is most assured to her selfe', may be intended to be understood as spoken by the object of the poet's love, here presented as an autonomous, if ironically ventriloquized, subject. At the heart of the sequence lies the problem of subjectivity itself, the issue of whether sexual desire necessarily entails the objectification of the desired.

Janet MacArthur has argued that Sidney's *Astrophil and Stella* and Spenser's *Amoretti* represent 'two different attitudes to life and love' but the similarities are as interesting as the differences (1989, 12). Both speakers might claim to be 'loving in truth, and faine in verse my love to show,/That the deare She might take some pleasure of my paine' (*Astrophil*, Sonnet 1). In Osgood's concordance to Spenser there occurs the suggestive note, 'Fain. Cf. Feign, which in Spenser sometimes is not easily distinguished in meaning from Fain' (1915, 262). What if we also apply that to Sidney's first line? Is it 'faine' in verse, or 'feign' in verse? His emotional 'truth' is being turned to fiction, the pain of unrequited love transformed into the 'pleasure' of poetry. Similarly, Spenser tells us 'thus I the time with expectation spend,/And faine my griefe with chaunges to beguile' (Sonnet 87). The association established in Petrarch between love and verse, Laura and poetic laurels, is seldom far from the surface: 'The laurel leafe, which you this day doe weare,/gives me great hope of your relenting mind' (Sonnet 28). The lady is therefore enjoined to 'fly no more...from Phebus chace,/but in your brest his leafe and love embrace'. Ideally, at least, 'fained' and 'true' love are not merely reconciled but serve as reciprocal instruments of reconciliation.

It is not usual in classical literature for the speaker of an epithalamion to be the bridegroom himself, and in engineering this break with convention Spenser further signals his concern with the relationship between love and art. He responds to his various classical models in a most personal manner, transforming what was traditionally a third-person celebration (with the important exception of *Canticles*) into a first-person journal—literally so in that it traverses the twenty-four 'hours' of the wedding day (cf. T. M. Greene 1957; P. W. Miller 1970; Tufte 1970; Welsford 1967). As a result, the epithalamion displays many of the preoccupations of the preceding sonnets. The speaker is a poet-groom: 'So Orpheus did for his owne bride,/So I unto my selfe alone will sing' (ll. 16–17). But, as both John Steen (1961) and Joseph Loewenstein (1986) have argued, the phrasing suggests darker possibilities.

According to Ovid, Orpheus's epithalamion was conspicuously ill-omened (*Metamorphoses* 10. 1–10), and the notion of singing a wedding song 'unto my selfe alone'—as the solitary, unrequited lover of *The Shepheardes Calender*'s June eclogue sings to himself (l. 72)—is disconcerting. Set in this context the reference to 'Eccho' in the first refrain inevitably recalls the Narcissus imagery of Sonnets 35 and 83. Although the epithalamion has often been regarded as resolving, if not transcending, the problems of the sonnet sequence, it rather participates in them (Cirillo 1968; Dubrow 1990; Klein 1992). Allusions to such tragic or perilous mythological figures as Tithonus (l. 75) and Medusa (l. 190) reflect the speaker's continuing anxiety. With the advent of nightfall the refrain alters from positive to negative (l. 314) as the verse attempts to ward off the many ills that may be lurking in the shadows (ll. 323–52). But the speaker's personal psyche is also conflicted. He wishes his marriage day to be a 'holy' day (ll. 249, 263) like that celebrated in Canticles but, also like that celebrated in Canticles, to be a day of sensual fulfilment (D. Anderson 1985). A certain tension between the 'sacred ceremonies' of 'th'high altar' (ll. 215–16) and the profane pleasures of the 'bed' (l. 301) is therefore fated to persist. As the concluding 'tornata' indicates, the 'endlesse matrimony' of the poem's middle line (l. 217) is set squarely in the context of transience (Neuse 1966). But transience has powerful artistic uses. Line 217 would not be the middle line were the poem not cut short 'through hasty accidents' (l. 429). Form is discovered even in the breach of form, and the curtal 'song' makes recompense for the inadequacies of the wedding day. The final stanza is reminiscent of the *Complaints* in expressing the hope that even a ruin may prove to be an 'endlesse moniment' if only, paradoxically, for 'short time'.

The developments that I have outlined in the critical approach to the *Amoretti and Epithalamion* may serve as paradigms for the shorter poems as a whole. Generally speaking we have tended to move from the more narrowly philological enquires of the 1930s and 1940s towards a more complex, and often self-problematizing, hermeneutic. The contrast is particularly evident where the apparent subject of interest is similar: for example, in the fields of patronage, persona, bibliography, genre or 'influence'. In the latter case we have tended to find 'subtexts' (Dasenbrock 1985; Dubrow 1995) where formerly there were merely 'sources' (Kastner 1908–09; McPeek 1936). T. M. Greene's *The Light in Troy: Imitation and Discovery in Renaissance Poetry* (1982) is seminal in this area in raising fundamental questions about the nature of literary mimesis particularly, for Spenserian purposes, in relation to Petrarch and Du Bellay. The issue now is not which authors Spenser used, but what form of intertextual dialogue or critique such usage promotes. What is involved, for example, in the use of Petrarch in the *Amoretti* (Klein 1992) or in the sudden turn from the Catholic Du Bellay to the Protestant Du Bartas at the very conclusion of *Ruines of Rome* (Fichter 1981)? At the same time attention has moved from the pursuit of biographical fact, from using literary materials as biographical 'sources' (Koller 1935; Mounts 1952), towards the recognition of the apparently 'auto-biographical' as a peculiar form of rhetorical discourse, as valuable for what it occludes as for what it reveals (D. Cheney 1984). The essays gathered in the fine anthology, *Spenser's Life and the Subject of Biography* (Anderson *et al.* 1996), are indicative of the profound shift in attitude in this area. Similarly, whereas the 'Old' historicism, as represented by Greenlaw (1932) and his school, was disposed to read many of the shorter poems as romans á clef, or to regard their relationship to contemporary power structures as essentially supportive, the 'New' historicism is more apt to detect textual resonances of the contradictory nature of official theory, or of Spenser's conflicted attitude towards it, and to regard the poems as interventionist rather than passive, as political acts in their own right (Montrose 1986a; Sinfield 1992). We have learned to attend to Spenser in his many roles as professional writer (D. L. Miller 1983), secretary (Rambuss 1993) and planter (Hadfield 1997), and generally to acknowledge the colonial context of the shorter poems, to recognise Ireland as a political theme, and as a metaphor for more abstract themes, rather than merely an accident of residence (McCabe 2002).

Modern commentators are far more disposed than their predecessors to distinguish between author and persona, or author and speaker (Gibbs 1990; Bates 1992), and to engage with the rhetorical and bibliographical strategies through which Renaissance writers construct an authorial identity (Helgerson 1983). One extremely significant result of these changes in emphasis has been the belated recognition of the importance of 'paratextual' materials such as title-pages, dedications, printers' letters and such like, materials that were generally ignored by earlier generations of critics or regarded at best as supplying contextual information. Their promotion to 'textual' status has facilitated new approaches to issues such as patronage and commercialism (Owens 2002). Similarly, whereas earlier generations of critics were often content to identify generic boundaries (Renwick 1925; Stein 1934), modern criticism is more concerned with the dynamic functionality of form, with the ways in which generic transgression may encode or promote other forms of transgression, other challenges to 'convention', whether sexual or political (Brown 1999). In retrospect it may well appear that Hallet Smith's essay, 'The Use of Conventions in Spenser's Minor Poems', published, most appropriately, in *Form and Convention in the Poetry of Edmund Spenser* (Nelson 1961, 122–45), marks a transitional point. Most of the contributions to that anthology were concerned with the creation of unity from diversity, coherence from fragmentation, and the subsequent recognition of the *Amoretti and Epithalamion* volume as multi-generic yet thematically, symbolically and even numerologically unified is indicative of its outlook (Kaske 1978; Miola 1980; C. Thompson 1985). Since the 1980s, however, Spenserian criticism has become more concerned with the uses of hybridity *per se* and with the less comforting aesthetics of irresolution

(Goldberg 1981; Cheney 2001). One very welcome by-product of such critical activity has been the growing awareness of the allusive power and wit of Spenser's poetic diction. Largely neglected by the New Critics of the 1930s in favour of the 'metaphysical' school (Radcliffe 1996, 172–4), Spenser's language is again beginning to be appreciated for its subtlety, precision and wordplay, qualities that are, perhaps, even more highly developed in the shorter poems than in the epic verse (Prescott 1986, 1994). We are rediscovering the pleasure of close, localised readings, and such rediscovery reminds us of our debt to the critical heritage. The tireless attention of such pioneering editors as W. L. Renwick (1928), C. G. Osgood and H. G. Lotspiech (1943, 1947) to the linguistic and allusive detail of the shorter poems provided an immensely rich storehouse for future generations of readers. And they themselves drew heavily on the work of earlier commentators from John Jortin (1734) to the redoubtable A. B. Grosart (1882–84). By attending to how Spenser was read in the past we learn to question our own critical criteria. It is sobering to remember, for instance, that the 'modern' perception of Elizabeth I's presence within the *Amoretti* was first bruited by George Chalmers in 1799 in a wholly different context but one which equally necessitated a 'political' reading (1799, 29–37)—he was trying to prove that Shakespeare was never so immoral as to write 'amourous' sonnets to a 'male object' but addressed them to the queen, emulating Spenser, his 'rival poet'. A salutary reminder, this, of how far an agenda may dictate a 'reading'.

In summary one can say that modern criticism, and particularly that of the last four decades, has engaged the critical tradition in an increasingly sophisticated debate in order to facilitate a new understanding of the importance of the shorter poems. What were previously categorised as 'minor' works, in every sense of the term, are now perceived to be deeply concerned with the major preoccupations of Spenser's artistic and political life. They are seen to employ their astonishing generic diversity to interrogate the aims and ideals of epic poetry while at the same time providing perspectives on England's Eliza, and Eliza's Colin, that *The Faerie Queene* is precluded from supplying. We have learned that they are no mere appendages to the 'great work' but vital, constituent elements of a greater canon in which it, and they, are contained and contextualised.

Further reading

Bernard, J. D. 1989. *Ceremonies of Innocence: Pastoralism in the Poetry of Edmund Spenser*, Cambridge: Cambridge University Press.
Brown, R. D. 1999. *'The New Poet': Novelty and Tradition in Spenser's Complaints*, Liverpool: Liverpool University Press.
Cheney, D. 'Spenser's Fortieth Birthday and Related Fictions', *SSt* 4 (1984 for 1983), 3–31.

Cheney, P. 1993. *Spenser's Famous Flight: A Renaissance Idea of a Literary Career*, Toronto: University of Toronto P.

Gibbs, D. 1990. *Spenser's 'Amorett': A Critical Study*, Brookfield: Scolar P.

Hieatt, A. K. 1960. *Short Time's Endless Monument*, Port Washington NY: Kennikat.

Hoffman, N. J. 1977. *Spenser's Pastorals: 'The Shepheardes Calender' and 'Colin Clout'*, Baltimore: Johns Hopkins University Press.

Johnson, W. C. 1990. *Spenser's 'Amoretti': Analogies of Love*, Lewisburg: Bucknell University Press.

Kay, D. 1990. *Melodious Tears: The English Funeral Elegy from Spenser to Milton*, Oxford: Clarendon P.

Loewenstein, J. F. 1986. 'Echo's Ring: Orpheus and Spenser's Career', *ELR* 16: 287–302.

MacArthur, J. H. 1989. *Critical Contexts of Sidney's 'Astrophil and Stella' and Spenser's 'Amoretti'*, Victoria, BC: English Literary Studies, University of Victoria.

McCabe, R. A. 1993. 'Edmund Spenser: Poet of Exile', 1991 Lectures and Memoirs, *Proceedings of the British Academy*, 80: 73–103.

———. 2002. *Spenser's Monstrous Regiment: Elizabethan Ireland and the Poetics of Difference*, Oxford: Oxford University Press.

Pigman, G. W. 1985. III, *Grief and English Renaissance Elegy*, Cambridge: Cambridge University Press.

Rasmussen, C. J. 1981. ' "How Weak Be the Passions of Woefulness": Spenser's *Ruines of Time*', *SSt* 2: 159–81.

Shore, D. R. 1985. *Spenser and the Poetics of Pastoral: A Study of the World of Colin Clout*, Montreal: McGill-Queen's University Press.

Smith, H. 1961. 'The Use of Conventions in Spenser's Minor Poems', in W. Nelson, ed., *Form and Convention in the Poetry of Edmund Spenser*, New York: Columbia University Press, 122–45

Stein, H. 1934. *Studies in Spenser's 'Complaints'*, New York: Oxford University Press.

10
The Faerie Queene (1596)
Theresa Krier

There is no denying that much of the 1596 *Faerie Queene*—for the
purposes of this essay, Books IV, V, and VI—is hard going. Book IV, the
Book of Friendship, leads readers through a tangled retelling and elaboration
of Chaucer's Squire's Tale and Knight's Tale, through increasingly violent
and ugly erotic episodes reflecting upon the dangers to which life in any
polity exposes the individual; through disquieting attacks on age and aged
characters; through precursor texts fascinated with death (Lucretius'
gorgeous philosophical poem *De rerum natura* and Statius' epic the *Thebaid*)
before it eases readers into the mythic richness of the Temple of Venus, the
abundance of the Marriage of Rivers, or the charm of the sea-epyllion of
Marinell and Florimell's union in the aquatic realm of the sea gods (cantos
x–xii). Book V, the Book of Justice, notoriously repels readers with its
violent, unsubtle protagonist Artegall, his iron henchman Talus, and their
exhausting, morally dubious efforts to enforce justice and liberate innocent
peoples from sadistic tyrants through military action. Book VI, the Book of
Courtesy, has often seemed to readers a guilty pleasure, retreating from the
harsh realities of *realpolitik* into folktale motifs, pastoral truancies, and
over-simple solutions to the problems of establishing community. Indeed
the general acknowledgment of earlier criticism's discontent with the 1596
books, and citations of those who have tried to rectify this situation have
become topos in themselves; scholar after scholar begins as Graham Hough
does in 1962:

> Complaints about the formal deficiencies of Book IV—and Books V and
> VI, too—have been even more vocal than those about Book III.... There
> is no quest; there is no single knight. Cambel and Triamond who give
> their names to the whole are the heroes only of an episode that is not
> central and has no general consequences. The illustration of the virtues
> of friendship seems faint and fluctuating at first sight, and the attempt to
> find an orderly narrative structure seems more completely doomed to
> failure here than in any other part of *The Faerie Queene*. The attempt has

nevertheless been made by Notcutt [1926] presumably on the principle of achieving a general victory by defending the least promising case. (Hough 1962, 180)

And yet... and yet. Books IV, V, and VI are as full as those of 1590, perhaps more full, with mythopoeic nymphs, satyrs, and deities; with babies, bears, shepherds, kind hermits and wild men, sheltering temples, benignly maternal personified virtues, and those endlessly alive woods. Moreover, Books IV–VI offer narrative exhilarations, intellectual pleasures, mythographic complexities. Readers have long speculated that Spenser may have been disappointed or disenchanted—with his professional prospects in the service of the English court, with Queen Elizabeth, her aging and her conduct of relations with Spenser's friends and her Ireland policy. But these days we say (with increasingly nuanced demonstrations) that Spenser sustains a lively willingness to *examine the conditions* of disappointment and disenchantment; to discover what poetico-narrative techniques of voice, diction, discourse, and tempo can allow him to think about brute force and political dirt; to risk the most harrowing or tired stories for their surprising payoffs in richness of orchestration and potentialities of idea. Readers differ widely on the effects of the 1596 poem's investigations of narrative conditions, but surely no generation raised on film and television genre series or on speculative fiction—familiar, that is, with narrative's ways of making something of narrative exhaustion, aging topoi, and the inundations of the relentless historical world—will find alien Spenser's investment in a never-ending story or our continuing conversation about it. In this chapter, I trace alternating currents of disappointment and engagement with the difficulties of the 1596 books, and at the same time a gradual movement toward recognition of their complex achievements. The long arcs of scholarship on the 1596 text are moving witnesses to readers' attraction to the poem, an attachment that springs not only from evident, easily argued pleasures of reading but also from more difficult effects in the reader, such as bewilderment, puzzlement, anger, disidentification, defensive boredom, resistance, even destruction. That the friendship between Spenser's poem and its readers in the last long century evokes and survives such a range of response is remarkable in itself, and suggests that we are still catching up with Spenser in understanding the nature of such friendship between readers and poems.

"Great matter growing of beginning small"

With this phrase from IV.ii.54, Spenser describes the way he will end one canto (a "beginning small") and start another (which will be "great matter"). The line offers a rationale for the poet's sense of narrative unit and proportion. But it also describes how his ceaseless, interlocking stories

unfold from the inner logic and movement of single stanzas—how the
Spenserian stanza gives rise to narrative possibilities.

When Britomart observes the embrace of Amoret and Scudamour
in the well-known lines following their hermaphroditic union at the
close of the 1590 *Faerie Queene*, she discovers in herself a little envious
disappointment:

> So seemd those two, as growne together quite,
> That *Britomart* halfe enuying their blesse,
> Was much empassiond in her gentle sprite,
> And to her selfe oft wisht like happinesse,
> In vaine she wisht, that fate n'ould let her yet possesse.

(III.xii.46 [1590])

When, in the 1596 *Faerie Queene*, Spenser unbinds the narrative threads of
1590 and launches his protagonists on new adventures, he carries all of
them into that future on a thematic current of disappointment, uncertainty,
anxiety, turbulent astonishment, and despair:

> But when the victoresse arriued there,
> > Where late she left the pensife *Scudamore*,
> > With her owne trusty Squire, both full of feare,
> > Neither of them she found where she them lore:
> > Thereat her noble hart was stonisht sore;
> > But most faire *Amoret*, whose gentle spright
> > Now gan to feede on hope, which she before
> > Conceiued had, to see her owne deare knight,
> Being thereof beguyld was fild with new affright.
>
> But he sad man, when he had long in drede
> > Awayted there for *Britomarts* returne,
> > Yet saw her not nor signe of her good speed,
> > His expectation to despaire did turne,
> > Misdeeming sure that her those flames did burne;
> > And therefore gan aduize with her old Squire,
> > Who her deare nourslings losse no lesse did mourne,
> > Thence to depart for further aide t'enquire:
> Where let them wend at will, whilest here I doe respire.

(III.xii.44–45[1596])

The two motives of envy and disappointment, small things beginning small
in these individual hearts, will unfold and become the great matter of the
poem's latter three books: its investigation of aggression toward the self and

toward the other in the very attempt to forge bonds and make a society. Disappointment and envy are complex affects in the discourse of heroic narrative generally, and especially so in the form of chivalric romance. In Spenser's Books IV–VI these conditions become the ground of fury against the self and of emulation and competition with others. Idealization followed by disenchantment—a dynamic explored with subtlety and range throughout Spenser's work, and perhaps most riskily in the 1596 books (see Gross 1985)—gives rise to aggressivity directed toward oneself. Aspiration to community through Friendship, Justice, and Courtesy (the titular virtues of Books IV, V, and VI) mysteriously provokes violence against the very parties with whom community is hoped for; the incessant clamor of the self for an enlarged, more gratified sense of life somehow also becomes a passion for death. This is sometimes true of the 1590 *Faerie Queene*—Miller (1988) argues this most forcefully—but in the 1596 books, Spenser risks sustained narrative speculations on the violence of such forces, and their engendering of violence in expanding social spheres.

Scholarship on the 1596 *Faerie Queene* was itself for a long time marked by perplexed disappointment—it would not be too strong to call it disenchantment. Even now, when the complex maneuvers of narratology, deconstruction, feminist and gender studies, psychoanalysis, and studies of nation and empire have stirred up productive readings, the critical scene is one of alternating indictments and reclamations of Spenser's Books IV, V, and VI. Yet the 1596 poem—willing to bore through the rock of narrative exhaustion, through unlikely precursor texts, through dark and bloody topical material, through disappointment and violent disenchantment— returns repeatedly to narrative exhilarations. Notwithstanding more recent concerns about gender, imperialism, continental politics, Ireland, and the question of Britain more widely, the best surveys of the books remain those in the 1990 *Spenser Encyclopedia* (Nohrnberg on Book IV, O'Connell on Book V, Tonkin on Book VI) as well as those in the *Variorum* and A. C. Hamilton editions of the poem. The narrative of debate leading up to and beyond those formidable pieces of scholarship, however, can offer new insights not only into the history of Spenser criticism but also into the conflicts within these disputed texts themselves.

Disappointments

In the late nineteenth century and the early twentieth, critics lamented changes from the first three books, changes which saddened them as signs of the falling off, or backing away, of a great poetic mind. Thus Herbert Ellsworth Cory in 1917:

> As the architectural lineaments of *The Faerie Queene* become, in the later books, more and more confused it would be an error for even the most

acute and ingenious scholar to attempt to work out the supposed allegorical significance of every detail.... As he strove courageously but tragically to fight against disillusioning realities, death and corruption, the allegory must have become at times but enigmatic gropings.... The political allegory is hopelessly episodical; the moral allegory is capricious and, when vital, almost invariably bitter. At the same time the fantastic and almost meaningless romances which we saw increasing in the third book grow more and more numerous and elaborate and confusing. (Cory 1917, 256; see also Church 1879, Lewis 1936, Hamilton 1961)

Cory declares Book IV "chaotic in structure... like a sky confused with cloud masses" (Cory 1917, 290); Lewis calls Book V "a stony plateau—for the fifth book would have been severe even if it had been successful" (Lewis 1936, 350). In 1962, Graham Hough says of Book V that

invention and narrative power are weaker [than elsewhere in the poem], the verse is often flat, the peaks of allegorical or pictorial concentration are lacking. The thematic material is less deeply felt than in I or III; it is largely social and political, and the historical allegory for the first time becomes quite inescapable... for much of the time we are contemplating a thin allegorical covering over a somewhat distorted version of particular historical events. (Hough 1962, 191; see also O'Connell 1977, 13 and MacCaffrey 1976, 336)

In 1968, Roger Sale titles a chapter "What Happened to *The Faerie Queene*" and takes it as his task to articulate and account for the poem's disenchantment and his own disappointment: "the parts undoubtedly written after 1590 all show that something 'has happened' to the poem.... The dourness expressed here in the proem to Book V is something new, marring, and troubling; beneath it is a resentment and an impulse to satire that can only alter the bearings of a poem like *The Faerie Queene*" (Sale 1968, 163, 165). J. C. Maxwell (1952) thinks that the narrative management of Book VI "betrays a mind not fully engaged by what it is doing." The narratives of Book IV are the least assured and most confused; in Book V history has embittered the poet, or made him careless, or he was infected by the evil policies that he enforced in Ireland; Book VI goes soft or dream-like, escaping from the hard realities of court life to the country-side or to fairy-tale motifs. To turn-of-the-century critics and those in their vein, Spenser's firm, epic-based structure gives way to mere episodic sequence; his romance world has been soured by the historical; at other times his over-luxuriant romance imagination grows even wilder and more tangled. It can be no accident that the best exception to these works objecting to the 1596 poem is also the best-informed in continental poetry and philosophy (Renwick 1925), and that one of the best refutations to such objections, James Nohrnberg's 1976 *The Analogy of* The Faerie Queene, is written by a Fryean reader with an inexhaustible appetite for poetic amplitude, narrative recurrence, and the significances of repletion. Yet the best of the disappointed critics also know that something eludes them in the 1596 books, and they make valiant efforts to give credit. Cory's long complaint includes what seems to be a reminder to himself: "but as we consider these things we must allow not only for disintegration in *The Faerie Queene* but for our own incapacity in reading Spenser" (257); he cites Bailey who charges Spenser with weaknesses and excess but envies him the poetic mind: Spenser "forgets that poetry, if it is to be a fine art, must dwell in Cosmos and not in Chaos, that order and limit are necessary parts of the constitution of the human mind, that the most poetical sort of confusion is still confusion and not creation, and that the end of confusion is weariness and sleep. Still these are faults that the rest of the world may envy. Just as we are not ethereal enough to live long with Shelley, we are not mobile enough, we have not enough of music in us to keep mind and ear long traveling with Spenser" (cited in Cory 1917, 257). The cloudy Book IV also has "clean shafts and pillars of the sunshine of a young and wilful spring" (Cory, 290); the maligned Book V is, in its very first canto, "inlaid with one jeweled episode" (Cory, 260). Professional readers of the late nineteenth and early twentieth centuries can be swift to respond to any moments that could please in these troubled books.

Finding fulfillments

For these readers, such moments of strength tended to be characterologically vivid, or tender, or obviously assured like the first face-to-face meeting between Britomart and Artegall, or symbolically dense like the Temple of Isis or the Mount Acidale episodes. If Spenser pursues the matter of an aggressivity originally against the self, and the paradox that characters most often come to this state in the pursuit of elusive love objects, he does so through narratives developed from the mythopoeic and characterological plenitude of the 1590 poem: Britomart, Florimell, Amoret, Belphoebe, and the males who encounter them—Artegall, Arthur, Timias, Marinell, Scudamour, Proteus, and Braggadochio. These narrative threads, cast into the future from the 1590 accounts, gradually introduce additional characters endowed with forms of interiority that make for a vivid array: Radigund, Tristram, Serena, the Salvage Man, Briana, Calepine, Pastorella, Matilda, among many others. These character-driven narrative threads have elicited powerful, shrewd analyses, especially in studies of eros and, after the rise of feminist and gender literary approaches, gender and erotic force. C. S. Lewis in the 1936 *Allegory of Love* was already reading characters, places, and "allegorical cores" with a lively, subtle sense of their medieval and especially their Italian matrices (Lewis 1936, 297–366). Throughout the middle decades of the twentieth century, studies of the whole *Faerie Queene* provided nuanced, often exhilarating accounts of the structure of the whole, its articulation of parts, and the functions of individual books and episodes (Hamilton 1961, Hough 1962, Nelson 1963, K. Williams 1966, Evans 1970). The disappointment of early readers—who from our vantage point may seem blinkered by a late Victorian medievalism and a neglect of the diversity of epic and romance traditions engaged by Spenser—never entirely disappears from the critical scene, but it does make room for developments in the symbolic structures of allegory. In this as in so many ways C. S. Lewis is the pivot between early and mid-century work: *The Allegory of Love* and the posthumously published *Spenser's Images of Life* (see also Lewis 1944, 1966), along with Rosemond Tuve's powerful *Allegorical Imagery* made possible the sturdy structural sense argued vigorously by A. C. Hamilton or lyrically by Kathleen Williams. Along with work on Renaissance iconography (by Ernst Gombrich, Jean Seznec, Edgar Wind, and Northrop Frye) they also laid the foundations for serious close readings of individual books in studies by Aptekar (1969), Berger (1957), D. Cheney (1966), Dunseath (1968), Fletcher (1971), MacCaffrey (1976), Nohrnberg (1976, 1990), Roche (1964), Tonkin (1972, 1990), and Williams (1967). All these works on what Frye (1963) calls "the structure of imagery" yield strong readings, opening up the complexity and iconographical richness of the poetry, especially of core cantos and of episodes focused on characters. Moreover they unfailingly add to the Fryean focus on narrative motifs, myth, image, archetype, and structure an informed attention to language, something in which Frye had virtually no interest. (The familiar point that Frye is not much interested in language ought to be more damning than it is. In fact, the generative power of what he does care about has been enormous; we have yet to unfold all the arguments and understandings implicit in even his brief remarks; some combination of Frye on romance and Lewis on story and faerie is essential to catching new readers of Spenser and holding them.)

Angus Fletcher's transformative 1971 book *The Prophetic Moment* provides a major contribution to our sense of big narrative poems by positing, for *The Faerie Queene*, five "typological matrices"—Biblical, Virgilian, Ovidian, Galfridian, and Hermetic—which structure and pervade the narrative as overlapping spheres that constantly shift and change their relationships to one another (Fletcher 1971, 57–132). This notion of permeating and permeable matrices is perhaps the most flexible and productive way of accounting for the challenging discursive mixes of the poem's 1596 books. Fletcher devotes half of his 1971 work to Book V, pursuing the typological matrices through which Spenser explores the difficult imperatives of the prophetic voice:

> The Fifth Book plots a troubled movement from chaos to cosmos, from desolate piratical violence to a cruel, taut, repressive, yet ever hopeful political settlement, which in turn will yield to the promise of Book VI:

an order of ceremonial grace. Every stage of this advance is threatened by divisive forces, and because (lacking utopian conditions) government remains balance of power, this poem of justice itself remains tragically poised between hope and despair. Book V recounts the liberation of Irena, but does not predict, though it does prophesy or "speak out for," a final peace. Beginning with its frequently ambivalent mythic materials, Book V enjoins an attitude of prophetic understanding, we might even say, prophetic sympathy. Yet even this impatient, wide-ranging fiction cannot contain all the main forces of political change in Spenser's imperialist world. The story of Artegall and Talus is flawed with doubt and ominous uncertainty, and while these are the normal tones of all major prophetic utterance, they have never comforted Spenser's readers. They testify that in the Legend of Justice ... Spenser wants to enforce the interdependence of justice and man's historical awareness. Book V ... no less than the other Books of *The Faerie Queene* is involved with the problem of conscience. (136–7)

No one has bettered Fletcher's learning and his ear for the individual word as well as for large narrative matrices; his development of Northrop Frye's formulation of a tragic hero entering a romance world (Fletcher 296; Frye 1957, 36–7) continues to generate subtle arguments about the thorny relationships of history to fiction in the 1596 poem—a point to which we will return—and allows us purchase on the way Spenser uses mixed genre to explore disappointment and disenchantment. Yet even Fletcher, who finds so much richness in the generic, discursive, and iconographic matrices of the poem's 1596 books, can slide into a sense that Spenser's disappointments and disenchantments lead to a disappointing poetry: "the story ... is flawed with doubt and ominous uncertainty" (136–7). Subsequent studies, however, gradually move to suggest that Spenser willingly engages or risks disappointment in order to find what narrative and poetry are possible after disenchantment with the prophetic voice and with feminine power.

There were demurrals from the massive influence of Northrop Frye and the very notion of structure, the most significant and influential being that of Paul Alpers in *The Poetry of* The Faerie Queene (1967; see also Sale 1968):

Books III and IV have traditionally been regarded as without structure, "merely episodic," because manifestly neither has a plot. However recent criticism has treated imagery (or alternatively, "myth") as structuring reality in these books. But consider what happens when Northrop Frye ... attempts to explain the ending of Book IV:

Painful or not, it is love that makes the world go round, that keeps the cycle of nature turning, and it is particularly the love of Marinell and

Florimell, whose names suggest water and vegetation, that seems linked to the natural cycle. Florimell is imprisoned under the sea during a kind of symbolic winter in which a "snowy" Florimell takes her place. Marinell is not cured of his illness until his mother turns from "watry gods" to the sun, and when he sees Florimell he revives

> As withered weed through cruell winters tine,
> That feeles the warmth of sunny beames reflection,
> Liftes vp his head, that did before decline
> And gins to spread his leafe before the faire sunshine

(4.12.34)

Alpers objects, "here, as elsewhere in his criticism, one feels that this is the poem as Frye would have written it; it is certainly not the poem that Spenser wrote" (Alpers 119–20). Alpers argues consistently against the notion of structure, with its strong implications of architectural firmness and foreconceit, and for the alternative of "organization," by which one canto or book is instead linked to another in a continual forward momentum. He also insists on the *rhetorical* quality of Spenser's verse, which means two things at least: (a) "In turning narrative materials into stanzas of poetry, Spenser's attention is focused on the reader's mind and feelings and not on what is happening within his fiction" (Alpers, 5); (b) we are constantly aware that Spenser is virtuosically performing, and transforming, genres and forms: "In reading *The Faerie Queene*, our delight is expressed by 'How fine a catalogue of trees!' 'How moving a love lament!' 'How lifelike a description of a tapestry!' 'How challenging or attractive a version of pastoral!'" (331).

Most influentially and with the most minute attention, Alpers (1967, 1977) argues that the narrator cannot be a dramatically consistent figure nor a character; rather the narrative voice speaks the truth of each unfolding moment in the narrative. This is a beautiful but surprisingly difficult, counter-intuitive proposal, one that later criticism has had to work out again and again, only to lose sight of it once more, and I want to linger with its peculiarity for a moment because it suggests so much about the allure and elusiveness of Spenser's narrative verse. It is difficult to speak about the poem in the classroom without handy recourse to a dramatically consistent narrator; while we can sometimes—as in Berger's work (discussed below)— grasp the narrative voice as belonging now to one episode's genre, now to another's, it is much harder to think consistently that narrative voice is in fact not attributed to a person. This is what I think Alpers is arguing, and it takes him onto some paths of thought that we still have not addressed fully. Thus in the 1967 book Alpers argues that, contrary to what one might assume about poetry—contrary to the way we read Shakespeare or Dante or

Milton—we ought not read too closely for minute verbal echoes across long stretches:

> if the reader remembers every verbal detail in a book of *The Faerie Queene*, he will be overcome with confusion, rather than awed by a sense of complex imaginative unity. . . . Spenser demands and rewards alert and detailed reading. But he does not expect our span of attention and retention to last for more than about a canto, or at most two. (124–5)

Again, "in *The Faerie Queene*, the details of expression are to be referred solely to the immediate poetic context in which they occur" (128). Alpers demonstrates with pairs of distant stanzas that, he argues, actually mislead us if we remember one while reading the other. But he can argue this at all because he takes seriously, and tries to account for, an inescapable aspect of Spenser's language that almost no one has addressed, Spenser's constant recourse to phrasal and literary commonplaces (the interesting exception is Anderson 1996). "For Spenser the meanings of locutions and formulas are inherent in them, and are as independent of a putative speaker as they are independent of specific dramatic situations within the poem" (96);

> in most poetry, apprehending so full a meaning requires a conscious recognition of its various elements. In Spenser the mind holds the phrase without analyzing it, and as if various meanings were resonances of the single verbal formula. . . . In using commonplace formulas, Spenser is able to count on an immediacy and obviousness that, far from robbing them of poetic effectiveness, is essential to the particular fusion of lucidity and suggestiveness that he achieves. (48)

Alpers and other critics interested in the narrative voice(s) of the poem come to perceive what readers earlier in the century had not. Where earlier critics had often taken the chivalric, political, and allegorical narratives as straightforward reflections of a disillusioned poet, the new scholarship gradually registered an understanding that the 1596 books bespeak an intensified, more explicit treatment of the conditions of storytelling *per se*. This understanding emerges in large-scale conversation by scholars with breadth of reading in epic and romance-epic (Berger (1961b) and many other essays; Durling (1965); Alpers (1967, 1977); Anderson (1971a); Hinton (1974); Braden (1975); Goldberg (1981); MacColl (1989); Bellamy (1994); and Nohrnberg (1976, 1990)). It would be too simple to think of it as a chronological development in criticism: it is a strand of thought that is picked up and re-examined by generations of the most perceptive readers of the poem. The notion of embracing the difficulty of narrative process, however, is one that is expressed with increasing confidence over the decades of critical engagement with the 1596 text.

Welcoming narrative frustrations

The influence of Northrop Frye, at once generative and provoking, is perhaps strongest in Frye's powerful condensing of the genre of romance—his supreme fiction—with the Freudian notion of the pleasure principle. Alpers' criticism of Frye and others in his vein is that they impose on the poem Frye's Blakean master-plot of the imagination's drive toward fulfillment in creating "a city, a garden, a home, a bed of love." In some ways drawing on what was implicit in Alpers' model (although also departing from it in radical ways), Jonathan Goldberg's 1981 *Endlesse Worke: Spenser and the Structures of Discourse* proceeds relentlessly from structuralist and deconstructive premises, and works hard the writings of Barthes, Derrida, and Lacan. By these means he makes much of the 1596 poem's narrative fractures, undoings, deferrals, losses, and refusals of fulfillment; he makes possible for the first time the articulation of entirely new kinds of responses, arising from the fierce exhilarations of readerly *frustration* and its invitation of increasingly intense wrestling with the text:

> Spenser's text offers continuous disequilibrium, frequent disruptions in narration, and characters who exist to disappear. Most often, when criticism takes stock of such traits of the narrative, it considers them as problems that could only be elucidated by pointing to some principle other than narration. Thematic unity, rhetorical addresses, allegorical meanings, are called forward in the service of explanation—often with the intention of explaining away—these disturbing features of the text. The frustrations of reading are thereby neglected, and so is something vital to the nature of Spenserian narration. (Goldberg 1981, xi)

The poem's very frustrations continually allow "the possibility of beginning anew, refiguring, re-entering, crossing normative limits in ways that keep narration going, but going where?" (Goldberg 1981, 19). The frustrations also catch, implicate, and situate the reader insofar as they make us aware of the kinds of desire generated by the text (see Gross (1982) for a review of Goldberg that emphasizes "the moral risk and inventiveness" (xvi) of Spenser's 1596 books).

The "endlesse worke" of Goldberg's title is a quotation from the opening line of Book IV Canto xii—a moment where Spenser looks back at the river marriage of the previous canto and contemplates the awful task of counting "the seas abundant progeny." In contrast to the "templar" structures seized on by critics in search of "fulfillment," those who embrace narrative frustration tend to fix on such acknowledgments of openendedness. The "Marriage of Thames and Medway" of IV.xi is, to adapt Fletcher's terms, a "labyrinthine" as much as "templar" moment. Set at the bottom of the sea in the Hall of Proteus (that archetypal shape-shifter and avoider of easy answers) the canto sees the mingling of all the rivers of the world but never actually witnesses the closure of the ceremony itself:

> So both agreed, that this their bridale feast
>> Should for the Gods in *Proteus* house be made;
>> To which they all repayr'd, both most and least,
>> Aswell which in the mightie Ocean trade,
>> As that in riuers swim, or brookes doe wade.
>> All which not if an hundred tongues to tell,
>> And hundred mouthes, and voice of brasse I had,
>> And endlesse memorie, that mote excell,
> In order as they came, could I recount them well.

(IV.xi.9)

The numerological analysis of Alastair Fowler (1964, 184–91) had discovered complex patterns in the catalogue that follows; for Fletcher (reaching back to Lewis) it is a moment at which there is "a union of epiphanic fixation and processional flow" (1971, 52). For those whose writing anticipates or follows Goldberg, however, it is the impossibility of order, the elusiveness of ending, that becomes the primary experience of the episode. After quoting the above stanza he tells us that "the narrator enters—to his loss—the violation of limit and the loss of voice to summon up the 'endlesse memorie' stored in other texts, and whose end he can never reach" (Goldberg 1981, 71). This, for Goldberg, encapsulates the condition of the poem. For while *The Faerie Queene* will never "represent the fullness and order of the world; it will represent the fullness of the *word*, and being endless will recount in its repletion and loss" (71, emphasis mine).

Goldberg offers one of the most productive rethinkings of the second installment's narrative: making us think about the elusive sources of the poet's authority as well the playfully readerly qualities of the narrative he has produced. Harry Berger's proliferating essays (1961a,b, 1968, 1989, and many more) have also been influential. They pose a particular problem for the historian of criticism because—while there is much that draws them together as a coherent vision of the poem—they also span the decades and respond acutely to the conditions of scholarly debate at the individual moments of their composition. The earlier pieces built on the models of Hough, Roche, and Hamilton and were an acknowledged influence on Fletcher, while the most recent draw directly on the readings of Goldberg. What remains a consistent feature of his approach is its focus on the "retrospective" nature of Spenser's narration: the way in which his poetry casts the reader's mind back—through devices such as archaism, irony, allusion, and repetition—to earlier episodes within or outside *The Faerie Queene* (see Montrose, "Introduction" in Berger 1988). He therefore differs in important respects from Alpers and Goldberg, but also shares something of their model of cumulative readerly experience. Berger thus embraces narrative frustration, and in doing so offers a mode of interpretation that proves especially rewarding for the second installment of *The Faerie Queene*. For him too the "Marriage of Thames and Medway" provides a self-reflexive instance of the action of composition: "the effect of this verbal pageant is a panorama which is not merely spatial and temporal but also cultural and mental—a panorama which could only be rendered in the medium of language because its sole locus is the poetic imagination and its sole time of occurrence is the sophisticated modern *now* of poetic utterance" (1968, 210). Instead of the declaration of incapacity ("not if an hundred tongues to tell") quoted by Goldberg, Berger offers the stanza which follows:

> Helpe therefore, O thou sacred imp of *Jove*,
>> The noursling of Dame *Memorie* his deare,
>> To whom those rolles, layd up in heaven above,
>> And *records of antiquitie* appeare,
>> To which no wit of man may comen neare;
>> Helpe me to tell the names of all those floods,
>> And all those Nymphes, which then assembled were
>> To that great banquet of the watry Gods,
> And all their sundry kinds, and all their hid abodes.

(IV.xi.10, italics in line 4 Berger's)

For Berger the poem is here "set before us as itself the culmination of the continual process of revising which began aeons ago . . . the latest form which the ancient reservoirs have nourished with their perpetual supply of vital energy" (1968, 210). That process might be said to drive the whole of the second installment, in which an explicitly modern narrative voice is repeatedly given the task of transmitting archaic subject matter. Certainly it lies at the heart of Berger's concepts of "revisionary play" and "Spenserian dynamics."

Berger's work draws equally on the strength of the narrative-frustration line of thought and the strengths of more structural, symbolic lines of thought, though he comes to be suspicious of gender, religious, and political assumptions in mid-century symbolic structures. The mix of genres and discourses continues as a productive problem in reading Spenser; Braden (1975), van Es (2002a), E. Fowler (2003), and Bellamy (2004b) explore the Marriage of Rivers and the union of Florimell and Marinell for their negotiations of, or their staging of fatigues, strains, clashes, and constantly renewed refreshments among discourses of poetic history, philosophy, law, political theory, chorography, history, or historiography. The riddle of the narrative voice in the poem, most frustratingly elusive and inconsistent in the 1596 books, also elicits a great deal of sophisticated, detailed work, from the 1960s onward. Among them is Anderson (1971a), who concentrates on IV.viii and its historical, topical pressures to argue for the poet's constantly shifting responsiveness involving shifts in style and speaker and the abandonment of half-completed plots. She, more than any other critic, may be said to develop the insights offered by Alpers. MacColl (1989) deploys Terence Cave to discuss the 1596 poem's celebration of narrative vigor, abundance, and buoyancy even, or especially, when acknowledging fatigue and apparent exhaustion of resources. She sees the poem as "the most striking Elizabethan expression of the principle of *copia* ... inexhaustible not just in its openness to interpretation and its resistance to the application of fixed meanings but in its enormous textual productivity" (27). Yet "the pursuit of copiousness and variety ... is both serious and joyful, and ... despite the demonstration, and the honest acknowledgment, of the incapacity of poetic language to encompass and control the material world, Spenser's endeavours are not self-defeating but triumphantly successful" (29; see also Gross 1985, 210–11).

A rather different focus on the 1596 poem's attention to the very conditions of narrative informs the two strongest studies of the 1596 books involving gender, desire, and the pleasures of narrative: Lauren Silberman's 1995 *Transforming Desire: Erotic Knowledge in Books III and IV of* The Faerie Queene and Dorothy Stephens' 1998 *The Limits of Eroticism in Post-Petrarchan Narrative: Conditional Pleasure from Spenser to Marvell* (see also Cavanagh 1994, Krier 1990). Silberman discovers a strong contrast between Books III and IV: the third book in its 1590 version setting up "an ideal of love" figured in hermaphrodite closure which is then rigorously exposed to the "social reality" of the 1596 text (4). In Book IV, Spenser "shows the reduction of the complex virtue of chastity to a fetishlike prize for the triumphant male as part of a larger cultural obsession with security" (10). It involves Spenser's examination and indictment of the pursuit of certainty, and his commitment to improvisatory risk, a commitment that finds its grandest vehicles in the last episodes of Book IV, the Temple of Venus and the marriage of rivers. For Silberman, the catalogue of rivers attendant at the marriage "both imposes and subverts linear order since the object of sequential reference is a system of flux" (131). By this point in Book IV, "multiple unfoldings of a greater plenitude provide an alternative to the castrating economy of absence and presence" (136), an economy that tyrannizes the discourse and behaviors of the violent knights, competing damsels, and their genres. Spenser's catalogue of rivers is indeed "endlesse," but that endlessness is offered as a powerful challenge to reductive authoritarian control.

Stephens' book argues for narrative representation's provisional nature, its versionality, its capacity for invention. She creates an interface between social and aesthetic through the conditional, multiplying nature of narrative representation, narrative voice, and reader situation. Thus she wonders, for example, not only "What does [Amoret's] story mean for female or male readers who do not desire the particular sort of closure that [her lover] Scudamour... desires?" but even more "why should we believe that the poem expects us to desire this particular closure?" (27); "there are other narrative positions possible besides ventriloquism on the one hand and subversion on the other" (32). From the 1596 books, Stephens draws on the episodes of Amoret, Æmilia, and the old woman in Lust's Cave, and Glauce and Ate, both in Book IV. The pleasures of narrative have become, in Silberman's and Stephens' books, risky, dangerous, and dark, which is to say that pleasure itself becomes conceptualized as deeper, larger, darker, or more ruthless than criticism earlier in the twentieth century had posited.

Force and form: From romance to history

Angus Fletcher comes close to identifying history with the tragic in the latter books of *The Faerie Queene*, and this makes sense if understood as proceeding from Northrop Frye's mid-century impulse to make a binary of romance (as fictive, imaginative, inward, serving the pleasure-principle) and the external, imposed brutalities of history and the reality principle. Frye's productive inclinations still stand behind many studies in the latter decades of the twentieth century which, if not explicitly endorsing such a binary, see by its light a Spenserian tension between public and private domains (D. Cheney 1984; Krier 1990; Rambuss 1993; Kennedy 2000). A polarized conflict between the very idea of history and an idea of romance also structures much early comment on the problem of Spenser and Ireland: misty and nostalgic visions of the island sadden and trouble late nineteenth- and early twentieth-century scholarship on Spenser, though in these years terms for critical analysis barely existed, and the mistiness occludes analysis even as it registers the difficulties of reading for the history in the poem. Coleman (1894) observed that most of *The Faerie Queene* "was composed on what to Spenser and his friends was almost a foreign land—on the conquered and desolated wastes of wild and barbarous Ireland" (92) and C. S. Lewis famously noted an affinity between Spenser's "poem of quests and wanderings and inextinguishable desires, and Ireland itself—the soft, wet air, the loneliness, the muffled shapes of hills, the heartrending sunsets" (1966, 126). A. C. Judson's biographical *Spenser in Southern Ireland* (1933) illustrates with photographs of sites relevant to Spenser studies, taken by the author.

Yet Fletcher also argues for complexity in Spenser's understanding and representation of violence as emerging from the same inwardness—call it the same structure of subjectivity—that desires happiness and acts through creative energy; one of Fletcher's sub-headings is "Rage: Ambiguous Energies of Culture" (249). The matter of Ireland particularly poses "an area of essential critical difficulty" (212). O'Connell (1977), Goldberg (1983), and Gallagher (1991) provide major, sophisticated treatments of many of the problems of history and ideology in the 1596 books, and posit various models of the relations between poetry and history. Fletcher briefly addresses the tragic rage of England in relation to Ireland in Spenser's poem. But this topic becomes a large and heated field in Spenser scholarship only later, with a welter of books and essays from the 1990s onward providing far more details of Irish history, culture, and language, and more details of English actions in relation to Ireland, than ever before. On many fronts this work makes openings in the blockages or helplessness of earlier work to know what to do with history and the written genres of history; on the other hand, the field of work on Spenser and Ireland seems to wrestle with its own disappointed anger of disenchantment, and can still disable its own strongest insights through obliviousness to the complex work that preceded it on narrative, poetry, genre, narrative voice, and representation. Thus the work that perhaps most fuelled interest in Spenser and Ireland, Stephen Greenblatt's chapter on the Bower of Bliss in *Renaissance Self-Fashioning* (1980), raises the germane issues in dominating prose but, in the view of many, undermines its promise by projecting Greenblatt's own fascination with absolutist power onto Spenser, rather than positing that Spenser could himself examine, critique, test, or deliberate about such power—as well as repression, pleasure, rage, violence—through the creation of fictions about it. Edward Said, Colin MacCabe, and Seamus Deane, likewise, make influential remarks that take as fact Spenser's brutality toward the Irish; they derive this datum from texts that, read carefully, pose outright and subtle difficulties to interpretation, placement of narrative voice, and functions of historical datum and genres in relation to poetic traditions.

It is, perhaps, the complex relationship between narrative form and political affiliation that has produced the strongest historically driven studies of the second installment. Richard McCoy's *Rites of Knighthood* (1989) illustrated ways in which romance depictions of knight errantry, read in the context of Elizabeth's court, themselves contained a kind of latent politics. Archaic visions of derring-do found in Arthurian legend did not simply glorify the monarch, they were also taken up by courtiers such as Spenser's patrons Leicester and Essex as cultural models endorsing a greater aristocratic independence from the center of power. It was this insight that helped stimulate Helgerson's 1992 reading of the poem, which postulates a conflict between the political values implicit in two of its principal literary modes: the romance polysemy of Ariosto's *Orlando Furioso* and the epic unity of Virgil's *Aeneid*. It was a clash, Helgerson argued, that was also to be found in Tasso's *Gerusalemme Liberata* (itself, of course, a source for *The*

Faerie Queene). In both Tasso's and Spenser's poems, changes across editions reveal tensions between these models. Helgerson's argument, therefore, has particular significance for the second installment:

> In its Virgilian intimations, its attempts at unity, and its celebration of Elizabeth, *The Faerie Queene* participates in this cult [of monarchical power] and these cultures of wholeness. But in its adherence to chivalric romance, it remains with [Tasso's] errant Rinaldo and the insubordinate Essex on the Gothic side of the great sixteenth-century cultural divide. Spenser came to know the danger of such errancy and insubordination. In Book 5 of *The Faerie Queene*, an incautious poet, who has spoken of Queen Mercilla, is found nailed by his tongue to a post. And since Mercilla's court is the poem's nearest representation of Elizabeth's, the warning is particularly telling. Nor is it the only sign of danger. A sense of peril hangs over the whole of the 1596 installment. Book 4, the first of the newly published books, begins with an acknowledgment that Spenser's own work has found disfavor in high places:
>
> > The rugged forehead that with grave foresight
> > Welds kingdomes causes, and affaires of state,
> > My looser rimes (I wote) doth sharply wite,
> > Fore praising love, as I have done of late.
>
> And Book 6, the last of the new books, ends with the Blatant Beast of envy and detraction threatening Spenser's "homely verse," which, as he again admits, has already been brought "into a mighty Peres displeasure." (Helgerson 1992, 52–3)

The dissatisfaction pervading the second installment had, of course, long been recognized. But Helgerson provided a mode of reading that connected literary form more intimately with politics. Politics was no longer a matter of allusion, it was to be found in structures of the poems itself. Along with an adventurous use of intertexts (from literary sources to maps and legal documents) Helgerson's sense of the political aspect of narrative tradition proved highly influential on a generation of historically minded critics. In particular, interest in the poem's fracturedness has been combined with attention to its Irish context to make the second installment of *The Faerie Queene* a new focus of interest. Escaping from Northrop Frye's binary between "history" and "romance" critics have gained purchase on material that had seemed simply awkward, reductive, and harsh. Narrative and political disenchantment are no longer seen as a source of frustration, instead they are the very object of study.

Book VI—the Legend of Courtesy set in a world of wild peoples, featuring a hero who neglects his quest in order to enjoy the pleasures of a pastoral sojourn—has proved especially fertile for critics concerned with the links between genre, gender, and politics. McCabe's recent study (2002), which reads *The Faerie Queene* alongside not only Virgil and Ovid but also a wealth of Irish bardic literature and English historical documents, is characteristic of this strand of current criticism in its responsiveness to both historical context and literary mode. McCabe observes that Calidore's apparent preference for pastoral leisure over heroic achievement had previously "given rise to the suggestion that the 'Legend of Courtesie' expresses Spenser's desire to retreat from the pressures of 'history', and the role of 'poet historicall', and supplant epic verse with lyric." In his assessment "exactly the opposite is the case" (McCabe 2002, 234). With the reintroduction of Spenser's pastoral persona, Colin Clout (VI.x.16.4), the political discontent of Spenserian pastoral is "infused into the heart of Spenserian epic: the poem has reached its most critically self-reflexive stage" (233). To complicate things further, the "monstrous regiment" of McCabe's title refers to both the native Irish *and* the specter of female monarchy of which Queen Elizabeth was herself the embodiment. The second installment thus becomes the battleground for two incompatible political visions: the desire to impose monarchical authority on the one hand and a profound skepticism about the form of that authority on the other. Historical readers have become fascinated by the treatment of female figures in Books V and VI. They have, for example, offered a series of readings of Serena (the damsel who is stripped and nearly killed by cannibals in Book VI Canto viii). For Fogarty (1989), Hadfield (1997, 177–81), Highley (1997, 129–31), and McCabe (2002, 241–3) the episode transforms romance and pastoral motifs concerned with wildness and feminine vulnerability to reflect upon both Irish wildness and the Queen herself. For those who write in this tradition, the profusion of narrative modes and literary influences in the second installment is thus inseparable from Spenser's engagement with history.

The strongest studies demonstrate that the field of "Spenser and Ireland" as a whole has not only grown bigger, embracing more episodes of the whole poem, but has begun to enrich itself with more complex strategies for reading than blame and indictment, which is to say that they respond to critical disappointment with intellectually fiercer sallies. They begin to offer subtle answers to the questions that perturb Spenser as well as scholarship about the relationship of force to form—iterary form, forms of nationhood, forms of subjects and subjectivity—in the 1596 books. Hadfield (1997) tracks unresolved, contradictory significances in the poem's manifold allegorical details, and ought to provoke further study of how to read such details allegorically. Willy Maley's *Salvaging Spenser: Colonialism, Culture and Identity* (1997), which provides the most patient sifting of all possible documents, scholarship, and opinions on Spenser and Ireland, argues that the Irish question needs to be recast in the context of the whole tangled British problem, and to include Scotland (see also Highley 1997); Maley, like others very recently, hypothesizes Spenser's incipient republicanism; Gregory

(2000) reads *The Faerie Queene* V.x–xii in light of the intersection between genres like chivalric romance and interventionist Protestant positions that considered not only insular but also continental religion and politics; Carroll (2001) persuasively calls for considering "how both Irish and English writers represented Ireland through the lens of European models in litera-ture, political theory and history, and through the medium of Irish and Latin as well as English" (1), and draws on gender as a tool of analysis in constructions of Ireland and the Irish. E. Fowler (2003) argues that Spenser uses constitutional theory and jurisprudence in episodes throughout the 1596 books, and that "there is a strong commitment through these final cantos [of Book IV] to value consent and denigrate conquest" (a point contested by those who use the *View* as a model for the poet's politics, such as Baker 1997, 66–123, and van Es 2002a, 78–111). Other scholars look at the 1596 books' complicated meditations on history by historicizing the genres that Spenser juxtaposes in them. Thus much of the 1596 poem works out implications of historical romance and ancient epic particularly asso-ciated with militarism and civil war—for example in Statius, Lucan, the Chaucer of the Knight's Tale, Malory, Ariosto (Hieatt 1975, Bellamy 1994, King, 2000, Krier 2001). The practice of *genera mixta* suggests that Spenser's problem-driven narrative works less by evoking readerly pleasure and iden-tification with characters than by evoking a kind of evenly hovering deliberation and evaluation. We have moved a long way from Fletcher's treatment of "romance" and "history" as a binary.

Form mediating force: The Spenserian stanza

Studies produced in the wake of Greenblatt and Helgerson's arguments offer new insights into the generic complexity of the 1596 *Faerie Queene*. Yet for those working in the aftermath of New Historicism there is still the danger that much subtle thinking on the experience of reading Spenser's poem can be forgotten in an all-encompassing search for political dissent and struc-tural tension. If so many issues and events of the 1596 books are as grim as historical studies suggest, how and why do we today continue reading outside the irresistible mythopoeic, templar, or joyous bits? If Spenser is so willing to entangle and complicate the narrative—through big massy chunks of narrative, relative flatness of character, proliferation of doubles and substitutes, and inundation of infolded layers of significance—then we might ask, baldly, where does he get the nerve? He seems to gamble on readers' willingness to stick with a proposed action's logic, even when it annoys or disturbs, until it exhausts itself: an obvious example would be Artegall's tortuous and increasingly violent efforts to impose Justice in Book V. The payoff, when frustrated readers arrive at moments of wonder and clarity in templar cantos like that of the Temple of Isis (V.vii), or when the narrative discovers new and happier social arrangements, as in moments of Book VI, or when we come to a new adventure about a comfortingly familiar character, is correspondingly great. Yet how can the poet impose this much discomfort on his readers? And is there anything in these books that frees us from that aggressivity toward the self that Freud later came to call the death drive? If, as Luce Irigaray remarks, "boredom in repeating the same story over and over again...is called, in part, the death instinct" (Irigaray 1985, 115), might we then also say that Spenser's *fascination* with repeating the same story—in different keys, with crucial variants, with new streams of discourse entering it—can be called, in part, a drive toward life?

One constantly surprising, constantly recurring release from the death drive into the elaborations of a life drive—a possibility of pleasure and even elation in reading the 1596 books—occurs in the stanza form, and especially in the breaks between stanzas, in the mind of the reader. The Spenserian stanza, with its steadiness, its unexpected openings of sound and sense, its relaxed syntactic movement, its suppleness of multiple meanings, the refreshment of the white spaces between stanzas, finds a new function in the 1596 *Faerie Queene*, in that its spaciousness accommodates the envy and disappointment out of which so many episodes arise. The buoyancy of the stanza allows commodiousness rather than straitening of thought. Its loose, sinuous syntax often surprises with a new possibility—a word, a condition— when the narrative or the analysis has reached an impasse. It is by tracing those new possibilities in the small beginning of an unexpected word or phrase that the "great matter" of these books carries us not only into chivalric plots about the mysteries of the death drive but into a poetic plot about movement and vitality: a drive toward life. The stanza creates, with every alexandrine, a threshold across which the new might grow, and so form extends generosity, sometimes even ease, to the reading of dark matter.

This is to rehearse only some of the remarkable treatments of the Spenserian stanza by careful readers—from Empson's famous remarks on the happy surprises and reliabilities of the stanza in *Seven Types of Ambiguity* (1930, pp. 33–4), through Alpers (1967), Fletcher (1971), to Gross (2004). For Empson:

> it is by the delicacy of this movement [of the stanza] that he shows his attitude towards his sentences, rather than by devices of implication in the sentences themselves.... *Ababbcbcc* is a unit which may be broken up into a variety of metrical forms, and the ways in which it is successively broken up are fitted into enormous patterns. The first quatrain usually gratifies the ear directly and without surprise, and the stanzas may then be classified by the grammatical connections of the crucial fifth line, which must give a soft bump to the dying fall of the first quatrain, keep it in the air, and prevent it from falling apart from the rest of the stanza.... it may [for example] add to the quatrain as by an afterthought, as if with a childish earnestness it made sure of its

point without regard to the metre, and one is relieved to find that the metre recovers itself after all. . . . In times of excitement the fifth line will be connected both ways, so as to ignore the two quatrains, and, by flowing straight on down the stanza with an insistence on its unity, show the accumulated energy of some enormous climax; and again, by being connected with neither, it will make the stanza into an unstressed conversational device without overtones of rhythm, picking up stray threads of the story with almost the relief of prose. . . . you have to yield yourself to [the stanza] very completely to take in the variety of its movement, and, at the same time, there is no need to concentrate the elements of the situation into a judgment as if for action. (Empson 1930, 1947, repr., pp. 33–4)

Paul Alpers amplifies and details these remarks, and structures them into a massive argument first about the stanza form, then about the organization—as opposed to the structure—of the poem. This is essentially an argument about temporality: we ought to read for the emerging organization of the poem, step by step, rather than seeking a static structure; the temporal argument itself emerges through the most patient and delicate study of the temporal process of reading the stanza that we have (Alpers 1967). This is an argument that only a Latinist could think to make—perhaps a Latinist whose native language is a germanic one—out of his own practice of yielding to the difficult movements of Latin syntax—and it serves Spenser beautifully. Alpers tries to account for that peculiarity of the verse that Gross recently termed, almost oxymoronically, "the cumulative independence" of the stanza's lines (2004). In doing so Alpers achieves the difficult end of keeping in view the internal mobility and process of discovery within the stanza:

When we say that the stanza we have examined has three major groupings . . . we do not mean that this is one fixed subtype of the Spenserian stanza that has been imposed from outside on the formulas and devices of the stanza. We are speaking of a set of choices that the stanza makes as it progresses. . . . Empson rightly says that the most important and frequent of such choices occur in and around the fifth line, but they can occur anywhere in the stanza. Groupings in Spenser's stanzas are almost always quite definite, because the independence of each line is not threatened by the combinations into which it enters. . . . Spenser's stanza is . . . an experience of language that is temporal and not spatial. (Alpers 1967, p. 40)

Throughout *The Faerie Queene*, at work in this stanza form day after day, year after year, Spenser works out an unfathomably various array of possibilities in his stanza, commodious occasions for elation in the play of rhyme scheme, sentence syntax, lineation, caesural pauses, and closing alexandrine (Hollander 1988; Fried 1981; Gross 1983, 2004; Dolven 2004).

In the 1596 books, even or especially in passages about aggressivity or a drive toward death, Spenser finds equal complexity and variousness in the spaces between the stanzas. Sometimes there is simple relief at the break after a stanza insistent on a violence it is determined to make us face. More interesting are the breaks that allow a recess from the strenuousness of thinking demanded by the most discursively mixed or iconographically dense stanzas—as if Spenser acknowledges the potential for fatigue in both reader and writer. The familiar sensation of wandering takes place not only in the poem's unending green world but in untrackable processes in the reader, between stanzas. Manifold combinations of active and passive thinking, or conscious and unconscious ideation, form a large part of the pleasure and fruitfulness of reading the most strenuous of Spenser's narratives. This is no small recompense for cleaving to the 1596 *Faerie Queene*, and suggests how the act of reading it, regardless of its subject matter, is occasion for jubilation. C. S. Lewis observed that if the poem is not exactly lifelike, the process of reading it is like living, and this is so not least in the way that engaging with the *form* of tireless stanzas activates the meaning-making processes of the unconscious as well as the conscious mind. Angus Fletcher was right to term his biblical, Ovidian, Virgilian, hermetic, and Galfridian contexts *matrices*; the stanza sequence, with the infinite variety of actions of condensing and disseminating that it evokes in the reader's mind, lead us through a complex form of the interactions between conscious and unconscious psychic process that is living.

Further reading

Eggert, K. 2000. *Showing Like a Queen: Female Authority and Literary Experiment in Spenser, Shakespeare, and Milton*, Philadelphia: University of Pennsylvania Press.

Fletcher, A. 1971. *The Prophetic Moment: An Essay on Spenser*, Chicago: University of Chicago Press.

Gallagher, L. 1991. *Medusa's Gaze: Casuistry and Conscience in the Renaissance*, Stanford: Stanford University Press.

Hadfield, A. 2001. "*The Faerie Queene*, Books IV–VII" in his *The Cambridge Companion to Spenser*, Cambridge: Cambridge University Press, 124–42.

Ivic, C. "Spenser and the Bounds of Race", *Genre* 32.3, Fall: 1–33.

Maley, W. 1997. *Salvaging Spenser: Colonialism, Culture and Identity*. Houndsmills, Basingstoke, Hampshire: Macmillan; New York: St Martin's Press.

Silberman, L. 1995. *Transforming Desire: Erotic Knowledge in Books III and IV of* The Faerie Queene. Berkeley: University of California Press.

Teskey, G. 2003. "'And therefore as a stranger give it welcome': Courtesy and Thinking", *Spenser Studies* XVIII: 343–59.

11

A View of the Present State of Ireland (1596; 1633)

Willy Maley

Reviewing the situation

No overview of the present state of Spenser studies would be complete without dwelling on the most vexed text in his corpus, a text which goes to the heart of Spenser's life, thought, and politics. *A View of the Present State of Ireland* provokes violent and varied reactions amongst critics: ignored because it is by Spenser, as a perplexing piece of prose that poses problems for the poetry; or obsessed over because it is by Spenser, as the key to his complex allegory, particularly Book V of *The Faerie Queene*, or simply as the finest example of English colonial ideology in the period. The 'present state' the *View* describes is one of ongoing anxiety, hence the embarrassment and unease it generates, and hence also the lasting political frisson (Fréchet 1980; Gardiner 2001). If Spenser is our contemporary then his continuing relevance is most dramatically figured in the *View*, a tale of invasion, conquest, and occupation, of the devastation of war and the rhetoric of reconstruction. What work of Spenser's could speak more powerfully to our present state than one that opens with a limited handover of sovereignty, offers an eyewitness account of a brutal beheading, lays bare the treatment of prisoners in a remote bay, and gives a chilling illustration of the fate of illegal combatants?

Commenting on his 1934 edition, W. L. Renwick remarks:

> Our concern here is not with Ireland's rights or wrongs, nor with belated apology, condemnation, or moralising, but with one man's surroundings and experience, which interest students of literature because that man was a great poet, and students of history because his is the best statement of official opinion at a difficult period. The two interests are not mutually exclusive. (223)

Renwick's claim, though calmly stated, is controversial. The jury is still out on whether Spenser was articulating 'official opinion', and many remain preoccupied with the rights and wrongs of Irish history. Moreover, despite Renwick's contention that Spenser's status as 'a great poet' should make the *View* of interest to students of literature, the opposite case could be made, that his reputation as a poet depends precisely on insulating him from the potentially negative effects of such an anti-Irish diatribe, if indeed that is what the *View* amounts to, rather than a reasoned dialogue. It has been read as a discussion of Irish origins, a practical political guide, a reform treatise, and hybrid text containing important elements of autobiography.

Several book-length works have been devoted exclusively to Spenser's Irish experiences (Henley 1928; Hadfield 1997; Maley 1997; McCabe 2002). But it is chiefly in the form of essays, and sometimes in the shape of short interventions, that much of the scholarship on the *View* exists. Those essays address the dialogue's three main themes of law, customs, and religion, but inevitably the 'customs' get most attention, translated into modern parlance as 'culture'. The absent state of Ireland in much Spenser criticism—an absence more often alluded to than demonstrated—arises from the very existence of the *View*. Had Spenser merely lived and worked in Ireland, but not written about it outside of his poetry and the letters he scribed as a secretary, then that sojourn could be viewed with a colder eye. For as long as the *View* has attached itself to Spenser, since at least the attribution by Sir James Ware in 1633, it has generated controversy.

The *View* poses a number of questions. Unpublished until 1633, when it formed part of Ware's *Ancient Irish Histories*, along with works by Edmund Campion and Meredith Hanmer, it was first credited to Spenser by Ware, an attribution reinforced by a manuscript copy initialled 'E. S.' It was Ware who furnished the first sustained life of Spenser in his 1633 edition. Jean Brink has cast doubt on Spenser's authorship, noting that no copy survives in his hand, and that Ware's claim is made posthumously, but most Spenserians, however unhappy they are with the *View*, are happy with the attribution on grounds of verbal and stylistic echoes between the prose and the poetry; shortage of other authorial candidates; dating; widespread circulation of manuscripts; and the attribution by Ware, belated but authoritative (Brink 1994a, 1997a; Hadfield 1994b, 1998a). Nonetheless, Brink's work, taken together with that of Catherine Canino, poses a major challenge to scholars of the *View* (Brink 1994a; C. Canino 1998). The *View*'s 65,000 words include not one single date, but the fact remains that a text entitled *A View of the [Present] State of Ireland* has attached itself to Spenser's corpus and continues to tax and vex critics and readers. In what follows—part snapshot, part survey—we will travel through time with the *View*, from its apparent suppression in 1598 to the disputes around its authorship that arose in the 1990s, from Ware to Wordsworth, from Yeats to Heaney, from Milton to McGuinness, Mahon, and Muldoon. The *View* is a text whose title has been taken up for various overviews of Spenser's work and of Irish studies more widely (Canny 1999; Hadfield and Maley 2000; Sharkey 1997;

Williams 1965). It is also a text that has been in the wars—its authorship disputed, its status in relation to the rest of Spenser's output debated, even its title laid open to question. The *Brief Note*, the minor prose piece that was its companion-in-arms for a century following Grosart's attribution, though included in the Variorum edition of 1949, had its authorship queried, first by Renwick in his 1934 edition, then by Ciarán Brady in *The Spenser Encyclopedia* (Brady 1990a). Renwick disputed the authorship of the *Brief Note*, but ironically endorsed the verses on the Earl of Cork's Lute printed in Ware's largely ignored edition (Miller 1996).

The 'edition' of the *View* used for this essay, and for this Guide as a whole, does not bear the title given to the first printed edition. Written in 1596 (Gottfried 1937; Martin 1932), unpublished until 1633, but not included in his collected works until 1679 (without Ware's notes), this controversial prose dialogue has in recent years generated the most significant body of cultural criticism in Renaissance studies, let alone Spenser studies. The range and richness of criticism on the *View* is astonishing. One of the most argued over pieces of prose in the Renaissance, it has attracted scholarship of an incredibly diverse nature. In part, this is due to the problematic place of Ireland in relation to both England and Britain. Despite protestations, the Irish question has taken over the asylum, or at least overrun Elysium, and the *View* has led the assault, closely coupled with Book V of *The Faerie Queene*. The kinds of issues raised by the *View* range from antiquarianism to violence with most stops in between, including historiography, language, law, mapping, sexuality, and translation (Maley 1991, 1996).

The history of scholarship on the *View* falls into three distinct phases, from antiquarianism to postcolonialism. First, there was the long period from its passage from manuscript to print under Ware on the eve of the Ulster Rising of 1641, through the Union of 1800, to the Irish Civil War and partition. This was the phase when criticism was chiefly biographical and historical, and its twin tracks can be seen in the difference between Ware's pacifying rhetoric and antiquarian reading and Milton's homing in on the text as a political tool. It reached its zenith with the founding of the *Journal of the Cork Historical and Archaeological Society* in 1891. This publication stimulated a steady flow of notes and observations which concentrated upon the local evidence for Spenser's stay in Ireland, consisting predominantly of essays on the poet's neighbourhood, neighbours, family and descendants, and much detailed work on the geography and government of Cork.

The second phase saw another twin-track approach. On one side, there was the perspective of figures such as Yeats, C. S. Lewis, and later Seamus Heaney that looked at the ways in which a poetic vision was compromised by contact with colonial violence. On the other side, there was the continuation and development of an historical approach enhanced by modern scholarly techniques and an increasingly sophisticated editorial approach.

The third and most recent phase of scholarship started with Stephen Greenblatt's New Historicist intervention (1980). Like Nicholas Canny's (1983) placing of the poet in a more layered landscape than was hitherto conceived, Greenblatt's essay combined the biographical and historical approaches. This third phase is arguably drawing to a close, as there is a shift towards comparative and interdisciplinary studies and a growing awareness of the intertwined nature of the antiquarian and the postcolonial and of the interplay of the rhetoric of race, religion, and sexuality in the *View* and in the English discourse on Ireland more broadly.

The sixteenth- and seventeenth-century view

The story of the *View* begins on 14 April 1598, when the following entry appears in the Stationers' Register: 'A viewe of the present state of Ireland. Discoursed by waye of a Dialogue betwene Eudoxus and Irenius'. Some critics conclude from this that the text was suppressed, but works entered in the register were sometimes queried because of turf wars between publishers. Matthew Lownes was a printer with piracy in his past (most notably over Sir Philip Sidney's *Astrophil and Stella*), so the *View* may have been caught up in a tug of war between rival printers. It may also have been caught up in a dispute regarding Spenser's poetry (Hadfield 1998a).

Most critics are aware that Book V of *The Faerie Queene* was the subject of an exchange of letters in November 1596 between Robert Bowes, the English secretary in Scotland, and Lord Burghley. Bowes conveyed James VI's displeasure at the depiction of his mother, Mary, Queen of Scots, as Duessa in Canto ix. Less often noted is that the matter was reprised two years later on 25 February 1598 when George Nicholson, a servant of Bowes, reported that Walter Quin, an Irishman based at St Andrews University in Scotland, was 'answering Spencer's book wherat the King was offended' (Maley 1994, 71). The timing of Nicholson's letter was crucial, since the prose partner-in-crime to Book V was about to be entered in the Stationers' Register.

Around twenty manuscript copies survive, including one which Essex may have had with him during his Irish campaign, suggesting that Spenser's work was not only mulled over by the mighty, but may have influenced policy. One surviving copy, Bodleian MS Rawl. B. 478, prepared for intended publication in 1598, has a note at the end from the Warden of the Stationers' Company to the Secretary: 'Mr Collinges/pray enter this Copie for mathew Lownes to be prynted when he do bringe other authoritie. Thomas Man'. This manuscript is collated in the Variorum, and was used by Renwick for his edition of 1934.

As noted earlier, the *View* was first published as *A View of the State of Ireland* minus the 'present'. This was its title for two centuries. Indeed, Ware was careful in the dedicatory preface to Sir Thomas Wentworth, the Earl of

Strafford, and in the introduction and notes, to contrast the troublesome period in which Spenser was writing with the relative calm of Caroline Ireland. This was of course wishful thinking as the *View*, a powerful piece of wartime journalism, was destined to be caught up in future conflicts that would make it pertinent even as it came to be seen as problematic. It has been said that the past is another country, but Ware's peaceful present of 1633 was another country too. Within a few short years of the publication of the first edition of the *View* Ireland was war-torn once again, and John Milton and his contemporaries were reading it, against the grain of Ware's wishes—and wishful thinking—as a guide to military practice in the midst of conflict.

Beginnings of scholarship

The *View*'s first and most famous recorded reader was John Milton, who noted two passages from Ware's edition in his commonplace book (Maley 1993, 194–6). The first, headed *Astutia politica*, reads: 'The wicked policies of divers deputies and governours in Ireland. See *Spenser* dialogue of Ireland.' Milton's second note, under *De disciplina militari*, reads: 'Provision for souldiers after the warrs to be consider'd. *Spenser* dialogue of Ireland from p. 84. &c.' It is obvious from these notes that Milton read the *View* for present policy, not for its antiquarian excursions. But as Linda Gregerson has argued, the *View* may have influenced Milton beyond his *Observations on Ireland*. Milton's ambitious *History of Britain* (1670), written in tandem with *Paradise Lost*, can usefully be read alongside Spenser's dialogue, which is as much a history of Britain as it is a view of the present state of Ireland (Gregerson 1999; Stevens 1995). Ireland was a testing-ground for English policy, and the *View* itself came to be regarded as a kind of commonplace book. But it was also, as Spenser, Ware, and Milton well knew, a crucial repository of knowledge about England and other nations. This uneasy alliance between antiquarianism and applicability, like the later unholy alliance between race and religion adumbrated by Paul Stevens (1995), persisted in the twentieth century.

The *View* continued to occupy the debatable land between antiquarianism and political commentary. The two areas were always subject to cross-border raids (van Es 2002). By the end of the eighteenth century the *View* had become a text that was brought into play for different reasons and in distinct ways, both as a useful archive for information on Irish culture and as a guide to a contemporary understanding of England's first colony. Maria Edgeworth cited it in the lengthy first footnote to *Castle Rackrent*, a novel initially published anonymously in 1800, referring to the Irish mantle and to Spenser's subtle understanding of its provenance. The reference is as gratuitous as some of E. K.'s glosses to *The Shepheardes Calender*, triggered by an innocuous allusion by her main character to his 'long great coat'. The use of Spenser shows knowledge of the text and awareness of its complexities. Edgeworth's text is as double-voiced as Spenser's. She notes that 'Spencer, in his "View of the State of Ireland", proves that it is not, as some have imagined, peculiarly derived from the Scythians, but that "most nations of the world antiently used the mantle"'. Edgeworth goes on to quote at length from the *View*, observing that 'Spencer knew the convenience of the said mantle, as housing, bedding, and cloathing' (Edgeworth 1995, 7–8). Edgeworth's glossing of the mantle seems innocent enough, but writing as she was at the time of the Union between Great Britain and Ireland, and predicting, ironically, the disappearance of 'Ireland' through that act of Union, she well knew the continuing relevance of Spenser's dialogue. Edgeworth is not just alerting her reader to the ironic nature of *Castle Rackrent*. She is showing that she knows the Anglo-Irish tradition of which she is now a part. Edgeworth's contemporary, Robert Southey, who served briefly as private secretary to Isaac Corry, chancellor of the exchequer for Ireland, and wrote in *The Vision of Judgment* (1822) on Richard Stanyhurst's translation of Virgil, is another Romantic writer with strong Irish connections who read the *View* with interest, making detailed notes (Southey 1850, 210–11). On 28 September 1803, Southey wrote: 'If the government want to extirpate disaffection in Ireland by the gallows, they must sow the whole island with hemp.' On perusing the *View*, and coming across one of its most pungent passages, the beheading of Murrogh O'Brien, Southey exclaimed: 'The foster mother at the execution!' (Southey 211; Variorum commentary 344). This was clearly a passage that appealed to the Romantic sensibility, but it is worth noting, with Edgeworth in mind, that Southey also picked out the 'Evil and misery of rack-rent' as one of the ills of Ireland identified by Spenser. Subsequent commentators remain caught between moral outrage and economic analysis.

The 1949 Variorum edition alludes to Southey's uncommon commonplace book reading of the *View*, but not to Milton's. Nor is there any mention of Southey's contemporary, William Wordsworth, who recommended in 1802 that a prospective buyer of Spenser's works 'purchase an edition which has his "State of Ireland" in it', adding that 'this edition may be scarce' (Marjarum 1940, 609). There were at this point three editions of Spenser's works that came with a *View*—the editions of 1679, 1715, and 1750. The dialogue was also available as a separate publication or printed with other Irish treatises in Ware's edition of 1633 and another of 1763. In 1829, Wordsworth discussed the contemporary situation in Ireland with reference to 'the writers of the time of Queen Elizabeth', by which time he would have had access to the first Variorum edition by Henry Todd, whose eighth and final volume was given over to the *View* (1805), and to the reprint of Ware's edition issued in 1809 (Marjarum 608).

By the mid-nineteenth century, interest in Spenser's Irish experiences was sufficient for one editor of his poetic works, George Stillman Hillard, to ask irascibly who can have much interest in the solution of the questions of whether the rebellion of the O'Neals be imaged in the episode of the babe with bloody hands, in the Second Book? or whether or not Sir Satyrane is a representative of Sir John Perrott? What are Sir John Perrott and the rebellion of the O'Neals to us? "What's Hecuba to him, or he to Hecuba?". (Radcliffe 1996, 113)

Ironically, the index to *The Cambridge Companion to Spenser* contains two entries for Sir John Perrot and none for Hillard. Poetic justice? Or a case of critics taking too prosaic a view of things? Hillard's use of *Hamlet* is fitting, as Brendan Bradshaw famously characterised the genre of colonial discourse to which the *View* belongs—while exonerating Spenser's dialogue from the charge—as 'Polonius prattling on through several folios' (Bradshaw 1979, 36). The *View* is the 'play within the play' in the Spenserian canon. It catches the conscience of critics.

Hillard's protests went unheard. Spenser's Irish experiences and their chief literary record continued to exert a strong influence over the rest of his work. Marx and Engels knew the importance of Spenser for English colonial history. While Marx's infamous pun on 'Elizabeths arse kissing poet [*der Elisabeths Arschkissende Poet*]', playing on the first Folio's designation of Spenser as 'England's Arch-Poet', has been replayed on many occasions (Riley 1990, 457), the more measured use of Spenser's *View* by Engels in his unpublished 'Notes for the History of Ireland' has gone largely unnoticed. In his notes on Goldwin Smith's *Irish History and Irish Character* (1861), Engels wrote: 'Arthegal in Spencer's *Faery Queen* is Lord Deputy Grey' (Marx and Engels 348). Using the 1809 reprint of Ware's edition, Engels cited the passage on the corruption of the clergy:

'...ye may find there...gross simony, greedy covetousness, fleshly incontinency, careless sloth, and generally all disordered life in the common clergyman. And besides...they do go and live like laymen, follow all kinds of husbandry and other worldly affairs as other Irishmen do. They neither read Scriptures, nor preach to the people, nor administer the Communion, but baptism they do,...they take the tithes and offerings and gather what fruit else they may of their living,...and some of them...pay, as due, tributes and shares of their livings to their bishops...'. Engels adds his own observation: '*All the above, apparently, refers to the Protestant priests of that time*'. (Marx and Engels 577, n. 327; emphasis in original)

Scholarship in the twentieth century

Milton and Wordsworth had agendas of their own, as did Marx and Engels, but from the late nineteenth century that political agenda takes a personal turn. Earlier writers read the *View* in isolation and for its political and historical content. From Yeats through C. S. Lewis to Heaney the perspective on poetry and politics shifts, and the question of responsibility, political, and ethical, comes to the fore (Gardiner 2001). Henceforth the *View* is caught up in a rhetoric of reproach. Yeats pioneered the poet-planter split and the aura of autobiographical angst:

> When Spenser wrote of Ireland he wrote as an official, and out of thoughts and emotions that had been organised by the State. He was the first of many Englishmen to see nothing but what he desired to see. Could he have gone there as a poet merely, he might have found among its poets more wonderful imaginations than even those islands of Phaedria and Acrasia. He would have found among wandering storytellers, not indeed his own power of rich, sustained description, for that belongs to lettered ease, but certainly all the kingdom of Faery, still unfaded, of which his own poetry was often but a troubled image. (Yeats 1961, 372)

The Ulsterman C. S. Lewis took a similar tack: 'When he wrote of Ireland, Spenser became a bad poet because he was in some respects a bad man... Spenser was the instrument of a detestable policy in Ireland, and in his fifth book the wickedness he shared begins to corrupt his imagination' (Lewis 1936, 348–9). Seamus Heaney, like Yeats, sees Elizabethan Ireland as a crucial formative period in the country's history, and Spenser as the key figure on the borderlands between literature and politics. In his poetry, Heaney homes in on the tension between Spenser's poetic ideals and the colonial ideology to which he appeared to subscribe. In poems about the Troubles and traditions such as 'Bog Oak' and 'Traditions' in *Wintering Out* (1972), 'Ocean's Love to Ireland' and 'Exposure' in *North* (1975), and 'Terminus' in *The Haw Lantern* (1985), Heaney presents Spenser as a writer whose work is shadowed and even at times overshadowed by colonial violence, by famine and the sword. In 'Bog Oak' he evokes the nightmarish image of victims of the Munster Famine as described in the *View* as a counterpoint to the poet's otherwise dreamy reflection: 'geniuses who creep / "out of every corner / of the woodes and glennes" / towards watercress and carrion' (Gardiner, 202). Neil Corcoran sees in Heaney's harping on the haunting of the author of *The Faerie Queene* by the ghost of his time in Ireland a reminder 'that such literary perfections as that great Renaissance poem were the flower of a culture whose roots lay in the brutal political realities described in the *State of Ireland*' (Gardiner, 201–2). Heaney's version of the personal poetic crisis is slightly more sophisticated than that of Yeats or Lewis, and recalls Walter Benjamin's observation that 'There is no document of culture which is not at the same time a document of barbarism' (Benjamin 1972, 248). Sue Petitt Starke poses the question of Spenser's poet-planter status differently in her essay entitled 'Briton Knight or Irish Bard' (1998).

There is predictably enough a strong Irish thread running through criticism of the *View*, from Ware's Dublin edition through the emergence of professional scholarship with the founding of the *Journal of the Cork Historical and Archaeological Society* and Henley's *Spenser in Ireland*, published by Cork University Press in 1928, to the holy trinity of Bradshaw, Brady, and Canny, and beyond to the important collections edited by Coughlan (1989) and Fogarty (1996). Richard McCabe is the Irish critic who comes closest to bridging the literary historical divide, particularly in his invaluable work on the Irish language. Other critics who have produced important work in this regard are Carroll (1996) and Ní Chuilleanáin (1996).

The second phase of scholarship also originated in Ireland, in Cork to be precise, with the appearance of Pauline Henley's *Spenser in Ireland* from Cork University Press in 1928. Despite a pejorative tone which contemporary reviewers attributed to its composition in the wake of the Irish Civil War and partition, Henley's ground-breaking monograph ushered in a new era of professional historiography. This 'old historicist' phase stretches from Henley to Heaney, from partition through to the outbreak of the Troubles. This was a period of much more intense activity, in which modern historiography was supplemented by editorial, linguistic, and textual scholarship. It was also coloured by a moral and ethical emphasis, especially marked in the comments of Yeats and C. S. Lewis on Spenser's culpability and on the matter of responsibility and the so-called corruption of the poetic imagination through the necessary but nasty activities of the planter-administrator. But this phase also witnessed a parallel development in terms of a sustained exploration of the *View*, chiefly by scholars based in Ireland and America. Those earlier critics—Frederic Ives Carpenter, Frank Covington, John Draper, C. Litton Falkiner, Rudolph Gottfried, Ray Heffner, Raymond Jenkins, H. S. V. Jones, William Clifford Martin, Constantia Maxwell, W. L. Renwick, and Roland Smith—pursued interests that were biographical, editorial, historical, and linguistic. This scholarship arose from a number of doctoral theses, including Gottfried's 1935 Yale Ph.D., the basis of the Variorum edition. I have drawn attention to this earlier scholarship elsewhere (Maley 1991). The Variorum edition was the crowning achievement of this period, eclipsing earlier editions, although Renwick's 1934 Scholartis edition and the 1970 Oxford modernised spelling version remain influential.

The third and most recent phase begins with the advent of New Historicism and the flurry of criticism prompted by the significant interventions of Greenblatt and Canny (Maley 1996). Two essays inaugurated this third stage of production around the *View*. Greenblatt's chapter in *Renaissance Self-fashioning* (1980) credited Spenser with a 'field theory of culture', and used the *View* to argue for an all-embracing Irish influence in the poet's work. Greenblatt's work opened the field afresh for literary and cultural critics.

The second decisive intervention was Canny's 1983 essay, focusing on the *View* 'as a fundamental contribution to the theory of colonization', and moving from sources and influences to contemporaries and successors, setting the scene for subsequent scholarship (Canny 1983, 1). Canny's key contribution was to map out a milieu for Spenser, preserving his special status as a singularly eloquent writer on Ireland, but saving him from social isolation by embedding him firmly within a particular planter community. Canny reminded readers that Spenser had contemporaries who had their own views on the state of Ireland, including Barnaby Rich, William Herbert, Richard Beacon, and John Davies. It would be tempting to see Canny as the originator of this kind of comparative approach, but earlier critics such as Gottfried had been just as willing to set the *View* alongside other examples of the genre (Gottfried 1938), and of course Ware himself introduced the text to the world in a context where it was presented alongside the work of key—and contradictory—contemporaries, Meredith Hanmer, a near-neighbour of Spenser's on the Munster Plantation, and Edmund Campion, a Jesuit priest executed at Tyburn in 1581.

Fellow Irish historians, most prominent among them Brendan Bradshaw (1988) and Ciarán Brady (1986), took issue with and added to Canny. Brady focused on faction, humanism in crisis, the law, and administrative change, while Bradshaw placed religion—in the shape of the poet's purported puritan convictions—at the heart of Spenser's politics. But Canny's particular brand of cultural and intellectual history best suited the historicist and ideological interests of literary critics. Canny presented Spenser as part of an emerging colonial elite, the post-Reformation New English, predominantly Protestant planters supplanting the largely Catholic Old English descendants of the original medieval colony. Between Greenblatt's 'cultural poetics' and Canny's colonial theory there was common ground, and not just because Greenblatt drew on Canny's earlier work on *The Elizabethan Conquest of Ireland* (1976). Behind both Canny and Greenblatt was the formidable figure of David Beers Quinn, whose ground-breaking work on Elizabethan Ireland went hand-in-hand with major studies of Raleigh and American colonization, areas that were also to preoccupy Canny and Greenblatt (Quinn 1966).

Ironies abound in the story of the recent resurgence of interest in the *View*. No sooner does one major Irish historian ask if we can go 'Beyond Spenser?' (Morgan 1999) than another tells us that 'Spenser Sets the Agenda' (Canny 2001). No sooner is Spenser planted firmly in *The Field Day Anthology*, with excerpts from the *View* incorporated ahead of women and Irish-language writers (Canny and Carpenter 1991), than scholars like Brink (1994a, 1997a) and C. Canino (1998) cast doubt on its authorship. In an intriguing twist on Greenblatt's suggestion that *The Faerie Queene* is all about Ireland, it has even been argued that the *View* is all about England, or at least that its proposals for radical reform are directed in large part towards Spenser's own nation (Shuger 1997; Bradshaw 1988). This may be true in two senses, for even if the *View* is all about Ireland, its targets for reform are the English in Ireland, Old and New.

Three passages into the present

Vital as the contributions of Greenblatt and Canny were, they ought not to obscure the fact that there was a long and venerable tradition of reading the *View*, both as an important historical document and as a literary text in its own right, one that impinged in significant ways on the rest of the Spenserian canon. Spenser's engagement with Ireland began long before the *View*, with *The Faerie Queene*, and not just Book V. But his prose dialogue is the magisterial culmination of that long engagement. Whatever Ware's reason for dropping the 'present' the *View* is preoccupied with presence—the presence of the monarch, lacking in Ireland; the (permanent) military presence proposed through a system of garrisons; and most problematic of all, the presence of the poet-planter himself, his self-presentation at the most dramatic—and traumatic—points in the dialogue. Had this exchange been staged between Colin and Hobbinol, the critical reception would have been different. Critics comfortably conflate author and character when it comes to the poetry, but shy away from such correspondences in the prose. Colin 'shadows' Spenser from *The Shepheardes Calender* to the 'Two Cantoes of Mutabilitie'. Irenius, the chief speaker in the *View*, 'shadows' Spenser in a more sinister way, as an unwelcome acquaintance. Judson called him 'Spenser's mouthpiece' (Judson 1945, 92), which would make Eudoxus his earpiece, but despite such easy identifications, and the various claims for Spenser as a 'spokesman' for a colonial community, critics remain suspicious of the relationship between the dialogue's speakers and its author.

Richard Morris, in his preface to the Globe edition of Spenser's works, speaks of restoring an 'inaccurate and incomplete' text to something approaching an imagined original: 'It seemed scarcely fair to Spenser's memory to let this single piece of prose remain in so unsatisfactory a state' (Morris and Hales 1869, iii). A footnote at this point informs the reader: 'The *title* itself as given by Ware is incorrectly stated. All the manuscripts, as well as the entry on the books of the Stationers' Company, read "A View of the PRESENT State of Ireland," but, curiously enough, the word "present" is omitted in all editions that I have seen' (emphasis in original). Thus, according to this nineteenth-century editor, the previous two centuries of published editions have followed Ware in omitting the 'present'.

Spenser's presence in Ireland is not in doubt, although the when and wherefore are open to question. The kind of presence invoked in the *View* is far removed from visions of exile or pastoral retreat. The text contains three key autobiographical digressions that can usefully be taken as focal points for an examination of the ways in which the text has been received and written about in particular periods: the Munster Famine; the Smerwick Massacre; and the execution of Murrogh O'Brien. Two of these passages are themselves the subject of considerable debate. Most critics accept that Spenser witnessed the Munster Famine, the catastrophic event that cleared the way for the Munster Plantation in the wake of the attainder of the Earl of Desmond, but remain sceptical about his implied presence in Ireland prior to his going there with Lord Grey in 1580, and his privileged position with regard to the Lord Deputy, which casts doubt on his witnessing of O'Brien's beheading in 1577, and his professed proximity at Smerwick three years later (Jenkins 1933; O'Rahilly 1938; Brady 1990b; Canino 1998; Hadfield 1999; O'Brien 2001). These passages raise many of the issues that pervade criticism of the *View*, and touch on the increasingly important matter of literary biography. While Greenblatt boldly declared him 'an agent of and an apologist for massacre', Canino questions whether Spenser was present at Smerwick, and, by extension, whether he is actually the author of the *View* (Greenblatt 1980, 186; Canino 1998).

The account of the victims of the Munster famine is the most visited passage in the *View*. This was a catastrophic event that emptied out a populous area of Ireland, killing 30,000 natives—one for every line of *The Faerie Queene*—to make way for 3000 settlers, including Spenser, a lot of collateral damage for a little cultural gain. Spenser's notorious description of the starving Irish may be the *View*'s most frequently cited passage, but critics remain divided as to whether Irenius is lamenting a human disaster, advocating ethnic cleansing, or merely worried about how such a tragic spectacle will affect the queen's continuing commitment to conquest. As with every textual crux, context is crucial. Eudoxus has just asked Irenius how his proposed strategy of quelling the natives will end. Irenius answers by adverting to the late wars in Munster, at the end of which 'a moste populous and plentifull Countrye sodenlye lefte voide of man or beaste, yeat sure in all that warr theare perished not manie by the sworde but all by the extreamitye of famine which they themselves had wroughte' (3267–70).

Again, the narrative seems torn between the suffering arising from starvation and morbid fascination with survivors resorting to cannibalism. In the course of the account, agency and responsibility shift from the English to the Irish. The Irish were 'kepte from manuraunce', and 'by this harde restrainte they woulde quicklye Consume themselves and devour one another', and 'broughte to soe wonderfull wretchednesse as that anie stonie harte would have rewed the same'. But by the end Irenius can claim that the Irish themselves have sown the seeds of their own destruction. Any compassion is cancelled out by this closing assertion. They wrought it, so they bought it.

This episode has to be read in its entirety, and not simply from the part beginning 'anie stonie harte would have rewed the same' (Heffner 1942, 512–15; Brady 1986, 17–19; *View*, 3235–302). The crucial reading is that of Eudoxus, who judges Irenius to be one of those 'Aucthors and Counsellours of suche blodye platformes', to whom Elizabeth, full of that hypothetical pity he had simulated at such an awful eventuality, would have given little thanks (*View*, 3300–302).

The account of the Smerwick Massacre, on a smaller scale than the Munster Famine, but with an international context that made it 'news' in Europe at the time, is equally problematic, if less ambiguous. Spenser's relationship with Lord Grey has engendered little discussion (Jones 1919; Jenkins 1937; Canino 1998). How closely Spenser accompanied Grey on his campaigns and how deeply 'embedded' he was in military operations remains a matter of debate. Irenius certainly claims to have been present at the notorious massacre at the Fort d'Oro (Golden Fort), Smerwick, on the Dingle Peninsula, on 9 November 1580, when the Lord Deputy put to the sword—after they had given themselves up—six hundred Spanish and Italian troops. In letters to Elizabeth and Burghley, scribed by Spenser, Grey justified his actions on grounds of expediency, and in the *View* Spenser defended his boss against charges that he was a 'bloody man'.

As with the description of the Munster famine, this report is prompted by a comment from Eudoxus, sidekick to the streetwise Irenius: 'But in that sharpe execucion of the Spaniardes at the forte of Smerwicke I harde it speciallye noted and if it weare trewe as some reported surelye it was a greate touche to him in Honour. ffor some saie that he promised them lief; others that at leaste he did put them in hope theareof' (3355–9). Irenius, ever ready to quash rumour, refute hearsay, and counter received opinion, knows better because he was there. 'Bothe the one and the other is moste vntrewe for this I cane assure youe my selfe beinge then as neare as anye' (3360–1). Irenius proceeds to run through the details of the negotiations and ultimatums, and his presence at the scene lends weight to his testimony. Irenius augments Grey's claim that the besieged fort's occupants, as foreign mercenaries—or illegal combatants—were strangers rather than subjects, and thus not entitled to quarter. Irenius offers two additional reasons for the denial of mercy, 'daunger' that they might regroup, and 'terrour' as an example to the Irish. Ironically, Spenser and his fellow planters were themselves foreign adventurers and fortune-seekers in disputed dominions. Indeed, under the terms of the Munster Plantation the 'undertakers' assigned 'seignories' were essentially private contractors, sub-contracted by the government. The difference between 'Mal' and 'Bon' was in the eye of the beholder—same text, different font. No stranger to ethnic cleansing and war crimes, Spenser knew the nastiness of modern conflicts, where mercy was viewed as lapse or luxury.

According to one historian, Ireland in the 1590s was 'England's Vietnam', meaning both a war in which a powerful nation was bogged down and one which generated bad publicity and engendered strong resistance (Outhwaite 1985, 32). Public opinion compelled those prosecuting the war to fight with one hand tied behind their backs—a familiar refrain. Grey did not live to see himself defended by his former secretary. Spenser's defence may have been prompted in part by the death of his former patron in 1593, followed a year later by the outbreak of the Nine Years War and the spectre of continuing violence in Ireland. That violence—its extremity, its language, and its official sanctioning—continues to attract some of the strongest scholarship on the text, and not just scholarship, but literature too. The Irish poet Nuala Ní Dhomhnaill, in verses entitled 'Ag Tiomáint Siar', translated as 'Driving Westward', confronts the legacy of violence by alluding directly to the Smerwick Massacre, and to a place:

> still peopled
> by a tale of *seven hundred beardless Seáns*
> butchered as the English
> marched on Dún an Óir.

(Gardiner, 203–4)

This is atrocity literature. Much criticism of Spenser and Ireland implies that the poet's planter status impoverishes his imagination. This is the view of Yeats and C. S. Lewis. Yet in addition to sparking some of the most exciting criticism in Spenser studies, the poet's dialogue with Ireland has inspired a novel, a novella, a play, and a great deal of poetry, including Marianne Moore's 'Spenser's Ireland', which the poet Paul Muldoon sees as emblematic of Moore's work (Moore 1981; MacBeth 1992; Welch 1994; McGuinness 1997; Muldoon 2003;).

Spenser specializes in theatrical beheadings. *The Faerie Queene* is littered with headless corpses, an orgy of violence in comparison with the *View*, but one of the most unsettling moments in the prose remains the peculiar passage in which Irenius recalls a decapitation strike of a particularly disturbing kind, namely the execution of 'A notable traitour', Murrogh O'Brien, in Limerick on 1 July 1577. The harrowing description captures beautifully Spenser's divided outlook. This is one of two places in the *View* where Spenser treats accusations of cannibalism, the other being that infamous passage on the devastation wrought by famine in Munster. What makes the account of O'Brien's judicial killing so perplexing is that it comes in the midst of a discussion of blood sacrifice among primitive peoples. Irenius is exploring Irish origins, but it is not while discussing the 'Scythians' who used 'to drinke a bowle of blodd togeather' (1823) that he raises the spectre of O'Brien's execution. Rather, this unsettling aside comes when he is considering the 'Gaules', who 'used to drinke theire enemyes blodd and to painte themselves therewith' (1934–35). Irenius interrupts himself to offer an anecdote of his own: 'And so have I sene some of the Irishe doe but not theire enemyes but friendes blodd as namelye at the execucion of A notable Traitour at Limericke Called murrogh Obrien I sawe an olde woman which was his foster mother take up his heade whilste he was quartered and sucked up all the blodd running theareout Sayinge that the earthe was not worthie to drinke it and thearewith allso steped her face, and breste and torne heare Cryinge and shrikinge out most terrible' (1935–42). As an example of bloodthirstiness this appears decidedly odd, because it is the English who carry out the bloodletting, and the foster mother is guilty of nothing more grievous than grief. At this point in the Variorum edition there is a blank space before the dialogue resumes with a blithe remark by Eudoxus which ignores the O'Brien anecdote altogether: 'Yee have verye Well run thoroughe suche Customes as the Irishe have derived from the firste olde nacions which inhabited that Lande Namelye the Scythians the Spanniardes the Gaules the Brittons' (1943–45). Is this merely a scribal interlude? Did Eudoxus 'blank' Irenius? Or is there more than Murrogh's head missing from the manuscript? This passage is a prime example of the interplay between past and present, antiquities and 'news' in the *View*. An exploration of origins turns into a contemporary account of primitive behaviour that is double-edged.

Eudoxus may have been content to pass over in silence O'Brien's execution, but others have not. Southey's exclamation—of horror or surprise—is one response. Later readers have been more detached. Andrew Hadfield speculates that the episode may be 'an anti-Catholic polemic' (Hadfield 1999). Hadfield draws a comparison between the execution of O'Brien and that of the Jesuit Robert Southwell in London in 1595, after which witnesses vied for blood and body parts. Southwell's remains were treated like relics. Hadfield's intervention dovetails neatly with the renewed concern for religious themes in the *View*. Robert Viking O'Brien looks at the question of sacrifice in another light in an important essay on cannibalism in *The Faerie Queene* (2001). O'Brien contrasts the condemnation of the practice in Book VI (6.8.35–6) with, first of all, the 'ghastly portrayal of famine-induced cannibalism' in the *View*, in the description of the Munster famine, and with the depiction of the bereaved bloodlust of Murrogh O'Brien's foster mother (O'Brien 37). O'Brien points out that the initial topic of warriors drinking the blood of their enemies is abandoned when Spenser goes on to describe the act of a woman consumed with a passion of a different kind: 'When O'Brien's foster mother drinks his blood, she expresses, not victory, but grief' (38). O'Brien goes on to argue that more pertinent analogies for cannibalism come from 'European narratives of the New World' (39). Both Hadfield and O'Brien effectively displace the question of cannibalism to communion and colonization, Old World religion and New World politics. Their subtle readings arguably underplay a specific Irish dimension. The fact that it is O'Brien's *foster* mother who takes up his head is crucial, as Southey's exclamation attests. Patricia Fumerton is head and shoulders above the rest when she argues that 'England had to put down Irish child exchange, which it perceived as rebellion . . . Fosterage . . . was an even more dominant feature of Irish than of English culture' (Fumerton, 253–4). What this old woman's hysterical act of mourning depicts is not cannibalism but the kind of close ties that can foster rebellion. Extended family networks were one of the evils identified by Irenius. Indeed, the English wished to cut off not only the literal heads of Irish rebellion but its metaphoric or symbolic heads too. Thus Irenius:

> And hearewithall woulde I allsoe wishe all the Oes and the mackes which the heades of the septes haue taken to theire names to be vtterlye forbidden and extinguished for that the same beinge an ordinaunce as some saie firste made by Obrien for the strenghteninge of the Irishe the Abrogatinge thereof will as muche enfeable them/(4860–4)

These three eyewitness accounts trouble readers, for they risk provoking the very pity the narrator wishes to ward off, and as records of barbarism they come dangerously close to being documents of civilization in their focus on sorrow and survivalist cannibalism rather than cold-blooded ritual. The cause of drinking blood and eating flesh is execution and enforced famine, events engineered by the English. In each case there's awkwardness in the argument. In the episodes of famine and execution, the Irish are cannibals only in the most extreme circumstances. This recalls *A Modest Proposal* (1729), the biting satire by Spenser's Anglo-Irish successor, Jonathan Swift. There, the English are urged to eat the Irish to save them from a more desperate demise. In Spenser's dialogue, the Irish eat themselves out of desperation. At Smerwick, the war on terror uses terror and the threat of future violence to dispense with traditional military notions of mercy and terms of surrender.

A View of the future: Four cornerstones and some cornicing

Since the first appearance of the *View*, successive critics, including some of the finest poets in the English language, have argued over its multiple themes and schemes. It has attracted comment on antiquities, authorship, barbarism, bards, cartography, censorship, civility, dialogue, exile, cultural practices such as fostering, gender and sexuality, history and historiography, humanism in crisis, language and linguistics, patronage, myth, the New English/Anglo-Irish colonial community, republicanism, relations with Spain, and violence, including war and conquest. In recent years four areas of enquiry have emerged as nodal points for research on Spenser's Irish treatise: race, religion, law, and sexuality. These may well prove to be the cornerstones for future research.

The *View* has held a special attraction for historicist and theoretical readings of Spenser. It is an exemplary postcolonial text, featuring in Edward Said's *Culture and Imperialism* (1993). Arguing that imperialism has been largely ignored by literary critics, Said asserts that 'it is generally true that literary historians who study the great sixteenth-century poet Edmund Spenser, for example, do not connect his bloodthirsty plans for Ireland, where he imagined a British army virtually exterminating the native inhabitants, with his poetic achievement or with the history of British rule over Ireland, which continues today' (Said 1993, 5). According to Said: 'Since Spenser's tract on Ireland, a whole tradition of British and European thought has considered the Irish to be a separate and inferior race, usually unregenerately barbarian, often delinquent and primitive' (284–5). The question of 'race' in Spenser's *View* is now attracting criticism more attuned to period and place than Said's broad brushstrokes, with critics drawing on anthropology, archaeology, and ethnology. Jean Feerick (2002), Andrew Hadfield (1993), Chris Ivic (1999), and Maryclaire Moroney (1999) are among those who have tackled this topic with sensitivity and subtlety.

In the 'Afterword' to *Worldmaking Spenser*, David Lee Miller asks: 'As postcolonialism and cultural studies provide increasingly dominant paradigms for literary study, will *A View of the Present State of Ireland* dislodge *The Faerie Queene* as Spenser's best known and most frequently studied text?' He then half-answers his own question by adding 'I hope not' (Miller 2000, 247). Miller puts his finger on the state of play in recent Spenser studies. The *View*, once an embarrassing outcast, now occupies a place close to the centre of Spenser studies. As Paul Stevens has remarked: 'For the last two decades in Spenser studies, certainly since the publication of Greenblatt's *Renaissance Self-Fashioning* in 1980, Spenser's Irish experience has been the only game in town' (Stevens 1999, 450).

If 'race' represents a growing area of interest in Spenser studies focused on the *View* then an equally significant move has occurred in the form of a return to religion and law, imagined anew as crucial components of a thoroughgoing strategy of 'reform'. Religion remains the great unspoken in the *View*, where the radical Protestantism of *The Shepheardes Calendar* is off the map. Brendan Bradshaw is the critic who has concentrated most on the theological impetus behind Spenser's dialogue, but his arguments, and those of other critics eager to see religion as central to his work, are apparently undermined by the scant attention paid to religion in the text. Arguably the most remarkable development in Spenser criticism has been the return to religion. The *View* is now the touchstone of Spenser's theological opinions. The broad claims of Bradshaw and others that Spenser was driven by Puritan zeal have been focused upon and finessed by critics concerned to tease out in subtler ways the extent to which Spenser viewed Ireland through the prism of the Reformation. Jacqueline McEvoy's analysis of biblical rhetoric in the *View*, taken together with Maryclaire Moroney's work on the dissolution of the monasteries, Paul Stevens' searching analyses of the interplay between colonialism and religion, and Andrew Hadfield's observations on anti-Catholic rhetoric, suggests a new critical configuration. Religion, a neglected area of study since the advent of new historicism, is now a fruitful area of inquiry. Although it has little to say on the *View*, Richard Mallette's *Spenser and the Discourses of Reformation* is part of a major reappraisal of the place of religion in Spenser's work which opens up the notion of reform beyond narrow theological premises or broad charges of 'Puritanism'.

Developments in the treatment of religion and gender have offered useful correctives to the pivotal work of Greenblatt and Canny. The 'colonial' model piloted by Canny, with its 'New World' analogue, was challenged by both Brady and Bradshaw, and their focus on law and religion, hitherto neglected or underplayed aspects of the *View*, has gained ground in recent years. Andrew Hadfield (1996a), Jacqueline McEvoy (1998), Maryclaire Moroney (1999), and Paul Stevens (1993; 1995) have revisited religion with telling consequences. David Baker (1986), Brendan Bradshaw (1987), Ciarán Brady (1989), David Edwards (1999), Elizabeth Fowler (2000), and Bryan Lockey (2001) are among those who have had another look at law, including common law and martial law, passing judgement in the process on the earlier tendency to downplay the thoroughgoing nature of Spenser's commitment to legal reform, and the extent to which the *View* is a study in legal imperialism, including martial law.

While Canny's colonial model was being expanded and expounded upon, Stephen Greenblatt's cultural model was being revisited and revised by critics eager to reverse its perceived displacement of gender politics by colonial politics. Greenblatt's alleged underplaying of matters of sexual difference has been challenged by a number of critics and the importance of sexuality has been pointed up in new ways, with the representation of women increasingly read within the specific national context where practices such as fostering and intermarriage are crucial, and also within a wider frame where an enhanced awareness of early modern sexualities can finesse our understanding of gender anxiety in the *View* (Cavanagh 1986; 1994; Fumerton 1986; Carroll 1990; Jones and Stallybrass 1992; Highley 1997; Craig 2001; Bowman 2003;). In an Irish context, colonialism and Catholicism, the two masters against which James Joyce struggled as a servant of art, create a sexual double bind. Recent Irish writers have used Spenser as a way of opening up the question of sexuality in modern Ireland. Both Frank McGuinness in his play *Mutabilitie* (1997), and Robert Welch in *The Kilcolman Notebook* (1994) queer the pitch of Spenser's sexual politics, while Derek Mahon, in his verse letter 'Beyond Howth Head', laments the loss of the 'Lewde libertie' that prevailed in Spenser's day, and which the poet railed against. Spenser's Puritanism is now the province of the Catholic Church, and Mahon upbraids 'that tight-arsed, convent-bred disdain' which is the mirror image of colonial appeals to purity (Gardiner 2001, 201).

A fifth focus for the future may be discerned in the form of a return to comparative studies. Too often Spenser's prose has been read in relation to his poetry, rather than in relation to texts located firmly within its own discursive field. Study of the text ought to be part of a study of Renaissance prose in general, and the dialogue form specifically. The *View* has been singled out for scrutiny in a way that skewers the place of his prose dialogue within a wider and more varied English discourse on Ireland. Comparative studies of the *View* have tried to place it within a colonial milieu, but none of Spenser's contemporaries, New or Old English or Gaelic Irish, has the profile that Spenser enjoys across history and literature. Those who did produce major treatises on Ireland in the period—Richard Beacon, Philip O'Sullivan Beare, Edmund Campion, John Davies, John Derricke, William Herbert, Geoffrey Keating, Fynes Moryson, Barnaby Rich, and Richard Stanyhurst—lack the cachet or kudos of Spenser. James Knapp is one of a number of critics who have argued that the originality and importance of Spenser's contribution has been exaggerated because of his literary reputation:

> It is safe to say that Edmund Spenser's *View of the Present State of Ireland* has been the most scrutinized of Elizabethan works on Ireland, despite the fact that much of its infamous content simply repeats anti-Irish tropes that had been circulating since the twelfth century. Almost from the moment of its publication in 1633, Spenser's status as an Elizabethan man of letters positioned his text as a central authority on the Elizabethan view of Ireland. Long viewed as a fiercely loyal subject of Elizabeth I, Spenser is thought to have had the unfortunate role of rendering widely-held anti-Irish sentiments in memorable verse and prose, his attitude representative of a community of zealous English Protestants. Only recently has the project of disentangling Spenser's Irish policy from the form of his presentation become central to the study of early modern Ireland. (Knapp 2000, 415–16)

Whether or not the *View* is read as an anti-Irish text—and its 'infamous content' is still subject to scrutiny and open to debate—one thing is clear: Spenser's prose dialogue has been the long-suffering victim of that which it is purported to perpetrate. The so-called suppression of the *View* has been ongoing since its entrance into the stationers register in 1598. Anti-Irish prejudice has fuelled critical reaction, by turns censorious and sensationalist. Paradoxically, the fact that Spenser chose to take Ireland as his muse in his longest foray into prose has also meant that interest in him is sustained. In his 'Memoir' of Spenser in Morris' Globe edition, J. W. Hales claims 'His poems are his best biography' (xv), but it is the prose—the letters (including the 'Letter to Raleigh'), the editorial apparatus of *The Shepheardes Calender*, and of course the *View*—that increasingly sets the agenda for biographical work on the poet-planter. 'The prose knows', as Stanley Fish says of Milton, and what it knows is that dialogue is the key to understanding Ireland's place in Spenser studies. Admiring the *View* is not something we are often urged to do. Spenser has led a double life, and the *View* has suffered for his art. From Ware to here, it is a vital and volatile text, one that impinges on Spenser's status as an English canonical author with indelible Irish connections.

Further reading

Brady, C. 1986. 'Spenser's Irish Crisis: Humanism and Experience in the 1590s', *Past and Present* 111: 17–49.

Brink, J. R. 1994. 'Constructing the *View of the Present State of Ireland*', *Spenser Studies* 11 (1994; intended for 1990), 203–28.

Canny, N. 1983. 'Edmund Spenser and the Development of an Anglo-Irish Identity', *Yearbook of English Studies* 13: 1–19.

Coughlan, P. ed., 1989. *Spenser and Ireland: An Interdisciplinary Perspective*, Cork: Cork University Press.

Deborah S. 1997. 'Irishmen, Aristocrats, and Other White Barbarians', *Renaissance Quarterly* 50: 494–525.

Greenblatt, S. 1980. 'To Fashion a Gentleman: Spenser and the Destruction of the Bower of Bliss', in *Renaissance Self-Fashioning from More to Shakespeare*, Chicago: University of Chicago Press, 157–92.

Hadfield, A. 1997. *Edmund Spenser's Irish Experience: Wilde Fruit and Salvage Soyl*, Oxford: Clarendon.

Ivic, C. 1999. 'Spenser and the Bounds of Race', *Genre* 32: 141–74.

McCabe, R. A. 2002. *Spenser's Monstrous Regiment: Elizabethan Ireland and the Poetics of Difference*, Oxford: Oxford University Press.

Stevens, P. 1995. 'Spenser and Milton on Ireland: Civility, Exclusion, and the Politics of .Wisdom', *Ariel* 26, 4: 151–67.

van Es, B. 2002. 'Discourses of Conquest: *The Faerie Queene*, the Society of Antiquaries, and *A View of the Present State of Ireland*', *English Literary Renaissance* 32, 1: 118–51.

12
Shorter Verse After 1595

Raphael Lyne

In 1596 Spenser published two major works: *Prothalamion*, a poem celebrating the double wedding of Elizabeth and Katherine Somerset, daughters of the Earl of Worcester, and *Fowre Hymnes* on Love, Beauty, Heavenly Love, and Heavenly Beauty (which appeared together with the second edition of *Daphnaida*). These were the final works published in his lifetime, but his last poem did not appear until 1609. In that year the bookseller Matthew Lownes published a new edition of *The Faerie Queene*, in which (under a separate title-page) *Two cantos of Mutabilitie* appeared for the first time. These cantos were presented as, and apparently are, additional material from the unfinished epic. These late works are rarely considered as a trio, and yet they do share interests. Critics repeatedly argue that they explore their own lateness in Spenser's career, and that they deliver notes of studied finality. Closure is implied in a turn towards comprehensiveness, a partial success in the quest for understanding, and in different versions of literary retraction, wherein a poet renounces some or all of his earlier work. These poems all have a scale one could call "philosophical": they explore ideas about transcendence, or ideas which in themselves transcend the everyday world. However, these works also have a material side, in that they interact with this everyday world, with time, bodies, politics, and the realities of a poetic career. The nature of the dialogue between philosophical and material is a vital critical question because it is centrally at issue in all three works, and because (in the *Mutabilitie Cantos*, most pressingly) its presence here urges a reconsideration of Spenser's earlier work.

Fowre Hymnes

The *Fowre Hymnes* are enigmatic poems based on numinous ideas of love and voluminous traditions of theory. Essentially, they revive an ancient tradition of the epic hymn (Rollinson 1971) and use it to marry neo-Platonic and Christian images of love. One of their most tantalising features is a dedication that states the first two hymns are earlier and more straightforwardly profane work, and the second pair are an attempt to correct this impulse:

> Having in the greener times of my youth, composed these former two Hymnes in the praise of Love and beautie, and finding that the same too much pleased those of like age and disposition [...] I was moved by the one of you two most excellent Ladies, to call in the same. But being unable so to doe, by reason that many copies thereof were formerly scattered abroad, I resolved at least to amend, and by way of retractation to reforme them.

The element of renunciation, alongside the aspiring tone and the late date, lend themselves to a note of finality in the collection. Modern critics have been sceptical of such an interpretation. Bjorvand (1975) asserts that despite Spenser's protestation that the two pairs should be read as distinct endeavours, they are in fact closely related, with the first pair incomplete without the second. Hyde (1986, 132–41) argues against the poems to Heavenly Love and Heavenly Beauty working simply as a retraction of the first pair—their aspiration to "reform" could be taken more generally. Johnson (1992) interprets this "retractation" as a renewed undertaking of ideas and vocabulary previously seen in the *Amoretti*. Oates (1983) sees it as a form of revision, and places the *Hymnes* as part of a developmental journey in Spenser's writing and thought. Having surveyed an earlier group of critics pursuing the idea of "retractation" in a more Chaucerian, negative way, the *Variorum* editors make a trenchant point:

> Perhaps the commentators have not made sufficient allowance for the conventionality of the literary "retractation" which many poets had declared from Petrarch down. (8.659)

The conventional element is indeed significant, though there is still a correspondence between the dynamic of the prefatory comment and the tendency towards a heavenly ideal then enshrined in the structure of *Fowre Hymnes*.

The move from earthly to heavenly qualities is vital, as the opening of the third hymn, to Heavenly Love, makes clear:

> Love, lift me up upon thy golden wings,
> From this base world unto thy heavens hight,
> Where I may see those admirable things,
> Which there thou workest by thy soveraine might,
> Farre above feeble reach of earthly sight,
> That I thereof an heavenly Hymne may sing
> Unto the god of Love, high heavens king.

(1–7)

This motion, which the fourth hymn calls a "transport from flesh into the spright" (259), is profoundly Christian but also reflects neo-Platonic thought, which revived Plato's distinction between a heavenly world of ideal forms and an earthly world of imitations. Neo-Platonism and the structure of the *Fowre Hymnes* offer ways of bridging the gap. Early twentieth-century critics strove to trace Spenser's poems back to distinct sources. The editors of the *Variorum* weigh in with more judicious observations after collating their efforts:

> The differing views presented in these extracts seem to point conclusively to the fact that Spenser was not following a pre-conceived plan of philosophical presentation, that while he undoubtedly understood the implications of the neo-Platonic stages of progression, he touched them but lightly as he passed along to give an appearance of philosophical development of his theme. (8.681)

In part this offers a valuable insight into the workings of the *Fowre Hymnes*. These poems are a set of interconnected, nuanced syntheses of a diverse tradition, but their style is that of inspired exploration rather than scholarly collation—it takes the *Variorum* to argue, decisively, that the *Fowre Hymnes* are not a Variorum themselves. However, Spenser's encounter with his sources is not really so light, and the evident importance of neo-Platonic thought led later critics to refine ideas of its presence in the *Fowre Hymnes* (Jayne 1952, Ellrodt 1960). There has been a move away from straightforward identifications of Spenser's poems with neo-Platonists' models of spiritual progression. For Welsford (1967) the framework of the Platonic ladder—one of the key metaphors—offers excessive clarity both in the progression and the hierarchy of the sequence. Instead, we have "two ideas of love, both of which are shown to be good and true" (62), and Spenser "only hints at a possible reconciliation" (63). For Hyde (1986, 132–41) the Platonic ladder is problematic when taken as an illustration of progress by strict stages: its original form implies a more organic process. Quitslund (1969) suggests that "Spenser, like many Renaissance thinkers, was fascinated by the diversity of truth, as manifested in many authorities and traditions, while at the same time he was anxious to reduce that diversity to concord and unity" (212). Applied to the *Fowre Hymnes*, this offers a way round the morass of interconnecting ideas: they derive from separate locations but part of the poet's endeavour has been to overcome that separateness by means of a heartfelt demonstration of hope and faith.

Not surprisingly those interested in neo-Platonic resonances, like Comito (1977), find the poems engaging with "the life of images", which "like the lovers' drama, unfolds on the margins of the ineffable" (301). Other critics have explored the ways in which the *Hymnes* might speak to the plainer world. Quitslund (1985, 202) reflects a more modern historicist tendency in testing the poems' images of love against the interests and experiences of their patrons and dedicatees (Margaret, Countess of Cumberland, and Mary, Countess of Warwick): "The ideals of the *Fowre Hymnes* are ironically related to the actualities of love as experienced by a widow and an estranged wife." Nevertheless, they do imply a movement towards "the light of an eventual happiness that poetry can only anticipate". Earlier Hill (1966) had argued that the poems have feet of clay in their fulsome praise of the Queen, and that this volume was a bid for financial rewards. Typically, however, critics have not resisted the movement of the poems away from worldly concerns and towards heavenly ideals. Patrick Cheney (1993, 195–224) finds a place for the *Fowre Hymnes*, as he does for *Prothalamion*, as a climactic part of Spenser's career trajectory: in embracing the hymn form, he aspires grandly towards Heaven.

Prothalamion

Prothalamion portrays its two brides as two swans swimming down the Thames, before tackling the poet's own troubles, giving snippets of London history, and praising the Earl of Essex. Its unusual combination of material has often been at issue in criticism. In 1715 John Hughes contrasted the allegorical practice of *Prothalamion* with his own recommended ideal:

> Another essential Property is, That the Fable be every where consistent with it self...Most of the Allegories in the *Fairy Queen*, are agreeable to this Rule; but in one of his other Poems, the Author has manifestly transgress'd it: the Poem I mean, is that which is call'd *Prothalamion*. In this, the two Brides are figur'd by two beautifull Swans sailing down the River *Thames*. The Allegory breaks before the Reader is prepar'd for it; and we see them, at their landing, in their true Shapes, without knowing how this sudden change is effected. (Hughes, "Essay on Allegory", in Cummings (1971) 256)

One might argue, in the face of such rigour, that the decorum of an allegorical epic differs from that of a short, occasional work such as *Prothalamion*, which makes its own rules within a smaller framework. These rules, however, have proved elusive, and critics of the poem's genre find it partly an innovation, and partly in debt to classical and renaissance predecessors. Norton (1951) is the fullest exploration of the English tradition. Osgood (1961) shows that both *Prothalamion* and the more conventional *Epithalamion* captured the imaginations of seventeenth-century writers of marriage poems, with numerous allusions as testimony. Smith (1959) sees it as an invented form which incorporates other topics as well as praising a marriage. Greene (1957) puts Catullus to the fore in an exploration of the classical epithalamion, but West (1974) finds the Roman poet Propertius the key antecedent for celebrating marriage in song.

Winbolt (1918, 140) raises a slight groan with his hoary naming of this "last complete poem published by Spenser" as a "swan-song", yet many have been interested in how it might play the role of a late work. Woodward (1962, 46) describes it as "a microcosm of Spenser's work in poetry", which "demonstrates the union of real and ideal which Spenser so passionately and eloquently hoped for in all areas of human life". The real–ideal dichotomy here parallels the philosophical-material interplay explored above in relation to *Fowre Hymnes*. What is striking about Woodward's account is the concrete "demonstration" of an often unrealisable union; other critics find the balance more precarious. The reception of this poem's flattery of patrons has a very different complexion when the prevailing assumptions about poetry change. Osgood (1930, 17) reflects an idealised notion of poetry's place in the world when he makes a sharp charge against the poet's motives:

> Spenser's desire for honor and gain, for prominent position and wealth, admits no denial. Ashamed as he was of it, he could never rise wholly superior to his ambition in politics and at court. With Spenser the infirmity was chronic and incurable.

It seems to a modern reader unsympathetic, even impertinent, for a critic to reflect (from a position of relative luxury) on a poet's weakness for patronage— something which could have been the difference between financial solvency and abject penury. In Spenser's case, there was an added political motivation for seeking favour with one of the few people with the influence and acumen to enforce the harsh policies he advocated in Ireland.

Spenser's life and work will not satisfy a reader's wish for poetry to transcend the venal or brutal aspects of reality. One, if not both, is often there, and critics of very different persuasions confront this issue again and again. Berger (1965), for example, starts with a question that identifies how it bears upon *Prothalamion*'s peculiar combination of material:

> *Prothalamion* is a simple-seeming poem.... In a poem of ten stanzas nominally celebrating the double marriage of "two Honourable and virtuous/Ladies" to "two worthie/Gentlemen", why are two stanzas devoted to the poet's own life and troubles, and a third to some patron-seeking praise of Essex? (363)

In Berger's account this is a question the poem itself addresses. It could hardly be more explicit, after all, in raising the question of patronage:

> Next whereunto there standes a stately place,
> Where oft I gayned giftes and goodly grace
> Of that great Lord, which therein wont to dwell,
> Whose want too well now feeles my freendles case:

But Ah here fits not well
Olde woes but joyes to tell
Against the bridale daye, which is not long,
Sweet *Themmes*, run softly till I end my Song.

(137–44)

The mood of this comment is difficult to gauge: it does not seem like a joke, but it is also hard to take it as bare-faced plea and complaint. In Berger's sensitive account the tone is one of acceptance. At the end of the poem the coexistence of two conflicting elements—the idealism of praise and the worldliness of patronage and fortune—is something accepted rather than embraced:

The poet is now fully aware that poetry cannot abolish actuality and ought not therefore be used as a means of escape. All it can do is change one's spirit, redirect the soul. (378)

For Manley (1982, 226), who puts the poem into city life, the link between the poem and the material world is a constructive one, and *Prothalamion* finds a positive location for the wedding in London: "Through its praise of brides and statesmen, the poem participates in the very process of culture-building that it celebrates and locates in the city". van Es (2002a, 73–7) shows the role it plays in Spenser's long-standing interest in chorography, writing that contemplates and describes the land. However, in Simon Shepherd's Marxist reading the poem's worldly interactions are burdensome, and thus the poem undertakes an "effort to explain and relate to the patronage system" that makes clear "the contradictions around the poet's role in this type of economic order" (Shepherd 1989, 105). This makes Spenser's candour a sharp response to the prevailing system. Eriksen (1993) shares this sense that the double marriage is the ostensible rather than the fundamental subject of the poem, and interprets *Prothalamion* as a series of "mannerist" manoeuvres all of which are ways of praising and impressing the Earl of Essex.

Some of the most illuminating accounts recognise the poem's intimate connection with their historical occasion. Alastair Fowler's analysis of the poem's metre, numerology, and zodiacal structure makes the poem seem deeply rooted in the very moment it describes:

The problem for the interpreter is to know how much of the resuscitated occasion—how much soil about the roots—to include in his synthesis. A purely critical account might afford more tact in selection; but it would falsify the proportion of the event. We may have to face a cruel paradox, that the monumental ideal made for expendability: for a poem uniquely suitable to a single unrepeatable occasion. (Fowler 1975, 86)

This sharp critique deems the problems of interpretation more or less intractable: the dialogue between material and philosophical may be unresolvable, even unexplorable, when the specific reference points are obscured. William Oram's account of the poem sees the occasion and the speaker in a dynamic relationship:

> The poem very likely builds, in ways we cannot now see, on the inflections of the occasion itself, which involved a uniting of families under the auspices of the queen's last favourite. It is thus very different from *Fowre Hymnes*, but like that poem, it depicts the unfolding drama of the speaker's active thought. (Oram 1997, 281)

Oram's interest in these late works' dramatisation of thought is traced back to an occasion which was as concrete for Spenser and his implied readers as it is lost to us. He goes on (290) to contrast the mood of this poem with both *Fowre Hymnes* and the *Mutabilitie Cantos*: here the marks of Spenser's ambition show him very much engaged in the world. However, Anne Lake Prescott is surely close to the truth when she argues that ultimately "the poignancy of living and writing in a changing world remains: for Spenser, the pillars of eternity are not found in London, not even at Essex House" (Prescott 2001b, 159). This strikes a note of finality in contrast to Oram's more lively vision. The frank wish for patronage usually tends against too much assertion that this poem acts out its role as a final work. Nevertheless, although the refrain is repeated, and the river keeps running, the imagined ultimate silencing of the poet's voice is ever-present: "Sweet *Themmes*, run softly till I end my Song".

Two cantos of Mutabilitie

The *Two cantos of Mutabilitie* announced themselves as part of the missing portion of the epic in which the legend of constancy would feature. One sensible suggestion as to how they came to light after Spenser's death is that of Burrow (1996, 41), who proposes that Lownes acquired them from William Ponsonby, the printer of the earlier *Faerie Queene*, whose stock and equipment he inherited. The scale of their plot is enormous: the titanness Mutabilitie is in dispute with the classical gods over who rules the world. Nature stands in judgement, eventually deciding that while Mutabilitie may indeed entirely dominate this world, the next world will elude her grasp. Their scale in themselves is small—two cantos (plus two additional stanzas) dwarfed by the seventy-two extant cantos in the rest of the poem. This discrepancy helps explain their problematic critical reception. For some, they revise the whole poem in retrospect, while for others they are a nagging yet marginal fragment. As part of the epic they are incorporated in the grand schemes of critics discussed in earlier chapters: for example, Nohrnberg (1976, 735–91) investigates their role within a huge allegorical network. However, they also receive attention in their own right as one of Spenser's shorter and later publications. Individual critics struggle with the same nuances and priorities identified in *Protha-lamion* and the *Fowre Hymnes*, yet with even greater intensity, as in doing so they are grappling with fundamental issues in the *Cantos*, in *The Faerie Queene*, and beyond.

The introduction to Zitner (1968) covers a great deal of the ground and summarises preceding speculations about the date and the relationship to the rest of *The Faerie Queene*. A central feature of criticism of the *Cantos* per se has been speculation as to their origin and intended context. John Hughes's 1715 *Life* filled in the gaps in the then orthodox theory that Spenser had completed his epic by telling the spurious story that "the six last Books (excepting the Two Canto's of *Mutability*) were unfortunately lost by his Servant, whom he had in haste sent before him into *England*" (Cummings 1971, 338). Given that these poems are about worldly vicissi-tude and the overriding power of change in the world, it makes a huge difference whether they were only ever an unfinished fragment. Scholarly consensus and also, not inconsequentially, critical taste have gravitated towards a view that the missing portion never was written. Evans (1880) denied they were part of *The Faerie Queene* at all—an idea which has persuaded few. Albright (1928) sees them as relics of the early drafts sent to Gabriel Harvey in the 1580s, and rejected by their first reader. Albright discovers some "salvaged" material elsewhere in *The Faerie Queene*—a perverse way of interpreting repeating themes in the poem. Greenlaw (1930) makes a series of trenchant criticisms of this view. Spens (1934, 39–50) constructs an ingenious but generally discredited theory that they were the final cantos in the eighth book of an eight-book *Faerie Queene*. Fowler (1964, 227–33) argues on mythological grounds that the subject matter suits a seventh book, which is the most plausible, if ultimately unprovable, explanation.

Other twentieth-century critics instead saw them and their incomplete-ness as a way of ascertaining how Spenser wrote. Lewis (1936) calls them "the core of a book without the fringe", and extrapolates from this Spenser's "habit of writing his 'cores' first and then draping the rest round them" (333). The work of Bennett (1942) established more fully that *The Faerie Queene* was not written in linear sequence, and so a surviving section such as this is not an aberration. Nevertheless the facts of their late arrival, and the notes of finality, have nagged readers and prompted critics to explore ways in which they are not necessarily incomplete or unfinished. Frye (1963, 71) deems them "certainly not a fragment: they constitute a single beautifully shaped poem that could not have a more logical beginning, middle, and end". It is indeed hard to argue that the final

lines, said to be the second stanza of an eighth canto, seem like the start
of something new:

> Then gin I thinke on that which Nature sayd,
>   Of that same time when no more Change shall be,
>   But stedfast rest of all things firmely stayd
>   Vpon the pillours of Eternity,
>   That is contrayr to Mutabilitie:
>   For, all that moueth, doth in Change delight:
>   But thence-forth all shall rest eternally
>   With Him that is the God of Sabbaoth hight:
> O thou great Sabbaoth God, graunt me that Sabaoths sight.

(VII.viii.2)

The thought that Spenser creates a truly dramatic ending here is beguiling
but there remains a feeling that in such an account the text is reflecting
rather than eliciting artful reading—and reading aimed at a formalist appreciation of the fragment rather than an attempt to locate the work in its
history. However, Colin Burrow has made the valuable point that there were
authoritative precedents for leaving an epic poem unfinished or indeed with
fragments hanging (Burrow 2001). Ariosto's *Cinque Canti* are the closest
analogy; Ovid's *Fasti* was also unfinished and remains with only six of
twelve books; the incompletely polished Virgil's *Aeneid*, the story goes, was
rescued from being burned despite its scrupulous author's wishes. The
classical connections of the *Cantos* were established in the 1930s, at least
partly in reaction to Albright (1929) who preferred to seek out non-pagan
antecedents. In direct opposition to this Greenlaw (1930) championed
Lucretius as an important source. Cumming (1931) made what now looks
like a decisive contribution to this debate by asserting the importance of
Ovid's *Metamorphoses*, though Bennett (1933) explored a neo-Platonist background. It is probable that critics of the early twentieth century found it
more difficult than modern readers to see playful, controversial Ovid in the
role of a philosophical source. Holahan (1976) argues, however, that
Spenser moves beyond Ovid in his supra-historical scale; Lyne (2001) sees
the exchange as more troubling on both sides.

Although critics vary in their interpretation of the mood of retrospection
therein, the dominant tendency has for some time been to read the *Cantos* as a
last word on Spenser's epic, and often on his whole body of work. Greene
(1963, 323) says that "although the *Cantos* differ strongly from the rest of the
poem, they also epitomise it". Blissett (1964) calls them "a detached retrospective commentary" and "a highly satisfactory conclusion to a foreshortened draft" (26). He also calls the final two stanzas a "retractation", implicit
where the dedication to the *Fowre Hymnes* is elliptically explicit (41–2).

Holland (1968) sees them as an encapsulation or a summary, with the timescale of the whole *Faerie Queene* contained within the *Cantos'* central myth. A different set of critical assumptions is implied in that conclusion of Campbell (1982, 58), that the poem embodies the suggestion that "the truth of this, or any other, poem is necessarily fragmentary". There is no resolution to the uncertainty, which is in keeping with a poem involved throughout in a dialogue between closure and deferral, but which also reflects critics' assimilation of post-structuralist doubts about the solidity of meaning.

Those who emphasise the interaction of the *Cantos* with the historical and political world do so both generally and specifically. Fletcher (1971, 217–28) describes them as an allegory of rebellion and revolution. Harry Berger (1988) says, of the *Mutabilitie Cantos* and Spenser's poetry more generally, "it is historical in two reciprocal aspects: the objective character of Spenser's vision is *evolutionary*; its subjective mode is *retrospective*" (243). The poems look back from "the here and now" (244) but tackle vaster processes. For Guillory (1983) the *Cantos* are engaged in a struggle with their own temporal nature:

> If the poet cannot escape the temporality of his medium, there cannot be sacred poetry. The *Mutabilitie Cantos* move inexorably to the enforcing of this dichotomy, redeeming time only insofar as it works toward its ultimate undoing. (65)

In the end the struggle must be successful—the concession of the world to Mutabilitie is made with a clear assertion of the limits of that world. Williams (1952) concludes a sensible analysis by placing the *Cantos* among similar passages in which the largest themes of *The Faerie Queene* are articulated. They are "a more explicit statement of the great theme which earlier books express by symbol and by arrangement of material" (128). The "great theme" is "this proper movement of all the richness of created things towards the unity which produces them and works through them" (130). Waller (1994, 179–86), like Williams, sees the *Cantos* fitting the mould of "last work" because of their ultimate resolution against this world. He sees them as an act of retrospection and rethinking that culminates in a kind of surrender (185).

Elsewhere these generalised historical themes are given more concrete reference points. Woodworth (1944) linked the Titaness herself with Arabella Stuart and plots in support of her claim to the English throne. Much more persuasive and influential, however, are those which explore the significance of the *Cantos'* Irish setting, something with which readers are confronted within the poem:

> Eftsoones the time and place appointed were,
>> Where all, both heavenly Powers, and earthly wights,
>> Before great Natures presence should appeare,

> For triall of their Titles and best Rights:
> That was, to weet, upon the highest hights
> Of Arlo-hill (Who knowes not Arlo-hill?)
> That is the highest head (in all mens sights)
> Of my old father Mole, whom Shepheards quill
> Renowned hath with hymnes fit for a rurall skill.

(VII.vi.36)

Spenser asks what is clearly a rhetorical question up to a point, but in doing so highlights the reader's separation from the immediate experience of the poet and his closest associates. For critics alert to the Irish situation the opposition to Mutability's rebellious tendency is not derived from morality but from the author's passionate allegiance to English dominion in Ireland. Nevertheless, Ringler (1965–66) weighed in against specific identifications of historical figures in the *Cantos* (as in Stampfer 1951–52 and others). To see Faunus as Tyrone, Cynthia as Elizabeth, and so on, was reductive. His analysis of the literary contexts for the Faunus episode is insightful: "it is a parody of the larger story in which it is embedded: it is a kind of anti-masque" (18). Nevertheless the story's evocation of known locations makes the worldly interpretations co-exist with the allegorical scheme. Lupton (1993) strikes a balance between the "largely philosophical" concerns of this part of *The Faerie Queene*, and its situation on "Spenser's much-debated property". Hadfield (1997, 185–202) argues that the *Cantos* include a wish that Elizabeth, like Diana in the Faunus episode, should intervene more strongly in Ireland. Alongside this, however, there is an implicit realisation that such an intervention was never going to happen. van Es (2002a, 102–11) argues that the *Mutabilitie Cantos* acknowledge this powerlessness through their dialogue structure, and should be understood in the context of a wider body of debates—including Irish assemblies—that resist the extension of monarchical rule.

Kathleen Williams (1966) makes the fundamental dialogue between the *Cantos* and the history rebound onto the reader's position:

> Mutabilitie is oddly convincing in action and speech; she is so, I think, because her character arises so directly out of the fluctuating experience which she personifies. She is as complicated a mixture as one of us, indeed she is one of us, and her attitudes express our own. (228)

Telling though this affinity may be, it is one that Spenser resists and tries to reject: humans are supposed to aspire outside Mutabilitie's range, and many interpret the final lines of the *Mutabilitie Cantos* as the poem's attempt to effect that aspiration. Some of the most stimulating recent criticism places the *Cantos* at the culmination of a long dialogue between moral philosophy and politics:

> Spenser's work dramatizes the differing, sometimes competing claims of moral philosophy and its elaboration of the ethical virtues, on the one hand, and the claims of an emerging political theory based on natural law and possessory right on the other. (Fowler 1995, 71)

The *Mutabilitie Cantos* could be seen as one of the crises caused by the competition between these claims: ultimately Spenser cannot assert moral value over the urgent potency of political context. In Teskey's ambitious and insightful account (1993, revised in Teskey 1996) the interaction within a related duality, politics, and metaphysics has a different quality: "we can get at the politics of *Mutabilitie* only by going through its metaphysics" (119). One of the most important things about Teskey's account is the way it raises the stakes, making the *Mutabilitie Cantos* engage with huge philosophical themes, but also with the earthly experience with which they interact.

The summary of the contribution of the *Cantos* to *The Faerie Queene* in Burrow (1996) demonstrates why the interaction of the philosophical and the material goes so deep:

> The *Mutabilitie Cantos* mark Spenser's poem not as an epic about the power of the poet to revive the heroic past in new, living images of virtue, but as an epic of mortality, in which heroes and poets are contained within a process of change. (41)

The overall message of this appendage to *The Faerie Queene* is indeed something close to this, but it is tempered by, or contrasts with, the last-gasp conclusion to the central debate. Nature's ruling allows the poem to gesture at a greater framework and at a new, next life. And thus it is not surprising that many critics have seen the *Mutabilitie Cantos* to achieve a kind of closure in relation to Spenser's epic poem and his epic ambitions. Fox (1972) argues that the poem's grand aim becomes less and less achievable until this final point, which "marks the end of Spenser's struggle in his poetry with death and despair" (40). For some these *Cantos* are Spenser's very final works. Stampfer (1951–52) boldly connects their rejection of worldly mutability with the sacking of Spenser's estate at Kilcolman; only at the last does the poet contrive a note of faith. No specific explanation overcomes the objection that the mood of the *Cantos* is derived from multiple sources (genre, theology, philosophy) and from dynamics within the rest of *The Faerie Queene* and indeed elsewhere in Spenser's verse.

Perhaps the crucial critical nexus is illustrated by Harry Berger's response to Thomas Greene (1963). The latter allows for the final stanzas to express a profound religious belief, but "if faith is indeed a refuge here, it is a lonely and bitter one" (323). Berger (1988) responds thus:

> Having oscillated between the elemental division of pagan pessimism and the organic harmony of medieval optimism, he attains a more complicated and dynamic equilibrium at the end, still looking backward, still pressing forward, still resolving doubts. (242)

It is hard not to conclude that these readings may well lie within the parameters of individual readers' diverse responses to such rich and elusive material.

Overview

Critics have often discovered related and very Spenserian interests in these works. The dialogue between the philosophical and the material, and an intrinsic sense of ending and mortality offer the prospect of a connected mapping of Spenser's late work. Yet critics have, in fact, rarely examined the three works together. One notable exception, Oram (1997), argues for the significance of the lateness of all three works:

> They differ greatly from one another, but like the second half of the epic, they all show a retrospective quality, looking back on the earlier poetry from the perspective of middle age. They deal in various ways with time, change, and the uses of the imagination. Each dramatises an act of *feigning* and of making things up as the speaker tries to understand the world and his place in it. In each case the speaker works through a sequence of imaginings toward a more comprehensive, if not to a final, vision. (263)

Oram cites key themes in these poems—time, change, "the world and his place in it"—that connect with the recurring concerns of critics examined thus far. In arguing for the perspective of middle age, he reminds us that Spenser died quite young, and that any interpretation of these works as distinctly final is benefiting from hindsight. Their interconnection is elusive and their shared interests are evident elsewhere in Spenser's work. However, they do represent a kind of phase in Spenser's career as it is perceived by critics, who cannot but wonder what kind of literary end he reached.

Further reading

Berger, H. 1965. "Spenser's *Prothalamion*: An Interpretation", *EIC* 15: 363–80.
Ellrodt, R. 1960. *Neoplatonism in the Poetry of Spenser*, Geneva: Droz.
Holahan, M. 1976. "Iamque opus exegi: Ovid's Changes and Spenser's Brief Epic of Mutability", *ELR* 6, 244–70.

Holland, J. F. 1968. "The Cantos of Mutabilitie and the Form of *The Faerie Queene*", *ELH* 35: 21–31.

Oram, W. A. 1997. *Edmund Spenser*, Twayne's English Authors Series New York: Twayne.

Quitslund, J. A. 1985. "Spenser and the Patronesses of the *Fowre Hymnes*: 'Ornaments of All True Love and Beautie'", in Margaret Hannay, ed., *Silent but for the Word: Tudor Women as Patrons, Translators, and Writers of Religious Works*, Kent: Kent State University Press, 184–202.

Rollinson, P. B. 1971. "A Generic View of Spenser's *Fowre Hymnes*", *SP* 68, 292–704.

Gordon Teskey. 1996. *Allegory and Violence*, Ithaca: Cornell University Press.

Welsford, E. 1967. *Spenser, Fowre Hymnes and Epithalamion: A Study of Edmund Spenser's Doctrine of Love*, Oxford: Basil Blackwell.

Williams, K. 1952. "'Eterne in Mutabilitie': The Unified World of *The Faerie Queene*", *ELH* 19: 115–30.

Woodward, D. H. 1962. "Some Themes in Spenser's *Prothalamion*", *ELH* 29: 34–46.

13
Texts and Resources

Andrew Zurcher

At the end of his well-known, magisterial reading of the twenty-second stanza of the ninth canto of Book II of *The Faerie Queene* (1628), Sir Kenelm Digby takes a moment to apologize to his friend, Sir Edward Stradling, for his presumption in handling the text of so great a poet:

> And now I return to you also the Book that contains my Text, which yesterday you sent me, to fit this part of it with a Comment, which peradventure I might have performed better, if either I had afforded my selfe more time, or had had the conveniencie of some other books apt to quicken my Invention, to whom I might have been beholding for enlarging my understanding in some things that are treated here, although the Application should still have been my own: With these helps perhaps I might have dived further into the Authors Intention (the depth of which cannot be sounded by any that is lesse learned then he was).[1]

Digby's sense of intellectual frustration, the need he perceives to match Spenser's learning before he can aspire to plumb his intention, is a feeling familiar to many Spenserians. His instinctive desire for 'the conveniencie of some other books' attests to the long tradition of reading this difficult, profoundly intellectual poet with a range of interpretive resources to hand. That tradition was never more in flourish than today, as critical readings, encyclopedias, glossaries, student guides, and other resources pour off the presses at an exhilarating, though sometimes bewildering, pace.

If Spenser is a poet who demands learned annotation and a capacious reference library, he is also a poet who coyly invites, and slyly resists, textual study. At a time when print was still considered mercenary for a poet

---

[1] Sir Kenelm Digby. 1643. *Observations on the 22. Stanza in the 9th. Canto of the 2d. Book of Spencers Faery Queen*, London, written 1628, p. 24; see R. M. Cummings. 1971. *Spenser: The Critical Heritage*, London: Routledge and Kegan Paul, pp. 158–9.

aspiring to literary credibility, Spenser charged into the printing house with innovative enthusiasm. From his earliest personal publication he played iconoclastically with print conventions. *The Shepheardes Calender* (1579) was fronted by woodcuts in the visual tradition of emblem books, and its eclogues were brazenly nested within an editorial apparatus attributed to 'E. K.'. In later publications he was no less individual. The first edition of *The Faerie Queene* (1590) includes a shocking eighteen separate dedications to prospective patrons (including a primary dedication to Queen Elizabeth), a presumptuous packaging that likely astonished his first readers. Similarly, the archaic language of many of his works, pastoral to epic, relies on an idiosyncratic orthography that makes his texts a notorious verbal minefield for editors as well as readers. Outstanding bibliographical problems attending some of Spenser's texts—for example, the relationship of the various extant versions of the manuscript treatise, *A view of the present state of Ireland* (1596), or the textual status of the fragmentary *Two Cantos of Mutabilitie* (first printed in 1609)—have also encouraged, and long frustrated, Spenser's editors.

Any scholar newly undertaking research on Spenser consequently faces a bewildering profusion of textual sources and critical resources; the dramatic explosion in both print and electronic materials over the past two decades has only complicated this picture further, and new texts and tools now appear so frequently that even seasoned Spenserians do best on their toes. This chapter provides a discursive introduction both to Spenser's texts, including the history of textual reception and the key textual issues at stake in editing and reading this demanding poet, and to the pre-eminent research resources currently available to Spenser scholars. Because the field is changing so rapidly in its medium, as well as its content, what follows contains some unavoidable speculative discussion of projects and even incipient trajectories not yet fully realized.

Spenser's texts

Any investigation of textual problems in Spenser, as in the work of any early modern poet, must be based on a sound technical understanding of the contemporary book trade, and its associated bibliographical concerns (paper and watermarks, printer's copy, composition, imposition, distribution, binding, etc.). The canonical guides to the technical tools of bibliographical investigation are still R. B. McKerrow's *An Introduction to Bibliography for Literary Students* (1927) and Philip Gaskell's *A New Introduction to Bibliography* (1974). Other key works—such as Fredson Bowers's *Principles of Bibliographical Description* (1949), or the seemingly countless groundbreaking studies in the journal of the Bibliographical Society, *The Library*, and in the journal of the Bibliographical Society of the University of Virginia, *Studies in Bibliography*— will also be helpful to the novice student of Spenser's texts. The traditional paper bible, Pollard's and Redgrave's *A Short-Title Catalogue of Books Printed in England, Scotland, and Ireland, and of English Books Printed Abroad, 1475–1640*, is now available in an electronic format on the Internet as part of the provision of the Research Libraries Group (see the chapter bibliography for access details). Further seminal articles in bibliography and textual editing— from W. W. Greg's 'The Rationale of Copy-Text' through the work of Bowers, D. F. McKenzie, Jerome McGann, and G. Thomas Tanselle, to the recent emphasis on 'un-editing' Renaissance texts in the work of Leah Marcus— can be traced in the bibliography to this chapter.

Sir James Ware wrote in the preface to his 1633 Dublin edition of *A View of the Present State of Ireland* that, ensconced in his house at Kilcolman, Cork, Spenser 'finished the later part of that excellent poem of his *Faery Queene*, which was soone after unfortunately lost by the disorder and abuse of his servant, whom he had sent before him into *England*, being then *a rebellibus* (as *Camdens* words are) *è laribus ejectus & bonis spoliatus*'.[2] Apart from the (equally dubitable) testimony of the Spenser–Harvey correspondence in 1580, no other references to Spenser's autograph literary remains survive, nor do the manuscripts themselves. Whether or not perfidious servants or feckless publishers were to blame, certainly the 'disorder and abuse' of time, at least, has rendered most of the textual problems of Spenser's poetry fairly straightforward. His major works, *The Shepheardes Calender* and *The Faerie Queene*, exist in only a small number of important early variants—all of them closely and genealogically related—while the texts of the shorter poetic works, as well as of the prose works, rely on single textual authorities. Apart from the contested status of the various early manuscript copies of Spenser's *A View of the Present State of Ireland*, then, an account of the textual history of Spenser's works would seem to offer a fairly simple tale. The devil, however, lurks in the detail.

The complexity of this detail is only too evident in the two venerable but still standard introductions to textual issues in the study of Spenser's poetry and prose: F. R. Johnson's *A Critical Bibliography of the Works of Edmund Spenser Printed Before 1700* (1933) and the various textual appendices and notes on variants appearing in the individual volumes of *The Works of Edmund Spenser, A Variorum Edition* (11 vols, 1932–49). The textual notes of Ernest de Sélincourt's 1910 edition of the *Minor Poems* (including *The Shepheardes Calender*), like those of J. C. Smith in his 1909 edition of *The Faerie Queene*, were a model of 'new bibliographical' clarity and forward thinking in their day, and are still useful; the observations made by Emma Unger on Spenser-related materials in the third volume of *The Carl H. Pforzheimer Library: English Literature 1475–1700* (1940) occasionally

---

[2] Sir James Ware, 'Preface' to *A View of the State of Ireland* (Dublin: Society of Stationers, 1633), ¶3[r].

complete or contest Johnson's conclusions; and the various short notes and lists of variants appended to recent editions can help to build up a picture of the textual problems in Spenser. C. G. Osgood's *Concordance to the Poems of Edmund Spenser* (1915) has now been partially superseded, for Books I–III of *The Faerie Queene*, by the superior concordance edited by Yamashita *et al.* (1990), a group that has gone on to produce a more general *Textual Companion to* The Faerie Queene *1590* (1993) in both electronic and print formats—containing important new bibliographical research on the printing of *The Faerie Queene* in 1590, particularly in relation to compositorial stints in John Wolfe's printshop. The rest of the data provided in that guide will, it is to be hoped, shortly itself be superseded by smart-searchable, scholarly, but free-access electronic texts—of *The Faerie Queene* as well as all the shorter poems and prose—such as those currently in preparation under the aegis of Oxford University Press. Of the existing general guides, the more focused and technical studies that support them, and the main issues raised and conclusions tendered by all of this work, the following discussion gives a more detailed view, disposed by text.

The Shepheardes Calender, Conteyning twelue Æglogues proportionable to the twelue monethes

The Shepheardes Calender, 56 leaves in quarto format, first hit the bookstalls of Hugh Singleton's shop, opposite Stationers' Hall on Creed Lane, in 1579. In the western shadow of old St Paul's toward Ludgate, Singleton's press was known for its connections to the Protestant community of Marian exiles, many of whom had returned to English bishoprics at Elizabeth's succession, under the patronage of the Earl of Leicester (Byrom 1933). At about the same time that he printed *The Shepheardes Calender*, Singleton also produced John Stubbs's incendiary polemic *A discoverie of the gaping gulf whereinto England is like to be swallowed by an other French mariage* (1579), which for its presumptuous meddling in the Queen's marriage negotiations with the duke of Alençon was suppressed by proclamation, costing Stubbs his hand. While Singleton was an experienced printer (his first publications probably date from before 1550), and his texts sound and polished, his religious politics and likely political connections were probably what drew the young, protestant Spenser to his shop. Singleton's politics may also have led him to relinquish his rights to *The Shepheardes Calender* soon thereafter; the copy was assigned to John Harrison the younger, a publisher and bookseller, on 29 October 1580, and the ensuing four quarto editions of the eclogues—of 1581, 1586, 1591, and 1597—all appeared under Harrison's imprint. This pattern of publication, with two editions following closely on the publication of the 1590 and 1596 instalments of Spenser's *The Faerie Queene*, suggests that Harrison considered *The Shepheardes Calender* a profitable little book.

The relative merits of the five quarto editions of *The Shepheardes Calender* were teased out by three centuries of increasingly attentive editors, and the main points summarized in de Sélincourt (1910, vi–xvi). Each successive quarto edition was printed from its predecessor, such that Q1 (1579) has the most textual authority, particularly on questions of orthography; the experimental spelling of *The Shepheardes Calender*, incorporating archaic and dialect forms, is well known, and is most in evidence in this first edition. While later quartos emended errors in Q1, they also introduced new errors, only some of which were afterwards properly corrected. Q4 (1591) and Q5 (1597), in particular, seem to show signs of pronounced haste in printing, and accelerate the inevitable process of orthographical normalization. In the face of this textual change, one element of the poems remained constant for almost forty years: the woodcuts prepared for Q1 were used in all subsequent editions of the eclogues up to F2 (1617), and have been thoroughly examined by Luborsky (1981, 1991), who contends that Spenser (or a very close associate) must have directed their design, that they were deliberately cut in an antique style, and that they were probably the work of a small group of (as yet unidentified) craftsmen.

The compositor setting Q5 famously omitted an entire eight-line stanza from the June eclogue (ll. 89–96, beginning, 'Now dead hee is, and lyeth wrapt in lead...'), which was not restored until the Hughes edition of Spenser's works in 1715. Its absence from the first of the seventeenth-century folio editions of Spenser's collected works, that of 1611 (F1), indicates that the printer Matthew Lownes, again, worked from a copy of the most recent quarto, Q5. As de Sélincourt notes (1910, xv–xvi), however, despite the reliance of F1 on the corrupt and normalized text of Q5 of *The Shepheardes Calender*, the sensible standard of emendation lives up to the claim of the title page, 'carefully corrected'. The woodcut blocks used in Q1–Q5 by Hugh Singleton and John Harrison here appear in the hands of the F1 printer, Matthew Lownes, suggesting that he had made some special arrangement with Harrison for *The Shepheardes Calender*, who still held the licence for this copy from the Stationers' Company; and indeed, when F2 was produced by Lownes in 1617, *The Shepheardes Calender* alone of all the constituent works appears under the imprint not of Lownes, but again of John Harrison, and clearly uses Harrison's type. The 1679 folio edition of Spenser's works (F3), printed by Henry Hills for Jonathan Edwin, relies mainly on the authority of F1, but corrects certain passages by recourse to F2, and recovers some dedicatory or otherwise ancillary material from the quartos. It also reprints the Latin translation of *The Shepheardes Calender*, the *Calendarium Pastorale* of 1653, ascribed to Theodore Bathurst of Cambridge; Bathurst's restoration of the missing stanza from the 'June' eclogue, both in his English text and in the Latin translation, is appended to the text of F3 in a note.

As *Variorum* 7 (692–6) notes, the textual history of *The Shepheardes Calender* from 1679 onwards illustrates the developing tendency of editors to return to the authority of Q1 wherever possible; Hughes (1715), Todd

(1805), and Collier (1862) resorted to Q1 with increasing frequency, and all the modern editions of the eclogues—from de Sélincourt (1910) and *Variorum* (1943) to the *Yale Edition of the Shorter Poems* (1989) and Richard McCabe's Penguin text (1999)—rely on Q1 as the base text. The one exception to this trend was Alexander Grosart's 1882–84 edition of Spenser's works, in which he claimed that, because Spenser was likely to have supervised the production of all the quartos of *The Shepheardes Calender* printed during his lifetime, Q5 ought to be taken as the base text, especially with respect to orthography. While the pattern of transmission of the text from quarto to quarto, and thence to the folios, fatally undermines Grosart's claims—Spenser almost certainly did not supervise the printing of any edition of *The Shepheardes Calender* after 1579—the glove Grosart threw down on Spenser's orthography is an important one, and not to be lightly dismissed in any area of the Spenser canon.

The Faerie Queene: Disposed into twelue books, Fashioning XII. Morall vertues

A parting comment in Spenser's 1580 (published) letter to Gabriel Harvey indicates that he had finished substantial work on *The Faerie Queene* before his departure into Ireland; the account of Lodowick Bryskett, Spenser's colleague in Lord Grey's Dublin administration, in his *A Discourse of Civill Life* (1606) apparently confirms that Spenser was still at work on the epic during the middle of the decade, and recent archival discoveries confirm that manuscript copies, or at least extracts, of the poem were circulating in London as early as 1588 (Black 2001). But *The Faerie Queene* did not appear in print until as late as 1590, during Spenser's brief return to court, when the first three books were printed in quarto by John Wolfe for William Ponsonby, who had staked his right to the copy by taking out a Stationers' Company license in December 1589. Ponsonby was to become Spenser's chief publisher throughout the last decade of the poet's life, and he seems to have put all of his resources to work for Spenser in the production of the 1590 edition of *The Faerie Queene* (hereafter Q1): as Johnson notes (1933, 16–17), Wolfe probably devoted at least two, and possibly all four, of his presses, to the simultaneous imposition of a large edition of Spenser's epic. While it is impossible to know exactly how many copies Wolfe printed, usual estimates of edition sizes in this period (see Gaskell 1974, 160–3) range from 1500 to 2000 copies of relatively popular volumes, and the intensity and professionalism with which Wolfe seems to have embraced the Spenser job suggest that he considered it a substantial and serious project. Certainly Wolfe—who after a period as a maverick but very shrewd agitator in the London booktrade during the early 1580s had been brought into the fold as the beadle of the Stationers' Company—had the resources and the expertise to produce a large edition of the poem on cost and on time (Hoppe 1933, Loewenstein 1988). About 75 to 100 full copies of this edition survive 'in sound condition' today (Johnson 1933, 13).

The earliest textual criticism of the late nineteenth century supposed that Q1 appeared in two distinct issues, distinguished by a series of corrections and flagged by a re-spacing of the date of publication on the title page, from '1590' to '1 5 9 0'. This argument was demolished by the first credible, if limited, collation of extant copies, by Johnson, who noted that Wolfe's printing house followed the normal contemporary practice of making corrections during the print run, retaining uncorrected copies of individual sheets alongside corrected copies, and then gathering individual copies indiscriminately from piles of mixed sheets. The idea of multiple *stages* in the printing of Q1, however, should not be totally discarded: evidence persists that the famous signed dedication to Queen Elizabeth, appearing in most copies on the verso of the title page, was an addition to the volume after printing began (see Johnson 1933, 15). Spenser certainly revised the set of dedicatory sonnets appended to the volume—significantly, adding a sonnet to Lord Burghley, Elizabeth's Lord Treasurer, and the most powerful of her councillors, along with six other new dedications—almost immediately after the original printing had finished (Johnson 1933, 15–16; Unger 1940, 1001–1002; Miller 1987; Loewenstein 1996; Brink 2003); the occasional failure to replace the leaves Pp6 and Pp7 correctly with the new sheet (or set of four leaves), signed Qq, has led to a number of variant states of the dedicatory sonnets in the surviving copies. The anomalous placement of the signed 'Letter of the Authors...to Sir Walter Raleigh', with the series of commendatory poems and dedicatory sonnets at the back of the volume (when all contemporary practice was to place such materials at the front), continues to demand the attention of bibliographers—it may well be that this curious arrangement reflects a sudden reorganization of the volume during printing, perhaps as a result of the Queen's interest in the new poem. Recent and current work on the letter to Ralegh, the dedicatory sonnets, and on the printing of the volume at large has argued for Spenser's particular and sustained attention to patronage issues in his composition, disposition, and publication of the volume, situating bibliographical evidence more and more securely in what we know of the historical and biographical context of the 1590 printing of the poem (Oram 1990, 2001; Erickson 2001; Zurcher 2005; but see Brink 2003).

Fifteen, rather than the full seventeen, dedicatory sonnets appear in Richard Field's 1596 quarto reprinting of the first three books of *The Faerie Queene* (Q2), indicating that Field must have set his type from an incorrectly bound copy of Q1—one lacking the dedications to Lady Carew and to the ladies of the court originally appearing on Pp8 of Q1. Many other errors, including significant mistakes in pagination and catchwords, migrate uncorrected from Q1 to Q2, confirming this hypothesis. On the other hand, only some authorial intervention can account for the addition of a stanza to

Book I (I.xi.3) and the revision of the end of Book III, canto xii, to accommodate the continuation of the poem in Books IV–VI. Having said that, Spenser
was almost certainly not responsible for the more specific, and ubiquitous
changes to the spelling apparent throughout the new edition: Q2 alters the
spelling of Q1 so dramatically (the *Variorum* editors calculate the revisions
at a rate of one word every two and a half lines; see *Variorum* 1, 521), and so
inconsistently, that we must suppose the revisions to be as accidental in the
spelling as in the punctuation—the preferences of the volume's compositors,
rather than its author. The significant, but only partial heed paid to the
corrections listed in Q1's 'Faults Escaped', too, suggests that Q2 (I–III) was
printed from a predominantly late-corrected copy of Q1, and not under the
supervision of the poet himself. Evans (1965) has gone so far as to suggest
that Ponsonby began publication of Q2 (I–III) before Spenser's arrival from
Ireland with Books IV–VI of the poem, which were duly printed by Field
shortly afterwards, presumably from the author's manuscript.

After Spenser's death, the Stationers' Company license for both parts of
The Faerie Queene passed from Ponsonby to Simon Waterson and thence, in
November 1604, to the young printer Matthew Lownes. Lownes sat on his
copy for almost five years before producing a new folio edition of Spenser's
epic in 1609 (hereafter *1609*). This was the first edition of *The Faerie Queene*
to include the 'Two Cantos of Mutabilitie', and it is possible that Lownes
inherited the manuscript for this section from Ponsonby by Waterson.
Because this copy was very shortly succeeded by Lownes's full folio edition
of Spenser's complete works (beginning in 1611, and known as F1), and
because leftover stocks of *1609* were, until exhausted, bound up with the
new material in 1611 to form part of the collected works, it can be difficult
to identify 'pure' copies of this edition. The bibliographical evidence of variants
indicates that *1609* was set from a copy—possibly a slightly annotated
copy—of Q2, a hypothesis supported by the fact that *1609* follows Q2 in
omitting 'A Letter of the Authors … to Sir Walter Raleigh' and most of the
other 'prefatory' matter appended to Q1.

Capitalizing on the success of *1609*, Lownes almost immediately set
about a new folio edition of the collected works of 'England's Arch-Poët',
the first copies of which were ready in 1611. As noted above, stocks of
1609 supplied this edition until they ran out, and the text of *The Faerie
Queene* needed to be re-set; the same went for other components of the
edition, which were printed in discrete batches that could be gathered and
compiled as needed, or sold separately, according to the demands of
customers. As Johnson notes in his painstaking analysis of F1 and the
1617 F2 (1933, 33–48),

> an examination of a number of copies of the collected editions of Spenser's
> works commonly designated as the 1611 and 1617 Folios, reveals that in
> no case were these editions printed as a unit. Instead, they were made up

by issuing as a single volume a number of separate sections which had been printed independently at periods often several years apart.

These seven sections were each set twice, and 'made up' into folio editions according to demand over the 1611–17 period, such that many surviving copies of these folio editions contain different constituent parts compiled in different sequences. It should be noted that Lownes did not include 'Mother Hubberds Tale' in the original collected edition of 1611, presumably out of respect for the antipathy of Robert Cecil, Burghley's ambitious son who had been created Earl of Salisbury by James, and had served the king as one of his most trusted councillors. After Salisbury's death in 1612, 'Mother Hubberds Tale' apparently went into immediate production, and was issued with the rest of the edition from late 1612 or early 1613; enough stocks were printed of this sensational fable to last Lownes and his successors until the mid-1620s.

Despite the generally arbitrary revisions of Q2 (I–III), and the further corruption of the complete text from F1 onwards, the choice of copy text for *The Faerie Queene* has been clouded for many editors by the piecemeal publication of Books IV–VI in Q2, and of 'Two Cantos of Mutabilitie' in 1609. Since the Hughes edition of 1715, editorial opinion has, as with *The Shepheardes Calender*, gradually reverted to the authority of the early quartos, with most recent editors choosing Q2 as the base, supplemented by the 'Two Cantos of Mutabilitie' from *1609*. The decision of the *Variorum* editors to prefer Q2 (I–III) to Q1 was based on the simple observation that the spelling of Q1 probably has no more authority than that of Q2, given that the compositors likely followed not Spenser's Q1 manuscript, but the house style of John Wolfe, its printer:

> If the spelling in the 1590 and 1596 quartos represents the practices of the printer, it cannot, as has often been supposed, be an indication of deliberate archaism in Spenser. In fact, the spelling of these quartos is no more archaic than that found in other books printed by the same printers, or other printers of the same period. (*Variorum* 1, 522)

Yamashita *et al.* (1993) have argued, however, that editors should prefer the textual authority of Q1 for Books I to III, except for the Q2 addition of a stanza in Book I, and substitution of several stanzas at the end of Book III— noting that, for all that Wolfe's house style may predominate in Q1, more of Spenser's spellings are preserved in Q1 than in Q2 (I–III). This argument is supported by Shaheen's study of rhyme-words (1980) and by the earlier, detailed bibliographical work of Frank Evans (1965), who showed conclusively that Q2 was produced in two consecutive phases (I–III, IV–VI) by two distinct pairs of compositors (probably comprising three men), and that the spelling revisions of Q2 (I–III), as well as the general orthographical tendencies of Q2 (IV–VI), reflect the spelling habits of these individuals. As Evans concludes, the spelling of Q1 is generally almost certainly closer to Spenser's own, and should be preferred to the normalizations of Q2 (I–III). This argument has guided the most recent scholarly edition of *The Faerie Queene*, edited by Hamilton, Yamashita, and Suzuki, (2001), and seems set to become the standard for future one-text editions.

Shorter poems and prose

Considerably less bibliographical study has been devoted to the texts of Spenser's shorter poems and prose, for obvious reasons: they are short works, mostly of uncomplicated textual status, and often survive only in manageably small numbers. It may be generally observed of all of these works that editorial practice, as for *The Shepheardes Calender*, has gradually restored the earliest quarto and octavo editions to their pre-eminent textual authority. Apart from Spenser's contributions to Jan van der Noodt's *A Theatre for Worldlings* (1569), all of the minor poems were published by William Ponsonby, using different printers, in the period 1591–96, and will be discussed in the order of publication (following Johnson) as shown below.

The first of Spenser's short poems to appear in print after Q1 of *The Faerie Queene* was *Daphnaïda, An Elegie vpon the death of the noble and vertuous Douglas Howard*, printed in quarto by Thomas Orwin for William Ponsonby in early 1591. The date and place of publication given in the poem's dedication, 'London this first of Ianuary 1591', have attracted the scrutiny of scholars for the last hundred years, and were considered at length by de Sélincourt (1910, xxi–xxiii): if Spenser dated *Daphnaïda* according to the old style (i.e. with the new year beginning 25 March), he would have been penning the dedication only five days after inscribing *Colin Clouts Come Home Againe* from his house at Kilcolman, in southwest Ireland, on 27 December 1591 (see below)—a nearly impossible feat. F. R. Johnson (1933, 24), like the *Variorum* editors, felt confident that we should read this date as new-style, thus placing *Daphnaïda* well in advance of *Colin Clouts Come Home Againe*, and closer to the death of Douglas Howard in the August of 1590; but the question has been reopened recently, and definitively closed, by Brink (1994a) and Weiss (1999). The importance of accurately dating this text lies in the way it connects Spenser to Sir Walter Ralegh and his cousin, Sir Arthur Gorges—the husband of the deceased Douglas Howard. As Sandison (1928) amply demonstrates, Spenser's timely participation in a serious power struggle between Gorges and his patron step-mother, the Lady Helena Marquesse of Northampton, on the one side, and the Howard family (and their Cecil connections) on the other, may have serious implications for how we understand the relationship of the (timeless) aesthetic to the (contemporary) political in Spenser's works.

Ponsonby's other Spenser publication of 1591, *Complaints: Containing Sundrie Small Poemes of the Worlds Vanitie*, is a collection of Spenserian translations and imitations, the poems loosely connected by a recurring plaintive and satiric character—and much more strongly joined by their sustained engagement in the partisan propaganda battles of factional politics at Elizabeth's court. Two of the poems in the volume—'The Visions of Petrarch' and 'The Visions of Bellay'—originally appeared (in different versions) in the 1569 protestant polemic, Jan van der Noodt's *A Theatre for Worldlings*. This earlier volume, which used Spenser's (juvenile) translations alongside a series of woodcuts that may have inspired the poet's later layout of *The Shepheardes Calender*, also includes four 'sonnets' paraphrasing text from Revelation, which did not subsequently appear in *Complaints*; these Revelation sonnets are often, nonetheless, attributed to Spenser (though see Satterthwaite 1960, 255–63). The main significance of *A Theatre for Worldlings* for Spenser scholarship is the very fact of its existence: it documents Spenser's early practice of poetry, it demonstrates some kind of affiliation to the energetic Dutch Protestant community in London, and it shows him pursuing the usual humanist poetical education of translation and imitation. The textual interest of the uncomplicated volume is slight, apart from the variant blank-verse states of some of the translations, which were later revised, with a looser relation to the French and Italian originals, to rhyming form (though see Loewenstein 1996, 121–2, and note).

By contrast, *Complaints* has rightly generated considerable bibliographical interest, again as a result of its incendiary politics. The textual composition of *Complaints* is at once apparently complex and disarmingly simple. A quarto volume of 92 leaves printed by Thomas Orwin, it contains the texts of nine individual poems (or sequences of poems), four with discrete title pages using the same ornamental border as that appearing on the cover of the volume. While the separate title pages seem to indicate that the 'volume' was printed such that its components might be sold separately— and here the anomalous 1590 title-page date of one poem in the collection, 'Muiopotmos', further suggests individual sale—the textual signatures for the volume run in an unbroken sequence from A–Z^4, incontrovertibly demonstrating that the volume was printed as an integral unit. Johnson's explanation of the problematic date of 'Muiopotmos', like his discussion of the separate title pages, has been widely accepted: the order of imposition of the volume seems to have been such that 'Muiopotmos' and its title page were printed last, after the rest of the volume's works; Johnson concludes that Orwin's press turned out the edition faster than they had anticipated, and that, recognizing that the edition would be ready for sale before the end of the year, it revised the date of the final element of the print-run from 1591 to 1590. While this is a plausible explanation of the discrepancy, it is perhaps undercut by the late date of Ponsonby's entry in the Stationers' Register: the copy was not registered until 29 December 1590. Still,

Ponsonby had not bothered to register *Daphnaïda* at all, and it may be that he had not planned upon staking out his right to *Complaints* until he realized, by the reaction of buyers as well as that of the government, that the volume was in fact highly explosive and in great demand.

For as Peterson (1998) has demonstrated, *Complaints* was officially 'called in' or suppressed by the Privy Council for its vicious lampoon of Lord Burghley and his son Robert Cecil in 'Mother Hubberds Tale', and Spenser had seemingly fled London for his house in Ireland by the middle of March 1591. This reading of the textual status of *Complaints* is consistent with its other main bibliographical claim to fame: the analysis of variants in extant copies (see Johnson 1933, 27; Stein 1934, 176–9; and *Variorum* 8, 680–5) indicates that the edition was carefully corrected during its production, and many of the corrections are of a nature and scope consistent with authorial oversight of the printing. It should be noted that the hypothesis of Spenser's involvement in the printing of *Complaints* seems to contradict Ponsonby's implication, in the introduction to the volume, that Spenser had already departed 'ouer Sea', and at least one recent critic (Brink 1991) has contested the traditional claim that Spenser was involved in the correction of *Complaints*. However, Brink's initial supposition, that we ought in the absence of better evidence to read Ponsonby's preface at face value, has been undermined by the witness of Sir Thomas Tresham's March 1591 letter, published by Peterson (1998): Spenser seems to have left for Ireland *as a consequence* of the poor reception of *Complaints*, suggesting that he was, in fact, in London throughout the printing of the volume. In this light, Brink's dismissal of the arguably substantive corrections made to some of the *Complaints* text looks too hasty, and it seems prudent to return to the widely accepted view that Spenser at least partially supervised the publication of this important, and notorious, text.

The next, and last, flurry of publication began in 1595, when Peter Short produced for Ponsonby the small octavo volume containing *Amoretti and Epithalamion*, an edition of eight gatherings of eight leaves, with an insertion of a half-sheet of four leaves, making 68 leaves in total. The half-sheet insertion, containing Ponsonby's own dedication to Sir Robert Needham along with two commendatory verses, is notable because it seems to demonstrate that Ponsonby sent his copy to Short to be printed before the dedicatory and commendatory material was drafted; indeed, the survival of at least one copy not containing this insertion indicates that some copies may have been sold or distributed before the prefatory material was included. That Spenser sent his manuscript of *Amoretti and Epithalamion* to London by courier from Ireland is attested in Ponsonby's dedication; he may have forwarded the older manuscript of *Colin Clouts Come Home Againe* by the same courier, or shortly thereafter, this time including his own dedication (dated 1591, as we have seen) to Sir Walter Ralegh. *Fowre Hymnes*, printed by Field for Ponsonby in a quarto volume that also includes a second edition of

Daphnaïda, followed in 1596. This time, as the analysis of variants again indicates, Spenser seems to have been present in London (or Greenwich, as he indicates in his dedications) for the publication, which would have coincided with the production of the second instalment, Q2, of *The Faerie Queene*. The short *Prothalamion* (1596), celebrating the double marriage of the daughters of the Earl of Worcester in November 1596, must have been published quickly in the closing weeks of the year. It was to be Spenser's final publication.

Of the shorter prose works, two items deserve at least summary mention. The *Three Proper, and wittie, familiar Letters* between Spenser and Gabriel Harvey, a fascinating but notoriously slippery window on Spenser's biography, appeared in a slim quarto booklet of 35 leaves from the press of Henry Bynneman in 1580. Capitalizing on the success of *The Shepheardes Calender*, the three letters advertise the 'learned wit' of Harvey's Cambridge circle in their discussion of the recent earthquake, as well as the issue of a reformed English versifying (i.e. quantitative verse). The occasional, perhaps even opportunistic, nature of the publication is further suggested by the addition of *Two Other, Very Commendable Letters, of the Same Mens Writing*, with a separate title page, at the back of the volume; the inclusion of these letters with their own title page—combined with the fact that all (six) surviving copies include both sets—may suggest that Bynneman received the last pair of letters after printing the first three, but before putting the volume out for sale.

The *Letters* provide a richly suggestive picture of Spenser's connection to Philip Sidney and his circle—the 'Areopagus'—at Leicester House in the Strand at this time, and it is the way these letters link the Spenser–Harvey circle of *The Shepheardes Calender* to the new Sidneian Areopagus that has to date most exercised Spenser's biographers and critics. But the bibliographical record here also has something to contribute. Bynneman's press seems to have been tied up throughout 1580 with the production of John Stow's *The Chronicles of England from Brute Vnto This Present Yeare of Christ. 1580*, a huge work in folio that seems, judging by the frequent editions of the next few decades, to have been considerably popular. Concurrent with this major work, though, his press produced a number of small pamphlets, like the Spenser–Harvey letters, with an interest in the earthquake, and the similarities in the topic, and between the authors, of these texts suggest that they may have been connected by more than an enterprising printer with a beef. It may be that Spenser was at this date associating with—or connected by a patron or friend to—his fellow poets Thomas Churchyard (*A warning for the wise, a feare to the fond, a bridle to the lewde, and a glasse to the good Written of the late earthquake chanced in London and other places, the. 6. of April 1580*, entered in the Stationers' Register by Bynneman, though printed by John Allde and Nicholas Lyng, in 1580) and Arthur Golding, the translator of Ovid's *Metamorphoses* (*A discourse vpon the earthquake that hapned throughe this realme of Englande, and other places of Christendom, the first of Aprill. 1580.*

betwene the houres of fiue and six in the euening, published by Bynneman in 1580); the likelihood of something more than a coincidental connection is reinforced by the dedication of Churchyard's work to Alexander Nowell, Dean of St Paul's—the patron whose family had supported Spenser's sizarship at Pembroke Hall, Cambridge. Spenser may also at this date have known John Florio, whose translation of Cartier's account of the exploration of New France (now eastern Canada) was also printed by Bynneman in 1580. Bibliographical study of early modern poets, dramatists, news-writers, and other intellectuals and hacks has tended to overlook the possible function of the printer as an agent, and the print-shop as a location, for the combination and collaboration of otherwise apparently unconnected authors; but as demonstrated by the example of Gabriel Harvey and Thomas Nashe—who both hovered in and around John Wolfe's shop before and during the grand spat that began in 1592—this kind of association may come to yield a significant new kind of evidence for our understanding of the bibliography, and the interpretation, of early modern literature.

The status of *Axiochus*, a Socratic dialogue on death, spuriously attributed to Plato and printed by Cuthbert Burby (i.e. Burbage) in a thin quarto in 1592, is finally uncertain. The title page claims that this short dialogue has been 'translated out of Greeke by Edw. Spenser', and it is certain that Burby meant to indicate Edmund, the poet, as he fingers him more precisely in the printer's dedication; given that many of Spenser's works were published anonymously or only with the abbreviated 'Ed. Sp.', this fairly common contemporary mistake makes sense. On the other hand, Burby may have been trying to capitalize on Spenser's popularity (and, after *Complaints*, notoriety) as a poet by falsely attributing this volume. We cannot finally know for certain whether or not this young, somewhat maverick printer had grabbed into his hands an authentic Spenserian manuscript; though from a bibliographical perspective it should be noted that Upton knew of the dialogue, considered it genuine, and planned in 1758 to publish it in his projected third volume of Spenser's works (which never appeared).

A View of the Present State of Ireland

The textual status of Spenser's 1596 prose dialogue, *A view of the present state of Ireland*, is more complicated and contentious than that of any of his poetic works. Unlike his poems, *A view* was never published during Spenser's lifetime, and all of the surviving manuscripts probably date from the time after his death. Brink (1994a, 1997a, 1999) has repeatedly called into question even the fundamental attribution of the work to Spenser, despite the fact that contemporaries clearly considered Spenser's authorship safe, and most scholars now accept it. While the dialogue was printed in

Dublin in 1633 by Sir James Ware, this early edition deliberately (and explicitly) excises several important but politically sensitive passages, and does not attempt to preserve some features of the manuscript tradition (including orthography) that might be thought to be Spenserian. Until the late nineteenth century, editors generally relied, like the printer of the 1679 folio collection of Spenser's works (F3), on the Ware text: Hughes, Todd, and Collier all relied on Ware relatively uncritically. It was Richard Morris's Globe edition of 1869 that first returned to manuscript sources, a trend followed (somewhat sloppily) by Grosart (1882–84) and (twice) by Renwick (1930–32, 1934); all of these editions attempted to produce an ideal single text collated from a number of manuscript sources.

However, the status of *A view* as a manuscript work, with no authorially sanctioned printed edition, makes it very difficult for the careful scholar to accept anything but a heavily annotated variorum presentation of the (apparently) most legitimate manuscript versions. Rudolf Gottfried's editorial apparatus to the *Variorum* edition (1949) demonstrates conclusively the dangers of relying on Ware's text, or indeed on any single text. His textual notes betray again and again the complicated process of correction and revision that must have characterized Spenser's drafting of *A view* up until 1596 at the least, and possibly until his death in 1599. The manuscript legacy, comprising many different textual states along at least two major stems (with many identifiable subdivisions), includes about twenty texts, and some fragments of texts. The most important (*Variorum* 10, 506–16), because they probably reflect Spenser's latest state of revision, are three nearly contemporary copies now located in the Huntington Library (Gottfried's *E*), the Gonville and Caius College Library, Cambridge (*C*), and the Bodleian Library, Oxford (*G*). These are closely related to two other versions: a manuscript derived from a very early state of Spenser's treatise, including many unique passages, now held in the Public Record Office, Kew (*P*); and a manuscript surviving in the Trinity College Library, Dublin (*T*). Another important, distinct group is that including the copy nearly printed in 1598—the Rawlinson manuscript in the Bodleian Library, Oxford (*R*)—and its two derivatives, manuscripts now held in Lambeth Palace Library (*L*) and Cambridge University Library (*D1*).

No modern edition after Gottfried's has improved upon his collation of the various manuscript traditions. The only current student text, Maley's and Hadfield's Blackwell edition (1997), reprints Ware's edition. The incipient development of scholarly publication in an electronic, Internet environment, however, holds particular promise for a text like *A view*, as it is possible in such an environment to represent variant manuscript states in an interlocking and mutually informative architecture without prejudicing or unduly elevating the value of any individual text. Driven by the editorial possibilities of the hyptertext publishing environment, the next few years will almost certainly witness a sustained return to and reappraisal of the individual manuscripts in the textual tradition of this important work. Full transcriptions of some of the important manuscripts (such as C) are already freely accessible on the Internet (see the next section for details), and it is likely that others will soon follow.

Textual traditions and new directions

Much has already been said above about the major movements in the textual tradition of Spenser's poetic and prose works, but it will be helpful to consider these trends as a whole, and to reflect on the dramatic changes that seem set now to take place in the textual reception of Spenser's works. Above all, it cannot be enough stressed that the combined legacy of the New Bibliography of the last century—which gave us so precise an understanding of the production of literary manuscripts and printed materials in the early modern period—and the 'new philology' of the last few decades—which has insisted on more parity in the approach to a 'network' of texts (Barthes 1971, Marcus 1996, 17–25)—has become in the age of cheap electronic publication the tool of textual enfranchisement for the average scholar, even the average reader. While the textual principles that guided bibliographical research and editorial strategy in the the last century continue to hold sway, new technology has made these principles increasingly the right, and the responsibility, of each individual user. Already the proliferation of 'un-edited' texts in electronic media has begun to displace 'ideal' texts, and to make historically aware readings standard, even *de rigeur*; as the production of transcriptions and contingent printed texts continues to boom, students and scholars will have unprecedented access to historical materials, and must answer this opportunity with sensitivity and restraint, as well as enthusiasm.

The history of Spenser's texts since the 'three' great folio editions of the seventeenth century has essentially defined a movement back to the earliest textual witnesses of his work, a tendency to restore 'his' orthography and the early uncorrupted readings of variant words and passages. While the texts of the shorter poems and the shorter prose never budged much from the quarto and octavo editions of the 1590s, the fates of *The Shepheardes Calender*, *The Faerie Queene*, and *A view of the present state of Ireland* were significantly more variable. It is only in the last century that editors, resorting to the earliest editions for their copy texts, and amending according to other early witnesses (and to good sense) in the production of 'ideal' texts, have produced really satisfactory versions of Spenser's three great works. We now often speak of two types of text, a student text and a scholarly edition. While some editors (notably Hamilton, Yamashita, and Suzuki 2001) have sought to combine these two types of text in a single printed edition, this kind of movement will become increasingly difficult in the emerging electronic publication environment. Spenser is already well-served on the Internet by freely available, student-serviceable texts from providers like Renascence Editions. These texts, however, are not appropriate for scholarly work, and scholars will likely turn increasingly to the arrays of 'un-edited' textual documents already beginning to appear in larger numbers. The result may be that, for many purposes, scholars will come to ignore textual issues at their peril, while students will have to be carefully guided to appropriate, 'representative' (or what in earlier days were known as 'ideal') texts.

Of course a related trend is equally evident in the development of editorial apparatus, biographical notes, glossarial supplements, and contextual materials appended to the publication of Spenser's works. The 1679 folio (F3) included a short glossary of Spenser's harder archaisms; by 1715 Hughes felt it appropriate to prepend a 'life' of Spenser, an essay on allegorical poetry, remarks on Spenser's writings, and a 25-page 'Glossary explaining the Old and Obscure Words in Spenser's Works'. John Upton's 1758 edition of *The Faerie Queene* is famous for its extended, and learned commentary; Upton's adherence to the textual and critical methods of Richard Bentley and Lewis Theobald, outlined in his 1751 *A Letter Concerning a New Edition of Spenser's 'Faerie Queene'*, resulted in one of the finest annotated editions of any English poet in the eighteenth century (John Radcliffe, 'Upton, John', in Hamilton 1990). It is a model of critical elucidation that looks back to Digby's claim that, to understand Spenser, one must master his learning (indeed, Upton printed Digby's letter to Stradling as an appendix to his 1758 edition of *The Faerie Queene*). The nineteenth-century editions of Todd (1805) and Grosart (1882–84) anticipated the later *Variorum* edition in their bulk and range of supplementary materials. Todd prefixed to his edition not only a 'Life', glossary, and 'Essay on Allegorical Poetry', but also a series of 'Remarks' on Spenser's individual writings. Though Todd's edition is not cumbered by the detailed annotations that so enriched Upton's, his edition is notable for its inclusion of Bathurst's 1653 Latin rendition of *The Shepheardes Calender*. But it was in the twentieth century that the scholarly edition fulfilled its potential, and in the eleven volumes of texts, notes, appendices, variant readings, and biographical details contained in *The Works of Edmund Spenser, A Variorum Edition* (1932–49) Spenser achieved a high-water mark of scholarly documentation which has yet to be surpassed (or even updated).

The more modest, student-oriented editions of *The Faerie Queene* produced by Roche (1978) and Hamilton (1977, 2001) contain ample annotation, mostly of a philological and literary nature. They thus characterize the decisive reaction against historicist readings of Renaissance authors that had dominated the nineteenth and early twentieth century. Gone are the detailed historical and philosophical discussions, in seemingly countless appendices, of the *Variorum* edition; gone, in fact, is the underlying principle, so abiding in the editorial reception of Spenser from Digby forward, that the reader ought to encounter Spenser not only in the texts of his poems, but in the whole corpus of political, philosophical, historical, mythological, and otherwise literary material that constituted Spenser's learning. Naturally constrained by the economies of paperback publishing, Roche's edition supplies only the barest skeleton of a life (in the now ubiquitous 'chronology' format) and a sparse, mainly glossarial set of annotations that define hard and obsolete words, identify characters and historical persons, document some literary allusions, and identify a scattered set of regular sources (the Bible, Homer, Virgil, Ariosto, Tasso, etc.). Hamilton's annotations, certainly the main attraction in his decidedly New Critical 1977 Longman edition of Smith's 1909 text of *The Faerie Queene*, are primarily philological in nature; as he remarks in his helpful introduction to the first edition, 'what is chiefly needed to understand the allegory fully is to understand all the words' (Hamilton 1977, 18). In its preoccupation with the philological and etymological texture of Spenser's wordsmithery, however, the edition does tend to lose sight of the allusiveness and erudition so palpable in Upton's notes (and preserved, haphazardly, in *Variorum*).

Hamilton remarks in the 'Preface' to his first edition of *The Faerie Queene* (1977, vii) that 'it became clear to me that the seventeenth-century Miltonic Spenser, that "sage and serious teacher" needed to be supplemented, if not supplanted for a while, by an earlier Renaissance Spenser, that skilled craftsman in words'. While the philological emphasis of Hamilton's annotations is a useful corrective, the 'Renaissance' authority that he claims for his bias is disputable. With the advent of New Historicism and the revival of 'new historical' readings in the last part of the twentieth century, Spenser's critics as well as his editors have returned to contextual materials. This trend is reflected in the expansion of Hamilton's annotations in the second Longman edition of *The Faerie Queene* (2001) and in the revival of interest in the encyclopedic *Variorum* approach to encountering Spenser. For the student or scholar new to Spenser's works, what is at stake in choosing between these editions can perhaps best be illustrated by an example. To take a piece of *The Faerie Queene* almost at random, we might consider how the various editions have treated Book I, canto xii, stanza 23, the first unveiling of Una to Redcrosse after his battle with the dragon. Upton's 1758 notes dwell on Spenser's classical sources:

> *The blazing brightness of her beautie's beame*—] Truth now appears in all her brightness and beauty.   Δεινὲς γὰρ ἂν παρεῖχεν ἔρωλας [ἡ Φρόνησις] ἔι τι τοιαῦτον ἑαυτῆς ἐναργὲς εἴδωλον παρείχιτο, εἰς ὄψιν ἰού. Plato in Phaedro. *Quam illa [Sapienta] ardentes amores excitaret sui, si videretur.* Cicero de Fin. ii. 16 *Forman quidem ipsam, et tanquam faciem honesti vides, quae si oculis cerneretur, mirabiles amores (ut ait Plato) excitaret.* Cic. de Off. i. 5. Dryden has expressed this very elegantly,
>
> > *For* TRUTH *has such a face and such a mien,*
> > *As to be lov'd, needs only to be seen.*
>
> But there is a particular reason why he mentions *her beautie's beame, and light of her sun-shyny face,* for so she is described in Revel. xiii. 1. *A woman*

clothed with the sun, and the moon under her feet, and upon her head a crown of twelve stars. (Upton 1758, 2, 424)

Upton goes on to query the original textual reading of 'ragged rimes' in this stanza, preferring 'rugged' on the basis of parallels in Macrobius and Horace, and noting Spenser's own parallel use of 'rugged' rhymes at *FQ* III.ii.3. Todd's 1805 'variorum' edition reproduces much of Upton's annotation for this stanza, but leaves out the parallels in Plato, Cicero, and Dryden; he adds his own parallels from Petrarch's *Rime* and Milton's *Comus*, and questions Upton's proposed emendation of 'ragged' to 'rugged' by citing the precedent of Skelton's well-known 'ragged' and 'to-jagged' verses. In a silence that speaks volumes, *Variorum* does not annotate this stanza at all, though it notes the more salient parallels with Revelation spotted by Upton in the surrounding stanzas, and pauses upon stanza 22 to ask, 'does not the betrothal of the Red Crosse Knight and Una refer rather to the union of England and reformed religion?' (*Variorum*, I, 308) Hamilton (1977) likewise gives no space to the classical sources and allusions that so exercised Upton, but briefly notes the reference to Revelation before concentrating in his usual style upon the semantic extension of one of the more interesting words in the stanza, 'enchace':

> **for to enchace:** to serve as a setting for; a fig. sense from the jeweller's art of setting gems. Upon the simplest level it means 'portray', 'display', 'adorn': the poet's words both reveal and enclose her heavenly image. (Hamilton 1977, 159)

Where Upton and Todd emphasize Spenser's classical education, and his legacy to the great poets like Milton and Dryden, *Variorum* sees historical context; and where *Variorum* reaches out to sixteenth-century religious history, Hamilton (1977) provides a New Critical close reading. In miniature, we can see both a strong current of continuity—the emphasis of all of Spenser's editors on the importance of his language, and the close links between this passage and Revelation—and at the same time pronounced differences reflecting the critical ideologies of the day—humanist allusion-hunting, historicist contextualization, practical criticism. For the student coming new to Spenser's works, it is absolutely crucial to remember that there is no one 'right' way of interpreting or elaborating Spenser's meaning, and that particular editors have generally plumped for a limited set of annotational emphases. Todd (1805) and *Variorum* (1932–49), however, went the furthest toward synthesizing previous scholarship, and the pluralistic critical communities of today have begun to return to the ethos of these editions.

In the climate of this renewed sense of Spenser's richness and the encyclo-paedic range of his meaning, a new project has been undertaken at Oxford University Press to re-collate and re-edit Spenser's texts from the earliest witnesses, and to document his work as a whole more fully and precisely in the light of the last seventy years of blossoming historical and literary research. It is to be hoped that this new editorial project will deliver us the most complete range of 'document' texts yet made available, as well as a range of 'representative' texts of Spenser's works for the consumption of the serious student and scholar; and will continue to expand upon the interrupted practice of contextualizing and interpreting Spenser's works through a range of ancillary materials. Instead of a single electronic texts of, say, *A View of the Present State of Ireland*, we will probably soon be speaking of a *View* 'archive' comprising collections of variant texts, intertexts, and materials from other media such as maps, emblems, and woodcuts. As early experience of online texts has already demonstrated, it will be an increasingly demanding task for scholars to determine the best available texts and materials. The next few decades of reading and research on Spenser are likely to be textually rich, but also textually unstable. The lesson of comparing extant editorial receptions of Spenser's works, with all of their profusion of annotation and interpretive resources, should suggest that this will also be a giddy time for Spenser resources. New editorial projects such as the Oxford Spenser, enabled by the new economies of electronic publication, will be able to deliver the entire history and breadth of Spenser scholarship with a thoroughness never before possible, or attempted; it will be up to the reader-user to sift and judge the relative value, and personal utility, of this material. Caveat lector.

Resources for research

At the end of the ninth canto of Book II of *The Faerie Queene*, the virgin Alma leads Sir Guyon and Prince Arthur to the topmost tower of her castle, where the three sage faculties of the rational mind—the prophetical Phantastes, the (anonymous) genius of the present, and the historian Eumnestes—reside and work. Any reader of *The Faerie Queene* will be struck by the buzzing and depainted chamber of the poetical Phantastes; but perhaps she will find herself even more dazzled by the energy and 'infinite remembraunce' of Eumnestes, with his 'old records from auncient times' and his sprawling library of 'antique Regesters'. As Spenser's earliest readers clearly recognized, the encyclopaedic range of his fantastical poetry—with its dense intertextual reference and voraciously interdisciplinary learning—seems to invite scholarly interpretation and exegesis, supported by such a heavy shelf of reading resources and the 'endlesse exercise' of a tireless Eumnestes. The artificial archaism of Spenser's diction, and the often arcane philosophical, historical, and literary arguments encoded in his poetry, encouraged editors to include interpretative aids—introductions, topical essays, glossaries—in editions of his poetry from as early as 1679. In this, Spenser's printers and editors might be thought to have been following the poet's own example, taking their cue from E. K.'s 'Epistle' to Harvey in *The Shepheardes Calender*, or Spenser's

'A letter of the Authors... to Sir Walter Raleigh' in *The Faerie Queene* (1590), introductory prefaces notorious for the strong influence they exert on the reader's reception of the poetry. Spenser's example is no less compelling today, when the reader's approach to his works is seemingly swamped with student guides, glossaries, encyclopaedias and chronologies, scholarly articles, academic books, internet tools, and many other types of research resources—even, alas, tiresome chapters *about* such resources. But because the present delightsome profusion of Spenser aids can seem daunting, sometimes even debilitating, it will be worth pausing to survey and review the best of the modern resources available to students.

The history of Spenser criticism up to the beginning of the publication of the *Variorum* volumes can be most conveniently accessed through the various notes, appendices, essays, source/analogue tables, and bibliographies contained therein. Much more, of course, exists for the specialist outside the summaries and excerpts provided in the *Variorum*, but on the whole the editors achieved their impressive goal of collating and presenting the full range of Spenser criticism to 1932. The volumes are also rich in supplementary essays—substantial and still relevant studies in their own right—of issues such as 'The Punctuation of *The Faerie Queene*'. It is important for readers handling these volumes to recognize that, because the *Variorum* was completed in stages over an almost 20-year period, each volume is the document of a particular year, and of a particular group of editors; the consequences of this serial publication can occasionally prove difficult to disentangle. The printed *Index* to the volumes, recently reprinted in paperback, is indispensable for the reader hoping to mine the collected notes and excerpts printed in the *Variorum* volumes on a given, particular subject (e.g., *justice, pastoral*). For those wishing to work back into the original editions, or annotations, of Hughes (1715, 1750), Jortin (1734), Birch (1751), Warton (1754, 1762), Church (1758), Upton (1758), Todd (1805), Child (1855), Collier (1862), Morris and Hales (1869), Grosart (1882–84), Dodge (1908), Smith and de Sélincourt (1912), or Renwick (1930), it will often be prudent to begin with a survey-dip in the relevant parts of the *Variorum*; further, more discursive guidance to pre-Victorian editions is to hand in Wurtsbaugh's *Two Centuries of Spenserian Scholarship (1609–1805)* (1936). The addition of the *Variorum* texts (unfortunately for the present without annotations or appendices) to the collection of Chadwyck Healy's *Literature Online* (or *LION*) will make these texts more widely available than hitherto, though for the time being at least Chadwyck Healy's services remain prohibitively expensive for many institutions and most independent users.

Since the publication of the *Variorum* volumes was completed in 1949, of course, the business of literary criticism has boomed—and Spenser scholarship has often been at the center of new critical trends. A number of routes to this scholarship exist, and can be pursued in different ways, depending on the nature of the study. Printed bibliographies of Spenser-related criticism have been published in book form on a number of occasions; two early guides—including a substantial amount of biographical documentation (some now deprecated, but the rest instructive), Carpenter's *A Reference Guide to Edmund Spenser* (1923), and Atkinson's *Edmund Spenser: A Bibliographical Supplement* (1937)—were only partially assimilated into *Variorum*, and remain useful for their subject divisions alone. Two more recent, complete, and reliable critical bibliographies are McNeir and Provost (1962) and Frushell and Vondersmith (1975). For criticism since 1970, the annotated reports and reviews of both articles and books in *The Spenser Newsletter*, now *The Spenser Review*, are indispensable; the reviews of this quarterly publication of the International Spenser Society have now been archived on the Internet as *Edmund Spenser World Bibliography*, and most back issues, after an eighteen-month delay, are freely searchable according to a number of limited search categories. More expansive critical searches are possible with the Modern Language Association's International Bibliography (MLAIB), available through many institutional libraries and via Chadwyck Healy's *Literature Online* (*LION*), which also delivers the Annual Bibliography of English Language and Literature (ABELL). More focused searches for materials relating to Spenser in Ireland can begin with the bibliographies compiled by Willy Maley (1991, 1996), both of which are also now freely available on the Internet.

Spenser scholarship has been organized, described, and documented most copiously, and by subject, in A. C. Hamilton's compendious helpmeet, *The Spenser Encyclopedia* (1990), which contains introductory articles on an exhaustive range of Spenser-related topics. An excellent cross-referencing index makes this printed resource, recently re-issued in an affordable paperback, particularly useful. For topics not covered by the *Spenser Encyclopedia*, students and scholars now have recourse to the community at large more directly through an active and collegial email discussion list, shared with Sidneians (the Sidney–Spenser list, currently hosted by the UK provider, JISCmail). Many Spenser scholars also subscribe to the wider, or related online communities of FICINO, SHARP-L, SHAKESPER, MILTON-L, and H-ALBION, among others. Such lists are most frequently used by scholars trying to build up bibliographies on a topic, or bidding for help to solve a defined, intractable problem; but they also occasionally host serious, sustained discussion and debate on topics central to the concerns of Spenserians. The now widespread practice of archiving email lists has transformed such exchanges from ephemeral common-room chat to often serious, if somewhat on-the-hop, academic discussion.

A range of journals dedicated to research in Renaissance English literature have supported Spenser studies over the years; currently foremost of these is *Spenser Studies: A Renaissance Poetry Annual*, which has produced nearly twenty volumes of serious research and commentary on Spenser (and his time) in the last two decades. *Spenser Studies* now offers a full table of contents and access to abstracts on the web. Other core journals of the field—*ELH, SEL: Studies in English Literature 1500–1900, English Literary Renaissance (ELR), Publications of the Modern Language Association of America (PMLA)* and *Modern Philology*—regularly publish articles on Spenser or of interest to scholars working on Spenser, and relevant studies occasionally appear in other journals such as *Renaissance Quarterly, Representations, Journal of English and Germanic Philology, Notes & Queries, Journal of the History of Ideas, Review of English Studies,* or in associated specialist journals such as *The Library, Studies in Bibliography,* or *Shakespeare Survey.* Many of these journals now make at least their tables of contents freely available on the web, and some participate in the JSTOR project, which makes the full texts of past issues available to subscribing institutions (note the relevant moving and fixed bars associated with Internet provision of each of these journals). While Internet-based journals have yet to make real purchase in this field, *Early Modern Literary Studies (EMLS)* regularly produces issues containing Spenser-related material, and this area of development may prove one to watch.

The notional Spenser student sitting at a computer terminal has, in addition to the Internet-based provisions noted above, two basic categories of research tool to call upon: specialized search-engines and databases, and online texts. Often, the two are combined in one resource—as is the case, for example, with Chadwyck Healy's Literature Online service (see below), which offers searchable, and often annotated, texts of most literary works in English, as well as databases of secondary literature in the field (ABELL and MLAIB). Such resources are either freely accessible, mere sites on the World Wide Web available to all those with Internet access; or they are subscriber-only services, available to those who are members of participating institutions (such as universities or major research libraries) or who pay for a private subscription. Free resources can be accessed simply by entering the appropriate URL into a web browser, but subscriber resources will probably need to be routed through a university/library server, and very possibly through a particular local resource, such as a university library's own access software. A student or scholar using a computer linked to a university network might well have all these categories of information-provision available. Sometimes a university library home page will provide a link to 'Electronic Resources', and that page will have relevant subject divisions (such as 'English' or 'Humanities') which will take the user to a specific service such as *LION*.

An eclectic group of such Internet-based research tools has increasingly come to support and even, incipiently, to change Spenser studies. Perhaps the two most breathtaking of these come from the ProQuest umbrella, which now includes University Microfilms (UMI) as well as Chadwyck Healy. *Literature Online (LION)* provides to paying subscribers the full (often annotated) text of most literary works in English from the earliest medieval texts right up to the twentieth century; and *Early English Books Online (EEBO)* delivers through PDF files (nearly) every book printed in England, Scotland, Wales, and Ireland, and books in English printed abroad, from the year 1475 to 1700. The unlimited access many scholars now have to facsimile texts of contemporary books, as well as searchable texts of the entire gamut of English literature, has steered Renaissance studies more generally back towards historical readings, contextual readings, and bibliographical concerns—a movement that has re-energized Spenser studies as well. The searchable database provided by the Research Libraries Group in their Eureka service, which includes *English Short Title Catalogue* (*ESTC*) (the successor to the printed *Short Title Catalogue*), has exerted a similar influence. A scholar wishing, for example, to document Spenser's debts to Protestant hagiography in Foxe's *Actes and Monuments* has merely to call up the PDF text of Foxe on *EEBO*. Similarly, a scholar looking to determine the frequency of Spenser's use of a particular word (e.g. 'maiden') can now simply type that word into the *LION* search box, suitably delimited, to obtain a total figure (in this case seven citations) as well as the relevant texts from Spenser's works. (Unfortunately, as anyone comparing this result to Osgood's *Concordance* will note, this is not the end of the story; for Spenser also spells the word 'mayden' in nine other instances in *The Faerie Queene* alone, which this search would not have registered; and it would likewise have missed the use of the word, for the same reasons, in *The Shepheardes Calender* and in *Epithalamion*. Similarly, this search picks up 'maiden-headed' from *FQ* IV.iv.17, but does not catch 'maidenhead', 'maiden-child', 'maiden's', 'maidens', or 'maidens''. Electronic searching has some way to go before it is as exhaustively reliable and time-efficient as an old-fashioned trip to the concordance.)

The revolutionary economics of Internet publication have seen in a new era of independent digital facsimiles, manuscript transcriptions, and other publications of similarly peripheral contextual material. Books, manuscripts, pamphlets, and other documents and materials once deemed too specialist or too unwieldy for profitable print publication are now at last seeing circulation in the unfettered electronic market. A case study in this development of new texts is offered by the recent online publication of Spenser's diplomatic letters (Burlinson and Zurcher, 2003), that set of documents produced by Spenser, or under Spenser's supervision, during his service as principal secretary to Arthur Lord Grey, Lord Deputy of Ireland from 1580 to 1582. While the texts of these documents cannot be said to be 'by' Spenser in any sense—the archive comprises letters from Grey to the Queen and Privy Council in London, and copies of other letters and documents relating to the service in Ireland—nevertheless the letters have great significance to Spenser scholars because of the contextual information they supply about Spenser's biography, the social and political environment in which he moved, and the kinds of language, thought, and business he was exposed to during his time as a secretary and clerk in the English administration in Ireland. Although in some ways a large corpus of materials—its text, in total, runs to about the same length as that of *A view*—this archive is easily and cheaply accommodated by a single university departmental server.

Scholarly access to manuscript resources has benefited in other ways from the online revolution in information delivery, too. Many libraries, collections, and other repositories now offer electronic catalogues of their holdings, in some cases with descriptive annotations, which at last make it possible to conduct significant searches for individuals, works, or even lines of text across a wide range of geographically and institutionally distributed holdings. A dedicated manuscript researcher may not, in this climate, find it impossible to add to even a definitive reference tool like Peter Beal's *Index of English Literary Manuscripts 1450–1625* (1980), which contains what is still the first port of call for research into Spenserian manuscripts. The largest and most important of the new Internet-based services, the British Library's online manuscripts catalogue (formerly MOLCAT; now incorporated into the 'Integrated Catalogue') and the online database of the National Archive (formerly the Public Record Office), are freely accessible to the public. Manuscripts formerly described in the reports of the Historical Manuscripts Commission are now re-emerging as part of the Access to Archives (A2A) database in the United Kingdom, which provides an umbrella, searchable database of local record-office, and small-institution manuscript holdings. Meanwhile the major period research libraries in the United States and the United Kingdom—the Folger Shakespeare Library, Newberry Library, Huntington Library, Houghton Library at Harvard, Beinecke Library at Yale, Bodleian Library at Oxford, and so forth—are regularly improving their online manuscript descriptions and search facilities. Other, supporting resources for manuscript research and publication—from online courses in early modern palaeography to web-publication tutorials and standards for SGML and XML—appear and improve regularly. Amid all of this explosive development, researchers have also thought to compile meta-lists of links to new as well as trusted research resources. The best of these are the relevant sections of Alan Liu's Voice of the Shuttle, Jack Lynch's Literary Resources, and the Humbul Humanities Hub. The links and resources of the Cambridge English Renaissance Electronic Service (CERES) make a digestible first course; for manuscript research see especially the document entitled, 'Routes Toward Early Modern Literary Manuscripts: A Prolegomenon', originally compiled by Jeremy Maule.

One important cautionary note on Internet resources should be sounded: resource authors and designers increasingly tend to create electronic materials that are, on the face of it, 'user-driven'. While the user has more power and flexibility in manipulating and searching through the contents of, say, an Internet site than a printed book, the editorial wisdom of the printed resource has sometimes been lost. It is, for example, crucial, when using

Internet-based research aids, to read the provider's documentation on content and, perhaps even more importantly, to understand the site's search facility. Users of the *Variorum* text of Spenser's works provided through *LION* will, of course, need to know that none of the annotations or appendices are included in the site's provision; these must still be searched out in the printed copies, and accessed through the printed index. Similarly, attempts to access recent journal article reviews via *Edmund Spenser World Bibliography*, or to read the most recent scholarship in *ELH* via JSTOR, will be useless, because of the invariable 'moving bar' protecting print copy. The same holds true for accessions to bibliographies like ABELL and MLAIB, which take time to add new materials. Library catalogues can be molar-grindingly idiosyncratic in the way they store or retrieve information, and often have very small but very important print about the limits of collection coverage. Some understanding of the way a site handles search parameters, such as boolean operators ('and', 'or', etc.), can make or break a search attempt, while search queries submitted in quotation marks (*'derring do'*) will turn up entirely different results from queries not so dressed (*derring do*). Searching through texts is always already complicated for Spenser students by the problem of orthography, which is generally not modernized in editions of any of Spenser's poems or even prose; this problem may be partly avoided by searching for word-stems or partial words instead of words (e.g. 'vanit' instead of 'vanity' or 'vanitie'), but some may continue to find the printed concordances, with their harmonized entries, easier to navigate.

Despite such unavoidable technical niggles, Spenser studies seem set, again, to move in the vanguard of scholarly innovation, both critical and methodological. Already students and scholars of Spenser's works have embraced the new resources, databases, texts, and other materials offered within the 'electronic university', and have taken the initiative (in true Spenserian style) to develop further research aids of wide use to the Spenserian community. New developments currently in the planning or production stage include facsimile texts of 'document' editions of Spenser's works, such as the texts of F1, F2, and F3, of Hughes (1715) and Todd (1805); facsimile editions of Spenser-related manuscripts, from the important recensions of *A View of the Present State of Ireland*, to state papers, to other contemporary manuscript romance and lyric works; electronic publication of Spenser-related visual material, such as emblems, heraldic designs, and allegorical illustrations; and the continuing and systematic conversion and updating of older resources into new, searchable, online aids. Whether these advances occur under the aegis of a single sponsor, such as the massive Internet publication project envisaged by the Oxford Spenser team, or by the incremental additions of the wider community, they will come. The future of Spenser studies has perhaps never dazzled so brightly.

Appendix 1: Summary census of Spenser editions, from 1569 onwards

[for fuller bibliographical detail, see http://www.english.cam.ac.uk/spenser/bibliography/]

Section 1: Editions of Spenser's works, 1569–1679

Jan van der Noodt. 1569. A Theatre wherein be represented as wel the miseries & calamities that follow the voluptuous Worldlings, *As also the greate ioyes and* plesures which the faithfull do enioy, London: Henry Bynneman. [Containing verse translations by Spenser.]

Edmund Spenser. 1579. *The Shepheardes Calender* Conteyning tvvelue Æglogues proportionable to the twelue monethes, London: Hugh Singleton.

Three Proper, and Wittie, familiar Letters: lately passed betvvene tvvo Vniuersitie men: Touching the Earthquake in Aprill last, and our English refourmed Versifying, London: Henry Bynneman, 1580. Includes: Tvvo Other, very commendable Letters, of the same mens vvriting: both touching the foresaid Artificiall Versifying, and certain other Particulars, London: Henry Bynneman, 1580.

E. S. 1581. *The Shepheardes Calender* Conteining twelue Æglogues proportionable to the twelue Monethes, London: John Harrison the Younger.

E. S. 1586. *The Shepheardes Calender, Conteining twelue Æglogues propor*tionable to the twelue *Monethes*, London: John Wolfe for John Harrison the Younger, 1586.

E. S. 1590. The Faerie Queene. Disposed into twelue books, *Fashioning* XII. Morall vertues, London: John Wolfe for William Ponsonby.

E. S. 1591. Complaints. *Containing sundrie small Poemes of the* Worlds Va*nitie*, London: printed for William Ponsonby.

E. S. 1591. *Daphnaïda*. An Elegie vpon the death of the noble and vertuous Douglas Howard, *Daughter and* heire of *Henry* Lord *Howard, Viscount Byndon, and Wife of Ar*thure Gorges *Esquier*, London: Thomas Orwin for William Ponsonby. [Reprinted 1596.]

E. S. 1591. The Shepheards Calender. *Conteining twelue Aeglogues proportionable to the twelue Monethes*, London: John Windet for John Harrison the Younger.

E. S. 1595. Amoretti and Epithalamion, London: Peter Short for William Ponsonby.

E. S. 1595. Colin Clouts Come home againe, London: Thomas Creede for William Ponsonby.

E. S. 1596. The Faerie Queene. *Disposed into twelue bookes, Fashioning* XII. Morall vertues, London: Richard Field for William Ponsonby. **Usually found with** E. S. 1596. The Second Part of The Faerie Queene. *Containing* The Fourth, Fifth, and Sixth Bookes, London: Richard Field for William Ponsonby.

E. S. 1596. Fowre Hymnes, London: Richard Field for William Ponsonby. [Including a second edition of *Daphnaïda*.]

E. S. 1596. Prothalamion *Or A Spousall Verse made by Edm. Spenser*. In Honour of the double mariage of the two Honorable & vertuous *Ladies, the Ladie* Elizabeth *and the Ladie* Katherine *Somerset*, Daughters to the Right Honourable the Earle of *Worcester* and espoused to the two worthie Gentlemen M. *Henry Gilford*, and M. *William Peter* Esquyers, London: Printed for William Ponsonby.

E. S. 1597. The Shepheards Calender: Conteyning Twelue Aeglogues, proportionable to the *twelue Moneths*, London: Thomas Creede for John Harrison the Younger.

E. S. 1609. The Faerie Queene, Disposed into XII. Bookes, Fashioning twelue Morall Vertues, London: Humphrey Lownes for Matthew Lownes.

E. S. 1611–17. The Faerie Queen: The Shepheards Calendar: Together With The Other Works of England's Arch-Poët, Edm. Spenser: Collected into one Volume, and carefully corrected, London: Humphrey Lownes for Matthew Lownes. [Including reprintings of constituent elements.]

E. S. 1633. A View Of the State Of Ireland, Written dialogue-wise betweene Eudoxus and Irenæus, ed. by Sir James Ware, Dublin: The Society of Stationers.

Theodore Bathurst, transl. 1653. Calendarium Pastorale, Sive Æglogæ Duodecim, Totidem Anni Mensibus accommodatæ [The Shepherds Calendar, Containing Twelve Æglogues, Proportionable to the Twelve Months], London: M.M.T.C. and Gabriel Bedell.

E. S. 1679. The Works Of that Famous English Poet, Mr. Edmond Spenser. *Viz.* The Faery Queen, The Shepherds Calendar, The History of Ireland, & c. Whereunto is added, An Account of his Life; *With other new Additions Never before in Print,* London: Henry Hills for Jonathan Edwin.

Section 2: Major editions of Spenser's works, 1715–1932

Hughes, J. ed. 1715. The Works of Mr Edmund Spenser. In six volumes. With a Glossary Explaining the Old and Obscure Words, London: Jacob Tonson.

Birch, Thomas D. D. ed. 1751. *The Faerie Queene* by Edmund Spenser, with an exact Collation of the two Original Editions . . . to which are now added a new life of the author and also a glossary adorn'd with thiry-two copper plates from the original drawings of the late W. Kent, 3 vols, London: Printed for J. Brindley and S. Wright.

Upton, J. ed. 1758. Spenser's Faerie Queene. A New Edition with a Glossary, And Notes explanatory and critical, 2 vols, London: Printed for J. and R. Tonson.

Church, R. ed. 1758. *The Faerie Queene* of Edmund Spenser, 4 vols, London.

Todd, H. J. ed. 1805. The Works of Edmund Spenser. In eight volumes. With the principal illustrations of various commentators. To which are added, notes, some account of the life of Spenser, and a glossarial and other indexes, 8 vols, London: Printed for F. C. and J. Rivington, T. Payne, Cadell and Davies, and R. H. Evans.

Child, F. J. ed. 1855. The Poetical Works of Edmund Spenser. The text carefully revised, and illustrated with James notes, original and selected, 5 vols, Boston: Little, Brown, and Co.

Gilfillan, G. ed. 1859. The Poetical Works of Edmund Spenser. With memoir and critical dissertations, 5 vols, Edinburgh: J. Nichol.

Collier, J. P. ed. 1562. The Works of Edmund Spenser, 5 vols, London: Bell and Daldy.

Morris, R. and J. W. Hales, eds 1869. The Globe edition [of the] Complete Works of Edmund Spenser edited from the original editions and manuscripts . . . with a memoir, London: Macmillan and Co.

Grosart, A. B. ed. 1882–84. The Complete Works in Verse and Prose of Edmund Spenser, 8 vols, London: privately printed.

Warren, Kate M. ed. 1897–1900. *The Faerie Queene* . . . edited from the original editions of 1590 and 1596, with introduction and glossary, 6 vols, London: Constable & Co.

Dodge, R. E. N. ed. 1908. The Complete Poetical Works of Edmund Spenser, Boston: The Cambridge Edition of the Poets.

Smith, J. C. and Ernest de Sélincourt, The Poetical Works of Edmund Spenser, 3 vols, London: Oxford University Press, 1909–12.

Renwick, W. L. ed. 1930–32. The Works of Edmund Spenser, 8 vols, Oxford: Basil Blackwell.

Greenlaw, E., C. G. Osgood, and F. M. Padelford, *et al.*, eds 1932–49. The Works of Edmund Spenser, A Variorum Edition, 11 vols Baltimore: Johns Hopkins Press.

Section 3: Selected editions of Spenser's works, 1932-Present

The Faerie Queene

Ed. by A. C. Hamilton, London: Longman, 1977. [A reprinting of J. C. Smith's 1909 text, buttressed by copious same-page New Critical annotation.]

Ed. by Thomas P. Roche, Jr., with the assistance of C. Patrick O'Donnell, Jr., London: Penguin Books, 1978. [An unmodernised text based on the early quartos, carefully annotated, with useful but not exhaustive textual notes.]

Ed. by A. C. Hamilton *et al.*, London: Longman, 2001. [A revised, unmodernised text based on the early quartos, and 1609 folio, of the poem, framed by the same elaborate annotation as the first edition.]

The Shepheardes Calender, etc.

The Yale Edition of the Shorter Poems of Edmund Spenser, ed. by William A. Oram, Einar Bjorvand, Ronald Bond, Thomas H. Cain, Alexander Dunlop, and Richard Schell, New Haven: Yale University Press, 1989. [An unmodernised text of Spenser's complete shorter poems, based on the original editions; carefully and faithfully laid out, and well annotated.]

E. S., Selected Shorter Poems, ed. by Douglas Brooks-Davies, London: Longman, 1995. [A modernised text based on the original editions; excellent annotations with a particular emphasis on Spenser's Platonism.]

E. S., The Shorter Poems, ed. by Richard McCabe, Harmondsworth: Penguin, 1999. [An unmodernised text of Spenser's complete shorters poems, built from a comparison of de Sélincourt's 1910 Oxford edition with the early quartos of individual works; scrupulously edited and copiously annotated. Apart from the pulp-paperback format, this is now the best affordable edition of Spenser's shorter poems.]

A View of the Present State of Ireland

A View of the State of Ireland, From the first printed edition (1633), ed. by Andrew Hadfield and Willy Maley, Oxford: Blackwell, 1997. [A faithful edition of Ware's 1633 text, with helpful prefatory material and appendices, including an annotated guide to further reading.]

Appendix 2: Internet resources for Spenser research

(URL information accurate at time of printing)

Edmund Spenser World Bibliography
http://www.slu.edu/colleges/AS/ENG/spenser/new/

Edmund Spenser Home Page
http://www.english.cam.ac.uk/spenser/

Spenser Studies: A Renaissance Poetry Annual
http://www.english.cam.ac.uk/spenser/studies/
The Spenser Review
http://www.english.cam.ac.uk/spenser/spenrev/
Sidney-Spenser Discussion List
http://www.english.cam.ac.uk/spenser/list.html

Haphazard: A manuscript resource for Spenser studies
http://www.english.cam.ac.uk/ceres/haphazard/

Literature Online (LION), including ABELL and MLAIB [by subscription]
http://lion.chadwyck.com [US]
http://lion.chadwyck.co.uk [UK]

Early English Books Online (EEBO) [by subscription]
http://eebo.chadwyck.com

Oxford Text Archive
http://ota.ox.ac.uk/

MLA database [by subscription]
http://www.mla.org/

Eureka (including ESTC and the RLIN Bibliographical File [by subscription])
http://eureka.rlg.org

Voice of the Shuttle
http://vos.ucsb.edu/

Jack Lynch's Literary Resources
http://andromeda.rutgers.edu/~jlynch/Lit/ren.html

Humbul Humanities Hub
http://www.humbul.ac.uk/

Cambridge English Renaissance Electronic Service (CERES)
http://www.english.cam.ac.uk/ceres/

Works Cited

Abbreviations used

CL	*Comparative Literature*
EA	*Études Anglaises*
EIC	*Essays in Criticism*
ELH	*English Literary History*
ELN	*English Language Notes*
ELR	*English Literary Renaissance*
ES	*English Studies*
HLQ	*Huntington Library Quarterly*
JEGP	*Journal of English and Germanic Philology*
JMRS	*Journal of Medieval and Renaissance Studies*
MLN	*Modern Language Notes*
MLQ	*Modern Language Quarterly*
MLR	*Modern Language Review*
MP	*Modern Philology*
N&Q	*Notes and Queries*
PMLA	*Publications of the Modern Language Association of America*
PQ	*Philological Quarterly*
REL	*Review of English Literature*
RES	*Review of English Studies*
SEL	*Studies in English Literature*
SP	*Studies in Philology*
SR	*Studies in the Renaissance*
SSt	*Spenser Studies*
TLS	*Times Literary Supplement*
TSLL	*Texas Studies in Language and Literature*
UTQ	*University of Toronto Quarterly*
YES	*Yearbook of English Studies*

Adamson, J. H. and H. F. Holland. 1969. The Shepherd of the Ocean: An Account of Sir Walter Ralegh and his Times, London: Bodley Head.

Albright, E. M. 1928. "Spenser's Reason for Rejecting the Cantos of Mutability", *SP* 25: 93–127.

——. 1929. "Spenser's Cosmic Philosophy and his Religion", *PMLA* 44: 715–25.

Allen, D. C. 1956. "On Spenser's *Muiopotmos*", *SP* 53: 141–58.

Allman, E. J. 1980. "*Epithalamion's* Bridegroom: Orpheus-Adam-Christ", *Renascence* 32: 240–7.

Alpers, P. J. 1967. *The Poetry of* The Faerie Queene, Princeton: Princeton University Press.

——. 1977. "Narration in *The Faerie Queene*", *ELH* 44: 19–39.

——. 1989. "Spenser's Late Pastorals", *ELH* 56: 797–817.

———. 1990. "Bower of Bliss", in *The Spenser Encyclopedia*, ed. A. C. Hamilton, Toronto: Toronto University Press, 104–7.

———. 1996. *What is Pastoral?*, Chicago: University of Chicago Press.

Anderson, D. 1985. " 'Unto My Selfe Alone': Spenser's Plenary *Epithalamion*", *SSt* 5 (for 1984): 149–68.

Anderson, J. H. 1971a. "Whatever Happened to Amoret? The Poet's Role in Book IV of *The Faerie Queene*", *Criticism* 1: 180–200.

———. 1971b. " 'Nat Worth a Boterflye': *Muiopotmos* and *The Nun's Priest's Tale*", *JMRS* 1: 89–106.

———. 1976. *The Growth of a Personal Voice: "Piers Plowman" and "The Faerie Queene"*, New Haven: Yale University Press.

———. 1982. " 'In Liuing Colours and Right Hew': The Queen of Spenser's Central Books," in *Poetic Traditions of the English Renaissance*, ed. Maynard Mack and George de Forest Lord, New Haven: Yale University Press, 47–66.

———. 1988. "Arthur, Argante, and the Ideal Vision: An Exercise in Speculation and Parody," in *The Passing of Arthur: New Essays in the Arthurian Tradition*, ed. Christopher Baswell and William Sharpe, New York: Garland Press, 193–206.

———. 1996. *Words That Matter: Linguistic Perception in the English Renaissance*, Stanford: Stanford University Press.

Anderson, J. H., D. Cheney, and D. A. Richardson, eds 1996. *Spenser's Life and the Subject of Biography*, Amherst: University of Massachusetts Press.

Aptekar, J. 1969. *Icons of Justice: Iconography and Thematic Imagery in the "Faerie Queene"*, New York: Columbia University Press.

Aristotle. 1946. *The Politics of Aristotle*, ed. and trans. Ernest Baker, Oxford: Oxford University Press.

Atchity, K. J. 1973. "Spenser's *Mother Hubberd's Tale*: Three Themes of Order", *PQ* 52: 161–72.

Atkinson, D. F. 1937. *Edmund Spenser: A Bibliographical Supplement*, Baltimore: Johns Hopkins Press.

Baker, D. J. 1986. " 'Some Quirk, Some Subtle Evasion': Legal Subversion in Spenser's *A View of the Present State of Ireland*", *SSt* 6 (for 1985): 147–63.

Baker. D. J. 1997. *Between Nations: Shakespeare, Spenser, Marvell, and the Question of Britain*, Stanford: Stanford University Press.

Barkan, L. 2000. "Ruins and Visions: Spenser, Pictures, Rome," in *Edmund Spenser: Essays on Culture and Allegory*, ed. J. K. Morrison and M. Greenfield, Aldershot: Ashgate, 9–36.

Barker, F. 1984. *The Tremulous Private Body: Essays on Subjection*, London: Methuen.

Barthes, R. 1971. "From Work to Text", trans. Josué V. Harari, in *Textual Strategies: Perspectives in Post-Structuralist Criticism*, Ithaca: Cornell University Press, 1979.

———. 1973. *S/Z*, trans. Richard Miller, Oxford: Blackwell, 1990.

Bates, C. 1992. *The Rhetoric of Courtship in Elizabethan Language and Literature*, Cambridge: Cambridge University Press.

Bath, M. 1988. "Verse Form and Pictorial Space in Van der Noot's *Theatre for Worldlings*," in K. J. Höltgen *et al.* eds, *Word and Visual Imagination: Studies in the Interaction of English Literature and the Visual Arts*, Erlangen, 73–105.

Baybak, M., *et al.* 1969. "Placement 'In the Middest' in *The Faerie Queene*", *Papers on Language and Literature* 5: 227–34; repr. in Hamilton 1972, 389–94.

Bayley, P., ed. 1977. *Spenser: The Faerie Queene*, Casebook Series, Houndmills, Basingstoke: Macmillan.

Beal, P., ed. 1980. *Index of English Literary Manuscripts, Volume I: 1450–1625*, London: Mansell.

Beilin, E. 1987. *Redeeming Eve: Women Writers of the English Renaissance*, Princeton: Princeton University Press.

Bellamy, E. J. 1987. "The Vocative and the Vocational: The Unreadability of Elizabeth in *The Faerie Queene*" *ELH* 54: 1–30.

——. 1991. "Em(body)ments of Power: Versions of the Body in Pain in Spenser", *LIT: Literature/Interpretation/Theory*, 2, 4: 1–30.

——. 1992. *Translations of Power: Narcissism and the Unconscious in Epic History* Ithaca: Cornell University Press.

——. 1994. "The Aesthetics of Decline: Locating the *Post*-Epic in Literary History", *SSt* 11 (for 1990): 161–85.

——. 1997. "Waiting for Hymen: Literary History as 'Symptom' in Spenser and Milton", *ELH* 64: 391–414.

——. 2004a. "Wind in Spenser's Isis Church", *SSt* 18: 9–23.

——. 2004b "Spenser's Marine Unconscious"., in *Irigaray and Premodern Writing*, London: Routledge.

Bell, I. 1998. *Elizabethan Women and the Poetry of Courtship*, Cambridge: Cambridge University Press.

Belsey, C. 1985. *The Subject of Tragedy: Identity and Difference in Renaissance Drama*, London: Methuen.

Benjamin, W. 1972. *Illuminations*, ed. Hannah Arendt, trans. H. Zohn, New York: Harcourt Brace.

Bennett, J. W. 1933. "Spenser's Venus and the Goddess Nature of the *Cantos of Mutabilitie*", *SP* 30: 160–92.

——. 1942, *The Evolution of* The Faerie Queene, Chicago: University of Chicago Press.

Benson, P. J. 1985. "Rule, Virginia: Protestant Theories of Female Regiment in *The Faerie Queene*", *ELR* 15: 277–92.

——. 1992. *The Invention of the Renaissance Woman: The Challenge of Female Independence in the Literature and Thought of Italy and England*, University Park, PA: Pennsylvania State University Press.

Berger, H., Jr. 1957. *The Allegorical Temper: Vision and Reality in Book II of Spenser's "Faerie Queene"*, New Haven: Yale University Press.

——. 1961a. "A Secret Discipline: *The Faerie Queene*, Book VI", in *Form and Convention in the Poetry of Edmund Spenser*, ed. William Nelson, New York: Columbia University Press, 35–75; repr. in Berger, *Revisionary Play*, 215–42.

——. 1961b. "The Prospect of Imagination: Spenser and the Limits of Poetry", *SEL* 1: 93–120.

——. 1965. "Spenser's *Prothalamion*: An Interpretation", *EIC* 15: 363–80.

——. 1968. "Two Spenserian Retrospects: The Antique Temple of Venus and the Primitive Marriage of Rivers", *TSLL* 10: 5–25.

——. 1969. "*The Faerie Queene, Book III*: A General Description", *Criticism* 11: 234–61.

——. 1971. "Busirane and the War Between the Sexes: An Interpretation of *The Faerie Queene III.xi–xii*", *ELR* 1: 99–121.

——. 1983. "Orpheus, Pan, and the Poetics of Misogyny: Spenser's Critique of Pastoral Love and Art", *ELH* 50: 27–60.

——. 1988. *Revisionary Play: Studies in the Spenserian Dynamics*, Berkeley: University of California Press.

——. 1989. "Kidnapped Romance: Discourse in *The Faerie Queene*", in *Unfolded Tales: Essays on Renaissance Romance*, ed. George M. Logan and Gordon Teskey, Ithaca: Cornell University Press, 208–56.

——. 1991. "Narrative as Rhetoric in *The Faerie Queene*", *ELR* 21: 3–48.

——. 1994. "Actaeon at the Hinder Gate: The Stag Party in Spenser's Gardens of Adonis", in *Desire in the Renaissance: Psychoanalysis and Literature*, ed. Valeria Funucci and Regina Schwarz, Princeton: Princeton University Press, 91–119.

——. 1998. "Displacing Autophobia in *Faerie Queene* I: Ethics, Gender, and Oppositional Reading in the Spenserian Text", *ELR* 28: 163–82.

——. 2003a. "Wring Out the Old: Squeezing the Text, 1951–2001", *SSt* 18: 81–121.

——. 2003b. "Archimago: Between Text and Countertext", *SEL* 43: 20–32.

——. 2004. "Sexual and Religious Politics in Book 1 of Spenser's *Faerie Queene*", *ELR* 34: 201–42.

——. 2005. "Resisting Translation: Britomart in Book 3 of Spenser's *Faerie Queene*", in *Translating Desire in Medieval and Early Modern Literature*, ed. Heather Hayton and Craig A. Berry, Tempe, Ariz: Medieval & Renaissance Texts & Studies Press, 207–50.

Berlin, N. 1966. "Chaucer's *The Book of the Duchess* and Spenser's *Daphnaïda*: A Contrast", *Studia Neophilologica* 36: 282–9.

Bernard, J. D. 1989. *Ceremonies of Innocence: Pastoralism in the Poetry of Edmund Spenser*, Cambridge: Cambridge University Press.

Berry, P. 1989. *Of Chastity and Power: Elizabethan Literature and the Unmarried Queen*, London: Routledge.

Berry, H. and E. K. Timings. 1960. "Spenser's Pension", *RES* n.s. 11: 254–9.

Bieman, E. 1983. " 'Sometimes I . . . mask in myrth lyke to a Comedy': Spenser's *Amoretti*", *SSt* 4: 131–42.

Bieman, E. 1988. *Plato Baptized: Towards the Interpretation of Spenser's Mimetic Fictions*, Toronto: University of Toronto Press.

Bjorvand, E. 1975. "Spenser's Defence of Poetry: Some Structural Aspects of the *Fowre Hymnes*," in Maren-Sofie Rostvig, ed., *Fair Forms: Essays in English Literature from Spenser to Jane Austen*, Totowa, NJ: Rowman and Littlefields.

Black, J. 2001. " 'Pan is Hee': Commending *The Faerie Queene*", *SSt* 15: 121–34.

Blissett, W. 1964. "Spenser's Mutabilitie", in Millar MacLure and F. W. Watt, ed., *Essays in English Literature from the Renaissance to the Victorian Age Presented to A. S. P. Woodhouse*, Toronto: University of Toronto Press; repr. in *Essential Articles for the Study of Edmund Spenser*, ed. A. C. Hamilton, Hamden, Conn.: Archon, 1972, 253–66.

Bloom, H. 1973. *The Anxiety of Influence: A Theory of Poetry*, New York: Oxford University Press.

Boderie, Guy Le Fèvre de la. 1582. *La Galliade*, ed. François Roudaut, Paris: Klincksieck, 1993.

Boehrer, B. T. 1988. " 'Careless Modestee': Chastity as Politics in Book 3 of *The Faerie Queene*", *ELH* 55: 555–73.

Bond, R. B. 1976. "*Invidia* and the Allegory of Spenser's *Muiopotmos*", *English Studies in Canada* 2: 144–55.

——. 1981. "Supplantation in the Elizabethan Court: The Theme of Spenser's February Eclogue", *SSt* 2: 55–66.

Bondanella, J. C. 1978. *Petrarch's Visions and Their Renaissance Analogues*, Madrid: José Porrúa Turanzas.

Bondanella, P. E. and J. C. Bondanella. 1971. "Two Kinds of Renaissance Love: Spenser's *Astrophel* and Ronsard's *Adonis*", *ES* 52: 311–18.

Borris, K. 1991. *Spenser's Poltics of Prophecy in* The Faerie Queen V, Victoria: University of Victoria.

Boswell, J. C. 2003. "Spenser Allusions: 1641–1700: Part I", *Spenser Review* 34: 24–40.

Bowman, M. R. 1990. " 'She There as Princess Rained': Spenser's Figure of Elizabeth", *Renaissance Quarterly* 43: 509–28.

——. 2003. "Distressing Irena: Gender, Conquest, and Justice in Book V of *The Faerie Queene*", *SSt* 17: 151–82.

Bradbrook, M. 1960. "No Room at the Top: Spenser's Pursuit of Fame", in *Elizabethan Poetry*, ed. John Russell Brown and Bernard Harris, London: Arnold, 91–109.

Braden, G. 1975. "Riverrun: An Epic Catalogue in *The Faerie Queene*", *ELR* 5: 25–48.

Bradshaw, B. 1979. *The Irish Constitutional Revolution of the Sixteenth Century*, Cambridge: Cambridge University Press.

——. 1987. "Edmund Spenser on Justice and Mercy", *Historical Studies* 16: 76–89.

——. 1988. "Robe and Sword in the Conquest of Ireland", in *Law and Government Under the Tudors: Essays Presented to Sir Geoffrey Elton on His Retirement*, ed. C. Cross, D. Loades, and J. J. Scarisbrick, Cambridge: Cambridge University Press, 139–62.

Brady, C. 1986. "Spenser's Irish Crisis: Humanism and Experience in the 1590s", *Past and Present* 111: 17–49.

——. 1989. "The Road to the *View*: On the Decline of Reform Thought in Tudor Ireland", in *Spenser and Ireland: An Interdisciplinary Perspective*, ed. Patricia Coughlan, Cork: Cork University Press, 25–45.

——. 1990a. "*A Brief Note of Ireland*", in *The Spenser Encyclopedia*, ed. A. C. Hamilton, 111–12.

——. 1990b. "Grey, Arthur, fourteenth Baron of Wilton (1536–93)", in *The Spenser Encyclopedia*, ed. A. C. Hamilton, 341–2.

Brink, J. R. 1991. "Who Fashioned Edmund Spenser?: The Textual History of *Complaints*", *SP* 88: 153–68.

——. 1994a. "Constructing the *View of the Present State of Ireland*", *SSt* 11 (for 1990): 203–30.

——. 1994b. "Dating Spenser's 'Letter to Ralegh' ", *The Library* 16: 219–24.

——. 1994c. "Documenting Edmund Spenser: A New Life Record", *American Notes & Queries* 7: 200–208.

——. 1996. " 'All His Minde on Honour Fixed': The Preferment of Edmund Spenser", in *Spenser's Life and the Subject of Biography*, ed. Judith H. Anderson, Donald Cheney, and David A. Richardson, Amherst: University of Massachusetts Press, 45–64.

——. 1997a. "Appropriating the Author of *The Faerie Queene*: The Attribution of the *View of the Present State of Ireland* and *A Brief Note of Ireland* to Edmund Spenser", in *Soundings of Things Done: Essays in Early Modern Literature in Honor of S. K. Heninger, Jr.*, ed. Peter E. Medine and Joseph Wittreich, Newark: University of Delaware Press, 93–136.

——. 1997b. "Edmund Spenser's Family: Two Notes and a Query", *N&Q* 44: 49–51.

——. 1999. "Spenser and the Irish Question: Reply to Andrew Hadfield", *SSt* 13: 265–6.

——. 2003. "Materialist History of the Publication of *The Faerie Queene*", *RES* n.s. 54: 1–26.

Brinkley, R. A. 1981. "Spenser's *Muiopotmos* and the Politics of Metamorphosis", *ELH* 48: 668–76.

Brown, R. D. 1999. *"The New Poet": Novelty and Tradition in Spenser's "Complaints"*, Liverpool: Liverpool University Press.

Bryan, R. A. 1972. "Poets, Poetry and Mercury in Spenser's *Prosopopoia: Mother Hubberd's Tale*", *Costerus* 5: 27–33.

Bryskett, L. 1606. *A Discourse of Civill Life: Containing the Ethike Part of Morall Philoso-phie, Fit for the Instructing of a Gentleman in the Course of a Virtuous Life*, London: William Aspley.

Buchanan, G. 1571. *Ane detectioun of the duinges of Marie Quene of Scottes.*

Burchmore, D. W. 1977. "The Image of the Centre in *Colin Clouts Come Home Againe*", *RES* n.s. 28: 393–406.

Burlinson, C. and Andrew Z. 2005. " 'Secretarie to the Lord Grey Lord Deputie Here': Edmund Spenser's Irish Papers", *The Library*, 7th Series, 6: 30–75.

Burrow, C. 1993. *Epic Romance: Homer to Milton*, Oxford: Oxford University Press.

——. 1996. *Edmund Spenser*, Plymouth: Northcote House.

——. 2001. "Spenser and Classical Traditions", in *The Cambridge Companion to Spenser*, ed. Andrew Hadfield, Cambridge: Cambridge University Press, 217–36.

Byrom, H. J. 1933. "Edmund Spenser's First Printer, Hugh Singleton", *The Library*, 4th Series 14: 121–56.

Cain, T. H. 1978. *Praise in* The Faerie Queene, Lincoln, Neb.: University of Nebraska Press.

Canino, C. G. 1998. "Reconstructing Lord Grey's Reputation: A New View of the *View*", *Sixteenth Century Journal* 29: 3–18.

Camino, M. M. 1998. " 'Methinks I See An Evil Lurk Unespied': Visualizing Conquest in Spenser's *A View of the Present State of Ireland*", *SSt* 12 (for 1991): 169–94.

Campbell, M. 1982. "Spenser's *Mutabilitie Cantos*", *Southern Review* 15: 44–59.

Canny, N. 1976. *The Elizabethan Conquest of Ireland: A Pattern Established, 1565–76*, Hassocks: Harvester Press.

——. 1983. "Edmund Spenser and the Development of an Anglo-Irish Identity", *YES* 13: 1–19.

——. 1996. "Reviewing *A View of the Present State of Ireland*", *The Irish University Review* 26: 252–67.

——. 1999. "Poetry as Politics: A View of the Present State of *The Faerie Queene*", in *Political Ideology in Ireland, 1541–1641*, ed. Hiram Morgan, Dublin: Four Courts Press, 1999, 110–26.

——. 2000. "The Social and Political Thought of Spenser in his Maturity", in *Edmund Spenser: Essays on Culture and Allegory*, ed. Jennifer Klein Morrison and Matthew Greenfield, Aldershot: Ashgate, 107–22.

——. 2001. "Spenser Sets the Agenda", in his *Making Ireland British, 1580–1650*, Oxford: Oxford University Press, 1–58.

Canny, N. and Andrew C. 1991. "The Early Planters: Spenser and His Contemporaries", in *The Field Day Anthology of Irish Writing*, 3 vols, ed. Seamus Deane, Derry: Field Day Publications, I: 171–234.

Carpenter, F. I. 1923. *A Reference Guide to Edmund Spenser*, Chicago: University of Chicago Press.

Carroll, C. 1990. "The Construction of Gender and the Cultural and Political Other in *The Faerie Queene* 5 and *A View of the Present State of Ireland*: The Critics, the Context, and the Case of Radigund", *Criticism* 32: 163–91.

——. 1996. "Spenser and the Irish Language: The Sons of Milesio in *A View of the Present State of Ireland, The Faerie Queene*, Book V, and the *Leabhbhar Gabhála*", *Irish University Review* 26: 281–90.

——. 2001. *Circe's Cup: Cultural Transformations in Early Modern Ireland*, Notre Dame, IN: University of Notre Dame Press.

Carruth, H. 1983. *Effluences from the Sacred Caves: More Selected Essays and Reviews*, Ann Arbor: University of Michigan Press.

Cartmell, D. 1986. "Beside the Shore of Silver Streaming Thamesis: Spenser's *Ruines of Time*", *SSt* 6 (for 1985): 77–82.

Casady, E. 1941. "The Neo-Platonic Ladder in Spenser's *Amoretti*", *PQ* 20: 284–95.

Cavanagh, S. T. 1986. " 'Such Was Irena's Countenance': Ireland in Spenser's Prose and Poetry", *TSLL* 28: 24–50.

——. 1994. *Wanton Eyes and Chaste Desires: Female Sexuality in* The Faerie Queene, Bloomington: Indiana University Press.

Chalmers, G. 1799. *A Supplemental Apology for the Believers in the Shakespeare-Papers*, London: Thomas Egerton.

Chamberlain, R. 2005. *Radical Spenser: Pastoral, Politics and the New Aestheticism*, Edinburgh: Edinburgh University Press.

Chambers, E. K. 1932. *The Oxford Book of Sixteenth-Century Verse*, Oxford: Clarendon Press.

Champagne, C. M. 1990. "Wounding the Body of Woman in Book III of *The Faerie Queene*", *LIT: Literature/Interpretation/Theory* 2: 95–115.

Chaudhuri, S. 1989. *Renaissance Pastoral and its English Developments*, Oxford: Clarendon Press.

Cheney, D. 1966. *Spenser's Image of Nature: Wild Man and Shepherd in* The Faerie Queene, New Haven: Yale University Press.

——. 1972. "Spenser's Hermaphrodite and the 1590 *Faerie Queene*", *PMLA* 87: 192–200.

——. 1984. "Spenser"s Fortieth Birthday and Related Fictions', *SSt* 4 (for 1983): 3–31.

——. 1997. "Afterword" in *Spenser's Life and the Subject of Biography*, ed. Judith H. Anderson, Donald Cheney, and David A. Richardson, Amherst: University of Massachusetts Press, 172–7.

Cheney, P. 1990. "The Old Poet Presents Himself: *Prothalamion* as a Defence of Spenser's Career", *SSt* 8 (for 1987): 211–38.

——. 1993. *Spenser's Famous Flight: A Renaissance Idea of a Literary Career*, Toronto: University of Toronto Press.

——. 1994. "Review of Richard Rambuss, *Spenser's Secret Career*", *SpN* 24: 5–9.

——. 1997. *Marlowe's Counterfeit Profession: Ovid, Spenser, Counter-Nationhood*, Toronto: University of Toronto Press.

——. 2001. "Spenser's Pastorals: *The Shepheardes Calendar* and *Colin Clouts Come Home Againe*", in *The Cambridge Companion to Spenser*, ed. Andrew Hadfield, Cambridge: Cambridge University Press, 79–105.

——. 2002a. "Introduction: 'Jog on, jog on': European Career Paths", in *European Literary Careers: The Author from Antiquity to the Renaissance*, ed. Patrick Cheney and Frederick A. de Armas, Toronto: University of Toronto Press, 286–301.

——. 2002b. " 'Novells of his devise': Chaucerian and Virgilian Career Paths in Spenser's *Februarie* Eclogue", in *European Literary Careers: The Author from Antiquity to the Renaissance*, ed. Patrick Cheney and Frederick A. de Armas, Toronto: University of Toronto Press, 231–66.

——. 2004a. "Dido to Daphne: Early Modern Death in Spenser's Shorter Poems", *SSt* 18: 145–63.

——. 2004b. *Shakespeare, National Poet-Playwright*, Cambridge: University of Cambridge Press.

Cheney, P. and Frederick A. de Armas, eds 2002. *European Literary Careers: The Author from Antiquity to the Renaissance*, Toronto: University of Toronto Press.

Cheney, P. and L. Silberman, eds 2000. *Worldmaking Spenser: Explorations in the Early Modern Age*, Lexington, KY: University Press of Kentucky.

Child, F. J., ed. 1855. *Works of Edmund Spenser*, 3 vols, Boston: Houghton, Mifflin.

Chinitz, D. 1991. "The Poem as Sacrament: Spenser's *Epithalamion* and the Golden Mean", *JMRS* 21: 251–68.

Christian, M., *et al*. 2001: "Spenser's Theology: The Sacraments in *The Faerie Queene*", Reformation 6: 103–177.

Church, R. W. 1879. *Spenser*, London: Macmillan 1901; repr. Detroit: Gale Research Group, 1968.

Church, R. W. 1879. *Spenser*, English Men of Letters, London: Macmillan.

Cirillo, A. R. 1968. "Spenser's *Epithalamion*: The Harmonious Universe of Love", *SEL* 8: 19–34.

Clarke, D. 2000. " 'In Sort as She it Sung': Spenser's *Doleful Lay* and the Construction of Female Authorship", *Criticism* 42: 451–68.

Cody, R. 1969. *The Landscape of the Mind: Pastoralism and Platonic Theory in Tasso's "Aminta" and Shakespeare's Early Comedies*, Oxford: Clarendon Press.

Cohee, G. E. 2000. " 'To Fashion a Noble Person': Spenser's Readers and the Politics of Gender", *SSt* 14: 83–105.

Coldiron, A. E. B. 2002. "How Spenser Excavates Du Bellay's *Antiquitez*: Or, the Role of the Poet, Lyric, Historiography, and the English sonnet", *JEGP* 101: 41–67.

Coleman, J. 1894. "Biographical Sketches of Persons Remarkable in Local History: Edmund Spenser", *Journal of the Cork Archaeological and Historical Society* 3: 29.

Collier, J. P., ed. 1862. *The Works of Edmund Spenser*, 5 vols, London: Bell and Daldy.

Collinson, P. 1967. *The Elizabethan Puritan Movement*, London: Jonathan Cape.

——. 1979. *Archbishop Grindal 1519–1583: The Struggle For a Reformed Church*, London: Jonathan Cape.

——. 1980. "A Comment: Concerning the Name Puritan", *Journal of Ecclesiastical History* 31: 483–88.

——. 1982. *The Religion of Protestants: The Church in English Society, 1559–1625*, Oxford: Clarendon Press.

——. 2003. *Elizabethans*, London: Hambledon.

Comito, T. 1972. "The Lady in a Landscape and the Poetics of Elizabethan Pastoral", *UTQ* 41: 200–218.

——. 1977. "A Dialectic of Images in Spenser's *Fowre Hymnes*", *SP* 74: 301–21.

Cooper, H. 1977. *Pastoral: Medieval into Renaissance*, Cambridge: D. S. Brewer.

Copeland, T. A. 1988. "Surrender of Power in *Epithalamion*" *Selected Papers from the West Virginia Shakespeare and Renaissance Association* 13: 58–65.

Cory, H. E. 1917. *Edmund Spenser: A Critical Study*, Berkeley: University of California Press.

Coughlan, P. 1996. "The Local Context of Mutabilitie's Plea", *Irish University Review* 26: 320–41.

——. ed. 1989. *Spenser and Ireland: An Interdisciplinary Perspective*, Cork: Cork University Press.

Court, F. E. 1970. "The Theme and Structure of Spenser's *Muiopotmos*", *SEL* 10: 1–15.

Craig, J. 2001. "Monstrous Regiment: Spenser's Ireland and Spenser's Queen", *TSLL* 43: 1–28.

Craik, K. A. 2001. "Spenser's *Complaints* and the New Poet", *HLQ* 64: 63–79.

Cullen, P. 1970. *Spenser, Marvell, and Renaissance Pastoral*, Cambridge, MA: Harvard University Press.

——. 1974. *Infernal Triad: The Flesh, the World, and the Devil in Spenser and Milton*, Princeton: Princeton University Press.

Cumming, W. P. 1931. "The Influence of Ovid on Spenser's Mutabilitie Cantos", *SP* 28: 241–56.

Cummings, L. 1964. "Spenser's *Amoretti* VIII: New Manuscript Versions", *SEL* 4: 125–35.

Cummings, R. M. 1970. "Spenser's *Amoretti* as an Allegory of Love", *TSLL* 12: 163–79.

——. ed. 1971. *Spenser: The Critical Heritage*, London: Routledge and Kegan Paul.

Cunningham, V. 2002. *Reading After Theory*, Oxford: Blackwell.

Dasenbrock, R. W. 1985. "The Petrarchan Context of Spenser's *Amoretti*", *PMLA* 100: 38–50.

de Grazia, M. 1991. *Shakespeare Verbatim: The Reproduction of Authenticity and the 1790 Apparatus*, Oxford: Clarendon Press.

de Man, Paul. 1979. *Allegories of Reading: Figural Language in Rousseau, Nietzsche, Rilke, and Proust*, New Haven: Yale University Press.

Dees, J. S. 1971. "The Narrator of *The Faerie Queene*: Patterns of Response", *TSLL* 12: 537–68.

——. 2001. "Colin Clout and the Shepherd of the Ocean", *SSt* 15: 185–96.

Deitch, J. 2001. "The Girl He Left Behind: Ovidian *imitatio* and the Body of Echo in Spenser's *Epithalamion*", in *Ovid and the Renaissance Body*, ed. Goran V. Stauivukovic, Toronto: University of Toronto Press, 224–38.

DeNeef, A. L. 1979. "*The Ruins of Time*: Spenser's Apology for Poetry", *SP* 76: 262–71.

——. 1982. *Spenser and the Motives of Metaphor*, Durham: Duke University Press.

Digby, Sir K. 1643. *Observations on the 22 Stanza in the 9th Canto of the 2d Book of Spenser's Faery Queene*, London: Daniel Frere.

Dixon, J. 1964. *The First Commentary on* The Faerie Queen, ed. Graham Hough, Stansted: Privately Published.

Dobson, M. 1992. *The Making of the National Poet: Shakespeare, Adaptation and Authorship, 1660–1769*, Oxford: Clarendon Press.

Dolven, J. 2004. "The Method of Spenser's Stanza", *SSt* 19: 17–25.

Donnelly, M. L. 2003. "The Life of Virgil and the Aspiration of the 'New Poet' ", *SSt* 17: 1–35.

Dowden, E. 1879. "Heroines of Spenser", *Cornhill* 39: 663–80.

Du Bellay, J. 1931. *Oeuvres Poétiques*, ed. Henri Chamard, Paris: Droz.

Dubrow, H. 1990. *A Happier Eden: The Politics of Marriage in the Stuart Epithalamium*, Ithaca: Cornell University Press.

——. 1995. *Echoes of Desire: English Petrarchism and Its Counterdiscourses*, Ithaca: Cornell University Press.

Duncan-Jones, K. 1991. *Sir Philip Sidney: Courtier Poet*, London: Hamish Hamilton.

Dundas, J. 1975. "*Muiopotmos*: A World of Art", *YES* 5: 30–8.

——. 1989. " 'The Heavens Ornament': Spenser's Tribute to Sidney", *EA* 42: 129–39.

Dunlop, A. 1969. "Calendar Symbolism in the *Amoretti*", *N&Q* n.s. 16: 24–6.

——. "The Unity of Spenser's *Amoretti*," in *Silent Poetry: Essays in Numerological Analysis*, ed. A. Fowler, London: Routledge and Kegan Paul.

——. 1980. "The Drama of *Amoretti*", *SSt* 1: 107–20.

Dunseath, T. K. 1968. *Spenser's Allegory of Justice in Book V of* The Faerie Queene, Princeton: Princeton University Press.

Durling, R. M. 1954. "The Bower of Bliss and Armida's Palace", *Comparative Literature* 6: 335–47; repr. in Hamilton 1972, 113–24.

——. 1965. *The Figure of the Poet in Renaissance Epic*, Cambridge, MA: Harvard University Press.

Eade, J. C. 1972. "The Pattern in the Astronomy in Spenser's *Epithalamion*", *RES* 23: 173–8.

Eagleton, T. 2003. *After Theory*, London: Allen Lane.

Edgeworth, M. 1995. *Castle Rackrent*, ed. George Watson, with an introduction by Kathryn J. Kirkpatrick, Oxford: Oxford University Press.

Edwards, D. 1999. "Ideology and Experience: Spenser's *View* and Martial Law in Ireland", in Hiram Morgan ed., *Political Ideology in Ireland, 1541–1641*, Dublin: Four Courts Press, 127–57.

Edwards, E., 1868. *The Life of Sir Walter Raleigh . . . together with His Letters*, London: Macmillan.

Edwards, R. R. 2002. "Medieval Literary Careers: The Theban Track", in *European Literary Careers: The Author from Antiquity to the Renaissance*, ed. Patrick Cheney and Frederick A. de Armas, Toronto: University of Toronto Press, 104–28.

Eggert, K. 1996. " 'Changing all that Forme of Common Weale': Genre and the Repeal of Queenship in *The Faerie Queene*, Book 5", *ELR* 26: 259–90.

——. 2000a. *Showing Like a Queene: Female Authority and Literary Experiment in Spenser, Shakespeare, and Milton*, Philadelphia: University of Pennsylvania Press.

——. 2000b. "Spenser's Ravishment: Rape and Rapture in *The Faerie Queene*," *Representations* 70: 1–26.

Elcock, W. D. 1951. "English Indifference to Du Bellay's *Regrets*", *MLR* 46: 175–84.

Ellrodt, R. 1960. *Neoplatonism in the Poetry of Spenser*, Geneva: E. Droz.

Emerson, O. F. 1918. "Spenser's *Virgil's Gnat*", *JEGP* 17: 94–118.

Empson, W. 1930. *Seven Types of Ambiguity*, repr. London: Chatto & Windus, 1947.

——. 1935. *Some Versions of the Pastoral*, repr. London: Chatto & Windus, 1950.

Erickson, W. 1989. "Spenser's Letter to Ralegh and the Literary Politics of *The Faerie Queene*'s 1590 Publication", *SSt* 10: 139–74.

——. 2001. "Spenser Reads Ralegh's Poetry in(to) the 1590 *Faerie Queene*", *SSt* 15: 175–84.

Eriksen, R. 1993. "Spenser's Mannerist Manoeuvres: *Prothalamion* (1596)", *SP* 90: 143–75.

Escobedo, A. 2004. *Nationalism and Historical Loss in Renaissance England: Foxe, Dee, Spenser, Milton*, Ithaca, New York: Cornell University Press.

Esolen, A. 1990. "The Disingenuous Poet Laureate: Spenser's Adoption of Chaucer", *SP* 97: 285–311.

Evans, F. B. 1965. "The Printing of *The Faerie Queene* in 1596", *Studies in Bibliography*, 18: 49–67.

Evans, M. 1970. *Spenser's Anatomy of Heroism: A Commentary on "The Faerie Queene"*, Cambridge: Cambridge University Press.

Evans, S. 1880. "A Lost Poem by Edmund Spenser", *Macmillan's Magazine* 42: 45–57; *Variorum* 6.433–4.

Falco, R. 1992. "Instant Artefacts: Vernacular Elegies for Philip Sidney", *SP* 89: 1–19.

——. 1993. "Spenser's *Astrophel* and the Formation of Elizabethan Literary Genealogy", *MP* 91: 1–25.

——. 1994. *Conceived Presences: Literary Genealogy in Renaissance England*, Amherst: University of Massachusetts Press.

Farness, J. 1996. "Disenchanted Elves: Biography in the Text of *Faerie Queene V*", in *Spenser's Life and the Subject of Biography*, ed. Judith H. Anderson, Donald Cheney, and David A. Richardson, Amherst: University of Massachusetts Press, 18–30.

Farrell, J. 2002. "Greek Lives and Roman Careers in the Classical *Vita* Tradition", in *European Literary Careers: The Author from Antiquity to the Renaissance*, ed. Patrick Cheney and Frederick de Armas, Toronto: University of Toronto Press, 24–46.

Feerick, J. 2002. "Spenser, Race, and Ire-land", *ELR* 32: 85–117.

Ferguson, M. W. 1982. " 'The Afflatus of Ruin': Meditations on Rome by Du Bellay, Spenser, and Stevens", in *Roman Images*, Selected Papers from the English Institute 8, ed. A. Patterson, Baltimore: Johns Hopkins Press, 23–50.

Fichter, A. 1981. " 'And nought of *Rome* in *Rome* perceiu'st at all': Spenser's *Ruines of Rome*", *SSt* 2: 183–92.

——. 1982. *Poets Historical: Dynastic Epic in the Renaissance*, New Haven: Yale University Press.

Fineman, J. 1986. *Shakespeare's Perjured Eye: The Invention of Poetic Subjectivity in the Sonnets*, Berkeley: University of California Press.

Fish, S. 1967. *Surprised by Sin: The Reader in "Paradise Lost"*, New York: St Martin's.

Fleming, J. 2001. "A View from the Bridge: Ireland and Violence in Spenser's *Amoretti*", *SSt* 15: 135–64.

Fletcher, A. 1971. *The Prophetic Moment: An Essay on Spenser*, Chicago: University of Chicago Press.

Fogarty, A. 1989. "The Colonization of Langauge: Narrative Strategy in *A View of the Present State of Ireland* and *The Faerie Queene*, Book VI", in Patricia Coughlan, ed., *Spenser and Ireland: An Interdisciplinary Perspective*, Cork: Cork University Press, 75–108.

——., ed. 1996. *Spenser in Ireland*: The Faerie Queene, *1596–1996*, Special issue of *The Irish University Review* 26.

Foucault, M. 1977. "What is an Author?", in *Language, Counter-Memory, Practice: Selected Essays and Interviews*, trans. Donald F. Bouchard and Sherry Simon, Oxford: Basil Blackwell, 113–38.

Fowler, A. 1964. *Spenser and the Numbers of Time*, London: Routledge and Kegan Paul.

——. 1970. *Triumphal Forms: Structural Patterns in Elizabethan Poetry*, Cambridge: Cambridge University Press.

——. 1973. "Neoplatonic Order in *The Faerie Queene*", in *A Theatre for Spenserians*, ed. Judith M. Kennedy and James A. Reither, Toronto: Toronto University Press.

——. 1975. *Conceitful Thought: The Interpretation of English Renaissance Poems*, Edinburgh: Edinburgh University Press.

——. 1989. "Spenser and War", in *War, Literature and the Arts in Sixteenth-Century Europe*, ed. J. R. Mulryne and M. Shewring, Basingstoke: Macmillan, 147–64.

Fowler, E. 1995. "The Failure of Moral Philosophy in the Work of Edmund Spenser", *Representations* 51: 47–76.

——. 2000. "The Rhetoric of Political Forms: Social Persons and the Criterion of Fit in Colonial Law, *Macbeth*, and *The Irish Masque at Court*", in *Form and Reform in Renaissance England: Essays in Honor of Barbara Kiefer Lewalski*, ed. Amy Boesky and Mary Thomas Crane, Newark: Delaware University Press, 70–103.

——. 2003. *Literary Character: The Human Figure in Early English Writing*, Ithaca: Cornell University Press.

Fox, A. 1995. "The Complaint of Poetry for the Death of Liberality: The Decline of Literary Patronage in the 1590s", in *The Reign of Elizabeth I: Court and Culture in the Last Decade*, ed. J. A. Guy, Cambridge: Cambridge University Press, 229–57.

Fox, S. C. 1972. "Eterne in Mutabilitie: Spenser's Darkening Vision," in *Eterne in Mutabilitie: The Unity of the Faerie Queene: Essays Published in Memory of David Philoon Harding, 1914–1970*, ed. Kenneth J. Atchity and Eugene M. Waith, Hamden, Conn.: Archon, 20–41.

Frank B. E. 1965. "The Printing of Spenser's *Faerie Queene* in 1596", *Studies in Bibliography* 18: 49–67.

Fréchet, R. 1980. "From 1979 to 1596 and Back: A Look at Edmund Spenser's *A View of the Present State of Ireland*", *Threshold* (Belfast) 31: 43–52.

Fredson, B. 1949. *Principles of Bibliographical Description*, Princeton: Princeton University Press.

Fried, D. 1981. "Spenser's Caesura", *ELR* 11: 261–80.

Friedrich, W. G. 1936. "The Stella of *Astrophel*", *ELH* 3: 114–39.

Frushell, R. C. 1999. *Edmund Spenser in the Early Eighteenth Century: Education, Imitation, and the Making of a Literary Model*, Pittsburgh, PA: Duquesne University Press.

Frushell, R. C. and B. J. Vondersmith, eds 1975. *Contemporary Thought on Edmund Spenser: A Bibliography of Criticism of* The Faerie Queene *1900–1970*, Carbondale: Southern Illinois University Press.

Frye, N. 1957. *Anatomy of Criticism: Four Essays*, Princeton: Princeton University Press.

——. 1961. "The Structure of Imagery in *The Faerie Queene*", *UTQ* 30: 109–27; repr. in *Essential Articles*, ed. A. C. Hamilton 1972, 153–70.

——. 1963. *Fables of Identity: Studies in Poetic Mythology*, New York: Harcourt, Brace, and World.

Frye, S. 1993. *Elizabeth I: The Competition for Representation*, New York: Oxford University Press.

Fukuda, S. 1987. "A Numerological Reading of Spenser's *Daphnaïda*", *Kumamoto Studies in Language and Literature* 29–30: 1–9.

——. 1991. "The Numerological Pattering of *Amoretti and Epithalamion*", *SSt* 9 (for 1988): 33–48.

Fumerton, P. 1986. "Exchanging Gifts: The Elizabethan Currency of Children and Poetry", *English Literary History* 53: 241–78.

——. 1991. *Cultural Aesthetics: Renaissance Literature and the Practice of Social Ornament*, Chicago: University of Chicago Press.

Gallagher, L. 1991. *Medusa's Gaze: Casuistry and Conscience in the Renaissance*, Stanford: Stanford University Press.

Gardiner, D. 1938. "The Debt of Fynes Moryson to Spenser's *View*", *PQ* 17: 297–307.

Gardiner, D. M. 2001. *"Befitting Emblems of Adversity": A Modern Irish View of Edmund Spenser from W. B. Yeats to the Present*, Omaha: Creighton University Press.

Gaskell, P. 1974. *A New Introduction to Bibliography*, Oxford: Oxford University Press.

Giamatti, A. B. 1966. *The Earthly Paradise and the Renaissance Epic*, Princeton: Princeton University Press.

Gibbs, D. 1990. *Spenser's "Amoretti": A Critical Study*, Brookfield: Scolar Press.

Gilman, E. 1986. *Iconoclasm and Poetry in the English Reformation: "Down Went Dagon"*, Chicago: University of Chicago Press.

Gleason, J. B. 1994. "Opening Spenser's Wedding Present: The Marriage Number of Plato in the *Epithalamion*", *ELR* 24: 620–37.

Gless, D. 1994. *Interpretation and Theology in Spenser*, Cambridge: Cambridge University Press.

Goldberg, J. 1975. "The Mothers in Book III of *The Faerie Queene*", *TSLL* 17: 5–26.

——. 1981. *Endlesse Worke: Spenser and the Structures of Discourse*, Baltimore: Johns Hopkins University Press.

——. 1983. *James I and the Politics of Literature*, Baltimore: Johns Hopkins University Press.

——. 1986. *Voice Terminal Echo: Postmodernism and English Renaissance Texts*, New York: Methuen.

——. 1989. "Colin to Hobbinol: Spenser's Familiar Letters", *South Atlantic Quarterly* 88: 107–26.

——. 1992. *Sodometries: Renaissance Texts, Modern Sexualities*, Stanford, CA: Stanford University Press.

Gorges, A. 1953. *The Poems of Sir Arthur Gorges*, ed. H. E. Sandison, Oxford: Clarendon Press.

Gottfried, R. B. 1937. "The Date of Spenser's *View*", *MLN* 52: 176–80.

——. 1938. "The Debt of Fynes Moryson to Spenser's *View*", *PQ* 17: 297–307.

Graves, R. N. 1989. "Two Newfound Poems by Edmund Spenser: The Buried Short-Line Runes in *Epithalamion* and *Prothalamion*", *SSt* 7: 199–238.

Greenblatt, S. J. 1973. *Sir Walter Ralegh: The Renaissance Man and His Roles*, New Have: Yale University Press.

——. 1980. *Renaissance Self-Fashioning from More to Shakespeare*, Chicago: University of Chicago Press.

Greene, R. 2001. "Spenser and Contemporary Vernacular Poetry", in *The Cambridge Companion to Spenser*, ed. Andrew Hadfield, Cambridge: Cambridge University Press, 237–51.

Greene, T. M. 1957. "Spenser and the Epithalamic Convention", *CL* 9: 215–28.

——. 1963. *The Descent from Heaven: A Study in Epic Continuity*, New Haven: Yale University Press.

——. 1982. *The Light in Troy: Imitation and Discovery in Renaissance Poetry*, New Haven: Yale University Press.

Greenlaw, E. 1911. *The Shepheardes Calender*, *PMLA* 26, 419–51.

——. 1930. "Spenser's Mutabilitie", *PMLA* 45: 684–703.

——. 1932. *Studies in Spenser's Historical Allegory*, Baltimore: Johns Hopkins University Press.

Greenlaw, E., C. G. Osgood, F. M. Padelford, and R. Heffner, eds 1932–49. *The Works of Edmund Spenser: A Variorum Edition*, 11 vols, Baltimore: Johns Hopkins Press.

Greg, W. W. 1950–51. "The Rationale of Copy-Text", *Studies in Bibliography* 3: 19–36.

Gregerson, L. 1991. "Protestant Erotics: Idolatry and Interpretation in Spenser's *Faerie Queene*", *ELH* 58: 1–34.

——. 1993. "Narcissus Interrupted: Specularity and the Subject in the Tudor State", *Criticism* 35: 1–40.

——. 1995. *The Reformation of the Subject: Spenser, Milton, and the English Protestant Epic*, Cambridge: Cambridge University Press.

——. 1999. "Colonials Write the Nation: Spenser, Milton, and England on the Margins", in *Milton and the Imperial Vision*, ed. Balachandra Rajan and Elizabeth Sauer, Pittsburgh, PA: Duquesne University Press, 169–90.

Gregory, T. 2000. "Shadowing Intervention: On the Politics of *The Faerie Queene* Book 5 Cantos 10–12", *ELH* 67: 365–97.

Grierson, H. J. C. 1922. "Spenser's Muiopotmos", *MLR* 17: 409–11.

Grosart, A. B. ed. 1882–84. *The Complete Works in Verse and Prose of Edmund Spenser*, 8 vols, London: Privately printed.

Gross, K. 1982. "Review of Jonathan Goldberg's *Endlesse Worke: Spenser and the Structures of Discourse*", *The Yale Review* 72: x–xvii.

——. 1983. " 'Each Heav'nly Close': Mythologies and Metrics in Spenser and the Early Poetry of Milton", *PMLA* 98: 21–36.

——. 1985. *Spenserian Poetics: Idolatry, Iconoclasm, and Magic*, Ithaca: Cornell University Press.

——. 2004. "Shapes of Time: On the Spenserian Stanza", *SSt* 19: 27–35.

Grossman, M. 1998. *The Story of All Things: Writing the Self in English Renaissance Narrative Poetry*, Durham: Duke University Press.

Grundy, J. 1969. *The Spenserian Poets: A study in Elizabethan and Jacobean Poetry*, London: Edward Arnold.

Guillory, J. 1983. *Poetic Authority: Spenser, Jonson, and Literary History*, New York: Columbia University Press.

Guy, J. 1995. *The Reign of Elizabeth I: Court and Culture in the Last Decade*, Cambridge: Cambridge University Press.

Haber, J. 1994. *Pastoral and the Poetics of Self-Contradiction: Theocritus to Marvell*, Cambridge: Cambridge University Press.

Hackett, H. 1995. *Virgin Mother, Maiden Queen: Elizabeth I and the Cult of the Virgin Mary*, Basingstoke: Macmillan.

Hadfield, A. 1993. "Briton and Scythian: Tudor Representations of Irish Origins", *Irish Historical Studies* 28: 390–408.

——. 1994a. " 'Who knowes not Colin Clout?': The Permanent Exile of Edmund Spenser", in *Literature, Politics and National Identity: Reformation to Renaissance*, Cambridge: Cambridge University Press, 170–201.

——. 1994b. "Was Spenser's *View of the Present State of Ireland* Censored? A Review of the Evidence", *N&Q* 240: 459–63.

——. 1994c. *Literature, Politics and National Identity: Reformation to Renaissance*, Cambridge: Cambridge University Press.

——. 1996a. "The 'sacred hunger of ambitious minds': Spenser's Savage Religion", in *Religion, Literature, and Politics in Post-Reformation England, 1540–1688*, ed. Donna Hamilton and Richard Strier, Cambridge: Cambridge University Press, 27–45.

——., ed. 1996b. *Edmund Spenser*, Longman Critical Readers, Harlow: Longman.

——. 1997. *Edmund Spenser's Irish Experience: Wilde Fruit and Salvage Soyle*, Oxford: Clarendon Press.

——. 1998a. "Certainties and Uncertainties: By Way of Response to Jean Brink", *SSt* 12 (for 2001): 197–202.

——. 1998b. "Was Spenser a Republican?", *English* 47: 169–82.

——. 1999. "Spenser's Description of the Execution of Murrogh O'Brien: An Anti-Catholic Polemic?", *N&Q* 46: 195–7.

——., ed. 1996. *Edmund Spenser*, Longman Critical Readers, London: Longman.

——., ed. 2001. *The Cambridge Companion to Spenser*, Cambridge: Cambridge University Press.

——. 2003a. "Robert Parsons/Richard Verstegan and the Calling in of *Mother Hubberds Tale*", *SSt* 17: 297–300.

——. 2003b. "Spenser and the Death of the Queen", in *Imagining Death in Spenser and Milton*, ed. Elizabeth Jane Bellamy, Patrick Cheney, and Michael Schoenfeldt, Basingstoke: Palgrave Macmillan, 28–45.

——. 2003c. *Shakespeare, Spenser and the Matter of Britain*, Basingstoke: Palgrave.

Hadfield, A. and W. Maley. 2000. "Afterword: A View of the Present State of Spenser Studies: Dialogue-Wise", in *Edmund Spenser: Essays on Culture and Allegory*, ed. Jennifer Klein Morrison and Matthew Greenfield, Aldershot: Ashgate Press, 183–95.

Hales, J. W. 1883. "Edmund Spenser", in *Complete Works of Edmund Spenser*, ed. R. Morris, London: Macmillan, xi–lv.

Hamilton, A. C. 1956. "The Argument of Spenser's *Shepheardes Calender*", *ELH* 23: 171–82.

——. 1961. *The Structure of Allegory in* The Faerie Queene, Oxford: Oxford University Press.

——., ed. 1972. *Essential Articles for the Study of Edmund Spenser*, Hamden, Conn.: Archon.

——., ed. 1977. Edmund Spenser, *The Faerie Queene*, Harlow: Longman.

——., ed. 1990. *The Spenser Encyclopedia*, Toronto: University of Toronto Press.

——., ed. 2001. Edmund Spenser *The Fearie Queene*, 2nd edn, Harlow: Longman.

Hankins, J. E. 1945. "Spenser and the Revelation of St. John", *PMLA* 60: 364–81; repr. in Hamilton 1972, 40–57.

——. 1971. *Source and Meaning in Spenser's Allegory: A Study of* The Faerie Queene, Oxford: Oxford University Press.

Hannay, M. 1999. "The Countess of Pembroke as a Spenserian Poet," in *Pilgrimage for Love: Essays in Early Modern Literature in Honor of Josephine A. Roberts*, ed. Sigrid M. King, Tempe, AZ: RETS/MRTS, 41–62.

Hardison, O. B., Jr. 1962. *The Enduring Monument: A Study of the Idea of Praise in Renaissance Literary Theory and Practice*, Chapel Hill: University of North Carolina Press.

Hardison, O. B. 1972. "*Amoretti* and the *Dolce Stil Novo*", *ELR* 2: 208–16.

Harris, B. 1941. "The Ape in *Mother Hubberd's Tale*", *HLQ* 4: 191–203.

——. 1944. "The Butterfly in Spenser's *Muiopotmos*", *JEGP* 43: 302–16.

Harris, D. and N. L. Steffen. 1978. "The Other Side of the Garden: An Interpretative Comparison of Chaucer's *Book of the Duchess* and Spenser's *Daphnaïda*", *JMRS* 8: 17–36.

Harrison, T. P., Jr. 1950. "Turner and Spenser's *Mother Hubberd's Tale*", *JEGP* 49: 464–9.

Harvey, E. D. 1992. *Ventriloquized Voices: Feminist Theory and English Renaissance Texts*, New York: Routledge.

Heffner, R. 1942. "Spenser's *View of Ireland*: Some Observations", *MLQ* 3, 507–15.

Helfer, R. 2003. "The Death of the 'New Poete': Virgilian Ruin and Ciceronian Recollection in Spenser's *The Shepheaerdes Calender*", *Renaissance Quarterly* 56: 723–56.

Helgerson, R. 1976. *The Elizabethan Prodigals*, Berkeley: University of California Press.

——. 1978. "The New Poet Presents Himself: Spenser and the Idea of a Literary Career", *PMLA* 93: 893–911.

——. 1983. *Self-Crowned Laureates: Spenser, Jonson, Milton, and the Literary System*, Berkeley: California University Press.

——. 1992. *Forms of Nationhood: The Elizabethan Writing of England*, Chicago: University of Chicago Press.

——. 2003. "Review of Richard McCabe's *Spenser's Monstrous Regiment: Elizabethan Ireland and the Poetics of Difference*", *Spenser Review* 34: 2–5.

Heninger, S. K., Jr. 1961. "The Renaissance Perversion of Pastoral", *Journal of the History of Ideas*, 22: 254–61.

——. 1962. "The Implications of Form for *The Shepheardes Calender*", *SR* 9: 309–21.

——. 1988. "The Typographical Layout of Spenser's *Shepheardes Calender*", in *Word and Visual Imagination: Studies in the Interaction of English Literature and the Visual Arts*, ed. Karl Josef Höltgen, Peter M. Daly, and Wolfgang Lottes, Erlangen: Universität Bibliothek Erlangen-Nürnberg, 33–71.

Henley, P. 1928. *Spenser in Ireland*, Cork: Cork University Press.

Herbert, M. 1977. "*The Triumph of Death" and other Unpublished and Uncollected Poems by Mary Sidney, Countess of Pembroke*, ed. Gary F. Waller, Salzburg: Institut für Englische Sprache und Literatur, Universität Salzburg.

Hester, M. T. 1993. " 'If thou regard the same': Spenser's Emblematic Centerfold", *American Notes and Queries*, n.s. 6: 183–9.

Hieatt, A. K. 1960. *Short Time's Endless Monument*, New York: Columbia University Press.

——. 1961. "The Daughters of Horus: Order in the Stanzas of *Epithalamion*" in *Form and Convention in the Poetry of Edmund Spenser*, ed W. Nelson, New York: Columbia University Press, 103–21.

——. 1962. "Scudamour's Practice of *Maistry* upon Amoret", *PMLA* 77: 509–10.

——. "A Numerical Key for Spenser's *Amoretti* and Guyon in the House of Mammon", *YES* 3: 14–27.

——. *Chaucer, Spenser, Milton: Mythopoeic Continuities and Transformations*, Montreal: McGill-Queen's University Press.

——. 1983. "The Genesis of Shakespeare's *Sonnets*: Spenser's *Ruines of Rome: By Bellay*", *PMLA* 98: 800–814.

——. 1987. "The Projected Continuation of *The Faerie Queene: Rome Delivered?*", *SSt* 8 (for 1987): 335–42.

——. 1990. "The Projected Continuation of *The Faerie Queene: Rome Delivered?*", *SSt* 8 (for 1987): 335–42.

Highley, C. 1997. *Shakespeare, Spenser, and the Crisis in Ireland*, Cambridge: Cambridge University Press.

Hill, E. M. 1966. "Flattery in Spenser's *Fowre Hymnes*", *West Virginia University Philological Papers* 15: 22–35.

Hill, W. S. 1972. "Order and Joy in Spenser's *Epithalamion*", *Southern Humanities Review* 6: 81–90.

Hinton, S. 1974. "The Poet and His Narrator: Spenser's Epic Voice", *ELH* 41: 165–81.

Hoffman, N. Jo. 1977. *Spenser's Pastorals: "The Shepheardes Calender" and "Colin Clout"*, Baltimore: Johns Hopkins University Press.

Holahan, M. 1976. "*Iamque opus exegi*: Ovid's Changes and Spenser's Brief Epic of Mutability", *ELR* 6: 244–70.

Holland, J. F. 1968. "The Cantos of Mutabilitie and the Form of *The Faerie Queene*", *ELH* 35: 21–31.

Hollander, J. 1987. "Spenser's Undersong", in *Cannibals, Witches and Divorce: Estranging the Renaissance*, ed. M. Garber, Baltimore: Johns Hopkins University Press, 1–20.

——. 1988. *Melodious Guile: Fictive Pattern in Poetic Language*, New Haven: Yale University Press.

Hoppe, H. R. 1933. "John Wolfe, Printer and Publisher, 1579–1601", *The Library*, 4th Series 14: 241–89.

Hough, G. 1962. *A Preface to* The Faerie Queene, London: Duckworth.

——. 1964a. "First Commentary on *The Faerie Queene*: Annotations to Lord Bessborough's Copy of the First Edition of *The Faerie Queene*", *TLS* Thursday April 9, 1964, 294.

——. 1964b. *The First Commentary on* The Faerie Queene, Privately Published.

Huffman, C. C. 1988. *Elizabethan Impressions: John Wolfe and His Press*, New York: AMS Press.

Hughes, J., ed. 1715. *The Works of Mr. Edmund Spenser*, 6 vols, London: Jacob Tonson.

Hulse, C. 1981. *Metaphoric Verse: The Elizabethan Minor Epic*, Princeton: Princeton University Press.

Hume, A. 1984. *Edmund Spenser: Protestant Poet*, Cambridge: Cambridge University Press.

Hunt, L. 1833. *Literary Criticism*, ed. Lawrence Huston Houtchens and Carolyn Washburn Houtchens, New York: Columbia University Press, 1956.

Hutton, J. 1941. "Cupid and the Bee", *PMLA* 56: 1036–57.

Hyde, T. 1986. *The Poetic Theology of Love: Cupid in Renaissance Literature*, Newark: University of Delaware Press; London: Associated University Presses.

Hyman, L. W. 1958. "Structure and Meaning in Spenser's *Epithalamion*", *Tennessee Studies in Literature* 3: 37–41.

Irigaray, L. 1985. *This Sex Which Is Not One*, trans. Catherine Porter, Ithaca: Cornell University Press.

Ivic, C. 1999. "Spenser and the Bounds of Race", *Genre* 32: 141–74.

Jauss, H. R. 1982. *Toward an Aesthetic of Reception*, trans. Timothy Bahti, Minneapolis: University of Minnesota Press.

Jayne, S. 1952. "Ficino in the Platonism of the English Renaissance", *CL* 4: 214–38.

Jenkins, R. 1933. "Spenser at Smerwick", *TLS* 32 S(May 11): 331.

——. 1937. "Spenser with Lord Grey in Ireland", *PMLA* 52: 338–53.

Johnson, F. R. 1933. *A Critical Bibliography of the Works of Edmund Spenser Printed before 1700*, Baltimore: Johns Hopkins University Press.

Johnson, W. C. 1974. "Spenser's *Amoretti* and the Art of the Liturgy", *SEL* 14: 47–61.

——. 1976. " 'Sacred Rites' and Prayer-Book Echoes in Spenser's *Epithalamion*", *Renaissance and Reformation* 12: 49–54.

——. 1990. *Spenser's "Amoretti": Analogies of Love*, Lewisburg: Bucknell University Press.

——. 1992. " 'Spenser's 'Greener' Hymnes and Amoretti: 'Retraction' and Reform' ", *ES* 73: 431–43.

——. 1993. "Gender Fashioning and the Dynamics of Mutuality in Spenser's Mutuality in Spenser's *Amoretti*", *ES* 74: 503–19.

Jones, E., ed. 1991. *The New Oxford Book of Sixteenth-Century Verse*, Oxford: Oxford University Press.

Jones, H. S. V. 1919. "Spenser's Defense of Lord Grey", *University of Illinois Studies in Language and Literature* 5: 7–75.

——. 1930. *A Spenser Handbook*, New York: Columbia University Press.

Jones, H. S. V. 1947. *A Spenser Handbook*, New York: F. S Rofts.

Jones, A. R., and P. Stallybrass. 1992. "Dismantling Irena: The Sexualising of Ireland in Early Modern England", in *Nationalisms and Sexualities* ed. Andrew Parker, Mary Russo, Doris Sommer and Patricia Yaeger, London: Routledge, 157–71.

Johnson, S. 1958–68. *The Rambler*, 3 vols in *The Yale Edition of the Works of Samuel Johnson*, ed. Allen T. Hazen, 8 vols, New Haven: Yale University Press.

Jortin, J. 1734. *Remarks on Spenser's Poems*, London: J. Whiston.

Judson, A. C. 1933. *Spenser in Southern Ireland*, Bloomington: Indiana University Press.

——. 1945. *The Life of Edmund Spenser*, Baltimore: Johns Hopkins Press.

——. 1946. "The Eighteenth-Century Lives of Edmund Spenser", *HLQ* 10: 35–48.

——. 1948. "Mother Hubberd's Ape", *MLN* 63: 145–9.

——. 1953. "The Seventeenth-Century Lives of Edmund Spenser", *HLQ* 16: 161–81.

Kaplan, M. L. 1997. *The Culture of Slander in Early Modern England*, Cambridge: Cambridge University Press.

Kaske, C. V. 1977. "Another Liturgical Dimension of *Amoretti* 68", *N&Q* n.s. 24: 518–19.

——. 1978. "Spenser's *Amoretti and Epithalamion* of 1595: Structure, Genre and Numerology", *ELR* 8: 271–95.

——. 1989. "How Spenser Really Used Stephen Hawes in the Legend of Holiness", in *Unfolded Tales: Essays on Renaissance Romance*, ed. George Logan and Gordon Teskey, Ithaca: Cornell University Press, 119–36.

——. 1990. "Rethinking Loewenstein's 'Viper Thoughts' ", *SSt* 8 (for 1987): 325–9.

——. 1999. *Spenser and Biblical Poetics*, Ithaca: Cornell University Press.

Kastan, D. S. 1999. *Shakespeare After Theory*, London: Routledge.

Kastner, L. E. 1908–09. "Spenser's *Amoretti* and Desportes", *MLR* 4: 65–9.

Kay, D. 1990. *Melodious Tears: The English Funeral Elegy from Spenser to Milton*, Oxford: Clarendon Press.

Kennedy, W. J. 2000. "Spenser's Squire Literary History", in *Worldmaking Spenser: Explorations in the Early Modern Age*, ed. Patrick Cheney and Lauren Silberman, Lexington: University Press of Kentucky, 45–62.

——. 2002. "Versions of a Career: Petrarch and His Renaissance Commentators", in *European Literary Careers: The Author from Antiquity to the Renaissance*, ed. Patrick Cheney and Frederick A. de Armas, Toronto: University of Toronto Press, 146–64.

Ker, W. P. 1897. *Epic and Romance: Essays on Medieval Literature*, London: Macmillan.

Kermode, F. 1962. "Spenser and the Allegorists", *Proceedings of the British Academy* 48: 261–79; repr. in Kermode, *Shakespeare, Spenser, Donne: Renaissance Essays*, London: Routledge, 1971, 12–32.

——. 1964. "*The Faerie Queene*, I and V", *Bulletin of the John Rylands Library* 47: 123–50; repr. in *Essential Articles* ed. A. C. Hamilton 1972.

Kerrigan, J., ed. 1991. *Motives of Woe: Shakespeare and "Female Complaint"*, Oxford: Clarendon Press.

King, A. 2000. *The Faerie Queene and Middle English Romance: The Matter of Just Memory*, Oxford: Oxford University Press.

King, J. N. 1982. *English Reformation Literature: The Tudor Origins of the Protestant Tradition*, Princeton: Princeton University Press.

——. 1986. "Was Spenser a Puritan?", *Spenser Studies* 6 (for 1985): 1–31.

——. 1986. "Spenser's *Shepheardes Calender* and Protestant Pastoral Satire", in *Renaissance Genres: Essays on Theory, History, and Interpretation*, ed. Barbara Kiefer Lewalski, Cambridge, MA: Harvard University Press, 369–98.

——. 1989. *Tudor Royal Iconography: Literature and Art in an Age of Religious Crisis*, Princeton: Princeton University Press.

——. 1990a. *Spenser's Poetry and the Reformation Tradition*, Princeton, NJ: Princeton University Press.

——. 1990b. "Queen Elizabeth: Representations of the Virgin Queen", *Renaissance Quarterly* 43: 30–74.

——. 2000a *Milton and Religions Controversy: Satire and Polemic in Paradise Lost*, Cambridge: Cambridge University Press.

Kinney, C. R. 1992. *Strategies of Poetic Narrative: Chaucer, Spenser, Milton, Eliot*, Cambridge: Cambridge University Press.

——. 2002 " 'What s/he ought to have been': Romancing Truth in *Spencer Redivivus*", *SSt* 16: 125–37.

Kinsman, R. S. 1950. "Skelton's Colyn Cloute: The Mask of Vox Poluli", in *Essays Critical and Historical Dedicated to Lily B. Campbell*, Berkeley: University of California Press, 17–26.

Klein, L. M. 1992. " 'Let Us Love, Dear Love, Lyke as We Ought': Protestant Marriage and the Revision of Petrarchan Loving in Spenser's *Amoretti*", *SSt* 10 (for 1989): 109–38.

Knapp, J. A. 2000. " 'That Moste Barbarous Nacion': John Derricke's *Image of Ireland* and 'The Delight of the Well Disposed Reader' ", *Criticism* 42: 415–50.

Knox, J. 1994. *On Rebellion*, ed. Roger A. Mason, Cambridge: Cambridge University Press.

Koller, K. 1934. "Spenser and Raleigh", *ELH* 1: 37–60.

——. 1935. "Identifications in *Colin Clouts Come Home Againe*", *MLN* 50: 155–8.

Kostic, V. 1959. "Spenser's *Amoretti* and Tasso's Lyrical Poetry", *Renaissance and Modern Studies* 3: 51–77.

——. 1969. *Spenser's Sources in Italian Poetry: A Study in Comparative Literature*, Beograd: Filososki Fakultet Beogradskog Univerziteta Monografije 30.

Krier, T. M. 1990. *Gazing on Secret Sights: Spenser, Classical Imitation, and the Decorums of Vision*, Ithaca: Cornell University Press.

——., ed. 1998. *Refiguring Chaucer in the Renaissance*, Gainesville: University of Florida Press.

——. 2001. *Birth Passages: Maternity and Nostalgia, Antiquity to Shakespeare*, Ithaca: Cornell University Press.

——. 2003. "Mother's Sorrow, Mother's Joy: Mourning Birth in Edmund Spenser's Garden of Adonis", in *Grief and Gender 700–1700*, ed. Jennifer C. Vaught with Lynne Dickson Bruckner, New York: Palgrave, 133–4.

Kucich, G. 1991. *Keats, Shelley, and Romantic Spenserianism*, University Park, PA: Pennsylvania State University Press.

Kuin, R. 1990. "The Gaps and the Whites: Indeterminacy and Undecideability in the Sonnet Sequences of Sidney, Spenser, and Shakespeare", *SSt* 8 (for 1987): 251–85.

Lake, P. 1982. *Moderate Puritans and the Elizabethan Church*, Cambridge, Cambridge University Press.

Lamb, M. E. 2000. "Gloriana, Acrasia, and the House of Busirane: Gendered Fictions in *The Faerie Queene* as Fairy Tale", in *Worldmaking Spenser: Explorations in the Early Modern Age*, ed. Patrick Cheney and Lauren Silberman, Lexington, KY: University of Kentucky Press, 81–100.

——. 2003. "The Red Crosse Knight, St. George, and the Appropriation of Popular Culture", *SSt* 18: 185–208.

Laqueur, T. 1990. *Making Sex: Body and Gender from the Greeks to Freud* Cambridge, MA: Harvard University Press.

Larsen, K. J. 1997. *Edmund Spenser's Amoretti and Epithalamion: A Critical Edition*, Tempe: Medieval & Renaissance Texts & Studies.

Lee, J., ed. 1998. *Edmund Spenser, Shorter Poems: A Selection*, London: Everyman.

Lerner, L. 1972. *The Uses of Nostalgia: Studies in Pastoral Poetry*, London: Chatto & Windus.

Lewis, C. S. 1936. *The Allegory of Love: A Study in Medieval Tradition*, Oxford: Oxford University Press.

——. 1954. *English Literature in the Sixteenth Century Excluding Drama*, The Oxford History of English Literature 3, Oxford: Clarendon Press.

——. 1966. *Studies in Medieval and Renaissance Literature*, ed. W. Hooper, Cambridge: Cambridge University Press.

——. 1967. *Spenser's Images of Life*, ed. Alastair Fowler, Cambridge: Cambridge University Press.

Lipking, L. 1981. *The Life of the Poet: Beginning and Ending Poetic Careers*, Chicago: University of Chicago Press.

Loades, D. 1991. *The Reign of Mary Tudor*, 2nd edn, London: Longman.

Lockey, B. 2001. "Spenser's Legalization of the Irish Conquest in *A View* and *Faerie Queene VI*", *ELR* 31: 365–91.

Loewenstein, J. F. 1986. "Echo's Ring: Orpheus and Spenser's Career", *ELR* 16: 287–302.

——. 1988. "For a History of Literary Property: John Wolfe's Reformation", *ELR* 18: 389–412.

——. 1990. "A Note on the Structure of Spenser's *Amoretti*: Viper Thoughts", *SSt* 8 (for 1987): 311–23.

——. 1996. "Spenser's Retrography: Two Episodes in Post-Petrarchan Bibliography", in *Spenser's Life and the Subject of Biography*, ed. Judith H. Anderson, Donald Cheney, and David A. Richardson, Amherst, MA: University of Massachusetts Press, 99–130.

——. 1998. "Authentic Reproductions: The Material Origins of the New Bibliography", in *Textual Formations and Reformations*, ed. Laurie E. Maguire, Newark: Delaware University Press.

——. 2002. *The Author's Due: Printing and the Prehistory of Copyright*, Chicago: University of Chicago Press.

Lotspeich, H. G. 1935. "Spenser's *Virgil's Gnat* and its Latin Original", *ELH* 2: 235–41.

Lowell, J. R. 1875. "Spenser" in *Literary Essays*, 10 vols, London: Macmillan, 1890, 4.

Luborsky, R. S. 1980. "The Allusive Presentation of *The Shepheardes Calender*", *SSt* 1: 29–67.

——. 1981. "The Illustrations to *The Shepheardes Calender*", *SSt* 2: 3–53.

——. 1991. "The Illustrations to *The Shepheardes Calender*: II", *SSt* 9 (for 1988): 249–53.

Lupton, J. R. 1993. "Mapping Mutability: Or, Spenser's Irish Plot", in *Representing Ireland: Literature and the Origins of Conflict, 1534–1660*, ed. Brendan Bradshaw, Andrew Hadfield, and Willy Maley, Cambridge: Cambridge University Press, 1993, 93–115; repr. in *Edmund Spenser*, Longman Critical Readers, ed. Andrew Hadfield, London: Longman, 1996, 211–31.

Lyne, R. 2001. *Ovid's Changing Worlds: English Metamorphoses 1567–1632*, Oxford: Oxford University Press.

Lyons, J. M. 1916. "Spenser's Muiopotmos as an Allegory", *PMLA* 31: 90–113.

MacArthur, J. H. 1989. *Critical Contexts of Sidney's "Astrophil and Stella" and Spenser's "Amoretti"*, Victoria, BC: English Literary Studies, University of Victoria.

MacBeth, G. 1992. *The Testament of Spencer*, London: Andre Deutsch.

McCabe, R. A. 1987. "The Masks of Duessa: Spenser, Mary Queen of Scots, and James VI", *ELR* 17: 224–42.

——. 1989. *The Pillars of Eternity: Time and Providence in "The Faerie Queene"*, Dublin: Irish Academic Press.

——. 1993. "Edmund Spenser: Poet of Exile", 1991 Lectures and Memoirs, *Proceedings of the British Academy* 80: 73–103.

——. 1995. " 'Little booke: thy Selfe Present': The Politics of Presentation in *The Shepheardes Calender*", in *Presenting Poetry: Composition, Publication, Reception, Essays in Honour of Ian Jack*, ed. Howard Erskine-Hill and Richard A. McCabe, Cambridge: Cambridge University Press, 15–40.

——., ed., 1999. *Edmund Spenser: Shorter Poems*, London: Penguin.

——. 2000. "Annotating Anonymity, or putting a gloss on *The Shepheardes Calender*", in *Ma(r)king the Text: The Presentation of Meaning on the Literary Page*, ed. Joe Bray, Miriam Handley, and Anne C. Henry, Aldershot: Ashgate, 35–54.

——. 2002. *Spenser's Monstrous Regiment: Elizabethan Ireland and the Poetics of Difference*, Oxford: Oxford University Press.

MacCaffrey, I. G. 1969. "Allegory and Pastoral in *The Shepheardes Calender*", *ELH* 36: 88–109.

——. 1976. *Spenser's Allegory: The Anatomy of Imagination*, Princeton: Princeton University Press.

MacColl, A. 1989. "The Temple of Venus, the Wedding of the Thames and the Medway, and the End of *The Faerie Queene*, Book IV", *RES* n.s. 40: 26–47.

McEachern, C. 1996. *The Poetics of English Nationhood, 1590–1612*, Cambridge: Cambridge University Press.

McEvoy, J. 1998. "Prophetic Authority and Error: A Biblical *View of the Present State of Ireland*", in *Renaissance Papers*, ed. T. H. Howard-Hill and Philip Rollinson, Columbia, S. C.: Camden House, 1–18.

Macfie, P. R. 1990. "Text and *Textura*: Spenser's Arachnean Art", in *Traditions and Innovations: Essays on British Literature of the Middle Ages and the Renaissance*, ed. D. G. Allen and R. A. White, Newark: University of Delaware Press, 88–96.

Maclean, H. 1978. " 'Restlesse anguish and unquiet paine': Spenser and the Complaint, 1579–1590", in *The Practical Vision: Essays in English Literature in Honour of Flora Roy*, ed. J. Campbell and J. Doyle, Waterloo, Ontario: Wilfrid Laurier University Press, 29–47.

McGann, J. J. 1983. *A Critique of Modern Textual Criticism*, Chicago: University of Chicago Press.

McGuinness, F. 1997. *Mutabilitie*, London: Faber.

McKenzie, D. F. 1969. "Printers of the Mind: Some Notes on Bibliographical Theories and Printing-House Practices", *Studies in Bibliography* 22: 1–75.

——. 1986. *Bibliography and the Sociology of Texts*, London: British Library.

McKerrow, R. B. 1927. *An Introduction to Bibliography for Literary Students*, Oxford: Clarendon Press.

McLane, P. E. 1961. *Spenser's "Shepheardes Calender": A Study in Elizabethan Allegory*, Notre Dame, Ind.: Notre Dame University Press.

McLaren, A. N. 1999. *Political Culture in the Reign of Elizabeth I: Queen and Commonwealth, 1558–1585*, Cambridge: Cambridge University Press.

MacLure, M. 1973. "Spenser and the Ruins of Time", in *A Theatre for Spenserians*, ed. J. M. Kennedy and J. A. Reither, Toronto: University of Toronto Press, 3–18.

McManus, C. 1997. "The 'Careful Nourse': Female Piety in Spenser's Legend of Holiness", *HLQ* 60: 381–406.

——. 2002. *Spenser's "Faerie Queene" and the Reading of Women*, Newark: University of Delaware Press.

McNeir, W. F. and F. Provost. 1962. *Annotated Bibliography of Edmund Spenser, 1937–1960*, Pittsburgh: Duquesne University Press.

McPeek, J. A. S. 1936. "The Major Sources of Spenser's *Epithalamion*", *JEGP* 35: 183–213.

Maley, W. 1991. "Spenser and Ireland: A Select Bibliography", *SSt* 9 (for 1988): 227–42.

——. 1993. "How Milton and Some Contemporaries Read Spenser's View", in *Representing Ireland: Literature and the Origins of Conflict, 1534–1660*, ed. Brendan Bradshaw, Andrew Hadfield, and Willy Maley, Cambridge: Cambridge University Press, 191–208.

——. 1994. *A Spenser Chronology*, Basingstoke: Macmillan.

——. 1996. "Spenser and Ireland: An Annotated Bibliography, 1986–96", *The Irish University Review* 26: 342–53.

——. 1997. *Salvaging Spenser: Colonialism, Culture, and Identity*, Houndmills, Basingstoke: Macmillan.

Mallette, R. 1979. "Spenser's Portrait of the Artist in *The Shepheardes Calender* and *Colin Clouts Come Home Again*", *SEL* 19: 19–41.

——. 1981. *Spenser, Milton, and Renaissance Pastoral*, Lewisburg: Bucknell University Press.

——. 1997. *Spenser and the Discourses of Reformation England*, Lincoln: University of Nebraska Press.

Manley, L. 1982. "Spenser and the City: The Minor Poems", *MLQ* 43: 203–28.

Marcus, L. 1996. *Unediting the Renaissance: Shakespeare, Marlowe, Milton*, London: Routledge.

Marinelli, P. 1971. *Pastoral*, London: Methuen.

Marjarum, E. W. 1940. "Wordsworth's View of the State of Ireland", *PMLA* 55: 608–11.

Mark V. 2002. "From Cursus to Ductus: Figures of Writing in Western Late Antiquity (Augustine, Jerome, Cassiodorus, Bede)", in *European Literary Careers: The Author from Antiquity to the Renaissance*, ed. Patrick Cheney and Frederick de Armas, Toronto: University of Toronto Press, 47–103.

Marotti, A. F. 1982. "'Love is Not Love': Elizabethan Sonnet Sequences and the Social Order", *ELH* 49: 396–428.

Martin, E. E. 1987. "Spenser, Chaucer, and the Rhetoric of Elegy", *JMRS* 17: 83–109.

Martin, W. C. 1932. "The Date and Purpose of Spenser's *Veue*", *PMLA* 47: 137–43.

Martz, L. L. 1961. "The *Amoretti*: 'Most Goodly Temperature'", in *Form and Convention in the Poetry of Edmund Spenser*, ed. W. Nelson, New York: Columbia University Press, 146–68.

Marx, K. and F. Engels. 1971. *Ireland and the Irish Question*, Moscow: Progress Publishers.

Maskell, W., ed. 1846. *Monumenta Ritualia Ecclesiae Anglicanae: Or Occasional Offices of the Church of England According to the Ancient Use of Salisbury, The Prymer in English and Other Prayers and Forms with Dissertations and Notes*, 2 vols, London: William Pickering.

Mason, R. A. 1982. "*Rex Stoicus*: George Buchanan, James VI and the Scottish Polity", in *New Perspectives on the Politics and Culture of Early Modern Scotland*, ed. John Dwyer, Roger A. Mason, and Alexander Murdoch, Edinburgh: John Donald, 9–33.

Maxwell, J. C. 1952. "The Truancy of Calidore", in *That Soueraine Light: Essays in Honor of Edmund Spenser, 1552–1952*, ed. W. R. Mueller and D. C. Allen, Baltimore: Johns Hopkins University Press, 63–9.

Mazzola, E. 1992. "Marrying Medusa: Spenser's *Epithalamion* and Renaissance Reconstructions of Female Privacy", *Genre* 25: 193–210.

——. 2000a. "Spenser, Sidney, and Second Thoughts: Mythology and Misgiving in *Muiopotmos*", *Sidney Journal* 18: 57–81.

——. 2000b. " 'O Unifying Confounding': Elizabeth I, Mary Stuart, and the Matrix of Renaissance Gender", *Exemplaria* 12: 385–416.

McCoy, R. C. 1989. *The Rites of Knighthood: The Literature and Politics of Elizabethan Chivalry*, The New Historicism, Vol. 7, Berkeley: University of California Press.

Meyer, S. 1969. *An Interpretation of Edmund Spenser's "Colin Clout"*, Cork: Cork University Press.

Meyer, S. 1962. "Spenser's *Colin Clout*: The Poem and the Book", *Papers of the Bibliographical Society of America* 56: 397–413.

Miller, D. L. 1979. "Authorship, Authority and *The Shepheardes Calender*", *MLQ* 40: 219–36.

——. 1983. "Spenser's Vocation, Spenser's Career", *ELH* 50: 197–231.

——. 1987. "Figuring Hierarchy: The Dedicatory Sonnets to *The Faerie Queene* Source", *Renaissance Papers*, ed. D. B. Randall and J. Porter, Durham: Southeastern Renaissance Conference, 49–59.

——. 1988. *The Poem's Two Bodies: The Poetics of the 1590 "Faerie Queene"*, Princeton: Princeton University Press.

——. 1990. "The Writing", *diacritics* 20: 17–29.

——. 1993. "Spenser and the Gaze of Glory", in *Edmund Spenser's Poetry*, Norton Critical Edition, ed. Hugh Maclean and Anne Lake Prescott, New York: Norton, 756–64.

——. 1996. "The Earl of Cork's Lute", in *Spenser's Life and the Subject of Biography*, ed. Judith H. Anderson, Donald Cheney, and David A. Richardson, Amherst: University of Massachusetts Press, 146–71.

——. 2000. "Afterword: The Otherness of Spenser's Language", in *Worldmaking Spenser: Explorations in the Early Modern Age*, ed. Patrick Cheney and Lauren Silberman, Lexington: University Press of Kentucky, 244–8.

Miller, J. T. 1979. " 'Love Doth Hold My Hand': Writing and Wooing in the Sonnets of Sidney and Spenser", *ELH* 46: 541–58.

——. 1997. "Mother Tongues: Language and Lactation in Early Modern Literature", *ELR* 27: 177–96.

——. 2000. "Lady Mary Wroth in the House of Busirane", in *Worldmaking Spenser: Explorations in the Early Modern Age*, ed. Patrick Cheney and Lauren Silberman, Lexington, KY: University of Kentucky Press, 115–24.

Miller, P. W. 1970. "The Decline of the English Epithalamion", *TSLL* 12: 405–16.

Miller, S. 2000. " 'Mirrours More Then One': Edmund Spenser and Female Authority in the Seventeenth Century," in *Worldmaking Spenser: Explorations in the Early Modern Age*, ed. Patrick Cheney and Lauren Silberman, Lexington, KY: University of Kentucky Press, 125–47.

Millican, C. B. 1932. *Spenser and the Table Round*, Cambridge, Mass.: Harvard University Press.

Mills, J. L. 1976. "Spenser and the Numbers of History: A Note on the British and Elfin Chronicles in *The Faerie Queene*", *PQ* 55: 281–7.

Miola, R. S. 1980. "Spenser's 'Anacreontics': A Mythological Metaphor", *SP* 77: 50–66.

Mohl, R. 1990. "Spenser, Edmund," *The Spenser Encyclopedia*, ed. A. C., Hamilton, Toronto: University of Toronto Press.

Montrose, L. A. 1979. " 'The Perfecte Paterne of a Poete': The Poetics of Courtship in *The Shepheardes Calender*", *TSLL* 21: 34–67.

——. 1980. " 'Eliza, Queen of Shepheardes,' and the Pastoral of Power", *ELR* 10: 153–82.

——. 1981. "Interpretting Spenser's February Eclogue: Some Contexts and Implications", *SSt* 2: 67–74.

——. 1983. "Of Gentlemen and Shepherds: The Politics of Elizabethan Pastoral Form", *ELH* 50: 415–59.

——. 1986a. "The Elizabethan Subject and the Spenserian Text", in *Literary Theory/ Renaissance Texts*, ed. Patricia Parker and David Quint, Baltimore: Johns Hopkins University Press, 303–40.

——. 1986b. "Renaissance Literary Studies and the Subject of History", *ELR* 16: 5–12.

——. 2002. "Spenser and the Elizabethan Political Imaginary", *ELH* 69: 907–46.

Moore, M. 1981. "Spenser's Ireland", in *The Complete Poems of Marianne Moore*, New York: Viking Press, 112–13.

Morey, J. H. 1991. "Spenser's Mythic Adaptations in *Muiopotmos*", *SSt* 9 (for 1988): 49–59.

Morgan, H. 1999. "Beyond Spenser? A Historiographical Introduction to the Study of Political Ideas in Early Modern Ireland", in *Political Ideology in Ireland, 1541–1641*, ed. Hiram Morgan, Dublin: Four Courts Press, 9–21.

Moroney, M. 1998. "Spenser's Dissolution: Monasticism and Ruins in *The Faerie Queene* and *The Vewe of the Present State of Ireland*", *SSt* 12 (for 1991): 105–32.

——. 1999. "Apocalypse, Ethnography, and Empire in John Derricke's *Image of Irelande* (1581) and Spenser's *Veew of the Present State of Ireland* (1596)", *ELR* 29: 355–74.

Morris, R., ed. 1883. *Complete Works of Edmund Spenser*, London: Macmillan.

Morris, R. and J. W. Hales. 1869. *Complete Works of Edmund Spenser Edited from the Original Editions and Manuscripts*, London: Macmillan and Co.

Mounts, C. E. 1950. "The Ralegh-Essex Rivalry and *Mother Hubberd's Tale*", *MLN* 65: 509–13.

Mounts, C. E. 1952. "Spenser and the Countess of Leicester", *ELH* 19: 191–202.

Mueller, W. R. 1959. *Spenser's Critics: Changing Currents in Literary Taste*, Syracuse: Syracuse University Press.

Muldoon, P. 2003. "Zigzag", *Parnassus: Poetry in Review* 27: 213–32.

Neely, C. T. 1978. "The Structure of English Renaissance Sonnet Sequences", *ELH* 45: 359–89.

Nelson, W., ed. 1961. *Form and Convention in the Poetry of Edmund Spenser*, New York, Columbia University Press.

———. 1963. *The Poetry of Edmund Spenser: A Study*, New York: Columbia University Press.

Neuse, R. 1966. "The Triumph over Hasty Accidents: A Note on the Symbolic Mode of the *Epithalamion*", *MLR* 61: 163–74.

Ní Chuilleanáin, E. 1996. "Forged and Fabulous Chronicles: Reading Spenser as an Irish Writer", *The Irish University Review* 26: 237–51.

Nohrnberg, J. 1976. *The Analogy of* The Faerie Queene, Princeton: Princeton University Press.

———. 1990. "*The Faerie Queene*, Book IV", in *The Spenser Encyclopedia*, ed. A. C. Hamilton, 273–80.

Norbrook, D. 1984. *Poetry and Politics in the English Renaissance*, London: Routledge and Kegan Paul.

———. 2002. *Poetry and Politics in the English Renaissance*, rev. edn, Oxford: Oxford University Press.

Norton, D. S. 1944a. "The Bibliography of Spenser's 'Prothalamion'", *JEGP* 43: 349–53.

———. 1944b. "Queen Elizabeth's 'Brydale Day'", *MLQ* 5: 149–54.

———. 1951. "The Tradition of Prothalamia," in *English Studies in Honor of James Southall Wilson, University of Virginia Studies* 4: 223–41.

Notcutt. 1926. "*The Faerie Queene* and Its Critics", *Essays and Studies* 12.

Oates, M. I. 1983. "*Fowre Hymnes*: Spenser's Retractions of Paradise", *SSt* 4: 143–269.

O'Brien, R. V. 2001. "Cannibalism in Edmund Spenser's *Faerie Queene*, Ireland, and the Americas", in *Eating Their Words: Cannibalism and the Boundaries of Cultural Identity*, ed. Kirsten Guest, Albany: New York State University Press, 35–56.

O'Callaghan, M. 2000. *The "Shepheards Nation": Jacobean Spenserians and Early Stuart Political Culture, 1612–1625*, Oxford: Clarendon Press.

O'Connell, M. 1971. "*Astrophel*: Spenser's Double Elegy", *SEL* 11: 27–35.

———. 1977. *Mirror and Veil: The Historical Dimension of Spenser's* Faerie Queene, Chapel Hill: University of North Carolina Press.

———. 1990a. "Dixon, John", in *Spenser Encyclopedia*, ed. A. C. Hamilton, 220–1.

———. 1990b. "Giant with the scales", in *Spenser Encyclopedia*, ed. A. C. Hamilton, 331–2.

———. 1990c. "*The Faerie Queene*, Book V," in *The Spenser Encyclopedia*, ed. A. C. Hamilton, 280–3.

O'Rahilly, A. 1938. *The Massacre at Smerwick (1580)*, Cork: Cork University Press.

Oram, W. A. 1981. "*Daphnaïda* and Spenser's Later Poetry", *SSt* 2: 141–58.

———. 1984. "Elizabethan Fact and Spenserian Fiction", *SSt* 4 (for 1983): 33–47.

———. 1990. "Spenser's Raleghs", *SP* 87: 341–62.

Oram, W. 1997. *Edmund Spenser*, New York: Twayne.

———. 2001. "What Did Spenser Really Think of Sir Walter Ralegh When He Published the First Installment of *The Faerie Queene*?", *SSt* 15: 165–74.

Orgel, Stephen. 2000. "Margins of Truth," in *The Renaissance Text: Theory, Editing, Textuality*, ed. Andrew Murphy, Manchester: Manchester University Press, 91–107.

———. 2002. *The Authentic Shakespeare and other Problems of the Early Modern Stage*, New York: Routledge.

Orwen, W. R. 1946. "Spenser's 'Stemmata Dudleiana'", *N&Q* 190: 9–11.

Osgood, C. G. 1915. *A Concordance to Spenser*, repr. Gloucester Mass.: Peter Smith 1963.

——. 1930. "Spenser and the Enchanted Glass", *Johns Hopkins Alumni Magazine* 19: 8–31; *Variorum*, 8.496.

——. 1961. "Epithalamion and Prothalamion: 'And theyr Eccho Ring' ", *MLN* 76: 205–8.

Osgood, C. G. and H. Gibbons Lotspeich, ed. 1943, 1947. Edmund Spenser, *The Minor Poems*, 2 vols, in Edwin Greenlaw *et al.*, *The Works of Edmund Spenser: A Variorum Edition*, Baltimore, Johns Hopkins Press.

Outhwaite, R. B. 1985. "Dearth, the English Crown and the 'Crisis of the 1590s,' " in *The European Crisis of the 1590s: Essays in Comparative History*, ed. Peter Clark, London: Allen & Unwin, 23–43.

Owens, J. 2002. *Enabling Engagements: Edmund Spenser and the Politics of Patronage*, Montreal and Kingston: McGill-Queen's University Press.

Padelford, F. M. and Matthew O'Connor. 1926. "Spenser's Use of the St. George Legend", *SP* 23: 142–56.

Paglia, C. 1990. "Sex", in *Spenser Encyclopedia*, ed. A. C. Hamilton, 638–41.

Parker, P. 1987. *Literary Fat Ladies: Rhetoric, Gender, Property*, New York: Methuen.

Pask, K. 1996. *The Emergence of the English Author: Scripting the Life of the Poet in Early Modern England*, Cambridge: Cambridge University Press.

Paster, G. K. 1993. *The Body Embarrassed: Drama and the Disciplines of Shame in Early Modern England*, Ithaca: Cornell University Press.

Patterson, A. 1986. "Reopening the Green Cabinet: Clément Marot and Edmund Spenser", *ELR* 16: 44–70.

——. 1988. *Pastoral and Ideology: Virgil to Valéry*, Oxford: Clarendon Press.

——. 1992. "The Egalitarian Giant: Representations of Justice in History/Literature", *Journal of British Studies* 31: 97–132.

——. 1993. *Reading Between the Lines*, Madison: University of Wisconsin Press.

Payne, M. and J. Schad. 2003. *Life.after.theory*, London: Continuum.

Pearcy, L. T. 1981. "A Case of Allusion: Stanza 18 of Spenser's *Epithalamion* and Catullus 5", *Classical and Modern Literature* 1: 243–54.

Peltonen, M. 1995. *Classical Humanism and Republicanism in English Political Thought, 1570–1640*, Cambridge: Cambridge University Press.

Peterson, R. S. 1998. "Laurel Crown and Ape's Tail: New Light on Spenser's Career from Sir Thomas Tresham", *SSt* 12 (for 1991): 1–35.

Petti, A. G. 1990. "Handwriting, Spenser's", in *The Spenser Encyclopedia*, ed. A. C. Hamilton, 345–6.

Phillips, J. E. 1964a. *Images of a Queen: Mary Stuart in Sixteenth-Century Literature*, Berkeley: University of California Press.

Philmus, M. R. R. 1999. "The Case of the Spenserian Sonnet: A Curious Re-Creation", *SSt* 13, 125–37.

Piepho, L. 2002. "*The Shepheardes Calender* and Neo-Latin Pastoral: A Book Newly Discovered to Have Been Owned by Spenser", *SSt* 16: 77–103.

——. 2003. "Edmund Spenser and Neo-Latin Literature: An Autograph Manuscript on Petrus Lotichius and His Poetry", *SP* 100: 123–34.

Pigman, G. W., III. 1985. *Grief and English Renaissance Elegy*, Cambridge: Cambridge University Press.

Poggioli, R. 1975. *The Oaten Flute: Essays on Pastoral Poetry and the Pastoral Ideal*, Cambridge, MA: Harvard University Press.

Pope, A. 1961–69. "A Discourse on Pastoral Poetry", in *The Twickenham Edition of the Poems*, ed. John Butt, 11 vols, London: Methuen, Vol. 1, ed. E Audra and Aubrey Williams, 1961.

Prescott, A. L. 1978. *French Poets and the English Renaissance: Studies in Fame and Transformation*, New Haven: Yale University Press.

———. 1985. "The Thirsty Deer and the Lord of Life: Some Contexts for *Amoretti* 67–70", *SSt* 6: 33–76.

———. 1986. "The Thirsty Deer and the Lord of Life: Some Contexts for *Amoretti* 67–70", *SSt* 6 (for 1985): 33–76.

———. 1991. "Marginal Discourse: Drayton's Muse and Selden's 'Story' ", *SP* 88: 307–28.

———. 1994. "Triumphing over Death and Sin", *SSt* 11 (for 1990): 231–2.

———. 1996 "Spenser (Re)Reading du Bellay: Chronology and Literary Response", in *Spenser's Life and the Subject of Biography*, ed. Judith H. Anderson, Donald Cheney, and David A. Richardson, Amherst: University of Massachusetts Press, 131–45.

———. 2000. "The Laurel and the Myrtle: Spenser and Ronsard", in *Worldmaking Spenser: Explorations in the Early Modern Age*, ed. Patrick Cheney and Lauren Silberman, Lexington: University Press of Kentucky, 63–78.

———. 2001a. "Complicating the Allegory: Spenser and Religion in Recent Scholarship", *Renaissance and Reformation* 25: 9–23.

———. 2001b. "Spenser's Shorter Pastorals", in Andrew Hadfield, ed., *The Cambridge Companion to Spenser*, 143–61.

———. 2002. "Divine Poetry as a Career Move: The Complexities and Consolations of Following David", in *European Literary Careers: The Author from Antiquity to the Renaissance*, ed. Patrick Cheney and Frederick de Armas, Toronto: University of Toronto Press, 206–30.

———. 2004. "Spenser's Religion Complicating the Allegory: Spenser's Theology in Recent Scholarship", *Renaissance & Reformation* 25: 9–23.

Pugh, S. 2004. *Spenser and Ovid*, Aldershot: Ashgate.

Quilligan, M. 1983. *Milton's Spenser: The Politics of Reading*, Ithaca: Cornell University Press.

———. 1987. "The Comedy of Female Authority in *The Faerie Queene*", *ELR* 17: 156–72.

———. 1990. "Feminine Endings: The Sexual Politics of Sidney's and Spenser's Rhyming", in *The Renaissance Englishwoman in Print: Counterbalancing the Canon*, ed. Anne M. Haselkorn and Betty S. Travitsky, Amherst, MA: University of Massachusetts Press, 311–26.

Quinn, D. B. 1966. *The Elizabethans and the Irish*, Ithaca: Cornell University Press.

———. 1990. "*A Vewe of the Present State of Ireland*", in *The Spenser Encyclopedia*, ed. A. C. Hamilton, 713–15.

Quint, D. 1983. *Origin and Originality in Renaissance Literature: Versions of the Source*, New Haven: Yale University Press.

———. 1993. *Epic and Empire: Politics and Generic Form from Virgil to Milton*, Princeton: Princeton University Press.

Quitslund, J. A. 1969. "Spenser's Images of Sapience", *SR* 16: 181–213.

———. 1985 "Spenser and the Patronesses of the *Fowre Hymnes*: 'Ornaments of All True Love and Beautie' ", in *Silent but for the Word: Tudor Women as Patrons, Translators, and Writers of Religious Works*, ed. Margaret Hannay, Kent: Kent State University Press, 184–202.

———. 1997. "Questionable Evidence in the *Letters* of 1580 between Gabriel Harvey and Edmund Spenser", in *Spenser's Life and the Subject of Biography*, ed. Judith

H. Anderson, Donald Cheney, and David A. Richardson, Amherst: University of Massachusetts Press, 81–98.

——. 2001. *Spenser's Supreme Fiction: Platonic Natural Philosophy and* The Faerie Queene, Toronto: University of Toronto Press.

Radcliffe, D. H. 1996. *Edmund Spenser: A Reception History*, Columbia, South Carolina: Camden House.

Rambuss, R. 1993. *Spenser's Secret Career*, Cambridge: Cambridge University Press.

——. 1996. "Spenser's Lives, Spenser's Careers", in *Spenser's Life and the Subject of Biography*, ed. Judith H. Anderson, Donald Cheney, and David A. Richardson, Amherst: University of Massachusetts Press, 1–17.

——. 2001. "Spenser's Life and Career", in *The Cambridge Companion to Spenser*, ed. Andrew Hadfield, Cambridge: Cambridge University Press, 13–36.

Rasmussen, C. J. 1981. " 'How Weak Be the Passions of Woefulness': Spenser's *Ruines of Time*", *SSt* 2: 159–81.

Raven, J., H. Small and N. Tadmor, eds 1996. *The Practice and Representing Reading in England*, Cambridge: Cambridge University Press.

Raysor, T. M., ed. 1936. *Coleridge's Miscellaneous Criticism*, Cambridge, MA: Harvard University Press.

Rebhorn, W. A. 1980. "Du Bellay's Imperial Mistress: *Les Antiquitez de Rome* as Petrarchanist Sonnet Sequence", *Renaissance Quarterly* 33: 609–22.

Renwick, W. L. 1925. *Edmund Spenser: An Essay on Renaissance Poetry*, London: Edward Arnold.

——., ed. 1928. Edmund Spenser *Complaints*, London: Scholartis Press.

——., ed. 1930–32. *Works of Edmund Spenser*, 8 vols, Oxford: Basil Blackwell.

——., ed. 1934. *A View of the Present State of Ireland, by Edmund Spenser*, London: Scholartis Press.

——., ed. 1970. *A View of the Present State of Ireland, by Edmund Spenser*, Oxford: Clarendon Press [reissue of 1934 edition with modernized spelling].

Riddell, J. A. and S. Stewart. 1995. *Jonson's Spenser: Evidence and Historical Criticism*, Pittsburgh, PA: Duquesne University Press.

Riley, A. W. 1990. "Marx & Spenser", in *The Spenser Encyclopedia*, ed. A. C. Hamilton, 457–8.

Ringler, R. N. 1965–66. "The Faunus Episode", *MP* 63: 12–19; repr. in *Essential Articles for the Study of Edmund Spenser*, ed. A. C. Hamilton, Hamden, Conn.: Archon, 1972, 253–66.

Roberts, J. 1990. "Radigund Revisited: Perspectives on Women Rulers in Lady Mary Wroth's *Urania*", in *The Renaissance Englishwoman in Print*, ed. Anne M. Haselkorn and Betty S. Travitsky, Amherst, MA: University of Massachusetts Press, 187–207.

Robinson, L. S. 1985. *Monstrous Regiment: The Lady Knight in Sixteenth-Century Epic*, New York: Garland.

Roche, T. P., Jr. 1961. "The Challenge to Chastity: Britomart at the House of Busyrane", *PMLA* 76: 340–4; repr. in Hamilton 1972, 189–98.

——. 1964. *The Kindly Flame: A Study of the Third and Fourth Books of Spenser's "Faerie Queene"*, Princeton: Princeton University Press.

Roche, T. P., Jr., ed. 1978. Edmund Spenser, *The Faerie Queene*, London: Penguin.

——. 1989. *Petrarch and the English Sonnet Sequences*, New York: AMS.

Rogers, W. E. 1977. "The Carmina of Horace in *Prothalamion*", *American Notes and Queries* 15:148–53.

Rollins, H. E., ed. 1931. *The Phoenix Nest (1953)*, Cambridge MA: Harvard University Press.

Rollinson, P. B. 1971. "A Generic View of Spenser's *Fowre Hymnes*", *SP* 68: 292–704.

Rosenberg, D. M. 1981. *Oaten Reeds and Trumpets: Pastoral and Epic in Virgil, Spenser, and Milton*, Lewisberg: Buknell University Press.

Rosenmeyer, T. G. 1969. *The Green Cabinet: Theocritus and the European Pastoral Lyric*, Berkeley: University of California Press.

Røstvig, M.-S. 1963. *The Hidden Sense and Other Essays*, Oslo: Universitetsforlaget.

———. 1971. "Images of Perfection", in *Seventeenth-Century Imagery: Essays on the Use of Figurative Language from Donne to Farquhar*, ed. E. Miner, Berkeley: Berkeley University Press.

———. 1975. *Fair Forms: Essays in English Literature from Spenser to Jane Austen*, Cambridge: Cambridge University Press.

Rovang, P. R. 1996. *Refashioning "Knights and Ladies Gentle Deeds": The Intertextuality of Spenser's "Faerie Queene" and Malory's "Morte Darthur,"* Cranbury, NJ: Associated University Presses.

Russell, D. 1972. "Du Bellay's Emblematic Vision of Rome", *Yale French Studies*, 47: 98–109.

Rustice, C. 1999. "*Muiopotmos*, Spenser's 'Complaint' against Aesthetics", *SSt* 13: 165–77.

Sacks, P. J. 1985. *The English Elegy: Studies in the Genre from Spenser to Yeats*, Baltimore: Johns Hopkins University Press.

Said, E. 1975. *Beginnings: Intention and Method*, New York: Basic Books.

———. 1993. *Culture and Imperialism*, London: Vintage.

Sale, R. 1968. *Reading Spenser: An Introduction to* The Faerie Queene, New York: Random House.

Sandison, H. E. 1928. "Arthur Gorges, Spenser's Alcyon and Ralegh's Friend", *PMLA* 43: 645–74.

———. 1934. "Spenser and Ralegh", *ELH* 1: 37–60, Adamson and Holland, 1969.

Sandler, Florence. 1984. "*The Faerie Queene*: An Elizabethan Apocalypse", in *The Apocalypse in English Renaissance Thought and Literature: Patterns, Antecedents and Repercussions*, eds C. A. Patrides and Joseph Wittreich, Ithaca: Cornell University Press, 148–74.

Satterthwaite, A. W. 1960. *Spenser, Ronsard and Du Bellay: A Renaissance Comparison*, Princeton: Princeton University Press.

Schleiner, L. 1990. "Spenser's 'E. K.' as Edmund Kent (Kenned/of Kent): Kyth (couth), Kissed, and Kunning-Conning", *ELR* 20: 374–407.

Schwarz, K. 2000. *Tough Love: Amazon Encounters in the English Renaissance*, Durham: Duke University Press.

Scott, S. C. 1986. "From Polydorus to Fradubio: The History of a Topos", *SSt* 7: 27–57.

———. 1987. "From Polydorus to Fradubio: The History of a Topos", *SSt* 7 (for 1986): 27–57.

Scott, Sir W. 1806. "Review of Todd's Edition of Spenser", *Edinburgh Review* 7: 203–17.

Sedinger, T. 2000. "Women's Friendship and the Refusal of Lesbian Desire in *The Faerie Queene*", *Criticism* 42: 91–113.

Shaheen, N. 1976. *Biblical References in* The Faerie Queene, Memphis: University of Tennessee Press.

———. 1980. "The 1590 and 1596 Texts of *The Faerie Queene*", *Papers of the Bibliographical Society of America* 74: 57–63.

Sharkey, S. 1997. "A View of the Present State of Irish Studies", in *Studying British Cultures: An Introduction*, ed. Susan Bassnett, London and New York: Routledge, 113–35.

Sharpe, K. and S. N. Zwicker, eds 2003. *Reading, Society and Politics in early Modern England*, Cambridge: Cambridge University Press.

Shaver, A. 1991. "Rereading Mirabella", *SSt* 9 (for 1988): 211–26.

Shepherd, S. 1989. *Spenser*, Harvester New Readings, New York and London: Harvester.

Shire, H. 1978. *A Preface to Spenser*, London: Longman.

Shore, D. 1985. *Spenser and the Poetics of Pastoral: A Study of the World of Colin Clout*, Kingston and Montreal: McGill-Queen's University Press.

Shuger, D. 1997. "Irishmen, Aristocrats, and Other White Barbarians", *Renaissance Quarterly* 50: 494–525.

Silberman, L. 1986. "Singing Unsung Heroines: Androgynous Discourse in Book III of the *Faerie Queene*", in *Rewriting the Renaissance: The Discourses of Sexual Difference in Early Modern Europe*, ed. Margaret Ferguson, Maureen Quilligan, and Nancy Vickers, Chicago: University of Chicago Press, 259–72.

——. 1987. "The Hermaphrodite and the Metamorphosis of Spenserian Allegory", *ELR* 17: 207–23.

——. 1995. *Transforming Desire: Erotic Knowledge in Books III and IV of* The Faerie Queene, Berkeley: University of California Press.

Sinfield, A. 1992. *Faultlines: Cultural Materialism and the Politics of Dissident Reading*, Oxford: Clarendon Press.

Smith, A. G. R. 1997. *The Emergence of a Nation State: The Commonwealth of England, 1529–1660*, 2nd edn, New York: Longman.

Smith, C. G. 1970. *Spenser's Proverb Lore*, Cambridge MA: Harvard University Press.

Smith, G. G., ed. 1904. *Elizabethan Critical Essays*, 2 vols, Oxford: Clarendon Press.

Smith, H. 1961. "The Use of Conventions in Spenser's Minor Poems", in *Form and Convention in the Poetry of Edmund Spenser*, New York: Columbia University Press, 122–45.

Smith, J. C. and E. de Selincourt, eds 1909–10. *The Poetical Works of Edmund Spenser*, Oxford: Clarendon.

Smith, J. N. 1959. "Spenser's *Prothalamion*: A New Genre", *RES* 10: 173–8.

Smith, R. 1958. "Spenser's Scholarly Script and 'Right Writing'", in *Studies in Honour of T. W. Baldwin*, ed. Don Cameron Allen, Urbana: University of Illinois Press.

Smith, Sir T. 1906. *De Republica Anglorum: A Discourse on the Commonwealth of England (1583)*, ed. L. Alston, Shannon: Irish University Press, repr. 1972.

Snare, G. 1969. "The Muses on Poetry: Spenser's *The Teares of the Muses*", *Tulane Studies in English* 17: 31–52.

Snyder, S. 1998. *Pastoral Process: Spenser, Marvell, Milton*, Stanford: Stanford University Press.

Southey, R. 1850. *Southey's Common-Place Book*, 3rd series, *Analytical Readings*, ed. J. W. Warter, London: Longman, Brown, Green, and Longmans.

Spens, J. 1934. *Spenser's Faerie Queene: An Interpretation*, London: Edward Arnold.

Spenser, E. Specific editions under editor's names, for select list of editions see Appendix.

Spenser, E. 1648. *The Faerie Leveller, or, King Charles his Leveller Descried and Deciphered in Queene Elizabeths Dayes by her Poet Laureat Edmond Spenser, in his*

Unparaleld Poeme Entituled, The Faerie Qveene, a Lively Representation of our Times, London.

Spenser, E. 1932–57. *The Works of Edmund Spenser: A Variorum Edition*, 11 vols ed. Edwin Greenlaw, *et al.*, Baltimore: John Hopkins University Press.

Spiller, M. R. G. 1992. *The Development of the Sonnet: An Introduction*, London: Routledge.

Stampfer, J. L. 1951–52. "The *Cantos of Mutability*: Spenser's Last Testament of Faith", *UTQ* 21: 140–56.

Stapleton, M. L. 1990. "Spenser, the *Antiquitez de Rome*, and the Development of the English Sonnet Form", *Comparative Literary Studies* 27: 259–74.

Starke, S. P. 1998. "Briton Knight or Irish Bard? Spenser's Pastoral Persona and the Epic Project in *A View of the Present State of Ireland* and *Colin Clouts Come Home Againe*", *SSt* 12 (for 1991): 133–50.

Starnes, D. T. and E. William Talbert. 1955. *Classical Myth and Legend in Renaissance Dictionaries*, Chapel Hill: University of North Carolina Press.

Steen, J. 1961. "On Spenser's *Epithalamion*", *Spectrum* 5: 31–7.

Stein, H. 1934. *Studies in Spenser's "Complaints"*, Oxford: Oxford University Press.

Steinberg, T. L. 1994. "Spenser, Sidney and the Myth of Astrophel", *SSt* 11 (for 1990): 187–202.

Stephens, D. 1991. "Into Other Arms: Amoret's Evasion", *ELH* 58: 523–44.

——. 1998. *Limits of Eroticism in Post-Petrarchan Narrative: Conditional Pleasure from Spenser to Marvell*, Cambridge: Cambridge University Press.

Stevens, P. 1993. " 'Leviticus Thinking' and the Rhetoric of Early-Modern Colonialism", *Criticism* 35: 441–61.

——. 1995. "Spenser and Milton on Ireland: Civility, Exclusion, and the Politics of Wisdom", *Ariel* 26: 151–67.

——. 1999. Review of Hadfield, A. (1997), *Spenser's Irish Experience: Wilde Fruit and Salvage Soyl*, Clarendon Press, Oxford, in *JEGP* 98: 448–50.

Stillinger, J. 1961. "A Note on the Printing of E. K.'s Glosses", *Studies in Bibliography* 14: 203–5.

Stillman, C. 1985. "Politics, Precedence, and the Order of the Dedicatory Sonnets in *The Faerie Queene*", *SSt* 5 (for 1984): 143–8.

Strickland, R. 1992. "Not So Idle Tears: Re-reading the Renaissance Funeral Elegy", *Review* 14: 57–72.

Strong, R. 1977. *The Cult of Elizabeth: Elizabethan Portraiture and Pageantry*, London: Thames and Hudson.

Stubbes, J. 1968. *"Gaping Gulf" and Other Relevant Documents*, ed. Lloyd E. Berry, Charlottesville, Va.: University of Virginia Press.

Stump, D. 1999. "A Slow Return to Eden: Spenser on Women's Rule", *ELR* 29: 401–21.

Summers, D. A. 1997. *Spenser's Arthur: The British Arthurian Tradition and* The Faerie Queene, Lanham, Maryland: University Press of America.

Suttie, P. 1998. "Edmund Spenser's Political Pragmatism", *SP* 95: 56–76.

Suzuki, M. 1989. *Metamorphoses of Helen: Authority, Difference, and the Epic*, Ithaca: Cornell University Press.

Tanselle, G. T. 1998. *Literature and Artifacts*, Charlottesville, VA: Bibliographical Society of the University of Virginia.

Taunton, N. 2001. *1590s Drama and Militarism: Portrayals of War in Marlowe, Chapman and Shakespeare's Henry V*, Aldershot: Ashgate.

Teskey, G. 1993. "Mutability, Genealogy, and the Authority of Forms", *Representations* 41: 104–22.

———. 1996. *Allegory and Violence*, Ithaca: Cornell University Press.

Thompson, C. 1985. "Love in an Orderly Universe: A Unification of Spenser's *Amoretti*, 'Anacreontics,' and *Epithalamion*", *Viator* 16: 277–335.

Todd, H. J., ed. 1805. *A View of the State of Ireland*, in *Works of Edmund Spenser*, 8 vol. 8, London: F. C. & J., Rivington.

Tolliver, H. 1971. *Pastoral Forms and Attitudes*, Berkeley: University of California Press.

Tonkin, H. 1972. *Spenser's Courteous Pastoral: Book Six of* The Faerie Queene, Oxford: Clarendon Press.

———. 1990. "*The Faerie Queene*, Book VI", in *The Spenser Encyclopedia*, ed. A. C. Hamilton, 283–7.

Traversi, D. A. 1936. "The Vision of Piers Plowman", *Scrutiny* 5: 276–91.

Tromly, F. B. 1986. "Lodowick Bryskett's Elegies on Sidney in Spenser's *Astrophel* Volume", *RES* n.s. 37: 384–8.

Tucker, G. H. 1990. *The Poet's Odyssey: Joachim Du Bellay and the "Antiquitez de Rome"*, Oxford: Clarendon Press.

Tufte, V. J. 1970. *The Poetry of Marriage: The Epithalamium in Europe and Its Development in England*, Los Angeles: Tinnon-Brown.

Turner, M. 1988. "The Imagery of Spenser's *Amoretti*", *Neophilologus* 72: 284–99.

Tylus, J. 1993. *Writing and Vulnerability in the Late Renaissance*, Stanford: Stanford University Press.

Unger, E. 1940. *The Carl H. Pforzheimer Library: English Literature 1475–1700*, 3 vols, New York: Carl H. Pforzheimer Library.

Upton, J., ed. 1758. *Spenser's Faerie Queene. A New Edition with a Glossary, And Notes Explanatory and Critical*, 2 vols, London: Printed for J. and R. Tonson.

Upton, J. 1987. *Notes on the* Fairy Queen, ed. John G. Radcliffe, New York, Garland, Originally published in 1758.

Van der Berg, K. 1978. "The Counterfeit in Personation: Spenser's *Prosopopoia*", in *The Author in His Work: Essays on a Problem in Criticism*, ed. L. Martz and A. Williams, New Haven: Yale University Press, 85–102.

van Es, Bart. 2002a. *Spenser's Forms of History*, Oxford: Oxford University Press.

———. 2002b. "Discourses of Conquest: *The Faerie Queene*, the Society of Antiquaries, and *A View of the Present State of Ireland*", *ELR* 32: 118–51.

Vaught, J. 2001. "Spenser's Dialogic Voice in Book I of *The Faerie Queene*", *SEL* 41: 71–89.

Vickers, N. J. 1981. "Diana Described: Scattered Women and Scattered Rhyme", *Critical Inquiry* 8: 265–79.

———. 1982. "Diana Described: Scattered Woman and Scattered Rhyme", in Abel, Elizabeth, ed., *Writing and Sexual Difference*, Chicago: University of Chicago Press, 95–108.

Villeponteaux, M. A. 1988. " 'With her own will beguyld': The Captive Lady in Spenser's *Amoretti*", *Explorations in Renaissance Culture* 14: 29–39.

———. 1993. "*Semper Eadem*: Belphoebe's Denial of Desire", in *Renaissance Discourses of Desire*, ed. Claude J. Summers and Ted-Larry Pebworth, Columbia: University of Missouri Press, 29–45.

———. 1998. " 'Not as women wanted be': Spenser's Amazon Queen", in *Dissing Elizabeth: Negative Representations of Gloriana*, ed. Julia M. Walker, Durham: Duke University Press.

Virgil. 1960. *Eclogues, Georgics, Aeneid I-VI*, trans. H. R. Fairclough, Cambridge, Mass: Harvard University Press.

Walker, G. 1988. *John Skelton and the Politics of the 1520s*, Cambridge: Cambridge University Press.

Walker, J. M. 1998. *Medusa's Mirrors: Spenser, Shakespeare, Milton and the Metamorphosis of the Female Self*, Newark: University of Delaware Press.

Wall, J. N. 1988. *Transformations of the Word: Spenser, Herbert, Vaughan*, Athens, GA: University of Georgia Press.

Wall, W. 1993. *The Imprint of Gender: Authorship and Publication in the English Renaissance*, Ithaca: Cornell University Press.

——. 2000. "Authorship and the Material Conditions of Writing", in *The Cambridge Companion to English Literature 1500–1600*, ed. Arthur F. Kinney, Cambridge: Cambridge University Press, 64–89.

Waller, G. 1994. *Edmund Spenser: A Literary Life*, Houndmills: Macmillan.

Ware, J. 1809. *A View of the Present State of Ireland, written dialogue-wise between Eudoxus and Irenaeus . . . in the years 1596*, in James Ware, ed., *Ancient Irish Histories*, 2 vols, Dublin, I: 1–266.

——., ed. 1633. *A View of the State of Ireland*, in *Two Histories of Ireland*, Dublin, 1633, 1–127.

Warkentin, G. 1990. "Spenser at the Still Point: A Schematic Device in *Epithalamion*", in H. B. de Groot and A. Leggatt, eds, *Craft and Tradition: Essays in Honour of William Blissett* Calgary:University of Calgary Press, 47–57.

Warton, T. 1754. *Observations on the Faerie Queene of Spenser*, London: R. and I. Dodsley.

Waters, D. D. 1970. *Duessa as Theological Satire*, Columbia: University of Missouri Press.

Watkins, J. 1995. *The Specter of Dido: Spenser and Virgilian Epic*, New Haven: Yale University Press.

Weatherby, H. L. 1984. "Una's Betrothal and the Easter Vigil: The Probable Influence of the Sarum Manual", in *Spenser at Kalamazoo*, ed. Francis Greco, Clarion: Clarion University of Pennsylvania, 6–20.

——. 1994. *Mirrors of Celestial Grace: Patristic Theology in Spenser's Allegory*, Toronto: University of Toronto Press.

Webster, J. 1981. "The Methode of a Poete: An Inquiry into Tudor Conceptions of Poetic Sequence", *ELR* 11: 22–43.

Weiner, A. D. 1985. "Spenser's *Muiopotmos* and the Fates of Butterflies and Men", *JEGP* 84: 203–20.

——. 1988. "Spenser and the Myth of Pastoral", *SP* 85: 390–406.

Weiss, A. 1999. "Watermark Evidence and Inference: New Style Dates of Edmund Spenser's *Complaints* and *Daphnaida*", *Studies in Bibliography* 52: 129–54.

Welch, R. 1994. *The Kilcolman Notebook*, Dingle, Co. Kerry: Brandon Press.

Wells, R. H. 1984. "Poetic Decorum in Spenser's *Amoretti*", *Cahiers Elisabéthains* 25: 9–21.

Wells, R. H. 1979. "Spenser's Christian Knight: Erasmian Theology in *The Faerie Queene*, Book I", *Anglia* 97: 350–66.

——. 1983. *Spenser's "Faerie Queene" and the Cult of Elizabeth*, London: Croom Helm.

Wells, W. 1945. " 'To Make a Mild Construction': The Significance of the Opening Stanzas of *Muiopotmos*", *SP* 42: 544–54.

Wells, W., ed. 1971–72. *Spenser Allusions in the Sixteenth and Seventeenth Centuries*, *SP* 68–9.

Welsford, E. 1967. *Spenser, Fowre Hymnes and Epithalamion: A Study of Edmund Spenser's Doctrine of Love*, Oxford: Basil Blackwell.

West, M. 1974. "Prothalamion in Propertius and Spenser", *CL* 26: 346–53.

Whitney, J. E. 1888. "The Continued Allegory in the First Book of the Faery Queene", *Transactions of the American Philological Association*, 19: 40–69.

Wickert, M. A. 1968. "Structure and Ceremony in Spenser's *Epithalamion*", *ELH* 35: 135–57.

Wiggins, P. DeSa. 1991. "Spenser's Use of Ariosto: Imitation and Allusion in Book I of the *Faerie Queene*", *Renaissance Quarterly* 45: 257–79.

Williams, A. 1967. *Flower on a Lowly Stalk: The Sixth Book of* The Faerie Queene, East Lansing: Michigan State University Press.

Williams, K. 1952. " 'Eterne in Mutabilitie': The Unified World of *The Faerie Queene*", *ELH* 19: 115–30.

——. 1961. "Venus and Diana Some uses of Myth in *The Faerie Queene*", *ELH* 28: 101–20; repr. in Hamilton 1972, 202–19.

——. 1965. "The Present State of Spenser Studies", *TSLL* 7: 225–38.

——. 1966. *Spenser's "Faerie Queene": The World of Glass*, London: Routledge and Kegan Paul.

Williams, W. P. 1990. "Bibliography, Critical", in *The Spenser Encyclopedia*, ed. A. C. Hamilton, 90–3.

Wilson, J. C. N. 1834. "The Fairy Queen", *Blackwood's Magazine*, 37: 408–430, 681–737.

Wilson-Okamura, D. S. 2002. "Spenser and the Two Queene", *ELR* 32: 62–84.

Winbolt, S. E. 1918. *Spenser and His Poetry*, London: George Harrap.

Wofford, S. L. 1988. "Gendering Allegory: Spenser's Bold Reader and the Emergence of Character in *The Faerie Queene III*", *Criticism* 30: 1–21.

——. 1992. *The Choice of Achilles: The Ideology of Figure in the Epic*, Stanford, CA: Stanford University Press.

Woodhouse, A. S. P. 1949. "Nature and Grace in *The Faerie Queene*", *ELH* 16: 194–228; repr. in Hamilton 1972, 58–83.

Woods, S. 1985. "Spenser and the Problem of Women's Rule", *HLQ* 48: 141–58.

——. 1991. "Amazonian Tyranny: Spenser's Radigund and Diachronic Mimesis", in *Playing with Gender: A Renaissance Pursuit*, ed. Jean R. Brink *et al.*, Urbana: University of Illinois Press, 52–61.

——. 1999. *Lanyer: A Renaissance Woman Poet*, New York: Oxford University Press.

——. 2000. "Women at the Margins in Spenser and Lanyer", in *Worldmaking Spenser: Explorations in the Early Modern Age*, ed. Patrick Cheney and Lauren Silberman, Lexington, KY: University of Kentucky Press.

Woodward, D. H. 1962. "Some Themes in Spenser's *Prothalamion*", *ELH* 29: 34–46.

Woodworth, M. K. 1944. "The Mutability Cantos and the Succession", *PMLA* 59: 985–1002.

Wordsworth, W. and D. Wordsworth. 1967. *Letters: Early Years, 1787–1805*, ed. Ernest de Selincourt, rev. Chester L. Shaver, Oxford: Clarendon Press.

Wurtsbaugh, J. 1936. *Two Centuries of Spenserian Scholarship (1609–1805)*, Baltimore: Johns Hopkins University Press.

Yamashita, H., H. Sato, T. Suzuki, and A. Takano, eds 1993. *A Textual Companion to* The Faerie Queene *1590*, Tokyo: Kenyusha.

Yates, Frances. 1947. "Queen Astrac", *Journal of the Warburg and Courtauld Institutes* 10: 27–82; repr. in Yates, 1975, 29–87.

Yates, F. 1975. *Astraea: The Imperial Theme in the Sixteenth Century*, London: Routledge and Kegan Paul.

Yeats, W. B. 1961. *Essays and Introductions*, London: Macmillan.

Zitner, S. P., ed. 1968. *The Mutability Cantos*, London: Nelson.

Zurcher, A. 2003. Correspondence posted to the Sidney-Spenser listserve, 15 March, Archive at http://www.jiscmail.ac.uk/archives/sidney-spenser.html.

———. 2005. "Getting it Back to Front in 1590: Spenser's Dedication, Ralegh's Equivocation, and Nashe's Insinuation", *Studies in the Literary Imagination* 38.

Index

Printed in the United States
65492LVS00001B/8